Law's Rule

Law's Rule

The Nature, Value, and Viability
of the Rule of Law

GERALD J. POSTEMA

OXFORD
UNIVERSITY PRESS

OXFORD
UNIVERSITY PRESS

Oxford University Press is a department of the University of Oxford. It furthers the University's objective of excellence in research, scholarship, and education by publishing worldwide. Oxford is a registered trade mark of Oxford University Press in the UK and certain other countries.

Published in the United States of America by Oxford University Press
198 Madison Avenue, New York, NY 10016, United States of America.

CIP data is on file at the Library of Congress
ISBN 978–0–19–064534–2

DOI: 10.1093/oso/9780190645342.001.0001

Printed by Integrated Books International, United States of America

Note to Readers
This publication is designed to provide accurate and authoritative information in regard to the subject matter covered. It is based upon sources believed to be accurate and reliable and is intended to be current as of the time it was written. It is sold with the understanding that the publisher is not engaged in rendering legal, accounting, or other professional services. If legal advice or other expert assistance is required, the services of a competent professional person should be sought. Also, to confirm that the information has not been affected or changed by recent developments, traditional legal research techniques should be used, including checking primary sources where appropriate.

(Based on the Declaration of Principles jointly adopted by a Committee of the American Bar Association and a Committee of Publishers and Associations.)

You may order this or any other Oxford University Press publication
by visiting the Oxford University Press website at www.oup.com.

For Leslie
sine qua non

Contents

Contents

Prologue

The rule-of-law idea, once an obscure notion more at home in law school lecture halls than in the mainstream media, is now the staple of the discourse of pundits, politicians, and protesters around the world. The rule of law enjoys broad international appeal. Ban Ki-moon, Secretary General of the United Nations, made this fact clear in 2012. "The rule of law," he said, "is like the law of gravity. It is the rule of law that ensures that our world and our societies remain bound together and that order prevails over chaos."[1] Unlike the law of gravity, however, the realization of the rule of law in a nation or beyond is not inevitable or invariable. Indeed, in the view of many observers, the rule of law is currently under grave threat. In 2005, the International Bar Association, the "global voice of the legal profession," observed with dismay "the increasing erosion around the world of the Rule of Law."[2] Several years later, this disturbing trend continued. In 2021, the European Union raised the alarm: "[P]ressure is mounting on the rule of law globally."[3]

Recently, the European Commission, with the backing of the European Court of Justice, sanctioned the Polish government for a deliberate and calculated legislative dismantling by Poland of the independence of the judiciary, a key component of the rule of law.[4] World leaders, journalists, and scholars have raised similar concerns about erosion of the rule of law in several countries, including Hungary, Brazil, Venezuela, Georgia, and Russia. Authoritarian-leaning leaders have seized opportunities created by the COVID-19 pandemic to expand their power and erode even further checks on their power. The global rule-of-law crisis reached a new low with the recent attack by Russian forces against Ukraine, which was a blatant violation of international law.

Established democracies have also seen dramatic declines in adherence to the rule of law. Notable in this group of backsliding regimes is the United States. According to the recent World Justice Project's (WJP) annual report, adherence to the rule of law in the United States has been in steady decline since 2016, especially in the areas of constraints on government power and criminal justice. The WJP *Rule of Law Index* for 2021 ranks the United States 20th of 31 in its north Atlantic region and 27th of 139 considered globally. It falls far behind Denmark, Norway, Finland, Sweden, the Netherlands, the United Kingdom, and Japan; but it also lags behind Lithuania, Estonia, and Uruguay. Its rank-order neighbors are Cyprus, Slovenia, Malta, and Costa Rica.

According to the International IDEA, a "historic turning point" occurred when then President Donald Trump challenged the legitimacy of the 2020 election.[5] He conspired to sabotage voting machines,[6] and his supporters attacked the Capitol violently, threatening the lives of member of Congress gathered to carry out their constitutional duty to ratify the results of the 2020 presidential election. The attack on the Capitol expressed the protesters' contempt for the US Constitution and the laws of the land. Representative Liz Cheney, member of the US House select committee investigating the January 6 attack, observed that the president's words and actions "demonstrated that he is at war with the rule of law."[7]

Still, those who exercise ruling power are often keen to claim the rule of law's halo for their own policies. They insist that they are offering a new model of constitutional democracy ("illiberal democracy") and a competing conception of the rule of law. And, when they stretch or even transcend the bounds of legality, they claim the actions are necessary to maintain "law and order." However, András Sajó argues in his recent book that "these claims are deeply deceptive—and constitute an abuse of constitutionalism and the rule of law, not a different conception of these ideas."[8]

These developments represent a grave threat not just to institutions designed to serve the rule of law but to our very understanding of the ideal. We literally don't know what we are talking about. Some critics dismiss talk of the rule of law as "ruling-class chatter," "mere rhetoric . . . reinforced by its intrinsic ambiguity."[9] Or, at least, the rule of law is, in the words of one legal scholar, the most puzzling "of all the dreams that drive men and women into the streets."[10] Never, it seems, has it been more important for us to get a proper measure of this dream. We need a clear, publicly persuasive account of the rule of law, its value, and the scope, force, and limits of its demands. This is the task of this book.

Although motivated by the serious national and international threats and challenges currently facing the rule of law, this work is not a manual for either building robust rule-of-law regimes or responding concretely to current threats to them. Rather, it seeks to articulate a coherent framework and foundation for thinking about the rule of law and planning strategies for building and defending it.

To answer fundamental threats to the rule of law we first must return to its foundational principles. This book articulates and defends a comprehensive, coherent, and compelling conception of the rule of law and defends it against serious challenges to its intelligibility, relevance, and normative force. This will involve uncovering the core aim of the rule-of-law ideal and the basic principles it entails. It answers our first question: What does rule of law mean? Two other equally compelling questions are: Why think it is important? and How does it work? To answer the former question, this book will identify and defend the moral foundations of the ideal. To address the latter question, it explores the institutions and practices of government and of civil society that realize this ideal—the institutional building, as it were, constructed according to the architect's abstract rendering.

The following work consists of two parts. Part I is devoted to articulating and defending its proposed conception of the rule of law. Chapter 1 locates the idea in the thought and writing of poets and philosophers, sages and scholars across time and cultures. It affords readers an intuitive grasp of key constituents of the rule-of-law idea. It ends with the proposal that at its core, the rule of law *promises protection and recourse against the arbitrary exercise of power using the distinctive tools of the law*. The organizing *aim* of the rule of law is to temper the exercise of power to avoid to the extent feasible its arbitrary exercise; it chooses law as the *means* of doing so. Chapter 2 refines this watchword into a working thesis, articulating each of the key notions that it comprises—power, arbitrariness, protection, recourse, and accountability, and describes the box of tools the law provides for tempering power. Chapter 3 defends three principles that immediately follow from this core idea of the rule of law: sovereignty of law, equality in the eyes of law, and fidelity. Sovereignty demands that those who exercise ruling power *govern with* law (legality), that law *governs them* (reflexivity), and only acts that are ordained by law are legitimate (exclusivity). Equality requires that law's protection and recourse is available on an equal basis for all who are also bound by it. Fidelity requires that all of its members, and not merely the legal or ruling elite, take responsibility for holding each other, and especially law's officials, accountable under the law.

Chapters 4 and 5 seek upstream sources of this articulated ideal. They uncover the moral foundations of the rule-of-law ideal and its place in the constellation of basic values of political morality. Chapter 4 argues that the rule of law is founded upon and serves the complex moral value of *membership*. This value combines in complementary relationships freedom, dignity, equality, and community in one integrated package. Chapter 5 explores the relationship between the rule of law and the core values of justice, human rights, and democracy.

The rule of law, like democracy, is by its nature an *institutionally realized ideal*. It exists only insofar as it is realized and articulated in institutions and practices—governmental and extragovernmental, formal and informal—in historical political communities. Chapters 6, 7, and 8 travel downstream to consider how the rule of law's principles are concretely realized in particular political communities. Chapter 6 sketches broadly the kind of institutions and practices that, in many polities, effectively serve the rule of law. Chapter 7 explores the material, cultural, and moral limits of the ideal—the conditions that must obtain for it to thrive and the limits on its moral force. Chapter 8 explores the kinds of threats to which the rule of law is most vulnerable. These include various ways in which key rule-of-law institutions and practices are sabotaged and subtler ways in which the moral culture in which the rule of law is rooted is coarsened and corrupted.

Part II takes up a number of important challenges to the intelligibility or feasibility of the ideal. Chapters 9 and 10 consider a challenge to a key theme of the conception defended in Part I: that the rule of law can be robust in a polity only when the ethos of fidelity—mutual accountability—takes hold in it. Chapter 9 addresses the challenge that fidelity drives out finality; that robust accountability justifies widespread civil dissent, which throws law into perpetual uncertainty, undermining the protection and order that the rule of law promises. In response, Chapter 9 explores the delicate dialectic between dissent and deference to authorities. Chapter 10 argues against critics that widespread accountability does not drive out trust, but rather underwrites it.

Chapters 11 and 12 explore four contexts in which the exercise of discretion plays a large and, for some, worrisome role. Chapter 11 argues that, despite the large role they assign to discretion, equitable judgment in the civil law context and mercy in the criminal law context are compatible with the rule of law. They are necessary complements to law, the chapter shows. Chapter 12 answers critics who charge that law must go silent in times of emergency, that ordinary checks and balances on executive decision-making are either ineffective or too dangerous to include within a constitutional order. On the contrary, the chapter argues, carefully calibrated law is most needed in these circumstances.

Chapters 13 and 14 take up the novel challenges posed by artificial intelligence and the growth of enormous power of digital power and digital platforms ("Big Tech"). Chapter 13 argues that law must also temper the power of these new Leviathans and explores in broad terms ways of doing so. Chapter 14 argues that artificial intelligence, suitably regulated, may have a role to play in ordinary operations of the law, but that it must not take the place of law.

The book concludes in Chapter 15, arguing for the importance of robust rule of law in the global domain against those who argue that it is either impotent or too costly.

The chapters of Part I fit closely together, giving shape and substance to the core conception of the rule of law. The chapters of Part II address several challenges to and applications of this conception. Readers interested in the rule-of-law idea in general are invited to read all of Part I, but they may wish to sample this or that chapter of Part II. The chapters of Part II depend heavily on the foundational work done in Part I, but they do not build on each other. Readers' interests can guide selection among them.

PART I
CORE AND CONSEQUENCES

1

The Idea of the Rule of Law

In the fifth century BCE, stone columns in the Cretan city of Gortyn promulgated a code of law.[1] The first sentence of the Gortyn Code asserts the supremacy of the legal process. It declares, "if anyone wishes to contest the status of a free man or a slave, he is not to seize him before a trial." Law and the legal process were to rule the actions and interactions of the citizens of Gortyn; but equally, law was to govern those who exercised power under color of law. Officials, even the *kosmos*, the city's highest official, were subject to the law. They could be fined if they failed to en-force the law properly. In the Gortyn Code, law was not merely an instrument of governance; law was meant to govern the governors and citizens alike. All need to be ruled, it assumed, not least the rulers. This is the simple, central idea of the rule of law.

Before we launch into a detailed analysis of the rule-of-law ideal, it would be helpful to get an intuitive sense of it. What more fully is the core, organizing idea lying at its center? What is the deep concern that motivates its partisans and gives life to the demands it places on institutions and individuals? This is the task of this chapter. The aim is not to give a systematic history of the de-velopment of the rule-of-law ideal. It is, rather, to illustrate the fact that, in a wide variety of political circumstances and cultures over a long period of time, writers who have thought about conditions necessary for the survival and flourishing of their political communities had recourse to a set of interre-lated ideas concerning the constitution of and constraints on social and polit-ical power.

The chapter approaches this task from two directions. First, just to sug-gest a rough idea of the rule of law, it looks briefly at two examples of its failure. Thinking about them affords a glimpse into what drives the ideal. Second, the chapter takes a longer look at attempts over the millennia to give expression to this intuitive idea. The chapter concludes with a sketch of the components of a coherent, articulated conception of the rule of law. It will be the task of remaining chapters of Part I to fill out the sketch provided in this conclusion.

Law's Rule. Gerald J. Postema, Oxford University Press. © Oxford University Press 2022.
DOI: 10.1093/oso/9780190645342.003.0001

Law's Failure

Red Coats or Red Gowns

To enrich our understanding of this idea, consider a story from mid-seventeenth-century England. Oliver Cromwell dominated the Commonwealth of England after King Charles I was violently removed from the throne during the Civil War. In 1654, shortly after the Bare Bones Parliament named him Lord Protector, Cromwell sought to consolidate his power by winning the support of England's legal establishment. He approached Matthew Hale, a highly esteemed member of the legal community who had a reputation for integrity, learning, and command of the Common Law. Cromwell offered Hale a position on the Court of Common Pleas. Hale expressed reluctance to take the position due to his deep reservations about the legal grounds of the Protector's authority. Impatiently, Cromwell replied that he possessed ruling power and he intended to keep it, but that he sought to rule with law and needed skilled men of the law to administer justice. He added, pointedly, that if he could not govern by red gowns, he would govern by red coats.[2] Hale accepted the position and served on the court until Cromwell's death in 1658. Richard Cromwell, Oliver's son and successor, urged Hale to stay on the court, but he refused, citing the younger Cromwell's lack of legitimacy. After the restoration, in 1660, Hale was appointed Chief Baron of the Court of Exchequer where he served until appointed Chief Justice of the King's Bench in 1671. Hale died in 1676, after a distinguished legal career.[3]

At first glance, we might read Hale's acceptance of Cromwell's commission as opportunistic collaboration with a government of dubious legitimacy; but if we consider his professional life prior to this event and long after it, a different reading suggests itself. His deepest loyalty—even deeper than his Royalist sympathies—was to the Common Law and its commanding place in the English scheme of government. It is more likely that he was moved by the conviction that ruling power, however structured, must be held accountable to the law. After all, Hale knew his Coke. Sir Edward Coke, the preeminent jurist of the previous generation, wrote that law is "the golden and straight metwand" by which all causes are to be measured.[4] Even more fundamentally, Hale's view of governance was shaped by Bracton, the early thirteenth-century jurist who wrote, "Let [the ruler] temper his power by law, which is the bridle of power."[5] Accepting the position gave him an opportunity to tether Cromwell to the law. Cromwell saw in the law only a source and instrument of power; however, Hale, inspired by Bracton and Coke, saw in law a power by which power itself is bridled. Law, in his conviction, must govern the governors. On this view, law is not simply a matter of rules, it is a matter of ruling, *the law's* ruling.

Kids for Cash

Another story, from a very different era and legal context, introduces us to further dimensions of the rule-of-law idea. Between 2003 and 2008, the presiding judge of the juvenile court in Luzerne County, Pennsylvania, summarily sentenced several thousand young people to extended detention in private facili-ties far from the young defendants' homes.[6] In hearings that lasted an average of four minutes, Judge Mark Ciavarella handed down harsh sentences for minor infractions or even innocent actions—for throwing a steak at the boyfriend of the defendant's mother, for example, and for calling the police when his mother locked him out of the house. He paid little attention to the evidence let alone any special features of the defendants' circumstances. In the American juvenile justice system, the legally mandated aim is not punitive but restorative. The law charges court officials with securing "the best interest of the child." This charge gives judges a degree of discretion to fashion arrangements to suit the needs and special circumstances of each defendant. Ignoring the law, however, Judge Ciavarella imposed sentences at his pleasure, in proceedings that mocked federal and state constitutional and statutory guarantees of due process. Although guaranteed the right to counsel through the whole process, juvenile defendants were urged systematically and illegally to waive their rights and to plead guilty. Well over 50 percent of defendants appearing before Judge Ciavarella waived their rights to counsel, and 60 percent of those who did were placed in extended detention, while only 20 percent of those who were represented by counsel were so placed. "The judge's whim is all that mattered in that courtroom," said the legal director of the Juvenile Law Center (which was instrumental in finally exposing the practices of Ciavarella's court). "The law was basically irrelevant."[7]

In early 2009, the public learned that Ciavarella's "zero tolerance" policy was motivated by nothing more than venal sinister interest. Ciavarella and his fellow judge, Michael Conahan, had been paid handsomely—$2.6 million over this period—to send juveniles to two private detention centers, while working to eliminate the public detention center run by the county. The judges were indicted and later convicted on a number of federal charges including conspiracy, money laundering, racketeering, and tax evasion. Judge Ciavarella denied that the money he received for sending juveniles to the private detention centers in any way influenced his judgment. The Pennsylvania Supreme Court disagreed. In October 2009, the Court expunged all the convictions, some three thousand, handed down by Ciavarella from 2003 to 2008.

While the venal motive was not uncovered until 2009, the practices of systematic denial of constitutional due process rights, excessively harsh and arbitrarily imposed sentences, and utter disregard for the law went entirely unquestioned by hosts of people—other judges, district attorneys, public defenders, court officers and staff, police, probation officers, school administrators, teachers, and counselors who witnessed these outrages but did nothing to challenge them. The Interbranch Commission on Juvenile Justice, established by the state legislature to investigate the scandal, opened its proceedings in October 2009, with these words:

> This morning our Commission begins its public hearings to assess the breathtaking collapse of the juvenile justice system in Luzerne County. Two judges stand criminally charged for conduct that had the unmistakable effect of harming children ... there is little doubt that their conduct, whether criminal or not, had disastrous consequence for the juvenile justice system ... Our concern, however, is not only the action of two Luzerne County judges. Our concern is also the inaction of others. Inaction by judges, prosecutors, public defenders, the defense bar, public officials and private citizens—those who knew but failed to speak; those who saw but failed to act.[8]

Many people personally witnessed hundreds of occasions on which the constitutional rights of children were violated. Clear dictates of the law meant to protect children from abuse by adults and the state were ignored in their presence. For six years, no one spoke up or spoke out—or nearly no one. In 2004, the Wilkes-Barre *Times-Leader* ran a series of stories on apparent irregularities in Ciavarella's court, but the news reports fell on deaf ears. Many in the community, especially school administrators, liked Ciavarella's zero-tolerance stance; others in the community regarded irregularities as par for the course in Luzerne County, which had a long history of corruption, nepotism, and mob-influenced politics. Apparently, fear, uncertainty, indifference to familiar moral corruption, or approval of the end result silenced the public's judgment and anesthetized its will to challenge.

The list of wrongs done and evils inflicted on the children and families of Luzerne County is long and disgusting, but, without denying or minimizing any of the other wrongs, I want to draw attention to just one. I do so not because it is the most important one from a moral point of view, but because it is easily overlooked. In Luzerne County, there was not only a breakdown of justice and a failure of fairness but also a collapse of law, a failure of law's rule. In crucial respects, the law offered no protection to the children of the county. Law did not matter. It did not count. In the words of the prophet, the law became slack, the wicked surrounded the righteous, and judgment came forth perverted (Habakkuk 1:4). The protections promised by the rule of law were not realized. The rule of law failed due to a failure of what in Chapter 3 I will call *fidelity*.

Bulwark, Bridle, and Bond

Often, in contemporary discussions, the idea of the rule of law is said to be a modern, even specifically Anglo-American idea. It is true that the phrase "rule of law" has relatively recent English roots. It is usually traced to the publication in 1885 of A.V. Dicey's *Introduction to the Study of Law of the Constitution*[9] (although the *Oxford English Dictionary* traces the use of the term to 1500 and again 1559). Terms in others languages—for example, *Rechtsstaat, État de droit*—which are now treated as near synonyms, also emerged in the nineteenth century; they and "rule of law" carry overtones of the parochial political histories from which they emerged.[10]

Our concern is not with the provenance of the words, but with the content of the notion. This notion has much deeper roots. Over a long period of time and in a variety of political cultures its various elements have found expression in histories, philosophical texts and legal treatises, in fables, poetry, and plays. Johannes Althusius (1603) sketched a map to guide our exploration of this rich story. Right or law, he wrote:

> [I]s the guiding light of civil life, . . . a bulwark of public peace and discipline, a refuge for the weak, a bridle for the powerful, and a norm and straightener of imperium. . . . It is also the precept by which political life is instituted and cultivated.[11]

In short, law provides a *bulwark* of protection, a *bridle* on the powerful, both those in positions of political authority ("imperium") and those in the community at large who seek to dominate and exploit the weak, and a *bond* constituting and holding together the polity and giving public expression to an ideal of association.

Bulwark

The fourth-century BCE Greek Sophist, "Anonymous Iamblichi," set the stage for our tour. He argued that by necessity (*anankē*), human beings are driven to live together, yet they cannot do so while living in a lawless condition, since "the penalty for lawlessness is even greater than for living alone." Thus, "because of all these constraints law and justice are king among us." People "must fight for the law," wrote Heraclitus, "as they would for the city walls." In his *History*, Thucydides observed that when some in society want to impose their wills on others, they first seek to "destroy without a trace the laws that commonly govern such matters." However, they fail to realize that "it is only because of these [laws] that someone in trouble can hope to be saved, and anyone might be in danger some day and stand in need of such laws."[12]

Similarly, Hyperides (fourth century BCE) wrote that, when people are "ruled by the voice of law, not the threats of man ... [they] need not be frightened by accusation, only by proof of guilt"; and their safety does "not depend on men who flatter their masters ... but on [their] confidence in the law."[13] "When laws are written down," wrote Euripides, "he who is weak and he who is rich have equal justice: the weaker ones may speak as ill of the fortunate as they hear of themselves, and a lesser man can overcome a great one, if he has justice on his side."[14]

This thought is no less prominent in modern thinking about the rule of law. Echoing Althusius, authors of the preamble to the *Book of the General Lawes and Libertyes* (of Massachusetts) (1660) wrote, "Laws are the people's Birthright. . . . By this Hedge their All is secured against the Injuries of men."[15] Less than a decade earlier, Thomas Hobbes wrote that laws are like "hedges" along roads not "set as an obstacle to travelers, but to prevent them from wondering off, with injury to their fellow citizens . . . for the end of laws is not to restrain people from a harmless liberty, but to prevent them from rushing into dangers or harm to themselves or to the commonwealth."[16] A contemporary legal scholar sums up the point this way: the rule of law enables "the little guy to say to the big guy, 'You can't do that to me.' The big guy can be the state, a large corporation, or a well-connected individual—anyone or anything that, in the absence of law, would be able to do basically what it wanted."[17]

This bulwark has two dimensions. It promises law's *protection* and *recourse* against those who seek to impose their will on those who are weaker. Law defines and enforces limits on the exercise of power over others. But it also provides to victims avenues of legal recourse against those who do them wrong. Chief Justice Marshall, in the course of his argument in the historic case *Marbury v. Madison*, reflected this twofold dimension of the rule of law. "The essence of civil liberty," he wrote, "consists in the right of every individual to claim the protection of laws, whenever he receives an injury ... One of the first duties of government is to afford that protection." Each individual not only must be protected, but must be accorded a legally protected means to *claim* that protection. Marshall then links this recourse notion with the rule of law in its classic version. "The government of the United States has been emphatically termed a government of laws, and not of men. It will certainly cease to deserve this high appellation, if the laws furnish no remedy for the violation of a vested legal right."[18] Every legal right must have a remedy at law—*ubi ius ibi remedium*—and every right holder is entitled to enlist the government's support of that right and accord him relief when it is violated.

Marshall here follows Blackstone, the great eighteenth-century English Common Law scholar, but the principle he relies on has deeper roots. Sir Edward Coke in his *Institutes* (1642) draws the principle from Chapter 39 of Magna Carta

(1215/1225)—the headwaters of our modern notion of due process. Coke writes, "every subject of this Realm, for injury done to him in *bonis, terris vel persona* [goods, land or person], by any other subject . . . may take his remedy by the course of law, and have justice, and right for the injury done to him."[19] The rule of law, on this historic view, requires both protection and recourse—both legal constraints and legal resources that an individual can mobilize.

Bridle

Threats of domination, in the view of these writers, may come from many different quarters of our communities. Yet to call on law to hedge about the powerful among us in effect puts the tools of power in the hands of a few. The exercise of political power has been a constant concern of those who reflect on the conditions of a decent civil life together. The Gortyn Code manifested this concern. In fourth-century Athens, Plato wrote that the city has a happy future "where law is master [*despotēs*] over rulers and the rulers are slaves [*douloi*] to the law."[20] Similarly, Aristotle declared boldly that "the law should rule everything"[21]—"everything" meaning all matters but also all members of the polis, including those who exercise political power. Law must rule (*nomon archein*). He argued further, "one who bids the law to rule . . . [bids] god and understanding [or reason] alone rule, whereas one who bids man rule adds on a wild beast as well."[22] This probably is one source of the familiar sloganized version of the rule-of-law idea: it is said that we seek "the rule of law rather than the rule of men." But what Aristotle meant is often misunderstood. When Aristotle contrasts "reason" with the "element of the beast," he is contrasting human passions with the deliberative capacities of human beings. Justice Brandeis of the US Supreme Court captured Aristotle's meaning when he wrote that we look to law to help us govern ourselves because we want "deliberative forces [to] prevail over the arbitrary."[23]

Plato, of course, was also a fan of reason, but he was less sanguine about the law's living up to reason's demands. In the classic debate over which is better, the rule of a good man or the rule of good law, Plato ultimately landed on the side of the rule of law, but he gave just two cheers for the second best.[24] In the course of his discussion of this problem, he exposed a key challenge for any robust defense of the rule of law. Laws in their necessary generality, critics argued, are blind to circumstances that are of relevance to just and reasonable decision-making and governance. Plato agreed, but argued reluctantly that we must embrace law anyway, because it is unlikely we will ever succeed in selecting for ruling power persons who combine in full measure the knowledge, discernment, and integrity necessary to warrant our trust. Plato was familiar with stories of tyrants who, as Aeschylus (fifth century BCE) put it, rule alone and "send accounts to no one's audit for the deeds [they] do."[25] "Will there ever be moderation in the rule of one man," wrote Herodotus (fifth century BCE), one who "can do as he will and never be brought to account?"[26] Plato concluded that law is the only device that promises some degree of constraint on the exercise of arbitrary power. But law cannot do that job on its own—someone must be in a position to hold those who rule to account, someone must hold the reins of the bridle on the powerful.

An English Franciscan friar captured a late medieval dialectic on this theme in a song composed in praise of Simon de Montfort, Sixth Earl of Leister, leader of baronial opposition to King Henry III, after Simon's triumph over the king in the Battle of Lewes (1264). The friar wrote, "[E]very king is ruled by the laws he makes. . . . Let him who makes law, learn that he cannot rule who observes not the law." He expressed this maxim poetically:

> Dicitur vulgariter "ut rex vult, lex vadit"
> Veritas vult aliter, nam lex stat, rex cadit.[27]
>
> [It is commonly said, "as the king wills, so goes the law."
> The truth wills otherwise, for the law stands, though the king falls.]

This dialectic was set in motion by discovery in Europe of Justinian's sixth-century code of Roman Law, the Corpus Juris Civilis. In one part of the Code, the compilers wrote, "What pleases the prince [ruler] has the force of law" (Digest 1.4.1) and "the prince is not bound by the laws" (Digest 1.3.31). However, to medieval legal scholars, this maxim sat uncomfortably alongside a maxim in another part of the Code. This maxim read, "It is a statement worthy of the majesty of a ruler for the prince to profess himself bound by the laws. So much does our authority depend on the authority of the law. And indeed it is greater for the imperium to submit the principate to the laws" (Codex, 1.14.4). The ruler is legibus solutus—above or free of the law—yet, it is a fitting expression of the ruler's majesty to submit to the law. Is this submission a matter of grace or the result of some effective demand? If the latter, what form does this demand take? This question shaped much of the thinking about the character and constitution of ruling power and constraints upon it in late medieval and early modern thought.

We caught a glimpse of this dialectic in Matthew Hale's echo of Bracton. In about 1235, Bracton insisted that law is the bridle of power, and therefore the ruler should temper his power with law. Directly citing the Codex maxim, he adds, "Nothing is more fitting for a sovereign than to live by the laws."[28] Law not only applies to those who exercise ruling power, but they must acknowledge and profess themselves bound by law. They must submit to it, acknowledge that they are subject to it. Recall Plato's striking image: rulers are slaves and law is master.

Who Holds the Reins?

How are we to understand this thought? It suggests that law rules when those whom law purports to govern *impose* its rule *on themselves*. Law's rule is *self-imposed*. However, early commentators on the Code, rejected this reading.[29] To be bound by self-imposed resolutions, or self-commands, they argued, is not to be bound *by law*. The problem is not that a personal resolve is difficult to keep, but rather that submission to law cannot be a matter of submission to *oneself*. We have now come to the crux of the problem of law's rule. To understand it, we must understand what it is to be subject to law, and in particular, what it is to submit to law, that is, to undertake the commitment to be ruled by law.

Bracton's response was twofold. First, he insisted that law is not merely a cloak that rulers can put on or take off at will, or after a pragmatic assessment of their circumstances. Rather, "law makes him the king"; there is no king where will rules rather than law—no *rex* without *lex*.[30] Law not only directs and constrains ruling power, it *constitutes* it and grounds it. Outside of law, there is only naked force. The English divine Richard Hooker, writing in the 1590s, reinforced Bracton's premise. No person or cause is free from subjection to the king's power, he wrote, yet that power is limited such that "unto all his proceedings the law itself is a rule. The axioms of our regal government are these, *Lex facit Regem*. . . . What power the king hath he hath it by law."[31]

Yet, second, Bracton still had to address the question: Who holds the reins of law's bridle? His answer: the barons or magnates of the kingdom.

> The king has a superior, namely, God. Also the law, by which he is made king. Also his *curia*, namely the earls and barons, because if he is without bridle, that is without law, they ought to put the bridle on him. That is why the earls are called the partners, so to speak, of the king; he who has a partner has a master.[32]

No doubt, Bracton was influenced by the recently negotiated Magna Carta (1215, 1225). The Charter is best known to British and American students of the rule of law through its Clause 29, which reads:

> No free man shall be taken or imprisoned or desseised or outlawed or exiled or in any way ruined, nor will we go or send against him, except by the lawful judgement of his peers or by the law of the land.[33]

This clause anticipates the doctrine enshrined in Amendment 5 of the US Constitution: "No person shall be deprived of life, liberty, or property, without due process of law."

Yet the Charter expressed a more general understanding of the law and its role in ruling. It imposed obligations of fealty on all parties. It called on both king and barons to keep faith with each other and with the principles that governed their lives together. Clause 61, to which Bracton implicitly referred, gave expression to this idea of joint responsibility. It required the king, on notification by his barons that he had violated the terms of the Charter, to cease and correct his violation, and, if he failed to do so, the Charter empowered an elected group of twenty-five barons to seek redress by any means short of harming the king and his family. They were entitled to "distrain upon and assail [the king] in every way possible, with the support of the whole community of the land." The Magna Carta embraced the idea that one who submits to the law must be held accountable to that law by others. Personal resolve and good intentions were thought to be insufficient. Institutions were created to secure accountability of those who exercise ruling power.

Although the Magna Carta may be the most famous late medieval expression of this principle, it was not unprecedented. Nearly a century earlier, the Count of Flanders (which territory at the time included parts of what we know as northern France) issued a number of charters to cities and other associations granting privileges to their residents. In one such charter, barons swore to support citizens if the count violated its terms.[34] This idea took root in France and emerged in the Reformation-era resistance manifesto, *Vindiciae contra Tyrannos*, which explored "the legitimate power of a prince over the people, and of the people over a prince."[35] It appeared seven years after the St. Bartholomew's Day Massacre (1572), in which thousands of Huguenots were murdered in a plot orchestrated by Catherine de' Medici to secure the reign of her son, Charles IX of France. Combining biblical language and Roman Law doctrines, the author of *Vindiciae* argued that God established a covenant with the king and the people that bound them in debt to God. Shrewdly, God made them each wholly liable for the entire debt, thereby each "by consequence are bound one for another and each for the whole." This empowered each party to hold the other to the terms of the debt.

Not long after, Johannes Althusius, scholar of Reformed theology and Roman Law and syndic of the Frisian city of Emden, develop this principle in an elaborate theory of association and government in *Politica* (1603/1614). "For what God is in the world, the navigator is in a ship, the driver in a chariot, the director in a chorus, the commander in an army, so law (*lex*) is in the city." He adds: "Law is thus over everyone. It is the superior above all, and each and every man recognizes it as the superior."[36]

This is a bold statement of the sovereignty of law: "Law is over all." But he did not leave the matter at that; rather, he sketched institutions to give effect to this principle. Taking a cue from his study of the constitution of Sparta, he charged officials elected from the elite of political society and acting on their behalf with the task of holding the supreme magistrate to the law.[37] This was not just their right; it was their solemn *duty*. The government of the supreme magistrate, in this constitution, holds the people of the commonwealth to obedience to its laws, but equally they, through their representatives, hold government officials to the law. Following the *Vindiciae* model, Althusius made the parties co-debtors, equally responsible for holding each other accountable to the terms of the covenant.[38] Against his absolutist opponents, Althusius insisted, "It is not absurd or contrary to nature that a king as the greater is subjected even to an inferior. For he who is greater or equal to another can be subjected to the jurisdiction of the other. Litigating parties can thus submit themselves to the decision of inferiors, and inferiors can judge in the case of superiors."[39] In England, half a century later, James Harrington echoed this principle. The polity, he wrote, must be "an empire of laws not of men." A defining feature of this empire is "that, as the hand of the magistrate is the executive power of the law, so the head of the magistrate is answerable unto the people that his execution be according to the law."[40]

Bond: Law as a Mode of Association

The idea of mutual accountability under law is companion to another theme that sounds through history. Anonymous Iamblichi associated *anomia*, the condition of lawlessness among human beings, with the condition of a war of all against all (later theorized by Hobbes), but he linked *eunomia*, the realized condition of mutual commitment to the law, with polity-wide trust. "The first result of lawfulness is trust,"[41] he maintained. Solon's legendary law-making efforts were said to result in *isonomia*, equal law, equality before the law,[42] or, perhaps, as Aristotle was to put it, a law for peers. But it was Cicero who clearly articulated the ideal. "Law is the bond which unites the civic association"; for "what is the city but an association or partnership in justice [or according to law—*iuris societas*]?"[43]

In sixteenth-century England, James Morice captured the same idea in the biblical language we encountered in *Vindiciae contra Tyrannos*.

> [A] better kynde of Monorchie hathe byne by common Assent ordayned and establyshed, wherein the Prince (not by Lycentious will and Imoderate Assertions but by the Law, That is by the prudent Rules *and* Preceptes of Reason agreed vppon *and* made the Covenant of the Common Wealth) may Justly governe and commande, and the People in due obedience saeflie lyve and quyetly enioye their owne.[44]

The king is to govern justly, according to law that made the commonwealth covenant. Harrington, likewise, characterized the "empire of laws" as that "whereby the civil society of men is instituted and preserved upon the foundation of common right or interest."[45] However, it was Althusius, in the early modern period, who articulated perhaps most richly this notion of law as social bond.

A polity or commonwealth is a *consociation*, he argued, a partnership of "symbiotes," who "pledge themselves each to the other ... to mutual communication whatever is useful and necessary for the harmonious exercise of social life."[46] Members not only live among one another, but are, in St. Paul's evocative phrase, "members one of another."[47] They "communicate" goods, services, and, most importantly, common rights and responsibilities. These things are not *allocated to* them, nor *exchanged between* them by negotiated bargain, but rather *entrusted to* each other and hence shared ("communicated"). Something more than exchange is involved, for both the reciprocal giving and the things given convey something of meaning; the movement brings the parties together, creating, reproducing, and enhancing unity. This ongoing activity gives rise to a set of rights, powers, and responsibilities proper to their consociation.[48] This law (*ius symbioticum*) is mutually established and mutually maintained. *Ius* emerges from, or supervenes upon, the covenantal activity of members of the commonwealth. On Althusius's view, *ius* is not a code of commanding laws, or discrete bill of rights and powers, but more generally *eunomia*, a spirit of mutual lawfulness, a mutual commitment to life governed by law.[49] *Ius*, then, gives rise to the rights and responsibilities *communicated* among its members, constituting them as a people and grounding the government that they constitute.

Althusius recognized that authority in the commonwealth entails an inequality of a kind, an asymmetry of power, but he insisted that this inevitable asymmetry is consistent with the mutuality that lies at the core of consociation. This is so for four reasons.

First, he subscribed to the medieval principle of double sovereignty. According to this principle, while the ruler is superior to any individual member of the community, the ruler is inferior and subordinate to the community as a whole (*maior singulis, minor universis*).[50]

Second, the ruler holds this position of superiority only by virtue of the polity's vesting of the person in the office, and the ruler retains it only so long as he legitimately remains in that office. Moreover, while in office "administrators," who "are called lords," must "regard their subjects not as slaves and bonded servants, but as brothers."[51] Likewise, members of the community are subordinate only to persons while they are incumbent in the office and only to powers vested in them by the office. The hierarchy is positional, not personal.

Third, and most importantly, while incumbents are empowered to exercise authority over members of the community, they can do so only according to law. Law is the ultimate sovereign and thus the office and power of the supreme magistrate, and all officials of its government, are ordained, constituted, and constrained by law. "All power is limited by definite boundaries and laws," he wrote. "No power is absolute, infinite, unbridled, arbitrary, and lawless. Every power is bound to laws, right, and equity."[52] Thus, as we have seen, law "is over everyone. It is the superior above all, and each and every man recognizes it as the superior."

Finally, and following on this subordination of all power to the law common to them, every governmental official, including the supreme magistrate, participates in an institutionalized network of mutual accountability. Officials are subject to accountability by the commonwealth through its official representatives. Authority, in Althusius's view, necessarily carries with it liability to being held accountable, liability that is shared with all members of the community. In exercising authority over others, one is bound to recognize the authority of others to hold one to account with respect to the law that is common among them.

The aim of the exploration we have just completed, as I mentioned at the outset, was not to give a systematic history of the development of the rule-of-law ideal but to illustrate how writers across time and cultures drew on a constellation of related ideas when thinking about the need for ruling power and for constraints on it. In Anglo-American societies, these ideas have congealed under the rubric "the rule of law." In other political communities and other languages many of the same concerns, conditions, and values have been yoked together. The rule-of-law rubric collects a complex set of ideas. This book seeks to bring some order to this complexity, to work out its implications for social and especially governmental institutions as well as the behavior of officials and citizens, and to understand more deeply the grounds and limits of its appeal and normative force. Our first task is to identify and clearly articulate the core organizing idea of the rule-of-law ideal.

The Rule of Law: The Core Idea

It is tempting to equate the concept of the rule of law with the straightforward thought that law must be in place and effective in a polity and that everyone must obey it. "The rule of law prevails," writes a prominent constitutional theorist, "where all individuals and all groups recognize an obligation to comply with law and act accordingly."[53] The rule of law, we might say, demands universal compliance.

This thought is not fundamentally mistaken, for the rule of law is robust in a community, in part, when members of the community "communicate" law and share a commitment to comply with it. However, this thought suggests both too little and too much. Even to get the rule of law going in a community it is not enough to see to it that there is "law and order" there, or that everyone complies with the law. After all, as Martin Krygier observed, "there were lots of laws under Stalin, and lots of rule, but there was not much rule of law."[54] Widespread compliant behavior may not stem from regard for the law or even an elementary understanding of it, but only from a savvy capacity, rooted in fear, to predict the next uniformed blow. The real experienced meaning of the "law and order" slogan is sometimes nothing more than arbitrary orders concealed beneath a tissue of law.

In addition, the rule of law in some circumstances may legitimate noncompliance with orders of those who hold positions of legal authority, and possibly the laws they enact if they violate rule-of-law standards. Not every case of dissent violates the ideal; in fact, the rule of law may be strengthened by conscientious defiance of demands of legal authorities who questionably claim legal warrant for their orders. We must look beyond the mere existence of law and universal compliance with it if we are to understand the rule of law's core ambition.

However, if we do so, we immediately see a dizzying array of proposed standards. Respected legal theorist Lon Fuller argued that the rule of law requires that laws be general, consistent, prospective, accessible, intelligible, and stable, and the behavior of officials be broadly congruent with these public rules.[55] In the spirit of this "formal" understanding of the rule of law, others add standards for governmental institutions, especially courts. They insist that the judiciary must be independent of political pressures especially from the executive branch of government, and that courts respect familiar principles of due process.[56] Yet critics argued that these principles of formal legality are thin and uninspiring and fail to capture the depth and force of the rule-of-law ideal. They insist on a larger and more robust set of standards. For example, in 2004, the UN Security Council adopted the following list of standards to guide their thinking about the rule of law in "post-conflict societies."

> The "rule of law" . . . refers to a principle of governance in which all persons, institutions and entities, public and private, including the State itself, are accountable to laws that are publicly promulgated, equally enforced and independently adjudicated, and which are consistent with international human rights norms and standards. It requires, as well, measures to ensure adherence to the principles of supremacy of law, equality before the law, accountability to the law, fairness in the application of the law, separation of powers, participation in decision-making, legal certainty, avoidance of arbitrariness and procedural and legal transparency.[57]

This is a mouthful. It is a lot to pack into a single concept of political morality, but some advocates add even more, arguing that the rule-of-law ideal incorporates robust principles of democracy or substantive economic and political equality, while others find "Asian" or communitarian values essential to the rule of law.[58]

Which of the above standards should we bring out to center stage? Sir Ivor Jennings once called the idea of the rule of law "an unruly horse,"[59] because the content of the rule of law has been hotly disputed. It is disputed by philosophers and legal theorists, of course, but also by public figures, politicians, and government officials, by domestic watchdog groups, and by international development organizations. The rule of law is a powerful political idea and ideal. It sets standards for laws and legal institutions, and more broadly, it articulates a distinctive mode of governance, seeking to temper and direct the exercise of ruling power; in addition, it gives shape to an ideal mode of political association. It occupies a key position in our repertoire of important values and principles of political morality alongside democracy, justice, fundamental human rights, liberty, and community. It supplies the architectural frame of a just and decent society and the infrastructure of democracy. It is a foundation stone of economic and political development. Establishing a robust rule of law is widely thought to be the first task in rebuilding nations shaken by civil wars or oppressed by authoritarian rule. While it enjoys a halo of legitimacy, it imposes irritating constraints on those who exercise power and necessitates compromises with other political goals. Consequently, it is vulnerable to capture and rhetorical abuse by those who would retain its halo and minimize its costs. Political ideals with this kind of scope, power, and visibility cannot escape controversy, not just at the periphery but also at its core.[60] How can we tame this unruly horse and chart a path through this controversy?

We can begin, I believe, by reflecting on the intuitive ideas examined earlier in this chapter. From them emerges a clear view of the motivating concern and ambition lying at the heart of the ideal. Repeatedly, our philosophers, theologians, poets, playwrights, politicians, and jurists trained their attention on the exercise of power—the power of those holding political office, but also of those in positions of power outside of government. They did not object to all exercises of power, because they recognized that asymmetries of power and authority are inevitable and often necessary and legitimate. The cause of their worry about power was what Martin Krygier calls power's "special disease," namely, "the propensity of power unconstrained to be exercised in arbitrary ways."[61] "Opposition to the exercise of arbitrary power" is the value animating the rule of law.[62]

But the rule of law is not just a negative idea, the idea of the *absence* of arbitrary power. It is positive and both more realistic and more sharply focused than this negative thought suggests. It is realistic in that it does not presume that we can eliminate the arbitrary exercise of power. Our best hope is to constrain it, to offer protections and, where they fail, recourse against it. It is positive and more sharply focused in that it looks to law for the protections and recourse, the remedy, against the disease of arbitrary power. A number of other devices or strategies might be employed against the arbitrary exercise of power; and they may be more or less appropriate to the social-political circumstances in which arbitrary power threatens the political community. But the rule-of-law ideal proposes a particular device for the tempering of power: the law. If other devices are also available, rule-of-law partisans may be willing to partner with others deploying them to secure even more effective constraints and modes of recourse.

Law is commonly set in opposition to that which is arbitrary as its logical contrary. In its Petition of Right (1610) addressed to James I of England, the House of Commons held up "amongst many other points of happiness and freedom" enjoyed by his subjects none more precious than to be "governed by the certain rule of the law . . . and not by any uncertain or arbitrary form of government."[63] Against the disease of ruling power, the cure is *law's* rule. As Euripides insisted long ago, law enables the vulnerable to stand up to the powerful and demand warrant for their intrusive or injurious behavior; it provides a forum in which they can challenge and criticize the exercise of power. In a word, the rule-of-law ideal seeks to enable legal subjects to "speak law to power,"[64] and thereby offer protection and recourse against its arbitrary exercise.

Thus, the core of the rule-of-law ideal is in one respect clear and straightforward, if not entirely simple. Throughout its long history, the idea is shaped by the following twofold thought: (1) a polity is well-ordered, and its members are accorded the dignity rightfully demanded by them in the name of their common membership, when its members are secured against the arbitrary exercise of power, and (2) law, because of its distinctive features, is especially and perhaps uniquely capable of providing such security. The rule of law imposes a moral demand upon political communities and their governments. It demands that they be structured in such a way that those who are subject to power, from whatever quarter, are provided protection and recourse against its arbitrary exercise though the law's distinctive features, tools, and modes of operation. In sum, when law rules in a political community, it *provides protection and recourse against the arbitrary exercise of power through law's distinctive tools.*

The rule of law is a moral ideal, a component of good, decent, and just political community. It seeks to temper power, protect against its abuse, *through law.* But we must hasten to add that law is not necessarily, or even always reliably, just. Defenders of the rule of law are clear-eyed about the potential for law to go wrong and do wrong. One way law can go wrong is to fail to meet the demands of the rule of law itself. But it can also go wrong by doing or enabling injustice of various forms. We will have to address the complex connection between the rule of law and principles of justice and respect for human rights in Chapter 5. However, first, we must elaborate the essential component principles of the rule-of-law ideal. This ideal embraces three immediately implied principles, which we saw repeatedly articulated in our tour of intuitive expressions of the ideal across its long history.

The first is law's *sovereignty*: Aristotle's idea that law must rule (*nomon archein*), that a political community in which law rules is, we might say, a *nomarchy*. This principle is, itself, a complex idea, embracing three closely related ideas. Nomarchy embraces (1) the principle of *legality*: the idea that governments must *rule by law*—that is, all governing power must be exercised through or by means of law. The rule of law calls for law as the infrastructure of life in the polity and the proper mode of exercise of governing power. Nomarchy embraces (2) *exclusivity*. This principle holds that all governing power is derived only from and is ordained exclusively by law. "To rule is an *office*, not an *empire*," declared a late sixteenth-century political text;[65] that is, government is a law-constituted institution; its powers are only those ordained by law. This is not to say that those who exercise governing power cannot act outside their law-ordained capacities, but only that they cannot *legitimately* do so. Nomarchy embraces (3) the crucial principle of *reflexivity*. "No one is above the law," we say in the vernacular, or, in Plato's words, "law is master and the ruler is slave." Less dramatically, Aristotle insisted, "rightly constituted laws should be the final sovereign." Law governs all, including—especially including—those who govern.

In addition to the major principle of sovereignty, two equally general principles follow directly from the core ambition of the rule of law: equality and fidelity. The first is associated with the political ideal of equality, but it is specifically tailored to the ambition of the rule of law. The idea is that all are subject to a common body of laws, and, importantly, each is entitled to its protection. Its concern is to include each person in a company of peers when it comes to the scope and range of the promise of the law's protection against the abuse of power. In the eyes of the law, this protection must be enjoyed by all who fall within the law's jurisdiction. Hence, the rule of law requires *equality in the eyes of the law*. This principle requires that all who are bound by law be entitled equally to law's protection and recourse of law against the abuse of power.

The audacity of the rule-of-law ideal is evident in a further feature of it and a third directly implied principle: *fidelity*. We should pause a moment to explain this notion. Law's sovereignty maintains that law must rule, that a political community in which the rule of law is robust is a nomarchy. However, as we shall see in Chapter 3, it is not just a little puzzling to figure out what it means for *law* to *rule*. The problem is that laws don't rule, people do. Chapter 3 will argue that law can rule only if a certain *ethos* takes root in the political community. The rule of law includes not only the formal, procedural, and institutional standards of legality, but it also comprises a set of relationships and responsibilities rooted in core convictions and commitments, which are essential for the realization of this ideal.

"Fidelity" is the term I will use to capture this idea. Law can rule only when it draws on the resources of civil society to breathe life into laws and institutions.

The fidelity principle maintains that *the rule of law is robust in a polity only when its members, legal officials and legal subjects alike, take responsibility for holding each other to account under the law.* A robust practice of holding each other accountable under the law is essential for the realization of law's rule. The soul of the rule of law is fidelity.

Taken together, *sovereignty, equality,* and *fidelity,* along with the deeper values they serve, constitute the complex ideal of the rule of law. We will carefully unpack these principles and trace their implications in the chapters to come. We will also explore the values they are said to serve to determine whether their bold claims need to be clipped back or perhaps strengthened.

Steps toward a Coherent Conception of the Rule of Law

Our watchword—the rule of law promises protection and recourse against the arbitrary exercise of power through the law's distinctive modes of operation—will guide our reflections from here on out. Yet its relative simplicity belies the fruitfully complex structure of a workable and defensible conception of the rule of law. Much of the confusion and controversy over the "definition" of the rule of law in the last half-century or more is due to a failure to grasp fully the structure of the core idea expressed by this watchword and its place in political morality considered more generally. Attempts to define the concept of the rule of law typically select and order various potential downstream institutions and standards by which to measure them. However, these efforts were distorted by looking exclusively to familiar institutions and practices rather than to the broader ambitions and values of the rule of law.[66] The chapters to follow adopt Krygier's approach. This will allow us to ask, concerning different political and social circumstances, in what ways and with respect to what features or tools of law can it contribute to the aim of providing the protection and recourse that it promises. We can ask, further, which downstream standards and which institutions and practices designed to serve them offer the best chance of realizing this contribution.

Several broad features of the conception provide a template for our discussion in the chapters to follow and generate some of the key questions they will seek to answer.

First, the core idea articulated in the previous section of this chapter has a distinctive structure. The focal and organizing *aim* of the rule of law is to temper the exercise of power to avoid to the extent possible its arbitrary exercise, while the *means* of doing so is provided by the law. Law seeks to constrain in advance the arbitrary exercise of power (protection) and to offer means of holding those who exercise power accountable after the fact (recourse). This aim implies constraints on government and its defining institutions, and on law itself, on the form law takes and on its implementation, as these are defined by the principles of sovereignty and equality; it also calls for an ethos imposing a set of mutual obligations and responsibilities on officials and lay members of the political community in which it takes hold, as defined by the principle of fidelity.

In Chapter 2 we take up the task of articulating with greater precision the key concepts in our watchword. In particular, we will seek to understand what is meant by power, what forms of power the rule of law is concerned with and when power is exercised arbitrarily. We will also explore at some length the features and tools of law on which the rule of law depends for protection and recourse against arbitrarily exercised power. In Chapter 3 we will articulate and defend the principles identified above: sovereignty of law, equality in the eyes of the law, and fidelity. Chapters 2 and 3 plant talk of the rule of law in a set of closely related, general ideas and principles that constitute the rule-of-law ideal.

Second, this ideal is grounded in yet more fundamental values of political morality and is realized more concretely in institutions, offices, associations, and practices of particular political communities. The rule of law is an important value of political morality, but it is one among others. It is a distinct principle, not reducible to or incorporating other familiar values like justice or democracy. It is a middle-level value that stands between more fundamental values of political morality, on the one hand, and the institutions or practices that realize it on the other. The moral standing and normative force of the ideal depend on the deeper values that it serves.[67] It also stands in important relations to other key values of political morality. Chapter 4 explores the moral foundations of the ideal, and Chapter 5 charts the complex relations that exist between the rule of law and the values of democracy, justice, and respect for fundamental human rights.

Third, this ideal gets concrete substance in particular political communities. It is realized in their legal systems, political institutions, associations, and organizations of civil society, and the practices in which they all are embedded. The rule of law makes demands on institutions of government, centers of social power, and the behavior of officials and citizens through a series of downstream standards adjusted to political and social circumstances that can vary across political communities. The deeper values served by the ideal define the scope of rule-of-law demands and the moral weight they bring to competition with other important values or principles of political morality. With an understanding of the deeper values on which the ideal rests, and some idea of the distinctive features of particular political communities, we can hope to introduce some order to the dizzying array of competing downstream standards and norms that, as we saw earlier, compete for allegiance. Chapter 6 is devoted to exploring the various institutions designed to realize the rule of law.

Fourth, we should keep in mind that behavior or political developments that appear to compromise the rule of law may not amount to failures of the political community measured against its standards, but may rather mark the limits of the ideal. Chapter 7 explores these limits.

These limits can take two forms. One kind of limit is moral. The rule of law's demands may be defeated by yet more pressing concerns of political morality. Political life is governed by multiple moral concerns that can come into conflict, and when this happens the concern of greater moral importance must prevail. A familiar, if controversial, line of thought argues that law must not intrude in domestic (household) relationships even to temper the exercise of power in them because privacy and individual liberty take precedence. If this is correct, one limit of the rule of law has been identified.

A second kind of limit has to do with the nature of the ideal itself. It is possible, some have argued, that given its nature, it may in some circumstances fail to constrain arbitrary power. It is said, for example, that in times of emergency, the normative force of rule-of-law constraints and devices is not merely defeated, but law itself is silenced. This, too, of course, is a controversial thesis, but it too must be addressed.

Part I concludes the task of articulating a conception of the rule of law by considering a number of threats to which it is especially vulnerable, while Part II addresses a number of challenges to this conception that emerge once we recognize that the rule of law has its limits. These challenges, we shall see, represent challenges *for* the rule of law, but not challenges *to* the ideal itself—challenges that must be addressed thoughtfully, but not threats to viability or normative force of the ideal.

In view of the complexity of the ideal, it is not surprising that it has been a cause of confusion and a magnet for controversy. Yet this complexity can be ordered in a way that makes possible reasoned reflection, analysis, and argument. The core idea articulated above provides an illuminating and broadly attractive structure in terms of which the various, often contested, elements of the rule of law—its constituent standards, institutions, and conditions—can be situated and related in a coherent and compelling conception of the rule-of-law ideal. This structure makes clear the connection between an important political value and salient features of law in a way that disciplines and directs debate over constituent elements. We can hope to make progress in understanding the ideal and its demands by paying attention to the level at which our analysis and argument are pitched and the kind of empirical and normative considerations that are likely to be most relevant to them.

2
Power, Accountability, and Law's Toolbox

In the preceding chapter, we considered a plausible candidate for the animating core of the rule-of-law ideal. The rule of law, we learned, *seeks to provide protection and recourse against the arbitrary exercise of power through the distinctive instrumentalities of the law*. This handy watchword is not yet an articulated conception of the ideal. (A conception would include a set core of principles, an argument that grounds them in deeper principles of political morality, and at least a general sketch of how the core principles are realized in the institutions and practices of particular political communities.) Still, the watchword offers a useful blueprint from which to begin building such a conception.

Yet, even with blueprint, the task is not easy. The English political philosopher, Jeremy Bentham, warned that "truths that form the basis of political and moral science . . . grow among thorns; and are not to be plucked, like daisies, by infants as they run."[1] Among the thorns to avoid are vague or inadequate understandings of the key terms of this watchword. So our first task is to refine our understanding of them. We need to understand more precisely (1) what kind of power the ideal seeks to protect against; (2) what forms of power are included within the scope of this idea; (3) what count as arbitrary exercises of it; (4) what is meant by "protection and recourse" against such exercises; (5) what contribution law and its distinctive modes of operation can make to realizing the ideal; and, related to this, (6) what kind of accountability might be fit for the rule of law. We will take some time in this chapter to fill out these key ideas. We begin with the notion of power.

Power

The rule of law is concerned not with the abuse of *law*, but rather with the abuse of *power* in social and political life. We can understand "power" in two ways. Power as *capacity* is the ability of certain agents to influence or control the decisions or actions of other agents. We can also think of power as the *position* or privilege created and sustained by law or social norms.

Consider a few examples. A mugger has power to make his victim hand over her purse; a slave master has power to make his slave pick his cotton; a military commander has power to order his troops into battle; a police officer has power

Law's Rule. Gerald J. Postema, Oxford University Press. © Oxford University Press 2022.
DOI: 10.1093/oso/9780190645342.003.0002

to order a crowd to disperse or to stop a person driving while intoxicated; an employer may have power to make his employee cut his hair or abandon his plan to marry his male beloved. In each case, an agent[2] has the ability to get others to do something they may not otherwise wish to do. Physical strength or possession of a weapon gives the mugger power. In other cases, power comes with a power wielder's position defined by law or social norms. Sometimes the ability is based wholly or nearly so on the position the power wielder holds; sometimes on both physical strength and position. In each of these cases, the power involves getting someone else to do something, so I will treat them as cases of power as capacity. In contrast, we sometimes think of power simply in terms of position or law-enabled privilege, without implying directly a capacity for getting other people to do things. For example, a homeowner has the power to sell his house, and an executive has power to appoint or hire an assistant or advisor.

The rule of law focuses primarily on abuse of power as capacity, but it is also concerned secondarily with abuse of power as position. We will consider power as capacity first and primarily and return more briefly at the end of this section to consider power as position.

Speaking very generally, power is the ability that something has to bring about a change in the world, as when the rain enlivens my thirsty hydrangeas or when I cut down a dead tree in my garden. The wielder of power can be a creature or force in the natural world—deer have power to destroy my hostas, and storms have power to knock down trees taking power lines with them; the power wielder may also be a responsible agent—I have the power to disturb your quiet Sunday afternoon by using my leaf blower for an hour.

We usually think of power as the ability to change the physical world in some way. Philosophers also talk about *normative*—moral or legal—powers, powers to bring about changes in the moral or legal world we inhabit. For example, by making a promise to you, I put myself under obligation to do what I promise and you acquire a right to rely on my doing what I promised; and when I sell my car to you, I enable you to exercise all the rights (and must perform all the duties) of an owner of that vehicle. In these cases, I exercise a power that I have to change the rights and duties we have with respect to each other and to others. Power as position in some cases involves exercise or abuse of normative powers.

Morality and law are typically concerned with the actions of responsible agents, rather than forces or denizens of nature. The class of responsible agents includes individual human beings, groups, associations, and organizations. Moral values other than the rule of law—for example, justice, kindness, or benevolence—consider the ability of agents to affect the well-being or interests of others. However, when the rule of law is concerned with power as capacity, it is concerned with the ways *agents* can *influence* or *control* the behavior of other *agents* (either with physical means or through exercise of its normative powers).

It is concerned with a special case of generic power, namely, the *power one agent has over another*. Xenophon, in the fourth century BCE, captured the notion well. Power, he wrote, is "the action of the stronger when he constrains the weaker to do whatever he chooses, not by persuasion, but by force."[3]

To understand the rule of law focuses on power over others consider distinctive features of this kind of power. First, it is *agent-regarding*: it is a capacity of certain responsible agents (power wielders) with respect to the decisions and actions of other responsible agents (power subjects). Deer can eat my hosta plants, and I may take steps to protect the plants, knowing that deer are in the neighborhood, but the deer (we assume) are not responsible agents exercising power over me.

Second, agent-regarding influence may be momentary, but the rule of law is concerned with capacities of agents that exist over time and are embedded in social, moral, or legal relations. Power relations are social, not natural, facts. Social arrangements enable wielders to subject others to their power. Thus, their power is *relational*: exercising and responding to this kind of power are ways *persons* relate to *other persons*. They involve decisions, choices, and actions of one responsible agent taken with an eye to influencing the actions of another agent. Alice's power to influence Bert is not a property Alice alone possesses but a social relation between Alice and Bert. We say Alice "has" power over Bert, but it is more accurate to say Alice is *in a position* to exercise power over Bert.

Third, these social relations are *unequal*, characterized by asymmetry between the power wielder and power subject. Usually, the power subject is *dependent* on the power wielder (or any interdependence between them favors the power wielder). Thus, power for rule-of-law purposes is *the socially embedded capacity of one agent to influence another in circumstances of marked dependency and inequality*. In light of these three factors, it is fair to say that the power wielder *has power over* the power subject, and the latter is *in the power of* the wielder.

Fourth, the rule of law recognizes a variety of *means* wielders use to exercise their power. They are not limited to coercion based on physical strength. Wielders may offer incentives or disincentives or exercise their authority (for example, a judge can order the tortfeasor to pay damages to the plaintiff or order a government official to give a congressional committee access to internal documents). Wealth and social standing are sources of social power, so too are differential access to technology and command over information. The means of power may also be psychological by which wielders manipulate the desires or wishes of agents or shape the parameters of their practical deliberation. The use of these means can be especially worrisome, because often the wielder can exercise the power without the subject's awareness of it and sometimes even with their (unwitting) agreement or participation. (In Chapter 13, we will discuss the power of digital platform—e.g., Facebook and Twitter—to manipulate behavior and desires.)

The rule of law is concerned with a wide range of means of exercising power, but not all forms of influence. In particular, it does not oppose deliberative forms of influence; on the contrary, it favors replacing other means of power with offering persons reasons for acting. Of course, sometimes we think of coercive incentives or disincentives as "reasons." We say the mugger's demand, "Your money or your life," gives you a "reason" to hand over your cash, but the mugger and victim do not engage in the sort of deliberative exchange the rule of law has in view. It opposes such nondeliberative modes of influencing behavior.

Finally, we usually think of power in terms of its exercise—my blowing leaves disturbs your quiet Sunday afternoon, or the mugger's demanding, "Your money or your life." Yet power exists even when wielders don't exercise it; and we have reason to be concerned about the *existence* of the power apart from any particular *exercise* of it. The mere existence of the power can in some circumstances influence the behavior of those subject to it and trigger the concern of the rule of law. Seeing a police car coming down the highway entrance ramp may motivate me to slow down; learning that the government has a free hand to crack down on protesters may keep me off the streets. Lunsford Lane, a former slave, wrote compellingly about this effect of power's existence.

> I endeavored so to conduct myself as not to become obnoxious to the white inhabitants, knowing as I did their power, and their hostility to the colored people . . . in every way I wore as much as possible the aspect of slavery . . . [Also] I had never appeared to be even so intelligent as I really was. This all colored people at the south, free and slaves, find it particularly necessary for their own comfort and safety to observe.[4]

African Americans (especially males) report that Lane's experience is not limited to the South during Reconstruction.

At least two points of view are available on the power relationship, that of the power wielder and that of the power subject. We may be inclined to focus our moral concern on the attitudes or intentions of the wielder. However, this must not be our sole focus, for one does not escape the position of power over others by not wishing to be in it or exercising that power benevolently. As Frederick Douglass put it, "My feelings [toward slave masters] were not the result of any marked cruelty in the treatment I received; they sprang from the consideration of my being a slave at all. It was slavery—not the mere incidents—that I hated."[5] Likewise, our moral concern might focus on the power subject's *experience* of subjection to power. But this concern, also, must not be our sole focus. For the experience of subjection depends to some degree on the agent's awareness of the subjection. However, the example of psychological manipulation we considered earlier makes clear that one may be subject to power without being fully aware of that subjection. In some cases, being *un*aware of manipulation may be more problematic from a moral point of view than subordination that is manifest to the subject. This, writes political scientist Steven Lukes, is "the supreme and most insidious exercise of power."[6]

Similarly, it is a mistake to think of power relations only as a matter of the actual attitudes or intentions of the parties involved. Power relations reside in the social meanings and the formal or informal norms that structure interactions between the parties. Thus, when we sketch in Chapter 4 the profile of the evils that the rule of law addresses and the values it seeks to serve, we must look beyond the *experience* of subjection. We must also attend to the social evil or wrong of people being *treated* in ways that publicly communicate the subject's inferior status.

Before we leave the topic of the nature of power, we must broaden the model of power relations that concern the rule of law. The intuitive model we have relied on takes the power relationship to be *dyadic* and *between individuals*—for example, the relationship between master and servant. However, the parties to the relation need not be individuals. Power-wielding agents may be collectivities, groups, associations, or institutions of various kinds. The wielders may be government officials, and the power subjects may be individual citizens, or small businesses, or large municipalities. The wielder may be a large employer and the power subjects members of its workforce. The wielder may be a nation-state (the United States, for example, or its officials), and the power subjects may be an international organization (the World Health Organization, for example). The rule of law is concerned with a wide range of power relations. (We will return shortly to consider the scope of the rule of law's concern.)

Likewise, the relationship need not be strictly dyadic. An individual agent may not be subject to the power of a single (individual or corporate) wielder, but rather to a decentralized aggregate of potential wielders.[7] More commonly, the agent may have some degree of freedom to escape the power of one wielder of the aggregate, only to fall under the power of another. In a community with a small number of employers, for example, a worker may be free to leave one oppressive employer but able only to attach himself to another perhaps no less oppressive. In such cases, exit from the power of one wielder does not result in exit from subjection to power but only from the power of one specific wielder.

The rule of law looks beyond the simple dyadic model in another way: it focuses on social, political, and legal (and sometimes, economic) *structures* that constitute, facilitate, and sustain power.[8] Efforts to contain or constrain power may involve restructuring the power relations to reduce or eliminate the imbalances that exist among agents. It is common among social theorists to speak of such structures as wielders of power, but this is misleading. Structures are not agents; rather, they are the products of the *actions* of agents, albeit not always the product of *design*. It is possible in some cases to see such structures as *forces* and thus possessing a kind of natural power, but it would be misleading, again, to see them as analogues of agents who exercise power. Because of the way a society is organized, some people can dominate others directly without necessarily wishing for domination or even approving of it.[9] It is not *systems* that dominate; rather, the systems put agents in a position to dominate others.

This captures the rule of law's concern with power as capacity. Before closing this section, we should return briefly to power as position. The rule of law is concerned with abuse or arbitrary exercise of position power especially when law constitutes and allocates that power. A police officer abuses this power when she pulls over a driver on a suspicion of criminal possession of drugs based only on the driver's race and gender. In this case, the officer abuses both power as capacity and power as position. The position makes possible the capacity. However, it is possible for officials to abuse their power in the sense of abusing their position without also getting someone to do something; abuse of power as position is not necessarily abuse of power over some other person. For example, the president of the United States abuses the power of the office when he grants pardons to family, friends, or associates. Similarly, he abuses the office by not paying his taxes, expecting the Internal Revenue Service to look the other way.[10] The rule of law is concerned with such abuses of power even when the power is not exercised over anyone, because they represent ways in which the official treats the law with contempt and seeks to slip its bonds.

In sum, the rule of law is concerned with two kinds of power: the power of position and the power of one agent over another agent. The power of position is the product of laws (or social norms) and can be abused; hence, it is a concern for the rule of law, even if it does not result in another person's being made to do something. In contrast, power over another resides in a relationship of inequality and dependence between power wielder and power subject. This is not necessarily a relationship between individuals nor is it strictly dyadic in form. Wielders of such power can draw on a variety of means of influencing the choices and actions of those who are subject to the power, but these do not include exchange of reasons for action. The rule of law is concerned with the existence and not merely the exercise of this power, and the power is manifest not only in the attitudes or subjective experiences of parties but in the social or legal structures that power relations are embedded in. Such power relationships attract the attention and concern of the rule of law when they provide opportunities for the arbitrary exercise of the power.

When Is Power Exercised Arbitrarily?

In 1788, the British House of Commons impeached Warren Hastings, the first Governor General of India. Edmund Burke set out the case for conviction in the House of Lords. Over four days Burke enumerated the list of high crimes and misdemeanors grounding Hastings' impeachment. Hastings argued that, as the magistrate in power, he had the right to act without law or procedure constraining him. Burke countered that no official had power outside the framework of law. In rebuttal, Burke declared, "Law and arbitrary power are in eternal enmity. . . . It is a contradiction in terms, it is blasphemy in religion, it is wickedness in politics, to say that any man can have arbitrary power."[11] Yet it is no easy matter to say, for purposes of the rule of law, what makes an exercise of power arbitrary.

Arbitrary power is capricious and arrogant. "I will do this, because I can," says the wielder of arbitrary power. To be subject to the arbitrary power of another is to be subject to the whim, the mere pleasure, of the wielder. The wielders' will is their only law; they are, we say, laws unto themselves. A will that is law unto itself is a feral will. Military intelligence officers chillingly expressed this capricious arrogance to a prisoner in the Guantanamo Bay prison camp: "You are in a place where there is no law," they said; "we are the law."[12] Nothing outside themselves constrained them, nothing but their absolute choice.

This is not to say that *no rules* govern their behavior, that *there are* no reasons to guide them; and, surely, it is not to say that arbitrary actions are *unpredictable*. Rather, wielders are utterly *indifferent* to rules or reasons. Gloucester, in Shakespeare's *Lear*, captured this sense of arbitrariness when he uttered the bitter line, "As flies to wanton boys are we to th' gods,/ They kill us for their sport."[13] Divine nature is so far beyond us that we are to them as flies are to us. We are not worth bothering about, utterly without standing to question or utter a vain protest; we are at the mercy of divine whim. To us, their behavior is unilateral, unaccountable.

Arbitrary power is *unilateral*. The wielder's perspective on the action is the only relevant deliberative perspective; no other side or perspective is considered. The wielder's judgment answers only the wielder's own will. Exercising power in this way is manifestly arrogant. The wielder's action says, "My will alone matters; yours is irrelevant. Do this for no reason you need to bother about but only because I say so." Thus, from the perspective of someone who is subject to this power, there is nothing to distinguish the wielder's reasoned judgment from mere whim, absolute choice. The subject of arbitrary power need not be uncertain about the wielder's behavior, or even find it unjustified; rather, the subject's perspective is irrelevant. His will is subjected to the mere will of the wielder; he is *subordinated* to that will. Subordination is the experience—or rather, the meaning—of the subject's role in the relationship; the meaning of the wielder's role is *domination*.

Arbitrary power is *unaccountable*. Not by definition. However, a signal feature of arbitrary power is that it is beyond accountability. "Fie, my lord, fie! a soldier and afraid?" taunts Lady Macbeth in her sleepwalk. "What need we fear who know it, when none can call our power to account?"[14] Power wielders may have their reasons, and their actions may even be reasonable (not Macbeth's, of course), and they may indeed be bound by law, but those who wield arbitrary power are exempt from giving reasons. They "send accounts to no one's audit for the deeds [they] do."[15] They are not answerable to any third party, and in particular not to the subjects of their power.

Opponents of absolutism in the seventeenth century found no comfort in the argument frequently pressed by its defenders that divine and natural law bound absolute rulers. Absolute rulers may await accountability before the divine court, but they claimed to be free of any mundane accountability. At best, they answered only to their own assessment of their compliance with transcendent norms. Opponents—Johannes Althusius, for example—insisted that accountability must be in the here and now; that rulers must be subject to and held to law of the land. This thought, we saw in Chapter 1, lies at the heart of the rule-of-law idea.

Before we leave our discussion of power and its arbitrary exercise, we should take a moment to warn against two common mistakes that defenders of the rule of law have found tempting. One is to equate arbitrariness with discretion; the other is to think that the remedy against arbitrariness lies in locating rule in something impersonal.

Arbitrary power is often confused with discretion. Discretion always involves the exercise of judgment, as does following any rule; but judgment may be discretionary *and* exercised within parameters, governed by standards or norms. Most importantly, it may be reckonable. The proper exercise of discretion is not arbitrary if the agent is answerable for actions based on discretionary judgment. The reasons that are meant to guide discretionary judgment may be open to audit. Discretion is arbitrary only when it is not accountable.

We argued that the rule of law is opposed to power when one party is subordinated to another's caprice. One might infer from this that the rule of law opposes only *personal subordination*, and is not opposed to forces that shape the lives or direct the actions of persons if these forces are not the expression of the will of some other person. This is the second mistake, for it has led some defenders of the rule of law to look for sources of order or legal norms that are *impersonal*, not attributable directly to the decisions and actions of human persons.

Defenders argue that, although social orders may limit the actions and direct the choices of people, they are consistent with stringent demands of the rule of law if they are "spontaneous," not the product of the design and execution of some identifiable persons. For example, the market, they believe, is a spontaneous order in this sense; hence, not a source of arbitrary power. Similarly, Frederick Hayek argued that English Common Law, in its classical form, was the product of a spontaneous order of case-by-case judicial decisions accumulated over long periods.[16] Unlike legislation, which has discrete and identifiable human sources, and hence represents a threat to the rule of law, Common Law norms, in his view, offered a paradigm of law that respects the rule of law.

This identification of nonarbitrary power with the impersonal cannot withstand scrutiny. It involves a good bit of self-deception, if not thinly veiled prevarication, about the actual working of such power. John Steinbeck ripped the veil from this deception in his classic novel, *The Grapes of Wrath*.[17] He tells the story of Dust Bowl farmers during the Great Depression driven from land they had worked for generations. They argue their case to visiting bank agents who delivered their eviction notices. They implored the agents to report their helplessness to bank officers. "The bank is something else than men," the agents reply; "every man in a bank hates what the bank does, and yet the bank does it. The bank is something more than men, I tell you. It's the monster. Men made it, but they can't control it." The agents represent the bank as an autonomous, impersonal force precisely to shift responsibility for disastrous consequences from human beings who make and execute decisions to something that allegedly lacks agency, and can bear no responsibility. But, of course, the bank is an institution, a structure of roles and rules, *and people* who occupy and follow them, some of whom also make them. The bank's institutional frame makes possible the exercise of power, but agents, employees, directors, and officers exercise the power. As responsible agents, they are—or should be—held accountable for their actions. If they are not held accountable, because a corporate veil is thrown over their activities, then their exercise of power is recognizably arbitrary, worthy of condemnation, and worthy of the concern of the rule of law. Moreover, the rule of law is equally concerned with the structures that constitute and sustain that power.

The Scope of the Rule of Law's Concern

The rule of law sets its face against social and political structures that create and sustain modes of power that equip agents and agencies to exercise that power arbitrarily. Power comes in many forms and people exercise power in many different domains. The ruling power of governing officials is a perennial focus; however, the rule of law can be limited to nation-states only artificially. The notion "extends to relations among citizens as much as it does to acts of governments or governance, indeed to the activities of all persons and institutions capable of exercising significant power in a society,"[18] Martin Krygier insists. Our task here is to elaborate this important claim.

In Chapter 7, we will address whether, and to what extent, the rule of law's *engagement* or *intervention* is appropriate, whether law can effectively contribute to tempering power in a particular domain (questioning law's *efficacy*), and whether, even if it can, it *may* or *must* do so (questioning its *legitimacy*). First, though, we aside put those questions to sketch a profile of the domains of the rule of law's *concern*.

State and Nonstate Governing Power

The modern nation-state, as conventionally understood, enjoys a monopoly of coercive power that is located in the hands of centralized, legally constituted authority. It is not surprising that the modern state attracts rule-of-law worries. Indeed, concern to bridle the tyranny of rulers has long dominated discussions of the rule of law. The ancient question, *quis custodiet ipsos custodes?*[19]—who guards the guardians?—captures this concern. However, Juvenal's formulation suggests a prior worry. Why, after all, must there be "guardians," rulers, at all? According to the rule of law's logic, those who rule with law must be ruled *by it* as well, but this suggests that law's ruling addresses a problem prior to its task of ruling the rulers. This was the story we told in Chapter 1. In the beginning, we might say, there was power, and law was created, in part at least, to protect people, thrown together by nature and necessity, from its arbitrary exercise. However, because "Leviathan fills our field of vision," we tend to be blind to other forms and centers of power to which people are subject.[20]

One of law's core functions, writes legal scholar Robin West, "is to protect individuals against what would otherwise be undeterred privations against them—not [only] by overreaching state officials, but [also] rather by undeterred private individuals, corporations, or entities."[21] Sources of arbitrary power are problematic from the point of view of the rule of law whether they are private or public.

Justice William O. Douglas once wrote, "[A]ll power tends to develop into a government in itself."[22] Although this statement is too broad as it stands, it alerts us to an important fact: nonstate enterprises often take on a distinctively "political" or "governmental" character. Large corporations are the most obvious examples of such enterprises. They are institutionalized, normatively constituted structures of authority that concentrate enormous power. In a straightforward sense, officers of these enterprises exercise governmental power.

The workplace is one site of nonstate governing power. Officers have responsibility for the enterprise, make rules by which their employees must live inside and outside the workplace, and enforce them directly or indirectly through their control of resources, opportunities, and activities needed by their employees and the conditions under which they work. Some companies inspect workers' personal belongings on the workers' unpaid time; others prevent workers from exchanging casual remarks, regarding it as "time theft"; others subject their workers to drug screening without suspicion, or pressure them to support favoured political candidates. The modern large business enterprise, organized as a firm, has the power to regulate many aspects of the lives of employees in the workplace and outside it, except where law explicitly limits that power. "Private government" exists, philosopher Elizabeth Anderson maintains, "when people are subject, in some part of their lives, to authorities that can order them around and impose sanctions for non-compliance."[23] For our purposes, the question is not whether wielders always or inevitably abuse this power, but rather that the power *exists*, and those who possess it can exercise it arbitrarily, if not regulated. The power can be as pervasive and invasive as state power.

State law constitutes this governance relationship, like that of the state. It does so with property laws governing command over resources and wealth, with laws defining and managing the labor market, and with laws defining the framework of the labor contract. Laws may also constrain the exercise of this power, for example, laws that seek to secure workplace safety, to prohibit certain forms of discrimination in the hiring process or in assigning tasks, and to provide opportunities for advancement. Law also constitutes the market in which the firm does its business and from which it draws its workers. In modern societies, the market is not a law-free zone. Its denizens are law-constituted, even when their actions are free of further legal constraint. Law enables this power, and the real possibility of its arbitrary exercise is reason enough to engage typical rule-of-law concerns.

Business enterprises can also exercise power beyond the workplace and the market. The company town, for example, was once a familiar form of social organization in the United States. The Pullman Palace Car Company made sleeping cars for the railroad industry. In the 1880s, it established Pullman, a town on the outskirts of Chicago. Other company towns sprang up around the country, for example, Kannapolis, North Carolina and Matewan, West Virginia. The Pullman Company provided living quarters for their workers, along with streets, sewer systems, stores, and private security officers. The company exercised control over the lives of its workers at work, at home, and in "public" spaces. Merle Travis captured the life of a coal miner in a Kentucky company town in his song, "Sixteen Tons."

> You load sixteen tons, what do you get? Another day older and deeper in debt.
> Saint Peter don't you call me 'cause I can't go,
> I owe my soul to the company sto'.

Sometimes corporations exercise power over people who are not even employees or residents of their company towns. In 1946, a case came to the US Supreme Court challenging one such exercise of power. The Gulf Shipbuilding Company owned Chickasaw, a suburb of Mobile, Alabama. Chickasaw had all the usual features of a small, Southern town. Town management adopted a regulation that permitted no solicitation of any kind in public places without written permission. On the authority of this regulation, town officials denied Grace Marsh a permit to distribute religious literature in front of the Chickasaw post office. When she refused to comply, she was arrested and convicted of the crime of remaining on premises after she was ordered to leave. Mrs. Marsh challenged the town's regulation and her conviction, on the ground that they violated her constitutional rights to freedom of religion and expression. The state of Alabama supported the town's prohibition and its action against Mrs. Marsh. The case eventually went to the US Supreme Court. The state argued that the corporation had a right to control the inhabitants of and visitors to Chickasaw just as homeowners have the right to regulate guests on their property. The Court rejected the analogy. Justice Black pointed out that Chickasaw performed the functions of a municipality and the corporation took on the role of government, so it was subject to constitutional limits on the exercise of governmental power.[24] The company exercised governing power over the community, not just the workplace. It acted as a private government.

It is easy to recognize other such private governing enterprises. Residential community associations come to mind. They provide many services to residents—for example, street maintenance, security, and refuse collection. They also subject residents to a regime of rules and controls that significantly shape their actions and lives. They govern their residents. That is enough to attract the attention and concern (if not ultimately the intervention) of the rule of law.

The widespread use of mass-market boilerplate provisions in commercial transactions is another good example of the kind of exercise of power that warrants rule-of-law scrutiny.[25] Firms using such boilerplate provisions attempt unilaterally to opt out of the existing legal regime of rights, duties, and protections. A combination of market conditions and law-created normative powers gives them the power. Unchecked, the use of such devices may be a genuine threat to the rule of law.

Private property regimes warrant scrutiny for the same reason. Defenders of private property argue that it is a bulwark against the intrusion of the arbitrary power of government. Ownership of property sufficient to sustain a decent life can provide a significant degree of protection. Yet private ownership of resources and wealth also poses a potential threat of arbitrary power. The problem posed by private property regimes is not incidental to those regimes; it arises from their very nature. Property regimes allocate decision-making power over the use of resources in a polity. This law-created and law-allocated normative power underwrites and amplifies social power. The owner gets to decide how resources are used.[26] This gives power to the owner, power over resources, and so, often, power over persons. In social contexts of vastly unequal ownership, this power can be great.

The power is valuable to the owner, of course, and can be valuable to the society as a whole, but may also be problematic from the point of view of the rule of law. In *Swann v. Gastonia Housing Authority*,[27] a US federal court of appeals agreed to protect a tenant against one such abuse. It held that a landlord could not evict a tenant without a full-fledged hearing showing good cause for eviction. In this case, the landlord participated in a government-funded rent subsidy program, and so the court did not regard it as a strictly private enterprise.[28] However, in *Robinson v. Diamond Housing Corporation*,[29] Judge J. Skelly Wright invoked the rule of law itself to justify preventing a landlord from unilaterally terminating a tenancy agreement in retaliation against the tenants' attempt to use the law to enforce their housing rights. The law provided recourse to tenants against landlords to force them to make improvements in their houses. The landlord's unilateral termination of the tenancy, Judge Wright argued, was a clear exercise of arbitrary power in an attempt to deny the tenants enjoyment of their legal rights. The same principled concern that justifies private property regimes—protection against governmental domination—called for legal limits on the exercise of the power created and allocated by the law. These limits are not imposed from the outside by values or principles in conflict with those that properly and persuasively underlie property; rather, they arise from the very principles on which the property regime rests.

Power beyond Borders

Thus far we have considered power exercised by agents and agencies within state borders over individuals, groups, or communities within those same borders. However, the rule of law's concern extends also to power exercised across and entirely outside state borders. This concern has become increasingly import in our time. We will discuss more fully in later chapters two such domains: the international or global domain and the domain of digital power.

Consider, first, power in the global domain. The exercise of power beyond national borders, especially the exercise of military power of one state against another, has been a concern of legal thought for centuries. The great classical texts providing the foundations of international law addressed problems of war, peace, and diplomacy; interestingly, they also addressed piracy, a much-feared nonstate exercise of power. No one doubts that power and agencies wielding it are dominant features of the global landscape, or that opportunities and means for arbitrarily exercising this power are manifold.

The question for us is whether law can contribute to the tempering of this power. We will address that question in Chapter 15. To prepare for that discussion, we will consider the kinds of power exercised in this vast domain and the agents that exercise them.

For centuries the main players were political entities—kingdoms, realms, empires, and hegemonic religious institutions like the church in Rome and Constantinople. In the early modern era, the global stage was mainly the domain of interstate, intergovernmental relations—with pirates working on its margins. Power among the states, of course, was vastly unequal, and many states depended greatly upon the hegemons in their region. Emerging about the same time were business enterprises that operated beyond the boundaries of their national homes, for example, the Dutch East India Company, founded in 1603. The numbers and power of transnational and multinational corporations has grown dramatically over the last century and a half.

The twentieth century witnessed the birth and growth of a wide array of non-state, international organizations —the International Labor Organization (1919), International Monetary Fund (1945), World Health Organization (1948), and a host of others. Some of these are intergovernmental organizations, bringing together numbers of states. The prime example, of course, is the United Nations (1945), but also the Association of Southeast Asian Nations (1961), the European Union (1993) (initiated in 1957 as the European Economic Community), and others. Nongovernmental organizations have also multiplied, some for humanitarian purposes (the International Committee for the Red Cross), others for economic purposes (the Bank for International Settlement), and others for cultural or scientific purposes (UNESCO). Perhaps the most dramatic increase of actors on the transnational stage in recent years has come in the domain of global governance. Among such actors are the General Assembly and the Security Council of the United Nations, adjudicatory institutions like the International Court of Justice, and an increasingly dense array of regulatory agencies, including the World Trade Organization, the World Bank, and the International Atomic Energy Agency. "A congeries of different actors and different layers" operate in an increasingly complex "global administrative space." This highly decentralized space comprises "a dizzying variety of global regulatory regimes, including international organizations, transnational networks of national regulatory officials, and private or hybrid private-public regulatory bodies."[30] As political scientists Ruth Grant and Robert Keohane observe, "The interdependence of states, globalization of business, expansion of the scope and authority of multilateral organizations, and rapid increases in the number of nongovernmental organizations

(NGOs) have heightened concerns about the way power is used and abused on the world stage."[31]

In this domain, as in the domestic realm, the power that is of concern to the rule of law is power of one state or nonstate entity *over* another—the differential ability of wielders to influence and direct the choices and decisions, the policies and practices, of those who are dependent on them. The most obvious form of such power is brute force, typically exercised by state militaries and sometimes nonstate actors (ISIS, for example). For example, in recent years China flexed its military muscles in the South China Sea to influence compliant behavior on the part of its neighbors; and in early 2022 Russia deployed its military to make clear its displeasure with moves in Ukraine to align more closely with the West.

Another familiar mode of power uses broadly economic tools—command over resources, capital, or markets—to direct the behavior of other actors on the global stage. The sheer size of a country's market gives it power to shape the way other countries organize their production and distribution of the goods they make. States and multinational corporations alike wield this power. For example, they make, withhold, or withdraw investment to shape the economic policies of developing countries, to force them to join military or ideological alliances, and, we must concede, to encourage dependent countries to develop rule of law or democratic institutions. Another example is the activity of the US government in 2021 to influence the operation of the World Health Organization, or punish it for past actions that it disapproved of, by withholding necessary financial contributions to it.

Power available to agencies and organizations in the domain of global governance represents a third mode of power. We might call this *authority-wielding* power. This includes a range of norm-making and norm-enforcing powers. Some are formal. Some are informal, for example, what some call "soft law." It is "soft" because its norms are not officially binding, but they can still influence the behavior of those who fall within their scope. The UN General Assembly exercises this kind of power, as does the World Trade Organization and other standard-setting organizations. Regulatory agencies that participate in the complex network of global governance exercise this power even when they lack formal enforcement powers.

This brings to light another feature of power in the global domain that is similar to its domestic analogue. The power available to actors in the global domain, and its differential distribution among them, is not simply a function of natural features of the actors or their circumstances. Rather, a major contributor is also the legal, or more broadly normative, systems in place. These normative systems *empower* some actors and *disempower* others.

Digital Power—The New Frontier

We live in the digital age. A wide range of digital technologies increasingly shapes our lives. They have generated a new and radically different form of power. The source of their power is knowledge, or rather information. Artificial intelligence technologies that collect, aggregate, and process information operate on all sorts of information, but the information that fuels the power of digital giants, so-called Big Tech, is a special sort. It is information about the users of computers and other devices and their uses of them, about the movements and moods of people, their "likes" and clicks, their friends and families, their passions and preferences. Simply used in the ordinary way, computers produce enormous amounts of data ("exhaust"). "Everything from our preferences, movement, habits, physical attributes, and a vast amount of seemingly inconsequential information about our devices is being logged when we browse the internet, use our phones, make transactions, and move around the physical world."[32] Digital actors collect, cook, and then consume the information in various ways, package it in useful new products, and sell it on ever-expanding markets.

These novel assets of the digital economy have enabled the industry, and its power, to grow exponentially. The economic power in this domain, producing hundreds of billions of dollars every year, is concentrated in the hands of a small number of digital platforms—Facebook, Google, Apple, Amazon, Twitter, and the like—and a network of data brokers that exploit opportunities created by the platforms. The appetite of digital actors for data is insatiable, so digital power wielders must engage users and keep them actively engaged, thereby generating more and more data. Internet-connected computers pervade our public and our private lives. Phones and a vast assortment of "smart" devices in our homes, cars, businesses, and public spaces—the "internet of things"—feed the demand for more and more data. Digital platforms manage the data behind an "algorithmic veil" of obscurity.[33]

Digital actors, controlling mass data and the technologies that analyze it, provide enormous benefits to the world; they also cause serious harm to individuals and communities. Moreover, control of mass data gives digital actors vast power *over* persons and communities. This power involves neither coercive force nor manipulations of incentives and disincentives. Rather, wielders of digital power work further out of view of our deliberation and choice, limiting or channeling our access to information, removing options from our awareness, shaping our preferences, manipulating our emotional vulnerabilities, and altering our means of communication with each other. Of course, law also seeks to influence our deliberation and choice, but wielders of digital power do so primarily by circumventing rather than addressing our deliberative capacities.

The legal environments in which digital actors operate enhance and sustain their power. With little legal resistance, digital platforms extract vast amounts of personal information from our computers, from our interactions on the web, from our phones, and from our movement through public spaces. Once they collect and aggregate it, they shield data from further access by legal trade-secret protections, nondisclosure agreements, and in some countries by constitutional protections of free speech.

Governments, heavily invested in digital surveillance, are members of the club of data power wielders. Other members of this club range from small-scale hackers and state-sponsored violators of cybersecurity, to a wide array of vendors of data analytics, and large-volume, sophisticated data brokers, to a small number of Big Tech companies. The latter dominate the digital domain. They represent the "new Leviathans." They, too, are worthy, of examination from the perspective of the principles and values of the rule of law, and, where feasible, constraint by resources mobilized to secure law's rule in the digital domain.

Law's Toolbox

The rule-of-law ideal concerns a wide variety of kinds and domains of power, but its proper scope is limited. It is not opposed to power per se, but only those modes or structures that tolerate, enable, or nourish its arbitrary exercise. Moreover, as we shall see shortly, it does not seek to eliminate or utterly shackle power, but only, as Martin Krygier suggested, to *temper* its exercise, offering protection and recourse against its abuse. Its remit is limited even more by the instrument it proposes to use for this power-tempering project. Law, and its sustaining partner, the ethos of fidelity, are its bridles of choice. The properties and capabilities of its chosen tool and the circumstances in which it is employed limit implementation of the ideal. Think of a cabinetmaker who sets out to make a piece of fine furniture, à decorative table, for example. He has a detailed idea what the table should look like, but he must adjust his project to match the tools he has on hand and the wood he has purchased. Certain designs he would love to follow are unfeasible because his tools, or his skill in using them, are not up to the task, or his materials won't lend themselves to the manipulation necessary to realize the design. Similarly, the nature of the legal tools and the social and cultural materials at hand limit realization of the rule-of-law project.

In addition, we must keep in mind that the rule of law is one value of political morality among others, and implementing its discipline brings with it significant political and moral costs. Thus, there may be moral limits to the rule-of-law project, domains of civil society or lives of its members that we may wish to keep free from law's intrusion, even if those who possess the power might arbitrarily exercise it. In Chapter 7, we will have to face questions regarding the moral and circumstantial limits of the rule of law and strategic questions about how much cost we are willing to bear for the protections promised by the rule of law. However, we can hope to make progress answering them only after we have a clear sense of the distinctive features and capabilities of law that our ideal proposes to utilize.

What can law contribute to the tempering of power? What does law have to offer to enable protection and recourse against its arbitrary exercise? The aim of our exploration at this point is not to identify features essential to law per se or to law wherever we might find it. Philosopher Jeremy Waldron, engaged in what appears to be a similar endeavor, sought "elementary requirements for a system of rules to qualify as a legal system."[34] This is not the object of our investigation. We are looking for salient and widely used features and devices of law, features that are characteristic of law, but not, in every case, so essential that we could not reasonably call something that lacks them a legal system. Our aim is not to mark the boundaries of the concept of law, but to identify items typically found in the toolbox of most legal systems that can be used to implement the rule of law.

Let's begin with a no-nonsense view of law's tools, removing any halo that law-lovers would like to give it. With its halo removed, law has often appeared to observers as a collection of hard-edged rules, backed by sanctions to enforce compliance with them. Rule-of-law theorist Lon Fuller conceded, "[F]or the man in the street or in the field, the most common response to the law is a gesture of helplessness and indifference. The law is like the weather. It is there, you adjust to it, but there is nothing you can do about it except get under cover when its special kind of lightning strikes."[35] *Law*, from this perspective, is a matter of *laws*, that is, rules created and imposed by the powerful through institutions that coercively enforce them.

There is no denying that rulers often deploy laws as instruments of power, but law is also capable of containing, constraining, and disciplining power. We do not restore an undeserved halo, but only look beneath the law's hard surface, when we seek to uncover important devices that we can use to serve these rule-of-law aims. The profile sketched in the preceding paragraph is a caricature, capturing but distorting some features of law through misrepresenting the features it includes and leaving out important ones.

The caricature correctly highlights two features of laws: they are *positive* and they seek to *order* behavior. By "positive," I don't mean affirmative or upbeat, but rather that the way law orders behavior is through means that are "posited"— that is, the law is a product of human activity or human processes, and thus it is contingent and subject to change. Law may not always be the product of explicit design; its rules often emerge from human activity undesigned, as customs do. Moreover, the law's mode of ordering is different from the sheer exercise of force. It is distinctive of law to order behavior through addressing rules or norms to agents who can grasp them and apply them to their own particular circumstances.

Law is not only positive; it is also distinctively *normative*. Thus, the law seeks to order or influence behavior not by *causing* that behavior, in the way that the snake charmer gets the snake to dance, but rather by addressing norms to law subjects, who are meant to take them up in their deliberations about what to do. Law seeks to work its magic not by getting people to do things, but by guiding their behavior through engaging their deliberative faculties. This is a further distinctive feature of law: it is *deliberative*. We will consider this feature presently, but first it is important to note two other dimensions of law's positivity.

Legal norms are positive in the further sense that they are (meant to be) fully *public*. Law does its characteristic work *in* public, *addressed to* a public consisting of agents that includes individuals, agencies, organizations, and associations, who are engaged in complex networks of social interaction. Their own understandings, and the understandings of the others with whom they interact, shape these interactions. Thus, the success of the law's ordering and guiding behavior depends on the uptake by those agents. That is, it depends on their understanding, their sense of the relevance and force of the norms, the public (the community) in which they act, and the extent to which their understandings are shared or overlap with other members.

Law's reliance on *formalities* is another dimension of its positivity. Law creates *ways* of doing or accomplishing things that are, in a sense, artificial but not pointless. To succeed in establishing a contractual relationship, for example, the parties must follow the recipe set out in contract law. Similarly, the sale of real property relies on proof of the seller's ownership of the property through tracing its title. Municipal laws provide warrants for the actions of government officials or citizens only if lawmakers follow formal procedures for enactment. In the place of natural processes and modes of customary interaction, the law institutes formalities to give public, legally recognized shape to actions by which people can order their relationships and give some determinacy to their future. Formalities are often seen as "mere" and hence in a way arbitrary, beside the point, indifferent to the real merits of actions. However, this is shortsighted, for law's formalities order behavior in public; they contain and constrain the power.

In addition, law works through *institutions*, especially, but not exclusively, courts or tribunals. The caricature we encountered earlier represents courts as institutions for imposing the orders of the powerful on the powerless, making them determinate and executing sanctions. But this fails to recognize features of judicial institutions that the rule of law seeks most to exploit. Essential to the rule of law are institutions for reasoned, principled, and public decision-making within and with respect to the law. The law, through its courts, proceeds deliberately and deliberatively. Three key features are characteristic of courts of law, Lon Fuller reminded us.[36] First, the law is identified and applied through the exercise of deliberative reason that receives and weighs evidence and arguments. Second, adjudication offers parties that come, or are brought, to the court a distinctive mode of participation. They are entitled to present evidence and arguments for their positions regarding the law and its bearing on their rights and duties. They can tell their stories, seek to make public sense of their actions, and articulate their grievances. Of course, they cannot do so in any way or using any language they please. The positive law provides a forum and a language for telling their stories. Third, the process itself, and the participants in it, are held to standards of behavior and judgment. The process must deal with the parties fairly—according each full and equal opportunities to offer arguments—and those who preside over the proceedings must be impartial, and they must base their judgments solely on the relevant evidence and arguments.

Legal philosopher Neil MacCormick called attention to another way in which courts serve rule-of-law aims.[37] The rule of law demands that all exercises of ruling power must be warrantable under the law—officials must have sound legal grounds for their actions, and their claims to act with warrant must be open to challenge. Mere assertion of warrant is never sufficient from the point of view of the rule of law. Courts offer forums for just such testing of assertions of legal warrant. This underscores again the *deliberative* character of law. Aristotle put us on the right track when he wrote, "[H]e who bids the law rule" bids "reason alone rule."[38] However, it is not Reason that rules, but rather *reasoning*—not some transcendent rational force or external standard of what is reasonable and right, but a disciplined practice of public reasoning. Law's governance is not governance by that which is rational, reasonable, or right, but rather by disciplined deliberative *reasoning*, by the disciplined giving, taking, and assessing of reasons. Recall the words of Justice Brandeis: we look to law to help us govern ourselves because we want "deliberative forces [to] prevail over the arbitrary."[39] Law's rule is, in an important part, the rule of deliberative reasoning.

MacCormick calls this the "argumentative" character of law.

> The dialectical or argumentative character of legal proceedings is a built-in feature of a constitutional [or more broadly, forensic] setting in which citizens are able to challenge the allegations of fact and the assertions of law on the basis of which government agencies of their own volition or at the instance of private litigants threaten to intervene coercively in their lives or affairs.[40]

Law is a discursive, deliberative discipline of practical reasoning. It thrives on giving and receiving, assessing and challenging, asserting and defending reasons for conclusions of law, conclusions that bear vitally on the actions and policies of those exercising power and the affairs and lives of those affected by them. What is characteristic of law, and vitally important to the rule of law, Waldron reminds us, is not merely the *existence* of norms, but what we—citizens, organizations, communities, government officials, and agencies—*do with them*.

> We do not just obey them or apply the sanctions that they ordain; we argue over them adversarially, we use our sense of what is at stake in their application to license a continual process of argument, and we engage in elaborate interpretive exercises about what it means to apply them faithfully as a system to the cases that come before us.[41]

Neither MacCormick nor Waldron shy away from the implication of this deliberative character of law: it opens law and legal processes to a degree of indeterminacy that undermines the view that law is designed to settle disputed matters with finality. Pragmatic or institutional features of particular legal systems may put limits on the opportunities for challenge of official and authoritative declarations of law, but in the view of rule of law such challenges are in principle legitimate. Chapter 9 will argue that dissent and disagreement are not threats to the rule of law, but essential ingredients of law's rule.

This is what we have learned about law's toolbox thus far: to meet the demands of the rule of law, law provides the focus, forums, and resources for accountability through fully public argument. It offers a disciplined practice of practical reasoning modeled by, but not limited to, its use in courts. This disciplined practice deploys standards that demand practical intelligence of officials and subjects of law; it also structures argument forensically and supplies positive text, precedents, and procedures from which arguments can be built and to which they are answerable. Law can rule when there is in place a robust discipline of public practical reasoning, shaped by its practice in a public forum and tethered to an interconnected body of rules, decisions, standards, and examples that are normative for the law's particular political community.

Distinctive of this mode of public practical reasoning is its *systematic* character. Law offers those it seeks to guide not a random collection of discrete rules or directives, but a system of interconnected norms related by their content—the meaning of particular legal rules is typically conditioned by their relationship to and interaction with many other rules and provisions.[42] The forensic, discursive, and argumentative dimensions of law are not merely a welcome accessory of law; they play an essential role in law's distinctive mode of normative guidance. In this way, law provides a framework for articulating conflicts in terms that can be addressed by means of reasoned, deliberative investigation and argument.

The law provides additional resources for ordering social life in meaningful and valuable ways. One such way is that it provides resources for publicly making and assessing claims of right or justice. Throughout the long history of reflection on law, we find an important argument about why human societies need law. Law is necessary for social ordering, some argue, because when we appeal directly to our sense of what is right or just (the Right), we find ourselves in intractable conflict with each other. We turn to law when appeals to the Right threaten to lead to perilous standoffs. Law, on this view, is a surrogate for the Right, a peace-promising *substitute for* morality. There may be truth to this thought— long centuries of offering and assessing this argument could not have been entirely unproductive—but it is at best incomplete. Perhaps, we should think of law not as *substitute for* morality (and the Right) but rather as a needed *complement to* morality.

The thought is that the moral dimension of right and justice not only demands behavior of certain kinds but it also requires reciprocity and publicity of Right-demanding and Right-respecting behavior. However, morality alone cannot provide them. For the Right to take hold in a polity, we must articulate it in positive structures and institutions that can provide the necessary publicity, recognition, and reciprocity. Law complements morality by making publicly available a distinctive discipline of reasoning and a distinctive framework for making and assessing claims of Right.

It does so in a second, more specific way, by giving a language and a forum for assertion of *rights*. To help us understand the distinctively valuable nature of rights, consider the following simple example. A pandemic forces Allan and Bobby, ages six and eight, to spend most of their days indoors playing with each other. They are prone to squabble, and Bobby sometimes takes advantage of his age and size and prevents Allan from playing with especially loved toy cars. One day their squabbling reaches a peak and their father no longer expects that they can work things out for themselves. He scolds them both for being unfair to each other, but he makes a special request of Bobby. He asks that Bobby promise that he will not take away Allan's cars when he is playing with them. Chastened, Bobby promises. In this situation, each boy has reason to play nice with and be fair to the other. Allan's interest in his cars is reason enough, perhaps, for Bobby to let him play with them undisturbed, but Bobby has a further reason to do so, his promise to his father. His promise gives Bobby an obligation not to disturb Allan's playing with the cars. Bobby owes the obligation not to Allan but to his father. Allan is the beneficiary of Bobby's keeping his promise, but Bobby owes this to his father.

Now consider *rights*. Rights are not objects that one possesses, or weapons one can wield against others; rather, rights constitute a certain kind of position or status in which one can stand with respect to others. Rights (legal rights, that is) are legally recognized claims to which obligations on some other party or parties are connected. Rights and obligations are correlative. "To have a right," John

Stuart Mill maintained, is "to have [an interest] which society ought to defend me in the possession of,"[43] by holding some other party to an obligation to respect or promote that interest. Further, rights are claims the *right bearer* can make, a *basis* for the bearer's demand on the actions, care or respect of another, and a recognized capability to *make* that demand *in the bearer's own behalf.*[44] Rights accord to their bearers a special kind of (normative) power, that of making an actionable demand on others to protect or promote that interest. The protection and the demand are grounded in the value of the interest, but even more fundamentally in *respect for the party* who has the interest. Thus, those who have the obligations typically entailed by rights owe them specifically *to* the bearer of the right, just as Bobby owed to his father his obligation to let Allan play with his cars. Rights mark the right bearers as the appropriate focus of the attention and respect of the parties who have the corresponding obligations.

What is important for purposes of the rule of law is that this notion of rights is not the special property of ordinary morality; rather, it is a key legal notion that plays an important role in the legal ordering of social life. The language of rights is distinctively, if not exclusively, juridical language. This is not the only language that law employs in its ordering of social life, but it is critical to the life and functioning of law. It is an important tool in law's toolbox.

We have called attention to the positive, normative, deliberative, and rights-defining dimensions of law. We need to bring to the foreground one more dimension, the *constitutive* dimension. This dimension is implicit in our discussion thus far. Consider the norms of law we brought into view earlier. These norms order social life and guide behavior by issuing directives to their subjects to perform certain actions or refrain from other actions. In addition, law plays a crucial constitutive role. The law defines or constitutes positions, statuses, roles, and associated procedures, and it bundles them together in complex combinations of rights, duties, powers, liabilities, disabilities, and responsibilities. In doing so, law shapes institutions and agencies and the associated powers they can wield. Perhaps, the most familiar such bundle is that which defines the duties, powers, and responsibilities of government enshrined in the state's "constitution." This creation of the law does not make use of or bring to bear preexisting extralegal power; rather, it creates that power, as it were, *ex nihilo.* No less important for the exercise and control of social power are statuses and relationship networks created by other departments of law, for example, family law and employment law; the law also enables the creation of business partnerships, trust arrangements, and the like. An important task of law is to allocate decision-making power to individuals, organizations, agencies, and communities. By giving legal definition to social relations, it orders social life, making certain activities possible, and enabling people to organize their lives and relationships with others in beneficial ways.

Tempering Power

Bracton, you may recall from Chapter 1, recommended that the king temper his power with the bridle of law. Rule-of-law defenders take this injunction to heart. We say that the rule of law aims to temper, or discipline, the exercise of power.[45] It seeks to do so by creating legal and other institutional structures, and by enabling and nurturing informal networks of accountability in civil society. Note the aim is not to enfeeble government officials, preventing them from abusing power by making it impossible for them to use it. Sometimes the rule of law ideal is associated with the small government ideology advocated by libertarians. Of course, small government does not mean no government; even small-government partisans recognize the need to allocate some powers to government agencies and institutions. However, the rule of law is not necessarily committed to small government, and certainly not debilitated government. It seeks *protection* against the abuse of power where possible, and *recourse* against it when recourse is practically feasible. That is, when there is suspicion that government officials or agencies have exercised power arbitrarily, victims, their surrogates, or other watchdogs may demand an accounting of their exercises of power and, where appropriate, seek a remedy.

The important implication of Bracton's centuries-old recommendation is that the rule of law seeks to *discipline* power. To discipline power is as much to enable and guide it as to constrain it; as much to give it resources, focus, and direction as to prevent its misuse. Plato insisted that law must be master and rulers servants of the law, but a different metaphor provides a more nuanced sense of the rule-of-law project. It requires officials to master the discipline of law, internalize it and make it their own, and thereby guide their exercise of power by its internal norms. Thus, to demand that government officials submit to the bridle of law is to require that they master the discipline law seeks to teach.

Law disciplines power in several ways. We are most familiar with its attempts to constrain and control through imposing duties and responsibilities, backed up, perhaps, by sanctions for misfeasance or malfeasance, thereby limiting what law subjects can do by blocking paths that must not be taken. The most visible constraints are formally enacted laws that outline duties of officials and add a schedule of penalties for failing to perform them properly. Yet, as we will see in Chapter 7, much of what gives shape and content to the law governing the vast agencies of the modern state are informal norms and conventions that are embedded in practices that develop over time. These conventions enlist the conduct and commitments of generations of incumbents in governmental offices. Such norms operate more like paths and roads for the effective exercise of power than barriers and obstacles to that exercise.

This suggests a second way in which law disciplines power. As we noticed in the previous section, law does not just block the exercise of power; it literally *constitutes* it. That is, law creates the tools of power, defines the domain and modes of exercise of that power, and determines how it is allocated, acquired, and transferred. The law empowers those to whom the power is entrusted: it invests with public authority governmental institutions and the officials who work in them, lays down procedures and formalities for the exercise of that authority, and determines not only what *may* or *may not* be done, but *how* it is to be done.[46] Political scientist Stephen Holmes helpfully suggests that we think of constitutional rules "as scripts, rather than ropes." If we do, he argues,

> it is easier to understand why powerful actors, looking for protocols to facilitate rapid coordination might be willing to incorporate them into their motives as obligatory principles of conduct. They are not incapacitating but capacitating. They are not shackles making unwanted action impossible, but guidelines making wanted action feasible.[47]

Also, law seeks to make the exercise of power *publicly visible* and to establish forums in which officials' actions, those contemplated and those completed, can be deliberately and deliberatively considered in a fully public manner. Law and legal institutions become, in a way, "a theater of debate."[48]

This enabling and distributing of governing power is a positive task, but, from the point of view of the rule of law, it also has an important negative implication, expressed in the exclusivity principle. This core doctrine of the rule of law holds that there is no legitimate governing power that is not ordained by law. This is not to say that there is no power, that no one is capable of exercising power, outside the law, but rather that to act outside the framework that law creates, orders, distributes, and oversees is to act without legitimate authority. Action *ultra vires* is action without the sanction of law, naked of its mantle of legitimacy.

To summarize, the main point of this section is that the aim of the rule of law is not to shackle power, or even to eliminate its arbitrary exercise; rather, the aim is to temper and discipline power in such a way that the underlying values of the rule of law are duly served through deploying the law's distinctive tools. Law provides *protection* against abuse of power prospectively through constituting and distributing power and through constraining its exercise, and retrospectively by imposing sanctions. Sanctions may take the form of imposing penalties on agents or agencies that violate these constraints; they may also take the form of invalidating official actions or the rules or regulations they enact, depriving them of legal standing. Protection *ex post* takes the form of making officials and agencies formally answerable for their actions, giving various institutions, agencies, and individuals the right to challenge the actions of the powerful. This also is part of the law's design to provide *recourse* against the exercise of power. Recourse has two key dimensions: response and redress. Law provides response through legal avenues and forums for holding those who exercise power accountable. Redress is available through legal forums that enable those who exercise power to vindicate their actions or require them to provide a remedy for their wrongful exercise of power.

Accountability

Accountability is key to law's rule. We wrap up this chapter's work of refining our understanding of the key terms in our watchword with a sketch of the notion of accountability.

"Accountability" refers not to an agent's *ability* to give an account, but rather to the agent's *liability* to another party's *demand* for an account. We might better call it as *account-liability* or *account-demandability*.

Holding someone accountable in its generic form has three defining features: it is an interpersonal, normatively structured, and discursive activity. Accountability is an *interpersonal* activity: two parties—an accountability holder and an account giver—engage in an asymmetrical relationship with respect to a domain of the giver's activity. The holder calls on the giver to provide, in a setting not entirely of his choosing, an account of the giver's activity in the domain, and the holder offers an assessment of the account given. The activity is *discursive*: the holder demands an explanation or reckoning, a narrative of reasons connecting the giver's act to relevant standards that might provide a warrant and grounds for the act. The account must justify the giver's actions or plans by offering reasons; and the holder, in turn, assesses the giver's actions in light of the reasons offered. The relationship is *normatively structured*: moral, legal, or organizational norms entitle the holder to call for the account from the giver, and make the giver liable to be called, and impose an obligation to the holder to provide the account. Norms define the powers, claims, and obligations that structure the accountability relationship, the domain of the giver's activities, and the giver's account and the holder's assessment. The holder's activity, like the giver's, is also subject to the norms of the relationship; the holder is liable to be held accountable for that activity.

Accountability on which the rule of law depends is a special case of accountability understood in this way. Rule-of-law accountability is a *public* activity; that is, the account is given in public, regarding public matters, and given to officers of the public or to the public generally. The norms defining the relationship and the domain of the giver's activity are the laws of the political community. The deliberative discipline of law governs and gives content to the discursive, reason-giving, accountability activity.

Each occasion of accountability is asymmetrical. The holder is entitled to demand an account from the giver, and the giver is obliged to give it; moreover, the giver is subject to the holder's assessment of the giver's account. This may tempt us to think that accountability is necessarily hierarchical. Since the holder, exercising authority over the giver, is subject to norms constituting and constraining that authority, the holder may be accountable to another party for adherence to norms governing the accountability relationship to the giver; and that third party, in turn, may be accountable to a fourth. This multiparty relationship can take hierarchical form, but accountability does not necessarily lead to hierarchy. Rather, their relationship may be reciprocal. A party may be entitled to hold another accountable in one domain, but may be liable to give account to the other in another domain. Also, reciprocity can be stretched. In larger groups, institutions, or organizations, there may be a network of crisscrossing lines of accountability. I will argue in Chapter 3 that in communities that enjoy a robust rule of law, individual instances of accountability-holding take place within a network of accountability relationships. Chapter 6 will explore in detail a variety of ways to institutionalize reciprocal accountability relationships within and outside of government.

Finally, authorization of the holder to impose sanctions on the giver may be included in the holder's remit, but sanctions are not a necessary feature of accountability. The holder's power to call the giver to account is normative, not physical. Although some means of compelling the giver to give an account may lie in the background, issuing the judgment itself may be the only means of enforcing the holder's judgment. Ombudsman offices and inspectors general within constitutional governments play a crucial role holding government officials and agencies to account without making their judgments enforceable in courts of law. Whether the accountability relationship should include a right of the holder to impose sanctions on the giver is a question of the effective design of the accountability relationship. Sanctions are adventitious or auxiliary relative to the activity of demanding and assessing an account; they are external incentives to encourage or compel compliance, not necessary components of accountability. There is nothing necessarily defective or incomplete about an accountability mechanism that does not build in sanctions to enforce the judgments of accountability holders.

Of course, the giver necessarily faces the judgment of the holder and possibly others, but we must not equate the giver's subjection to the holder's *judgment* with the giver's liability to suffer *punishment* at the holder's hand. Adverse public judgment or denunciation of an accountable agent may be undesirable from that agent's point of view, but it is misleading to think of this consequence as a moral sanction; for, unlike criminal or civil penalties, the force of the criticism depends directly or indirectly on the criticized party's conscience or internalized norms. Criticisms that appeal to norms one feels no allegiance to may cause discomfort, but they lack the force of criticisms that claim that one has violated a shared value. Some will shrug off criticism for jaywalking or disloyalty to the group; others will take it personally.

The requirement to provide reasons for the exercise of power appeals to common norms of law and to the presumed commitment of the giver and the holder to make these norms effective. Consequently, the holder's judgment engages the giver's integrity, or at least the giver's concern for the holder's esteem or good offices (or those of the public). These motivations connect with the giver's presumed commitment to law. The giver may find the holder's adverse and public judgment painful and unwelcome, but that is because the giver takes seriously her commitment to the law and the holder's judgment implicates this commitment and may cast unfavorable light on it. This feature of accountability will play an important role in Chapter 10, where we will address the challenge that accountability is rooted in deep distrust and drives out trust.

Conclusion

The task of this chapter was to elaborate in detail the key concepts that populate our proposed understanding of the core aim of the rule of law: to provide protection and recourse against the arbitrary exercise of power, through the law's distinctive tools. The relevant *power* is the power of one party over another in relationships characterized by dependency and inequality (although positional power was also brought into view). This power is arbitrarily exercised when its exercise is unilateral and not subject to accountability. The rule of law is concerned with private as well as public governing power, within the boundaries of nations and beyond them, including the newly emerging power of digital platforms. The law's available tools include its positive, directive, deliberative, systematic, rights-defining and protecting, and constitutive dimensions. With these tools, the rule of law seeks to temper rather than disable governing power, to discipline it in its distinctive ways and thereby provide protection and recourse against its abuse. A key to the success of law's rule lies in effective mechanisms by which those who wield power are held accountable for its exercise.

However, these elaborations leave our core idea still in an abstract and aspirational form. We must now consider the principles implied by this core idea and, after that, the institutions in which it can best be realized.

3

Sovereignty, Equality, and Fidelity

Walter McMillian, a black resident of Monroeville, Alabama, sat on death row convicted of the murder of a white girl on the testimony of two witnesses, Ralph Myers and Bill Hooks. Since Myers was an accomplice, Hooks's confirming testimony was critical to the state's case according to Alabama law. After reading the court record of the case, Bryan Stevenson, the lawyer for McMillian's appeal of his murder conviction, was convinced that many people in the community, including the police and prosecutor, "were willing to ignore evidence, logic, and common sense to convict someone and reassure the community that the crime had been solved and the murderer punished." His assessment was confirmed when he received a phone call from Darnell Houston. Houston had gone to the authorities twice with evidence that Hooks had lied on the stand. Houston called to tell Stevenson that the authorities had arrested him and charged him with perjury, based on what he had told McMillian's lawyers a year earlier. When Stevenson pressed the district attorney (DA) on the matter, he learned that Houston had been indicted for perjury without any investigation or evidence that his statement was false—another violation of Alabama law. Stevenson concluded that the DA sought to intimidate the witness and discourage his coming forward with evidence that contradicted the state's case. "This is clearly inappropriate and legally indefensible," Stevenson told the DA. The DA was unmoved. "I knew I was talking to someone who didn't care what the law said," Stevenson writes. "I'd seen the abuse of power in many cases before, but there was something especially upsetting about it here, where not only a single defendant was being victimized but an entire community as well."

Driving home to Montgomery frustrated, appalled, and worried, Stevenson looked out on the rural farmland and hilly countryside, thinking "about what life here must have been like decades ago." But, he adds, "I didn't have to imagine it. Darnell's despair, his sadness in recognizing that they could do whatever they wanted to him with impunity, was utterly disheartening. From what I could see, there simply was no commitment to the rule of law, no accountability, and little shame."[1]

What Stevenson sought to recall was, of course, the near century of "Jim Crow" in the American South. (Isabel Wilkerson's chilling account of life under "Jim Crow" in *The Warmth of Other Suns*[2] forces one to recognize that this common term, referring to a happy, clownish blackface figure from vaudeville,

Law's Rule. Gerald J. Postema, Oxford University Press. © Oxford University Press 2022.
DOI: 10.1093/oso/9780190645342.003.0003

trivializes the structures and practices of systematic racial oppression.) A legally supported regime of systematic oppression of black Americans persisted from the late 1870s until 1960s and beyond. Although racial segregation in some of its institutional manifestations may arguably have been legal at the time, the blatant, intentional, and publicly humiliating inequality of access to public facilities of all sorts arguably were not (they were separate *and un*equal). The systematic violence that reinforced the practices of segregation was not merely brutally unjust, it was morally and legally criminal. Violence in support of racial domination involving rape, kidnapping, terror, and murder was common—not isolated acts of rogue individuals, but widespread and systematic activities of private citizens that were tolerated, sanctioned, and abetted by police, prosecutors, courts, and elected officials. No one could reasonably argue that these violent actions were legally permissible, or that the legal protections provided to white citizens did not extend to their intended black victims. The violence targeted a specific social group with the undisguised aim of securing and maintaining their subordination to the community wielding arbitrary power. Citizens and officials up and down the governmental ranks systematically ignored or public flouted the law. During this period, and arguably beyond it,[3] there was a systematic, officially entrenched, public practice of illegality.

"The rule of law requires that law *counts*," Martin Krygier rightly insists, and this "in turn requires that it be widely expected and assumed to count."[4] In the South under Jim Crow, there was law, but it did not count. The law promulgated did not match the practice of legal officials or citizens. This failure was not due, as in Nazi Germany, to a lethal mix of public and secret laws; rather, the mismatch was entirely and intentionally public. The message was, "if you are black, law does not apply to you; we, the white community, are the law." There was little uncertainty about who was the intended subject of this power. The informal rules of the culture accorded arbitrary power to white individuals and officials in defiance of existing law. This was a failure of law; law failed to rule. It failed not through a defect of the legal norms or procedures themselves but through a failure of the community's commitment to secure law's sovereignty, to hold ruling power accountable. State agents and private citizens alike defied the rule of law, and they denied its promise to fellow citizens to whom they owed duties of fidelity.

In the previous two chapters, we learned that the rule of law, at its core, seeks to provide protection and recourse against the arbitrary exercise of power through law's distinctive instrumentalities. This is an ideal fundamental to any polity, the moral foundation of social life anywhere. At bottom, it is not about disorderly behavior; it is about disorderly power. Stevenson's story and the story of racism in the United States illustrate multiple failures of the rule of law. This chapter, elaborating the discussion begun in the preceding two chapters, will unpack the principles by which we measure these failures.

In 2004, the United Nations articulated its understanding of the rule of law. The rule of law is "a principle of governance" that makes demands on "all persons, institutions and entities, public and private," the United Nations declared. The practical demands of the ideal take shape in three concepts and principles associated with them, "supremacy of law, equality before the law, [and] accountability to the law."[5] For reasons that will become clear as we proceed, I prefer slightly different terms for the same ideas: *sovereignty* of law, *equality* in the eyes of the law, *fidelity* with respect to the law. These three concepts address three fundamental questions about law's ruling: *Who* are bound and *in what ways* are they bound? Who *benefits*? and *How is it possible* for law to rule?

Sovereignty of the Law

According to the UN report, the rule of law is a principle of governance according to which all entities that exercise power, public or private, govern with and are governed by law. We must not fail to appreciate the boldness of the rule of law's claim. Its unequivocal demand is for law alone to rule. Law is Sovereign. Note, the rule of law demands that law rules over the exercise of power, not over all behavior or over all domains of life. It demands sovereignty for law, not ubiquity. Italian fascists claimed that their state was more entitled to be called a rule-of-law state (*stato di diritto*) because law regulated every aspect of daily life. This, Geoffrey Walker rights observed, is a ghastly parody of the rule of law.[6] Law's claim of sovereignty is demanding and unequivocal, but not totalitarian.

The rule of law focuses on power over others—on *governance*, as the United Nations put it. It prescribes a model for governance, an ideal *mode of governance*, to which political communities must aspire and by which we measure their performance. However, it is not the only mode of keeping order. Mao Zedong, for example, instituted *rule by Party* in China. Every Party meeting and resolution is law, he declared.[7] Lon Fuller called this governance by "managerial direction."[8] More extreme, but not less familiar, is *rule by repression*. Unpredictability of government intrusion in the lives of citizens can serve the purposes of some rulers. "Keeping things fluid can be an especially appealing strategy for a certain type of ruler," Stephen Holmes observes. "Injecting uncertainty into social situations is a well-known mechanism of control. If a subject population never knows what is going to happen to it, it is unlikely to present a serious challenge."[9] In contrast, the rule of law prescribes a mode of governance defined by the principle of law's sovereignty.

The idea of law's sovereignty comprises three subprinciples: legality, reflexivity, and exclusivity. These principles are analytically separable, but interdependent. The meaning and practical import of any one of them is distorted if ripped from its connections to the others. They offer three windows onto a single, unified demand on the exercise of governing power. We will look at each in turn, keeping in mind their complements.

Legality

The rule of law demands, in part, that those in power exercise their power through the law; their exercise of power must take legal form. Scholars often use "rule with law" or "rule by law" for this notion, but a better term is "legality" (although some writers use "legality" for other, cognate concepts).

We should distinguish this idea from others often associated or equated with it. First, a political community does not satisfy the requirement of legality merely by having a legal system. There could be many laws in a country but no rule of law. At a minimum, rule with law is a demand addressed to those who exercise ruling power. One way of translating the Chinese word for the rule of law is "to use law to rule the country."[10] This still is not an adequate rendering of the notion of "legality," but it puts us on a more promising track.

Second, we must distinguish legality, or rule by law, from "law and order." This slogan, used in highly politicized contexts, is not merely an incomplete rendering of the idea of legality; it is a distortion of it. "Law and order" links two ideas: strict order and "law" as its cause or means. Its goal is quietude or immobilization (order), and the means of achieving and sustaining it is by the manifest assertion of force through commands of authorities (orders). We can better render it, "orders and order" or "order by orders." Politicians use "law and order" when government forces, with only a thin veil of legal warrant, quash disruptive social behavior. For example, then President Trump defended deploying border control forces to overpower protestors in Portland, Oregon, in June 2020, as restoring "law and order."

"Law and order" so used is a distortion of the rule of law because the first and governing concern of the rule of law is not with broken rules but with the abused power. The rule of law recognizes that governments may exercise power to deal with disruptive behavior, of course, but they may do so only when they manifestly stay within the limits of law. In May 1977, former President Richard Nixon, in a behind-the-scenes interview with David Frost, said, "[W]hen the president does [something,] that means that it is not illegal . . . the president's decision . . . enables those who carry it out, to carry it out without violating a law."[11] Nixon echoed, no doubt unknowingly, the absolutist's maxim: what pleases the ruler has the force of law. As we saw in Chapter 1, medieval legal scholars challenged this principle, and the dispute over it helped shape our idea of the rule law. The rule-of-law ideal stands resolutely opposed to this thought, demanding *at a minimum* that what the ruler "pleases" must take the form of law.

This demand imposes a discipline on the exercise of power. Law is the *medium* through which rulers must exercise power; and rulers must undertake a *commitment* to rule through this medium. It demands, among other things, that ruling power take the form of public standards, articulated in general, prospective, consistent terms, accessible to all, underwriting claims of right that can be submitted to tribunals empowered to assess them with the participation of those subject to that power. Legendary legal scholar Lon Fuller called this discipline "the inner morality of law."[12]

Lying at the center of the requirement of legality, behind these canons requiring that law meet certain formal conditions, is the principle that law must not be used as a tool of abuse against those who are subject to the law.[13] Law commits such abuse when, for example, it imposes inconsistent obligations on people, when it is applied retroactively, and when its rules are not sufficiently general or publicly accessible. Law is also abused when politicians use it to undermine or weaken institutions designed to protect against, or provide recourse against governmental abuse of power, for example, when legislation weakens judicial institutions. (In Chapter 8, we discuss recent attempts of the ruling party in Poland legislatively to undermine the independence of the Polish courts.[14])

Reflexivity

Ruling *with law* is not sufficient to satisfy law's sovereignty. Philosopher-historian David Hume tells us that England's Edward I "took care that his subjects should do justice to each other; but he desired always to have his own hand free in all his transactions, both with them and with his neighbors."[15] Law, to King Edward and hosts of other rulers before and after him, was a convenient tool of governance. Those who exercise ruling power grasp the political advantages of rule with law and embrace it publicly—as long as they are not bound by it. When rulers can exercise political power more efficiently without submitting to the fussy technicalities of law, they see no reason to use law. But this willingness to ignore law when it serves their purposes cannot be widely known in the political community without jeopardizing the benefits of ruling with law that they seek. The formalities of law prove useful to those in power precisely because it is widely believed by those subject to their governance that law constrains the exercise of that power. That is to say, those who are inclined to rule with law realize that law is an effective tool of governing just insofar as it is possible to mask their use of it as a mere tool. The utility of ruling with law to those in power is parasitic on its successfully masquerading as something more, as being subject to the demand of reflexivity: those who rule with law and in its name are at the same time ruled by it. The central demand of law's sovereignty is *reflexivity*.

The principle of reflexivity holds, first, that the law applies to and tempers ruling power, and second, it does so by subjecting the exercise of power to institutions and arrangements of accountability. The rule of law is robust in a polity only when there are strong and effective institutions empowered to bring that exercise to account, institutions that are themselves likewise accountable. (We will draw out this implication of the reflexivity presently when we discuss fidelity.)

Reflexivity emphasizes one dimension of the rule-of-law demand of universal subjection to law. All are subject to the law; hence, as we put it in the vernacular, "No one is above the law." All are subject to its demands and to accountability for exercising that power in accord with it. Indeed, as we shall see at the end of the next subsection of this chapter, those who exercise ruling power are subject to the law in a way that ordinary citizens who have no immediate access to that power are not.

Recently, with the rise again of authoritarian and quasi-authoritarian governments around the world, scholars have begun to speak of "illiberal democracies" and "authoritarian rule of law."[16] It is an interesting, if troubling, question whether a democracy can be "illiberal"; however, it is clear that the phrase "authoritarian rule of law" involves a contradiction. Authoritarian rulers, by definition, put themselves above the law, using law to their advantage, but not submitting to its discipline. However, a polity respects the rule of law only when law rules those who rule with law.

Exclusivity

In the late nineteenth century, the US Supreme Court articulated a key principle when it wrote, "[A]ll the officers of the government, from the highest to the lowest, are creatures of the law and are bound to obey it. It is the only supreme power in our system of government."[17] The International Commission of Jurists in its report of the Delhi Congress (1959) cited as one of two fundamental principles of the rule of law "that all power in the State should be derived from and exercised in accordance with the law."[18] That is to say, law claims sovereignty over every exercise of governing power. This is what we called in Chapter 1 the *exclusivity* principle.

According to this principle, institutions and state functionaries operate with legitimate authority only when ordained by law. "Law doesn't just have a little sphere of its own in which to operate, but expands to govern and regulate every aspect of official practice,"[19] writes legal philosopher Jeremy Waldron. There is no legitimate exercise of governing authority outside the purview of the law. This might look like a trivial tautology[20]—"legal authorities cannot act illegally"— but it is not a tautology, and it is far from trivial. It is a bold and demanding normative principle, which many rulers and political theorists have vigorously rejected, defending their special prerogatives. It also has profound implications for our understanding of the constitutional powers of the executive. A short detour into late medieval Christian theology will help us understand its secular use, meaning, and force.

Medieval theologians sought to reconcile God's omnipotence with an orderly natural and moral world. Although some argued that God was not even constrained by laws of logic—holding that it was within God's power to lift a stone He is powerless to lift—most agreed that God's omnipotence was limited to the power to do, or make, or bring about anything that was logically possible. However, they agreed, the laws of nature are contingent, products of God's free creative act, as are the laws that order the moral world. Do these natural and moral laws bind God? they asked. At this point, theologians introduced a distinction they found useful. They distinguished God's *absolute* power from God's *ordained* power. Ordinarily, God exercises power ordained by His creation of the laws of the natural and moral world. Creating them, God bound Himself; the laws God ordained constrain God's power. However, these theologians argued, creation did not affect God's absolute power, which exists in some sense apart from God's ordained power. Hence, while God is bound by ordained power, God's absolute power remained free.

This solution itself created more disagreement. As time went on, two competing interpretations of the distinction between God's absolute and ordained power vied for orthodoxy. One understanding, adopted by theologians like Albert the Great, held that God did not have two *powers*—one absolute, one ordained—but that there are two ways that we mortals can intellectually grasp God's power. (Hence, we can call this the Two Views view.) Viewed in the abstract—that is, apart from God's benevolence and "prior" to God's benevolent willing—God's power is absolute. But considered in light of God's benevolence and creative activity, God's power is ordained, and God wills only "ordinately," that is, logically and, if you will, "lawishly," and not arbitrarily.

The alternative understanding—the Two Powers view—held that that the distinction marked out two different divine powers. God exercised *absolute* power in creating the world and ordaining its natural and moral laws; and God exercises *ordained* power in God's interaction with the natural and moral world, *for the most part*. However, divine absolute power always remains available, part of God's omnipotence repertoire. Thus, it is always open to God to change the natural or moral order, or suspend its laws. God holds divine absolute power in reserve for special purposes.

It should come as no surprise that political theorists, writing theological position papers for their rulers (and high Church leaders), favored the Two Powers view. It became a staple of political thinking well into the seventeenth century, a favorite of absolutist rulers and their defenders. The claim was not that rulers may rule by *diktat*, but that they always hold in reserve, available when needed, powers beyond those ordained by law.

Ernst Fraenkel's analysis of Nazi Germany's state is a chilling example of the political application of the reserved power view.[21] The German state, under Nazi rule and according to Nazi theory, was bifurcated, he argued. For all "ordinary" social and economic matters in the state, all private or nonpolitical matters, law prevailed. This "Normative State" fit the model of the *Rechtsstaat*—law-defined and law-governed state—that matured in Germany over the previous century. Lurking in its shadows, however, was another political state in which the authorities', and ultimately the Leader's, decision alone reigned. It prevailed over all "extraordinary" matters, a lawless vacuum, where no legal rules governed and was "regulated [only] by arbitrary measures (*Massnahmen*) in which the dominant officials exercise their discretionary prerogatives." Fraenkel called it the "Prerogative State" (*Massnahmenstaat*).[22] These two domains did not exist side by side; rather, the Prerogative State suffused and compromised the Normative State, because the definition of the line between "ordinary" and "nonpolitical" matters, on the one hand, and the "extraordinary" and "political" matters, on the other, was exclusively in the hands of political authorities, beyond the oversight of courts or other institutions of accountability. "Jurisdiction over jurisdiction rest[ed] with the Prerogative State."[23] The result was that the entire realm of the "private" was at the same time potentially political. The Nazi State was a nightmare realization of the Two Powers view.

Challenging the Two Powers view, the exclusivity principle of sovereignty rejects out of hand any claim of reserve absolute ruling powers. It maintains that *all* governing power that is not ordained by law is null, invalid, and without legitimacy. It rejects the idea that there is a reserve of extralegal power that authorities may legitimately draw upon when they think doing so might be necessary or useful. Unlike the power of an omnipotent deity, the *only* legitimate governing power, in the view of the rule of law, is legally ordained, legally constituted power.

Backed by the exclusivity principle, law's capacity to *constitute* power—to constitute institutions, offices, and procedures of governing (recall Chapter 2)— affords a potent mechanism of constraint on power. Sir Matthew Hale, England's premier jurist in the mid-seventeenth century, called it law's *potestas irritans*— law's "irritating" (or rather, nullifying) power.[24] Acting within their offices, with warrant of law, officials enjoyed legal cover, as it were, protecting them from liability for the injuries or indignities that they may cause in the exercise of their official duties. Officials acting *ultra vires*—without that warrant—are exposed to liability. Law, Hale suggested, has the capacity to *invalidate* actions, strip them of their claimed legitimacy, and subject officials to liability for threatening or violating legally protected interests. If, as the exclusivity principle insists, the rule of law recognizes only *ordained* power, law's capacity to constitute offices entails a capacity to *constrain* governing power by channeling it and removing legal cover from other exercises of power over people.

However, we might wonder whether the law could explicitly constitute an office that confers unconstrained power on its incumbents, that *ordains* such power. We do not have to go very far to find historical examples of such an arrangement. One example is the traditional doctrine of royal prerogative in English constitutional law. John Locke, in the late seventeenth century, defined the prerogative as the "power to act according to discretion, for the public good, without the prescription [or further warrant] of the law, and sometimes even against it."[25] The late nineteenth-century English constitutional theorist A.V. Dicey puts an even sharper point on the concept. Prerogative, he maintained, is "the residue of discretionary or arbitrary authority which at any given time is legally left in the hands of the Crown."[26] But there are also recent troubling examples of legally ordained lawlessness. We can find them, for example, in various nations' attempts to respond to alleged emergencies. Governments create "legal black holes"[27]—where law is used "to suspend law, thus creating an exceptional regime alongside the regime of ordinary law."[28] Legal philosopher David Dyzenhaus argues that such was the case when the United States detained alien enemy combatants offshore in Guantanamo Bay. The US government claimed the detention camp was beyond the jurisdiction of the federal courts. In many such cases, law creates a space in which state actors are unconstrained by law, unaccountable to the law—a law-created lawless void.

If we take the exclusivity principle seriously—and care about the arbitrary exercise of power—we must conclude that prerogative powers, legal black holes, and other such devices are condemned by the rule of law. It is resolutely opposed not only to the claim that there is some extralegal domain of power legitimately exercised by those entrusted with positions of governing authority but also to the legal creation of such a domain. To create it is to use the law against the rule of law, to subvert it. As the example of law in times of crisis might suggest, the exclusivity principle is controversial. We will address serious challenges to it in Chapter 12.

Before we close this section, we need to make one clarification of the exclusivity principle. As I have formulated it, the principle applies to official, that is to say, governing power. The rule of law requires that law be everywhere in government, but not everywhere in life. Law's sovereignty does not entail law's ubiquity.

However, we must recognize a certain asymmetry between governing officials and ordinary citizens. From law's point of view, ordinary citizens in a polity may do *whatever is not prohibited* by law; government officials, however, may *do only what is permitted or authorized by law*. For the citizen, anything not prohibited is permitted, but for officials nothing is permitted, unless it is explicitly authorized by law. The main reason for this asymmetry is that the rule of law recognizes two kinds of agents who are subject to law: natural persons and legally constituted artificial persons. Artificial persons include, at least, government offices and agencies (we will consider later whether nonstate entities, corporations for example, are included). They have no moral standing outside the law; natural persons do. As the court in *US v. Lee* put it, "all the officers of the government, from the highest to the lowest, are creatures of the law and are bound to obey it."[29] Officials exist as creatures and functionaries of the law. This is not true of ordinary citizens.[30] Ordinary citizens, as natural persons, have moral standing independent of the law. This asymmetry will play an important role in our discussion in Chapter 15 of the place of the rule of law in the global domain, a domain in which states and other artificial persons are the primary actors.

Equality in the Eyes of the Law

Equality is regularly said to be a foundational principle of the rule of law, along with sovereignty, but this claim needs defense. Moreover, it is easy to mistake the aim of equality as it serves the rule of law; so we must clarify the claim before we attempt to defend it.

First, the primary concern of equality in this context is not material or economic equality, nor the political equality associated with democracy. (We will explore these further dimensions of equality in relation to the rule of law in Chapter 5.) In the United Nations' language, echoing common usage, the rule of law calls for "equality before the law"—before a tribunal, but not only then. Its focus is on the daily operation of the law.

Second, we should not think of it as requiring the *same treatment* between some set of persons and *different treatment* for others. Although "equality" implies comparison, the relevant idea here is that of a comparison class, and *inclusion* in that class. That is, its concern is inclusion in a company of peers when it comes to the scope and range of the promise of the law's protection against the abuse of power. In the eyes of the law, all who fall within the law's jurisdiction must enjoy its protection. Thus, we shall call it the principle of "equality in the eyes of the law."

The early career of a famous clause of the Magna Carta illustrates the idea of equality at work here. In 1215, English barons forced King John to sign a charter of liberties. Among the most influential portions of the Charter is the text from Chapter 29. (We also looked at it briefly in Chapter 1.)

> No freeman shall be taken or imprisoned, or be disseised of his Freehold, or Liberties, or free Customs, or be outlawed, or exiled, or any other wise destroyed; nor will We not pass upon him, nor condemn him, but by lawful judgment of his Peers, or by the Law of the Land. We will sell to no man, we will not deny or defer to any man either Justice or Right.[31]

This clause might have been designed to protect all English men (not women, of course), but it explicitly extended the protections of law only to "freemen." Over the next decades, the restriction of the scope of these protections became a pressing issue. In 1354, Edward III clarified the scope of Chapter 29 with the following statutory language.

> That no Man of what[ever] Estate or Condition that he be, shall be put out of Land or Tenement, nor taken nor imprisoned, no disinherited, nor put to Death, without being brought in Answer by the due Process of the Law.[32]

This clause, rooted in Magna Carta Chapter 29, inspired the Fifth Amendment of the Constitution of the United States, which reads, "No person shall . . . be deprived of life, liberty, or property, without due process of law." The Magna Carta of 1215 seems to extend its protections of law to "freemen," while the US Constitution purports to protect all persons. A late nineteenth-century judgment of the US Supreme Court makes the demand of legal equality with force. A citizen of the United States, it argues, "knows no person however near to those in power, or however powerful himself, to whom he need yield the rights which the law secures to him when it is well administered."[33]

   We know, however, that, despite the Constitution's language, Fifth Amendment protections were not extended to all persons resident in the United States for the first seventy years of the life of the American democracy, and even well after that. Former slaves and their descendants did not enjoy the protections, even formally, until the passage of the Fourteenth Amendment in 1868, and not in reality until a century later (if then), and women even later, since the Equal Rights Amendment has not yet been ratified. The rule of law's equality principle insists on wide scope, like that promised in Edward III's statute and the US Constitution's Due Process clause—promised real, not parchment protections, protections available to all within the jurisdiction of the law.

   The theme of law's wide scope is ancient. In fifth-century Athens, Euripides made the link between this notion of equality and the core notion of the rule of law. He wrote:

Nothing means more evil to a city than a tyrant.
First of all, there will be no public laws.
But one man will have control by owning the law,
himself for himself, and this will not be fair [*or* that is the end of equality].
When the laws are written down, then he who is weak
and he who is rich have equal justice:
the weaker ones may speak as ill of the fortunate
as they hear of themselves, and a lesser man
can overcome a great one, if he has justice on his side.[34]

He ends with the query, "What greater equality can there be in a city?" This is a remarkable passage. The despot, he argues, puts himself above the law—violating the reflexivity principle—and acts as if he *owns* the law. This implies that there is no public law, that is, law common to all, and thus equality is at an end. Why? Because, he argues, where there is law, it protects the weak and the strong, the rich and the poor alike. The weak have the same recourse to the law as the strong, and, with law's protection, the weak are not frightened into subservience but can resist the calumny of the rich without fear.

Euripides' argument retains its force millennia later. We can put the argument in terms of our preceding discussion. The rule of law—promising protection and recourse against the arbitrary exercise of power—demands reflexivity. Reflexivity calls for subjection of officials as well as lay persons to the law. All are included in the scope of law's demands. Law is common to all, binding all. The scope of law's protections as well must be universal. If the ruler claims to stand above the law, he claims to be above all others, to be *exceptional*. We can demand of him, "What makes you so special?" Thus, to concede that one is subject to the law is to oppose the designation of being special in the eyes of the law. Reflexivity requires that the laws be common to all; it calls for common subjection to the law.

The argument thus far considered views the matter in its "vertical" dimension, but we can make a similar point regarding law's "horizontal" dimension. Just as the law does not countenance people elevating themselves above the law, so it prohibits treatment that puts people beyond the scope of law's protection. The rule of law requires that, when it comes to law's protection, social, economic, cultural, or personal distinctions do not count. As an anonymous seventeenth-century English lawyer wrote, "If we could perfectly execute justice wee must make no difference between men for their friends[hi]p, parentage, riches, pov[er]tye, or dignitye."[35] Nothing of this kind puts them above the law, beyond its demands and burdens, and nothing of this kind puts them outside the benefits of the law. Those who enjoy law's protection and benefits are subject to law's burdens; likewise, those who are subject to law's burdens are entitled as well to the benefit of its protection.

When, inevitably, law draws distinctions and thus treats people differently, the question must be asked, "What's so special about these people who get preferential treatment or on whom special burdens are placed?" Compelling reasons must support the different treatment, and these reasons must not be demeaning to those excluded from law's benefits. The law's treatment of members of the political community governed by law must meet what political philosopher Philip Pettit calls "the eyeball test." However different the treatment, those who are subject to the law "should be able to look one another in the eye without fear or deference." This test "allows for departures from substantive equality in . . . material matters, directing us instead to the importance of equality in the interactions that people are capable of enjoying with one another."[36]

The Recourse Principle

The benefits of law, from the point of view of the rule of law, include not only law's *protection* but also effective *recourse* when one judges that one has been the victim of an abuse of power. Law that is common to all, binds all, protects all, and offers recourse to all. The recourse principle is a complement to the equality principle. Seeds for both were planted in Chapter 29 of the Magna Carta.

According to Chapter 29, Sir Edward Coke reports, "[e]very Subject of the Realm, for injury done to him . . . by any other Subject . . . may take his remedy by the course of law."[37] On Coke's reading, due process of law requires that any act of government that may adversely affect an individual's life, liberty, or property must proceed only by law and through fair and reasonable process of law. In addition, it requires that any subject of the law who suffers injury at the hands of another party, whether government or private subject, is entitled to call on the law on his own behalf to remedy the wrong.

The recourse principle requires that victims be accorded a fair (not merely formal) opportunity to seek legally ordered relief. On this principle, the rule of law implies a duty on governments to provide law subjects rights of recourse—that is, *every subject of law is entitled to a right of action in law against any other subject of law (governmental or private).* This right of action is a right (1) on one's own motion, (2) to submit to a court of law or other regular legal process a legally recognized claim, (3) and to defend that claim in a full and fair procedure, and (4), upon proof of the claim, to obtain judicially ordered relief.[38]

This right locates in law subjects a *power* to call on the assistance of law and government, which have a duty to respond, and a *liberty* to do so (on their own motion). By allocating this power and liberty, however, the law also creates opportunities for abuse. So it imposes limits on the exercise of this power and subjects it to law's formal procedures. Thus, the right also entails for the right bearer a duty and liability: a *duty* to respect the limits of the power and a *liability* to be called to account for the exercise of the right. The right entails reciprocal rights of others. In particular, rights on the part of one accused of wrongdoing or causing injury to defend against the claim in a full and fair process and a right of recourse against anyone who abuses the right of recourse. Thus, the principle of recourse calls for a legally structured scheme of reciprocal rights, powers, liberties, and liabilities.

The recourse principle engages subjects of law in what we might call the accountability project that is at the heart of the rule of law. But it does so on a somewhat different ground than the fidelity principle that we will discuss presently. Viewed from the perspective of individual subjects of law, the accountability project has a public and a personal dimension—a common project of holding those who exercise power accountable to the law and a personal right of holding those who injure one through their abuse of power accountable *to oneself*. The common project of holding power accountable to law is the domain of the fidelity principle; the recourse principle structures the personal one.

The recourse principle's concern is mutual empowerment, rather than mutual obligation or responsibility sustaining law's rule. It aims to put resources at the disposal of subjects of law rather than enlist them in a collective project. The idea from which it stems is the idea that the rule of law requires all members of the community to be subjects of (not subjected to) a common body of law, and it provides resources and opportunities to be more than passive beneficiaries of the effective definition and execution of laws; it empowers their active involvement in their protection.

Law as a Mode of Association

The rule of law represents not only a mode of governance but also an ideal mode of association. Philosopher Michael Oakeshott argued that the rule of law is the "vernacular language" of moral association.[39] The rule of law affirms a distinctive social formation, a way in which members of a polity regard, recognize, and relate to each other. This is the thought implicit in the claim that the rule of law obtains in a community in which all members are subject to a common set of laws and hence are equal before the law (or perhaps we should say *equal in and through* the law). This expresses an important fact about, and constraint upon, a government's treatment of the governed, but it also expresses a fact about, and commitment implicit in, relations among co-members of the polity.

Rousseau captured the reciprocity at the center of this model. In his *Letters from the Mountain*, he wrote: "[F]reedom consists less in acting at will than in not being subjugated to the will of another; it also consists in not subjugating the will of another to our own."[40] Rousseau used the language of freedom, but Kant found the language of equality more apt. The core element of his notion of the "rightful condition," he argued, is "the equality of human beings as subjects within a commonwealth."[41] In Chapter 1, we encountered the rich conception of moral association sketched by Johannes Althusius. On his view, law's mode of association is that of a public constitution, a largely explicit social ordering, of rational self-directing "symbiotes," pledged to mutual communication of reciprocal rights, duties, and responsibilities. Rather than keeping them apart, to prevent violent interactions, law enables members to *come together*, providing them with public means of mutual recognition and a medium for common and public deliberation. Law's covenant, to use the language of sixteenth-century lawyer James Morice, is a covenant among people *with respect to* law—a network of mutual commitment to regard their polity as ordered by that law and to take responsibility for it. This covenant is at the heart of law, for law can rule in a commonwealth only if law's ethos has taken hold, only if it is rooted in mutual faithfulness to differentiated and interconnected responsibilities.

Fidelity to the Law and to Each Other

Now we must address a fundamental challenge. The rule of law's bold claim is that *law rules*. However, we know that law does not, it cannot, rule. Law rules only through the efforts and agency of human beings ordered in their institutions and practices. So what can we make of law's bold claim?

How Does Law Rule?

The rule of law imagines, in James Harrington's words, "an empire of laws, not of men."[42] But, as we learned in Chapter 2, these familiar words have led scores of writers over several centuries to undertake a fool's errand, seeking an understanding of law that removes human beings from its ruling. They sought to locate law's rule in some impersonal, human-effort transcending force—in God, divine law, natural law, or some form of "spontaneous order." However, this strategy simply replaced law, that is, proper civil or positive law, with something else. It does not answer the question that has perplexed us for so long. We want to know how *law* can rule—that is, how law can produce order and, more importantly, provide protection and recourse against the arbitrary exercise of power.

The sad story of Walter McMillian and Darnell Houston that we told in the opening of this chapter is the story of a society with a narrow and twisted sense of what members owe to each other. The story of "kids for cash" told in Chapter 1 does the same. These stories illustrate a major thesis of this book: that law can only do its job of constraining the abuse of power when there is in place the ethos of *fidelity*. This ethos involves more than a general willingness to submit to law's governance and to give deference to its limits and requirements—what social theorist Philip Selznick called "a culture of lawfulness."[43] It is not enough that people *believe in* the rule of law and see it as "a necessary and proper aspect of their society."[44] Most crucially, the rule of law needs, in addition, the active engagement of officials and citizens in holding each other to their responsibilities under the law.

The history of Jim Crow teaches further that law's rule fails when power is held to account only when it serves the interest of those doing the holding. Where Jim Crow was firmly in place, law did not count in and for relations between the whites and blacks in the community. A young white man from Neshoba County, Mississippi, confessed, "I didn't know it was against the law to kill a black man. I learned that when I joined the army. When they told me, I thought they were joking."[45] No doubt, officials and citizens in the white community needed to see their behavior as justified in light of existing social standards, but the law was not among those standards. The white community's commitment to law failed precisely at the point where its protections were meant to extend to the people that they sought to subjugate. No one who had the resources and opportunities to do so exercised the responsibility of holding these lawbreakers accountable under the law.

Scottish Enlightenment writer Adam Ferguson sketched a striking portrait of the ethos underwriting the rule of law. Law's capacity to rule, he argued, lies in "the influence of men resolved to be free; of men, who, having adjusted in writing the terms on which they are to live with the state, and with their fellow-subjects, are determined, by their vigilance and spirit, to make these terms be observed."[46] Lon Fuller argued that the rule of law established a partnership between those who rule and those who are ruled, a partnership characterized by reciprocal compliance with the law—each willing to comply given assurance that others will do as well. However, Ferguson insisted the rule of law needs and demands more. It needs and demands that all members of the community, officials and laypersons alike, take responsibility for holding their partners in the relationship to their respective duties. The fidelity ethos involves mutual accountability as well as reciprocal compliance. The *fidelity thesis* maintains that *the rule of law can be robust in a polity only when all of its members, and not merely the legal or ruling elite, take responsibility for holding each other, and especially law's officials, to account under the law.*

Fidelity has a societal or "horizontal" as well as strictly political or "vertical" dimension. Moreover, the rule of law fails if law does not extend and sustain its protections across the whole community. The scope of fidelity's responsibilities is community-wide, extending over the full reach of the law. Fidelity's responsibilities are owed *by all* who enjoy law's benefits *to all* who are subject to law's burdens; moreover, they are *owed* not to the government, nor to the law, but *to each other*.

Why Mutual Accountability?

We have seen that the rule of law demands that those who exercise power in the political community do so only within the frame of law-ordained authority and that the same law applies to them. That is, it implies exclusivity and reflexivity. Thus, those who exercise ruling power do not merely wield coercive power, they also hold others accountable to the law, and do so legitimately only if they have proper legal warrant for doing so. The warrant provides the agent *standing* to exercise a kind of authority over another along with a *standard* guiding the exercise of authority. Law defines the relationship between the parties, and each is subject to that law. Thus, the rule of law demands that those who exercise power in the polity are also subject to the law.

But to be subject to the law involves *submitting* to the law's governance, acknowledging one's subjection to it and undertaking a commitment to treat it as a norm for one's deliberation, decisions, and actions. Further, as Thomas Hobbes argued, to commit to the law is to submit to the judgment of others, to allow oneself to be held accountable to others. He that "setteth the Lawes above the Soveraign, setteth also a Judge above him."[47] We encountered a suggestive reason for this thesis in Chapter 1. To submit to law but not to another to judge one's performance according to that law is to submit to *self-imposed* rule; however, we argued, to be bound by self-imposed resolutions is not to be bound *by law*. Submission to law cannot be a matter of submission to *oneself*. We can develop this thought in two ways, one pragmatic, the other conceptual and principled.

Consider, first, the pragmatic argument. Machiavelli tells the tale of Pluto, who addressed the council of the princes of Hell. "Since by heavenly decree and irrevocable destiny I hold this kingdom," Pluto asserted, "I cannot be bound by any judgment whatever, be it earthly or heavenly; nevertheless, because it is a sign of great wisdom when they who have supreme power allow themselves to be ruled by law and take due note of other people's opinions, I have decided to seek your advice."[48] Wherein lies this wisdom? Machiavelli based his argument on the premise that one can effectively rule only with the largely voluntary cooperation of the people.[49] The people will cooperate voluntarily only if they believe those who exercise power over them will also comply. Successful exercise of ruling power, on this view, requires reciprocal compliance. However, it is not enough that rulers' commitments are voluntary and sincere; they must be publicly credible, and not easily withdrawn. Any reason for people to suspect that their ruler's behavior could change with a shift in policy or preference, or with their self-serving interpretation of the law, will weaken the people's willingness to comply. The best way for rulers to make a credible commitment to comply with the law, so the argument goes, is to establish and submit to a framework of accountability, to institutions or arrangements for holding them to their commitments.

However, this version of the argument is problematic because only a subset of the people need to cooperate voluntarily for rulers to maintain effective ruling power, and it is possible to secure their cooperation without submitting to public accountability. We have far too many examples from history—and sadly, in contemporary politics—of those who hold supreme power co-opting and corrupting those on whose cooperation they depend (see Chapter 8). Those who rule need the voluntary cooperation of a *portion* of the political community, and they can secure cooperation in a variety of ways; they can secure compliance of the remainder through coercion and intimidation.

The principled argument takes a more promising tack. It proceeds in two stages. The first stage sets out to establish Hobbes's thesis that to be subject to law is to be subject to the judgment of another. Philip Hunton, writing in 1643, put the rule-of-law position succinctly. To subject someone with ruling power to a law "and then make him judge of his own deviation from the law is to absolve him from all law . . . It is the same to assign him no judge as to make him his own judge."[50] That is to say, for one to claim to be subject to the law but to be the sole judge of one's compliance with that law involves one in a contradiction. Why?

Suppose someone claims to hold another person accountable and in that way exercise authority over that person. This, as we have seen, is to claim that one acts with warrant of law. That is to claim that one's act falls under the law and that the law is binding on one. But *saying* so does not *make* it so. Rather, the claim is a judgment, and judgments necessarily point *beyond* their *makers*. To claim that the law warrants one's act is to make a claim that transcends the judgment maker. However, to claim at the same time that one is the sole judge of compliance with the law is simply to say that one's *saying* so *is* sufficient warrant for its *being* so. It is so just in virtue of one's saying so. But, then, claiming that one acts with warrant of the law and that one is the sole judge of that warrant is to express a contradiction.

Thus, as Hunton put it, to be only self-accountable is to be accountable to no one; and self-validating judgments are not merely false judgments, they are failed judgments—utterances that fail as judgments. Consequently, submission to the law can never be a matter of self-imposition or self-authorization. Self-authorizing is failed authorization. To be subject to the law just is to be accountable to another, and an *unaccountable accountability-holder* is a contradiction in terms.

Immanuel Kant pressed this argument to its second stage. He wrote, "[N]o one can bind another to something without also being subject to a law by which he in turn can be bound in the same way by the other."[51] According to Kant, to submit to law is, necessarily, to submit to *reciprocal* accountability. Kant's idea is that for one party to hold another party accountable is not merely for the first to exercise power over or to manipulate the other; rather, it involves *addressing* the other party, and it depends on the other party's uptake—their grasp and appreciation of the order addressed to them. The addressee is not caused by the order to act, but rather *responds* to the first party's intervention. The addressee regards the responsive behavior as *owed to* the one holding the other accountable. So relations of accountability-holding (and authority in general) are in middle voice, as it were. Like greeting another, embracing another, or coordinating activities with another, exercising normative authority and holding another accountable involve reciprocity.

Must accountability be reciprocal? Could not Alice be accountable to Bert and Bert to Cleo? Could there not be an accountability chain? Hobbes thought there had to be one; and he exploited the consequence of this to insist that the sovereign ruler cannot be subject to law in the first place. His argument was simple.[52] Either this accountability chain stops, for example, with Cleo, or it goes on to Darren to Eli to Fritz, and so on. But, then, Hobbes argued, either the chain proceeds ad infinitum or it stops somewhere. If it stops, then there *must* be an unaccountable accountability-holder. However, we have already concluded that the idea of an unaccountable accountability-holder is a contradiction in terms, so the one who holds others to the law may wield power, but is not subject to the law. This is the conclusion Hobbes drew, because he thought that the other option, the chain proceeding ad infinitum, is a manifest practical absurdity. It is absurd, in his view, because it leaves everyone uncertain about who, if anyone, is in authority with standing to hold others accountable.

However, there is a way out of Hobbes's compelling dilemma. Hobbes's argument rests on the assumption that authority or accountability relations are essentially hierarchical, that if one is subject to the authority of another, one is in every respect subordinated to that party. The way out of Hobbes's dilemma is to reject this assumption. The medieval maxim, *par in parem non habet imperium* ("an equal has no command over an equal"), was understood historically to preclude authority relations among equals. However, this maxim could also be rendered as "an equal is not subject to the *unilateral* authority of an equal." Philip Hunton put the point well: "[T]his power of judging argues not a superiority of those who Judge over him who is Judged."[53] To be accountable to another is not to be subordinate to that other party. Alice may be subject to Bert's authority with respect to one matter, but this does not preclude Bert's being subject to Alice's authority in another matter. Scholars of ancient Athens argue, for example, that in Athens, "citizens were both subjects and objects of power—accounted and accountants."[54]

Kant envisions a structure of reciprocal accountability, but typically, accountability that supports the rule of law forms a loop or network. The fidelity thesis maintains that such a network of accountability is not only possible, it is essential to the realization of the law's rule in a political community. Law is capable of ruling only where all members of the community—officials of all ranks and citizens alike—submit to and participate in a network of mutual accountability. The law's ability to rule in a community depends on a robust commitment of its members to make law effective by holding each other accountable to the law. While one individual may hold another accountable, fidelity is not limited to this kind of direct interpersonal relationship. Upholding law's rule is a cooperative endeavor. One's own efforts can contribute to that endeavor, but its success will depend on the efforts of many others as well. Thus, fidelity responsibilities typically involve doing one's part in a common, cooperative endeavor, responsibilities owed to each other as members similarly committed and bound. Each party subject to law submits to and participates in a network of mutual accountability. The lines of accountability may intersect in many different ways. Although each occasion of accountability-holding is asymmetrical between the holder and the giver, on other occasions, the holder is liable to give an account to some other holder, perhaps for his calling the initial giver to account. These connections form a network rather than a hierarchical chain.

What might an accountability loop or network look like? We will answer this question in detail in Chapter 6, but we can give here an idea of what is involved. One familiar example is intragovernmental checks and balances within a constitutional regime. Constitutions not only divide and allocate governmental powers to different relatively autonomous branches, but the jurisdiction of each branch penetrates to some extent the jurisdictions of other branches. Intragovernmental accountability depends on a network of agencies empowered to hold each other accountable.

"Bottom-up" accountability in the "vertical" political dimension is also familiar. Where the rule of law is adequately realized, the exercises of power by government authorities taken under color of law can be challenged in court. Not only can people demand a public showing of the alleged operative facts on which the exercise of power is premised, but those subject to this power or their surrogates can demand that the authorities produce their warrant for so acting. Citizens are accountable to authorities, but so also are authorities accountable to citizens, through the offices of the court.

Organizations of civil society might also be involved. One example of such accountability-holding occurred in 2004 in Greensboro, North Carolina.[55] Twenty-five years earlier, members of the Ku Klux Klan and the American Nazi Party attacked labor union activists and members of an organization with ties to the Communist Workers' Party during a demonstration in a low-income neighborhood in Greensboro. City police were notably absent from the demonstration. Five demonstrators were killed and ten severely injured. In subsequent trials, all Klan and Nazi defendants were acquitted. City officials sought to move on after what was called the "Greensboro Massacre," and the local media did little to resist their efforts. However, racial and civic tensions kept resentment alive. In 2004, a group of citizens sought support from the city council to establish a truth commission on the model of the Truth and Reconciliation Commission of South Africa. The city council refused to support and sought to quiet the attempt, but Greensboro citizens persisted. They set up an ad hoc truth commission with financial support from a local private foundation. At the commission hearings, evidence and testimony exposed failures of the city police department, city government, and criminal and civil justice system.[56] This citizen-initiated, privately funded effort illustrates how a community's sense of responsibility to hold official accountable, even twenty-five years after the fact, can be given concrete form.

Recent attempts to restrict abortion in the United States brings to mind what we might at first blush think as another example of citizen involvement in accountability-holding. In 2021, the state of Texas enacted a law that bans abortion after six weeks of pregnancy. What is unique about this law is its enforcement provisions. It prohibits state officials from enforcing the law and empowers Texas citizens to sue abortion providers and others who assist them, awarding them $10,000 per illegal abortion if their suit is successful.[57] The Texas law outsources enforcement of the law, in effect deputizing ordinary citizens to do the work normally assigned to state officials. The constitutionality of this law— its ban on abortion and its unique mode of enforcement—was widely doubted,[58] but for our purposes, the question is whether it is a proper example of the community involvement in holding fellow citizens accountable to the law.

The answer is that this is not community accountability-holding but rather nothing more than vigilantism. The problem is not that the Texas law enables law enforcement officials to deputize citizens to assist them on an ad hoc basis. The problem, rather, is that the law enables people to abuse those who are subject to the law; it violates that core principle of legality discussed earlier in this chapter. It incentivizes civilians to exercise state power without adequate protections against partiality and guarantees of competence. There is no provision in the law for a mechanism by which the civilian enforcers are themselves held accountable. What is more, it allows for the possibility—surely not beyond the intentions of the lawmakers—of dozens or more separate cases filed across the state over the same handful of abortions with the same defendants. Even if the defendants were able to win every case, the burden of having to defend themselves in multiple courts with no protection against double jeopardy would be intolerable. The law, in effect, and likely in design, mobilizes the full power of the state to attack individuals and organizations that cannot possibly defend themselves. This is not a case of duly moderated mutual accountability but a radical challenge to procedural rights that lie at the heart of the rule of law's demand of legality.

The Ethics of Fidelity: Responsibility for the Whole

According to the fidelity thesis, along with *standing* to hold others accountable comes *responsibility* to do so. Fidelity makes a powerful claim about the obligations and responsibilities of members in a community that aspires to realize the rule of law. The claim is that, in a community characterized by a robust rule of law, accountability is a communicated—distributed and shared—normative power. All members of the community have a mutual responsibility to exercise this power. Each member owes this obligation to each other member and to all—it is *mutual* and *general*.

The argument for this remaining part of the fidelity thesis proceeds from two claims. The first is that accountability holders have both the normative power to hold others accountable, and, second, a responsibility to exercise this power (in appropriate ways, under appropriate circumstances, of course). The latter claim is clear if we consider what it means to accord standing to someone to hold another accountable. The point of one's according such status to another is rooted in the point of mutual submission to law's rule, namely, protection against the arbitrary exercise of power. But that point is realized only if those to whom the power is given accept and exercise the power. Fidelity to law entails a commitment on the part of each to take responsibility for holding each other accountable under this common law. Combine this with the claim, which we defended earlier, that each owes fidelity-responsibility to each as members of law's commonwealth because the good of a robust rule of law is an essentially *public* good, and it follows that this responsibility is community-wide.

We can think in either of two complementary ways about the implications of this public-good understanding of the rule of law for the direction and scope of fidelity responsibilities.

First, the *fair play* perspective regards vigilant efforts to hold those who exercise power accountable as a cooperative enterprise for mutual benefit. Seen in this way, the fidelity principle entails doing one's part in a common, cooperative endeavor, a responsibility owed to each other as members similarly committed and bound. Sharing the burdens of law's governing involves doing one's part in the cooperative enterprise of accountability-holding. Each bears this obligation, and it is owed in fairness *to each other*.

Second, we can also look at this endeavor from the *solidarity* perspective suggested by *Vindiciae Contra Tyrannos*, the sixteenth-century work that we briefly encountered in Chapter 1. According to *Vindiciae*, the covenant of mutual obligation and accountability between the king and the people was rooted in and shaped by a deeper covenant between God and the two parties. While the king was needed to hold the people to their duties, God recognized that to leave the king unaccountable was "hazardous," and so God also empowered the people "to stand as surety." Each pledged, to God and to each other, "jointly and not separately." "On that account they [were] bound for the whole sum," just as "creditors are accustomed to do with unreliable debtors, by making many liable for the same sum, so that two or more promissory parties are constituted for the same thing, from each one of whom the sum can be sought as if from the principal debtor."[59] Drawing on Roman Law doctrine of joint liability for debt, the author argued that God gave each party standing and incentive to hold the other accountable to God's laws by requiring of each of them commitment for the whole. Each was "bound one for another and each for the whole."[60] Rashi, the Talmud sage, offered a model of this interwoven caring in his understanding of the covenantal undertakings at Sinai. While God gave the law to the people of Israel, each member of that people was a guarantor on behalf of all the others. For each Israelite, there was not just one covenant, but 603,550 covenants.[61]

By analogy, we can argue that the public good of protection against the arbitrary exercise of power promised by law's rule calls for a multilateral joint commitment among members of law's commonwealth "each for the whole." The good sought is public, so it is a good for each in and through its being a good for all. The responsibility of each is first of all responsibility for the whole in that sense, but, because that whole can only be achieved through cooperative efforts of the members, each is, first, bound to *do one's part*, and second, bound also *for one another*—that is, bound to encourage and empower each other and, where necessary, hold each other accountable.

The solidarity perspective has one important implication. Because the responsibilities of fidelity are responsibilities to participate in a cooperative endeavor, they will be limited to an extent by the reliable participation of other parties. That is, the obligations are in an important respect conditional. *Fiat fidelis ruat caelum*—do what fidelity requires and let the heavens fall—is not part of the fidelity ethos. To attempt to hold another accountable under the law in the face of widespread infidelity in the community is not an overriding obligation. However, from the solidarity perspective, the participation of others in the cooperative endeavor is not merely a fact to be observed or lack to be lamented. Rather, the fidelity-responsibility of each includes efforts to empower and encourage others to participate, to take their corresponding responsibilities seriously.

Fidelity obligations are not absolute. They are limited to an extent by the participation of others. They are also limited in another respect. The exercise of fidelity-responsibility is constrained by considerations of appropriateness of time, place, and manner, which are themselves rooted in the ultimate aim of protecting against the arbitrary exercise of power. Fidelity rejects any proposed exercise of accountability-holding that is incompatible with that aim or that cannot contribute to its promotion. We will explore in Chapters 7 and 9 the scope and limits of this mutual responsibility.

From the fair play and from the solidarity perspectives it follows that the scope of fidelity's concern is commonwealth-wide. We argued earlier that subjection to law's obligations and responsibilities implies the reciprocal benefit of its protection; there is no burden of compliance without benefit of law's protection. The fidelity principle is interleaved with this aim of equality in the eyes of the law. The argument we have pressed entails that the network of accountability must secure the promised protections. So any one person's or group's fidelity-responsibility is not limited to securing law's benefits for that person or group, but rather extends to all those who fall within the scope of law's demands and hence law's protection. In this further sense, we are bound for each other and for the whole.

Alienation and Infidelity

Law's rule fails when law becomes irrelevant, when it or some significant portion of it does not count. Alienation, apathy, and resigned acceptance of corruption sap the rule of law of its vitality. However, we must take care here. The widespread sense of the irrelevance of law to daily life may manifest a massive failure of fidelity, but it might also manifest a different failure of law.

In conditions of legal pluralism—where more than one system of norms exist in a community and may vie for the allegiance of its members—formal, government-imposed law may fail to take root in the community it purports to govern. Where this is true, it is possible that robust fidelity focuses on some other common, albeit informal, set of norms. Recall, fidelity is not a matter of mutual faithfulness to government or the state, or to government's law, but of faithfulness of members of the community to each other with respect to some common governing norms. Thus, widespread alienation from government's law in a community may not signal *anomy*—the *lack* of law or the failure of law to count—but *polynomy*—the existence of more than one set of relatively autonomous sets of law—and commitment of the bulk of the polity to norms other than government's law. In some cases, a more accurate characterization of the community would not be that law fails to rule but that a *different law* rules. This may be the case in societies where colonial powers impose foreign formal law that fails to sink its roots into the local communal soil.

However, we must not be too quick to accept that the rule of (informal) law is robust in a community. It is possible that the informal norms of a community do not honor the core standards of the rule of law. Just as government's law may fail to meet formal or procedural rule-of-law standards, so too informal, customary forms of law may fall short. Fidelity is a necessary condition of the realization of the rule of law; it is not sufficient.

What do these caveats imply for our analysis of the culture of the US South in the Jim Crow era discussed earlier in this chapter? It is true that white citizens ignored or defiantly disobeyed the law that promised protection against violence to all citizens. They treated it as irrelevant to their behavior and to their assessments of their neighbors' behavior insofar as it applied to and protected black citizens. In some respects, they followed an informal code that supported and encouraged racial oppression. Nevertheless, for two reasons their behavior manifested a serious failure of fidelity and in consequence a failure of law to rule. First, the informal racist code that guided the white community itself failed to meet the fundamental test of protecting all members of law's commonwealth against the arbitrary exercise of power. It violated the equality principle. Second, it was a failure of fidelity in particular because white citizens were not alienated from the law in general; rather, they defiantly refused to acknowledge its application to fellow citizens whom they sought to oppress. Law failed to rule because, when it was needed to make good on its promise to protect those governed by it, those who were bound to each other to vigilant efforts to sustain law's protection failed to take their responsibilities seriously. The rule of law failed not because the government's law failed to take root in the community but rather because members of the white community failed to take their responsibilities with respect to that law seriously, responsibilities they owed to all members of their community.

Elements of a Conception of the Rule of Law

Philosophers distinguish between the *concept* of some important idea and *conceptions* of that concept. The distinction is artificial, but it can be helpful. We might think, for example, that justice requires doing right by people, as in the ancient formula, "justice renders to everyone their due." We might propose this as the concept of justice, but to understand what justice requires of us, we need to spell out what the scope of "each" is, what each is "due," and how, when, where and by whom it must be rendered. We need principles to guide us in answering these questions and in seeking to do justice ourselves and securing a just society. We need a *conception* of justice, an ordered set of principles that fill out and give substance to the concept.

Recall the passage we quoted near the beginning of this chapter taken from the 2004 declaration of the United Nations regarding the rule of law. Here's the whole passage:

> The "rule of law" is a concept at the very heart of the [United Nations'] mission. It refers to a principle of governance in which all persons, institutions and entities, public and private, including the State itself, are accountable to laws that are publicly promulgated, equally enforced and independently adjudicated, and which are consistent with international human rights norms and standards. It requires, as well, measures to ensure adherence to the principles of supremacy of law, equality before the law, accountability to the law, fairness in the application of the law, separation of powers, participation in decision-making, legal certainty, avoidance of arbitrariness and procedural and legal transparency.[62]

We might think of this as the United Nations' proposed conception of the rule of law. However, although the passage mentions a number of desirable values and goals, it reads like a laundry list. It does not meet the philosophers' ideal of a conception of the rule of law. It does not present a compelling structure for understanding the idea or an ordered set of principles to fill out that structure. That is not surprising, after all, since those who composed this paragraph were not writing philosophy.

The present work does seek to meet that ideal of a conception. In the first three chapters, a conception of the rule of law has begun to emerge. In Chapter 1, we sought to isolate the common core, the organizing idea, of the rule-of-law ideal. Chapter 2 clarified and put into order the component notions gathered into that core idea. The present chapter articulated and defended principles that follow directly from that core idea—sovereignty, equality, recourse, and fidelity. These principles, if realized, promise to serve the goal proposed by the core idea. These efforts have given us the outlines of a compelling conception of the rule of law. But it is not yet complete. A number of tasks remain.

For one thing, we need to work out the relationship between the rule of law and other key concerns of political morality, most importantly, justice, democracy, and respect for human rights. Another task is to seek out the institutions and practices that are needed to realize this still quite general conception in particular political communities. We might think of this as the task to identify *downstream* components of our conception. Third, we need to defend the conception set out in the first three chapters by identifying the deeper values of political morality that the rule of law is meant to serve. We must identify the *upstream* source of the rule-of-law ideal. The first remaining task will be taken up in Chapter 5 and the downstream task in Chapter 6 and beyond that in the chapters of Part II. But in the next chapter we will take up the upstream task. We will seek out the moral headwaters of the rule of law in order to assure ourselves of its validity and provide a measure of its moral force. Once we have articulated and defended this conception, we can take on in Part II a number of challenges to the conception to test its strength and durability in the rough and tumble of modern politics.

4

Moral Foundations

The rule of law, wrote historian E.P. Thompson, is "an unqualified social good."[1]
Few who think seriously about the rule of law believe that even when it is fully
realized the rule of law is literally an unqualified good—that it is a good that
cannot be achieved without some loss or cost, or without struggle. Political theorist Michael Ignatieff wrote, "I cannot help thinking that liberal civilization—
the rule of laws, not men, of argument in place of force, of compromise in place
of violence—runs deeply against the human grain and is only achieved and
sustained by the most unremitting struggle against human nature."[2] Surely,
achieving and sustaining the rule of law is not costless, and its costs at times can
be morally significant; and even its most ardent defenders recognize that sometimes its demands must yield to other more pressing moral concerns. Although
the rule of law claims sovereignty of law over persons, institutions, and centers
of power, it does not pretend to sovereignty over all other competing moral
principles.

Still, if we articulated the ideal fairly and accurately in the preceding
chapters, we must concede that the ideal is remarkably bold and demanding.
It entails standards to which we hold governments and political authorities
from the lowliest to the most exalted, standards to which we likewise hold
our civic associations, our fellow citizens, and ourselves. It demands that law
reigns. By what right? It calls on all members of the political community to
participate in an ethos of mutual accountability that underwrites and makes
possible law's rule. What justifies this kind of active allegiance? These bold
demands, if they are to maintain their grip on our judgments and our actions,
cannot float free of any more fundamental moral ground, resting only on incidental benefits.

We have learned over the course of the previous chapters that the rule of
law is a complex, multidimensional ideal. This ideal gives shape to a distinctive mode of association as well as distinctive mode of governance, implies
standards of legality, and engages an ethos practiced by citizens and officials
alike, and holds sway not only in the halls of government, but also in civic life,
not only within domestic political communities and beyond. Our account of
the grounding value of this ideal must speak to and seek to justify these large
ambitions.

Law's Rule. Gerald J. Postema, Oxford University Press. © Oxford University Press 2022.
DOI: 10.1093/oso/9780190645342.003.0004

Incidental versus Grounding Value

The ideal takes its place in political morality alongside other values or principles. To press the inquiry to uncover its deeper moral roots might strike us as imprudent. Wouldn't it be wise simply to present the ideal in its Sunday best and leave the matter at that? We might hope in that way to attract the widest possible fan base. However, our task here is not to swell the ranks of rule-of-law devotees, but to uncover the values that provide it focus and force. The values that the rule of law purports to serve inevitably and properly shape the standards, institutions, and practices that carry out its instructions. Indeed, the ideal is contested widely and vigorously in good part due to disagreements over the values that people think it servers. We cannot understand the content and moral force of the ideal by listing various things it is good for, without paying close attention to values it is founded on.

Some Advantages of the Rule of Law

For scholars and advocates of the rule of law, for government and corporate advisors, it is relatively easy to identify the advantages of establishing the rule of law in a political community. Some will argue that the rule of law enhances, or even provides the necessary infrastructure for, economic development, social modernization, and political stability. The United Nations insisted, "The rule of law is not a mere adornment to development."[3] And the UN General Assembly asserted in 2012:

> We are convinced that the rule of law and development are strongly interrelated and mutually reinforcing, that the advancement of the rule of law at the national and international levels is essential for sustained and inclusive economic growth, sustainable development, the eradication of poverty and hunger and the full realization of all human rights and fundamental freedoms, including the right to development, all of which in turn reinforce the rule of law.[4]

Similarly, the world development community (including the World Bank, the International Monetary Fund, and the Asian Development Bank) has long embraced the rule of law as an instrument of development. Martin Loughlin reported in 2018 that these agencies, since 1989, have devoted well more than one billion dollars to projects designed to build and sustain the rule of law in developing countries.[5] In 2017, the World Bank maintained, "The rule of law is widely recognized as necessary for the achievement of stable, equitable development. Indeed, over the last few decades no other governance ideal has been as universally endorsed."[6]

However, scholars who have looked closely at the impact of this attention and funding on actual economic performance of underdeveloped and developing countries remain somewhat skeptical.[7] China appears to be an example of remarkable economic development despite very weak adherence to rule-of-law norms. Moreover, even when these arguments for the promotion of the rule of law stand up to scrutiny, they fail to answer adequately the question we have posed. At best, they lend support to a thin version of the rule-of-law ideal that does not approximate the rule of law defended in previous chapters. They cannot support the rule of law's bold claims. Even the best of them highlight only incidental, and often highly contingent, consequences of establishing the rule of law in a political community. They cannot explain the depth of commitment it calls for or its ability to stand up against competing principles of political morality and justify adapting their demands to the requirements of the rule of law.

We seek values intrinsic to the rule of law that thrust roots into fundamental concerns of political morality. To do this adequately and persuasively will take some time and effort, because the ground of the rule of law is complex. Defenders tend to locate its ground either in freedom of some kind, in individual dignity, or in some understanding of social or political equality. However, I will argue here that the best explanation of the focus, force, and scope of the rule of law locates its source in a complex interweaving of them all as components of a deeper notion of community that I will call "membership."

Membership puts individual dignity, equality, and freedom from subordination to the will of another in close internal, mutually qualifying connections. They find their home and best expression as components of an especially valuable kind of community. Moreover, law, when it meets the demands of the rule of law, has features that enable it to play a key role in securing and nurturing communities aspiring to realize the value of membership. The task of this chapter is to give articulate expression to the moral idea of membership and use it to illuminate the deep, intrinsic value of the rule of law.

But first, we must consider the most salient competing conception of the rule of law's grounding value, individual liberty. There is no denying that the rule of law can contribute greatly to enhancing individual liberty; however, taking it as the grounding value is likely to mislead us about the focus and scope of the ideal.

Freedom

Freedom is a complex value of political morality. We will not explore that full complexity here; rather, we will consider briefly two broad understandings of freedom, nondomination and individual liberty.

Nondomination

Recall our watchword: the rule of law promises protection and recourse against the arbitrary exercise of power through law. The rule of law seeks to temper the power some parties have *over* others—that is, unequal or asymmetrical power that some have over those who are dependent on them in some substantial way. This suggests strongly the value of *nondomination* inspired by theorists of the Roman Republic.[8] They opposed domination—being subject to the arbitrary will of another. This suggestion puts us straightaway in the camp of those who argue that the rule of law fundamentally, and not merely incidentally, serves individual *freedom*, the opposite of domination.

However, this proposal does not offer a very satisfying explanation of the rule of law's value. After all, "nondomination" is the name we are likely to give to the condition of being protected against the arbitrary exercise of power. This explanation does not go very deep. Neither does it, yet, suggest a way of understanding the *law's* role in this project of protection. Is law merely a convenient means, or is the law's role more tightly woven into the fabric of freedom? Can nondomination show us how? Can it explain law's claim to *sovereignty*? Does it explain the importance of fidelity to the rule of law? To answer these questions we should look more closely at the principle of nondomination and its link to individual freedom.

At this point, early in our exploration, we encounter a deep divide between two ways of understanding, of capturing the moral significance of, the values we will consider in this chapter. One such view takes the perspective of individuals immersed in their social and political relationships. It takes account of the meaning these relationships have for these individuals and the standing accorded to them in these relationships. Call this the "relational" perspective. Alternatively, a "nonrelational" perspective views the value the rule of law to individuals abstracted from their social and interpersonal relationships.

We can view the value of freedom as nondomination from each of these two perspectives. From the nonrelational perspective, to be free of domination is to be free of actual or potential interference with one's choice and action. Domination is one form of interference with one's free movement; it concerns behavior that puts obstacles in the way of achieving one's goals. It is not different in kind from natural obstacles to one's actions, like the bear standing in the way along a mountain trail. Of course, it usually does make a difference to us whether it is a person that stands in our way. A person is morally responsible, while the bear presumably is not. It will often be important to know why someone put the obstacle there. It is important in part because it helps us predict what they will do next; it will shape our expectations about their future behavior. Of course, we can also accuse them (not the bear) of wrongdoing.

However, why they stand in our way may be important for a deeper reason. Their behavior may have meaning for us. The answer to the why question tells us something about their attitude toward us and how they *regard* us; it may tell us something about our relationship and how they regard it. What they *do*, or are capable of doing, says something about *who we are to each other*. In that case, we are on the verge of taking up the rather different, *relational* perspective. We will explore presently the idea of freedom as nondomination in this relational perspective, but first we must consider what is in modern times the more familiar, nonrelational perspective on freedom.

Individual Liberty

Throughout its long history the rule of law has been associated with freedom. "We are servants of the law so that we can be free," Cicero declared. The political community, he argued, is "held together by the laws"; it is "the foundation of our liberty."[9] From Cicero's Roman perspective, law was the source of freedom of the political community, of citizens as free persons, or rather as persons who were free by virtue of being citizens of a free polity.

In contrast, from the typical modern, especially Western, perspective, freedom is a matter of individual liberty. On this view, we look to law to define and protect a sphere of action free from interference from others. Of course, in social life, others inevitably will interfere with one's own actions and plans. Law that meets rule-of-law standards defines a social environment that individuals can count on; they can predict the actions of fellow citizens and government officials and navigate the limits they pose. Freedom is possible because individuals know in advance how the law will operate, how they have to act to avoid its interference, and how others will act to achieve their goals while avoiding its interference. This enables us to make plans and autonomously organize our lives. "Provided I know beforehand that if I place myself in a particular position, I shall be coerced and provided that I can avoid putting myself in such a position, I need never be coerced," writes Frederick Hayek. "The laws of the state have the same significance for me as the laws of nature."[10] The laws of nature, as it were, limit an individual's choices and actions, but they do not subject one to anyone's arbitrary will. They are *impersonal*, not the expression of the will of any person. Although one's choices and actions are restricted, one is not dominated. Thus, individual liberty is freedom from *interference* by other *persons*. Likewise, Hayek argued, legal rules that are truly general, not made to serve the interests or block the interests of any particular persons, are impersonal. This is especially true if the rules are products of "spontaneous" processes—as, for example, the rules of common law that emerge from the accumulation of particular judicial decisions over time.

The rule of law is essential for achieving this degree of individual liberty and autonomy, Hayek argued. Law meeting rule-of-law standards can play this role because its rules are fixed, general, optimally determinate, public, and consistent, settling with finality matters that would otherwise be contested. *Predictability* is the signal contribution that law makes to individual liberty. "Liberty finds no refuge in a jurisprudence of doubt," the US Supreme Court wrote in its landmark case, *Planned Parenthood v. Casey*.[11] The formal rules of law are "certain," that is, they leave little room for doubt or discretion. Rules that are certain in this sense make the behavior of fellow citizens and government officials predictable. Likewise, the rule of law secures predictability of government action with arrangements that hold all exercises of governing power to the formal rules of the law. In this way, the rule of law is the guardian of individual liberty, its grounding virtue.

There is no denying the attractiveness of this explanation, or its impact on modern thinking about the rule of law. Nevertheless, it goes wrong at three points: it is incomplete; its goal is unattainable, and a single-minded pursuit of it, paradoxically, is likely to enhance arbitrariness; and it lacks moral depth. Let's take a brief look at each of these deficiencies.

First, this explanation of the rule of law's value is *incomplete*. If it succeeds, it accounts for only part of the bold ideal we articulated in Chapters 2 and 3. It leans heavily on the legality strand of the rule-of-law ideal, but it does not fully explain the reflexivity or exclusivity principles, and it has nothing to say about equality or fidelity. This is due largely to the fact that it operates with a very narrow view of the resources that law provides for protection and recourse against arbitrary power. It focuses exclusively on fixed general rules, ignoring law's constitutive and deliberative capacities. It also rests very heavily on the alleged determinacy and certainty of legal rules, in the hope of making the behavior of law subjects and officials predictable.

Second, this goal is *unattainable*; vagueness and indeterminacy of language, and hence of legal rules, is inevitable.[12] Montaigne called attention to this fact in the late sixteenth century. "I am not pleased by the opinion of [Justinian, the great codifier of Roman law,] who sought to rein in the authority of the judges with his great many laws, cutting their slices for them. He was quite unaware that there is as much scope and freedom in interpreting laws as in making them."[13] Justinian, he wrote, sought to cut the law into little, intellectually digestible slices so that judges and citizens could follow them without exercise of mature and prudent judgment. However, prudent judgment—*juris prudence*—cannot be eliminated from the process of understanding and applying or following the law. Laws seek to guide decisions and actions, but, as philosopher Timothy Endicott observed, the notion of a "guide" would be incoherent "if we counted nothing as a guide unless it answered all questions. No map, for instance, would be a guide."[14] The orderly behavior that rules make possible depends on the exercise of judgment. We all know that "working to rule"—scrupulous adherence to formal rules rigidly interpreted—is a way for workers to go on strike without formally calling a strike. To work to rule is a way of subverting the rules by following them without prudent judgment. "In the real world we expect people to make innumerable minor adjustments that rules cannot capture, and if they refuse to exercise discretion, the enterprise will grind to a halt."[15] Discretion and judgment may be inevitable elements in legal ordering, but the problem from the rule of law's point of view lies not in relying on judgment, but rather in leaving those authorized to exercise judgment free to do so without discipline and accountability. For this, the full resources of the law—all its tools—appropriately shaped to rule-of-law standards, are needed.

Moreover, when we seek to diminish the vagueness of a standard by reducing as far as possible reliance of decision makers on their judgment, we risk increasing the arbitrariness of their decisions.[16] Bentham, in the late eighteenth century, exposed the risk of arbitrariness in trying to hold decision makers rigidly to fixed rules. He argued that when the rules require decisions that manifestly fail to serve their purposes or are inconsistent with other concerns of manifestly greater importance, decision makers face a choice. They can either stick to the rule, and portray themselves as deeply principled, or set it aside in favor of the competing concerns, and show themselves to be persons of liberality and immanently reasonable judgment. Thus, paradoxically, the attempt to restrict judicial decision-making to rigid rules has the effect of freeing the judge to decide more or less as he or she wishes. This is the paradox of inflexibility.[17]

Frances Bacon, in the seventeenth century, counseled a different view of legal rules. He argued that we should think of rules not as fixed texts, but as "magnetic needles: they point at the law, but they do not themselves settle it."[18] Later in his career, Hayek also came to appreciate the limits of rigid formal rules. Rules, he conceded, could be only "a very imperfect formulation of principles which people can better honor in action than in words."[19] It's easier done than said. To regard the rule of law as simply the rule of rules, as Antonin Scalia once put it,[20] offers a strategy to cabin arbitrary power that is bound to fail.

Finally, by focusing on the law's impact on the lives and actions of individuals abstracted from their relationships with others, this understanding of the rule of law *lacks moral depth*. It fails to appreciate the moral concern that motivated defenders of the rule of law over its long history. For one thing, as we have seen, the rule of law models a desirable mode of association, not only a mode of governance. Civic community is a partnership according to and bound by law, Cicero argued. Similarly, Immanuel Kant thought of the polity, the commonwealth, as a community of equals subject to a common body of law.[21] The individual liberty account relies on a narrower understanding of law. Law is something that keeps us out of each other's hair, not something that binds us together.

Further, the individual liberty account fails to understand the *kind of moral wrong* done by subjecting a person to another's arbitrary will. The problem lies not (merely) in one agent's actual or likely interference with the actions of another, but rather in the nature of the relationship between the parties. It lies, specifically, in the fact that one party is *subordinated* to another. The deeper moral objection is that one party is *in a position* to exercise unilaterally its will over another. The victim's will is not his or her own, but is a tool in the hands of the dominator. The victim and dominator alike experience this relationship as one of inferiority and superiority. For this objectionable relationship to exist no actual interference or even manifest threat of it is necessary. Rather, it defines the horizon of the social environment in which the parties interact, the practice that gives the relationship its meaning and morally objectionable public character.

The Evil of Subordination

Edmund Burke took this relational perspective on freedom in his speech to Parliament on March 22, 1775. In this speech, he urged conciliation with the rebellious colonies on the North American continent. Burke traced the ferocity of the rebellious colonists to the "high and haughty" "spirit of liberty" among the slaveholders of the southern colonies.[22] Burke insisted, paradoxically, that their passion for freedom stemmed precisely from their status as slave masters. They regarded freedom not merely as absence of the ability to do as they choose, but rather as their right and privilege to dominate the wills of the slaves, just as they used any other piece of property they owned. This freedom was the source of their identity and the ground of their standing in society. Living daily among slaves, masters were especially sensitive to invasions of their privilege, the loss of their rights, and interference with their untrammeled choice. "In such a people," Burke argued, "the haughtiness of domination combines with the spirit of freedom, fortifies it, and renders it invincible." Slave masters know more about domination than most of us, he argued, and more acutely feel its pain when they perceive another exercising domination over them.

Domination, on Burke's rendering of the perspective of the American slaveholders, was not merely an interference with choice or action; it was the expression of an especially hateful subordination, of their ultimate inferior status. To submit to the power of England reduced them, in their eyes, to the status of slaves. As legal scholar Jedediah Purdy observed, "Freedom meant independence from such power, being the one whose will commanded, not the one who cowered before a willful commander."[23] Masters did not merely make people do things they would otherwise not wish to do, they exercised their will over them, making clear through their exercise of legally authorized power their superiority and the slave's debasement. Hayek tried to express the evil of domination in terms of restrictions of individual liberty, but the slave masters did not think of it in that way. Freedom as nondomination was freedom from the status that put them under what they regarded as the arbitrary will of another master. Of course, the slave is subjected to an extreme form of subordination, but it is not the extreme nature of the example but the social meaning and structure of it that we need to explore. This rendering of the idea of freedom as nondomination offers promise of a deeper understanding of the value underlying the rule of law.

We can start by identifying the evil of subordination. Subordination is matter of being vulnerable to the arbitrary will of another in conditions of dependency. The evil of this condition lies not just in the fact that the victim can only do what the dominator permits; neither does it reside in the dominator's potential for cruelty, for he may not be cruel. The evil resides more deeply in the nature of the relationship itself. The victim is publicly held to be inferior to the dominator. This status is most evident through the dominator's command or cruelty, but it persists and remains manifest even in the absence of the dominator's actions, in the perceptible possibility of the victim's committing the crime of impudence. The victim knows that at any moment, on any occasion, for any reason or no reason at all, the dominator can bring his will to bear on the victim's actions, life prospects, and even desires and wishes. His will is superior; it commands the victim's inferior will. This ongoing relationship of subordination makes the condition of inferiority public, visible to the victim and, as the victim knows, usually to others.

This is simultaneously two evils. It debases the victims, publicly denies their dignity, and manifests a fundamentally evil social relationship. These are closely related negative dimensions of a single complex value. We might think of it in terms of equality—not equal treatment, treating people the same way, but rather treatment *as an equal* or peer. Equality of this kind is not a matter of what one has, relative to what others have, but rather what we *are* to, or with *respect to, each other*. The relationship of the dominator to the dominated is not a relationship of peerhood. Still, equality of this kind is only part of the complex value we need if we are to explain the good of nondomination and the evil of subordination. We do not have a familiar term for this value. I will call it *membership*.

Membership

Wendell Berry set several of his novels and short stories in a small Kentucky town. In them, he paints a detailed portrait of "the Port William membership."[24]

The idea of membership he explores in these stories is not the formal kind of relation that exists between elements of a set; rather, it captures a certain kind of community, one in which members are bound by history, interdependency, and a deep-rooted mutual regard that respects the distinctive features of each member and their ability to contribute to the whole. "Membership," in Berry's use, like its cousin "friendship," refers to a kind of value as well as instantiations of that value, to the relationship between, for example, David and Jonathan, or between Thelma and Louise, and to the value these friends cherish. The Port William membership is more than a social fact, a town on the map. A deep and complex value shapes the lives of its citizens and measures their interactions. I propose to borrow Berry's term to capture a vision of community that publicly embraces the dignity and diversity of individuals who find themselves a part of that community and that seeks to structure and sustain a domain of social life in which each relates to each as equals. "Membership" represents the interwoven complex of freedom, dignity, equality, and community. Let us explore these values and their interrelationships more closely.

Dignity and Equality

Dignity is a widely cherished but often contested idea. Often it is offered as the foundation of human rights, and sometimes put forward as the ground for human equality, a secular version of the theological idea that each human being is created in God's image. Article 1 of the Universal Declaration of Human Rights holds that "[a]ll human beings are born free and equal in dignity and rights."[25] Defenders naturally link the rule of law to dignity. The International Commission of Jurists at their Delhi Congress (1959) defined the rule of law as that set of "principles, institutions and procedures" shown "to be important to protect the individual from arbitrary government and to enable him to enjoy the dignity of man."[26] Critics, however, charge that this notion is all affect without content.[27]

We can give the notion content by looking at the impact of its manifest denial. Living in conditions of subordination typically leads to victim self-censorship and servility. Victims experience humiliation and are made to feel inferior. The feeling is painful. It is akin to shame because victims are forced to see themselves through the eyes of the dominator and the public as degraded. Crucial to the experience is the sense that the degrading treatment is wrong or mistaken. However, we must not focus exclusively on the subjective experience of subordination. The evil fundamentally lies in the quality of the treatment—or more precisely in the quality of the relationship that might at any point issue in such treatment. This evil is brought home to victims through their awareness, but the shame is the subjective marker of the wrong done, not the wrong itself. The evil is not lessened or mitigated if victims are unaware of it; indeed, it is greater if they come to see the treatment as justified. There is at least a remnant of dignity available to those who recognize the wrong done to them, who are aware of the demeaning treatment *as wrong*.

Thus, the wrong does not lie wholly in the experience of subordination, but in the fact of it, and the nature of the relationship that sustains it. That wrong consists in the denial or denigration of the victim's status in the dominator's and the victim's community, denial of the standing that is properly the victim's due. This is a denial of the victim's dignity. Dignity is the standing that is due a person, a rightful position a person occupies vis-à-vis others. One whose dignity is respected can stand eye to eye with others in one's community; one can demand this respect in one's own right. Thus, dignity is not a valued *property* of a person, but rather a *mode of regard*, a socially recognized position that carries with it rights and responsibilities in and to the community.

This mode of publicly available regard carries with it recognition and respect, not reducible to the attitudes of individuals, but embedded in the community's practices and institutions recognizing members of the community as equals. "As I would not be a slave, so I would not be a master," wrote President Abraham Lincoln. "This expresses my idea of democracy. Whatever differs from this, to the extent of the difference, is not democracy."[28] Lincoln's attitude stands in stark contrast with the attitude of slaveholders that Burke reported. The slaveholders passionately demanding *their* "freedom," a status that they understood in opposition to status of their human property on whose unfreedom they depended. Lincoln's attitude stemmed from the connection he felt to others.

Lincoln put his point in terms of "democracy," but he was talking about a mode of social regard, not about a structure of government. (Or perhaps a mode of regard that he assumed lies at the heart of democratic government.) "Equality" is the word we might more naturally use; not equality of possession that measures what I have by comparing it with what you have, but, rather, equality that measures the quality of relationships among members of a community. It embraces a vision of a society that recognizes status, positions of regard (dignity) to which rights and responsibilities attach. A society characterized by this kind of equality is a "single status society"[29]—a domain of social life in which all members relate to each other on the footing of equality, from which no member or resident is excluded. Excluded from the society of peers, one is rendered publicly invisible.[30] Equality of this kind does not entail the obliteration of all differences and distinctions, all hierarchies or asymmetries, but it permits such differences only if they can be justified starting from this standpoint of equality and can only take forms that sustain this fundamental status,[31] only if they pass the "eyeball test."[32]

Seen in this light, the concern about subordination, about being under the power of another, is concern about social inequality as well as freedom. The salient evil of subordination lies not in being treated differently, but being treated as an inferior, as one excluded from the association of peers and equal regard, and thus made publicly invisible. We can measure this evil in terms of its impact on individuals, but also in terms of its stain upon and distortion of the community in which it occurs. The community falls short of, it fundamentally violates, the ideal of membership.

Members of One Another

Aristotle spoke of an ideal mode of association on the model of interpersonal friendship. He called it *civic friendship*.[33] Friendship offers an attractive model of the kind of community I have in mind here, but I find more apt St. Paul's suggestive image. He wrote, "Speak every man truth with his neighbor, for we are members one of another [*esmen allelōn melē*]," and only on that condition are we "subject to one another [*hypotassomenē allēlois*]."[34] *Membership* rather than friendship is the model. This rich image implies *inclusion*. Members are not merely parts of, and swallowed up by, a group or collectivity; rather, they are members *of each other*. They are not subordinated to any other person or to the group, but only, qua members, subject reciprocally to each other. As I read it, this involves three further elements: *mutuality*—each has a place and responsibilities that fit together with those of other members; *peerhood*—as I am included in you, you are included in me, we stand face to face as peers; and *diversity*—neither you nor I lose our identities by being submerged in the community, rather *as members* we occupy the same status. Let's look briefly at each dimension.

First, a membership community is a fellowship of *mutuality*, an engagement of mutual commitments, rooted in and nourished by deep interdependency, and structured by a network of mutual responsibilities aimed at maintaining a widely inclusive social order. In Johannes Althusius's apt phrase, these responsibilities are communicated: their burdens and their benefits circulate among and engage members (recall Chapter 1). This movement involves active reciprocal giving and taking rather than passive reception of benefits. Members entrust these responsibilities to each other, rather than exchange them between each other. This reciprocal giving conveys something of meaning, and the essentially public movement brings the parties together in an integrated whole.

Members care for each other in ways structured by their mutual responsibilities; but they also care about the membership. They value it and take care of it. Hence, they care about how other members contribute to this care taking and take responsibility for other members' exercise of responsibility. Each is bound *to* each other and *for* each other. I am my brother's keeper, but more: as poet Micheal O'Siadhail put it, I am "keeper even of your keeping me."[35]

That said, we should also recognize that membership-inflected relationships need not be intimate or emotionally intense, and they need not presuppose a rich set of shared values. Members share a commitment to the mutual responsibilities that provide the relationship's infrastructure. Membership relationships may be intimate and ideologically homogeneous, but they can also be at arms' length and ideologically diverse.

Second, among human beings, relationships of genuine mutuality cannot survive without maintaining a robust form of equality. Being members of one another entails *peerhood*. As I am included in you, you are included in me. We stand face to face, on a par, on a footing of equality. A scheme of mutual responsibilities is not by itself proof against domination due to arrogant exercise of rank or exploitation of weakness. Thus, in their enactment and enforcement of mutual responsibilities, membership communities must be vigilant about the opportunities for oppression that they may create. They must also be aware of the ways in which characteristic activities of diverse members, and typical structures of their responsibilities, may tend to push some members to the margins or exclude others. The ideal of membership is compelling only if membership communities are communities of peers, whose practices and institutions publicly create and sustain opportunities to participate in community life as equals.

Third, membership demands inclusion of each person in the community in a way that respects *diversity*. Inclusion does not entail assimilation to fixed, ascribed identities; rather, each is due an effort at identification.[36] Inclusion does not require abandoning one's distinctive identity. As I am a member of you, you are a member of me. Neither you nor I lose our identities, because as members we occupy the same status. The aim of membership is, in philosopher Danielle Allen's words, *wholeness*, not *oneness*.[37] The motto of a membership community is not *e pluribus unum*—out of many *one*, unison—but, as it were, *e pluribus fugum*—out of many a *fugue*, a polyphony uniting voices in counterpoint. Each member, like each musical line in a fugue, has its own identity and complements other lines. The musical meaning of each phrase, incomplete in itself, is completed by its place in the harmonic and melodic structure comprising the contributions of all the voices.

Difference is not a threat to membership communities, but a key to its vitality. The structure of mutual responsibilities utilizes and coordinates the diverse capabilities of members. Their responsibilities are not the same, but they fit into a coordinated scheme, which, when it works according to plan, enables the efforts of each to complement and complete the activities of others and sustain their common life.

In this way, the community publicly honors the *dignity* of each member. Each has a recognized and secure place from which they can participate with others on an equal basis; they are guaranteed a place to see each other eye to eye. According to philosopher John Rawls, political morality requires systematic and public recognition of the separateness of persons. Separateness is recognized when each member is treated as a unique and fundamental source of moral claims. It is secured in membership communities without detachment from or isolation within the community. Recognition of the dignity of each member is baked into the practices and institutions of the membership community.

Membership relationships, like many other kinds of relationships, can bring rich benefits to members; they can be of great value *to* members. Moreover, they are often the objects of deep attachment for their members. For members, the value of the relationships, their practical force, lies in part in this historically contingent attachment.[38] However, this value to or for members does not exhaust the value of membership relationships. The relationships are objectively valuable, valuable in themselves and apart from the subjective valuations of individual members. Hence, membership relationships are worthy of respect and promotion by nonmembers as well as by those who find themselves participating in them. For this reason, they are worthy of members' attachment.

Membership is a public good. It is public in the sense that it is a good available to any one member just when it is available to all; and it is available to all only through the continued cooperative efforts of members to nurture and sustain it. It is a public good also in the sense that it includes but is not reducible to the good it provides for individual members. It underwrites cherished attachments of individual members to each other and to the community.

Membership and the Rule of Law

Understood in this way, the notion of membership brings under one normative roof the values of freedom, dignity, equality, and community. This moral-political value stands alongside justice, peace, democracy, and respect for human rights. It explains our deep concern about and objection to subjection to the arbitrary power of another. Domination of some members in the community by others, and especially by those exercising ruling power, is inconsistent with respect for their standing as peers and their dignity as members. Our discussion grounds robust opposition to domination in the complex value of membership. Yet, if we are to account for the value and normative force of the rule of law, we must explain law's role in efforts to protect against such domination. If the preceding discussion is persuasive, we understand why protection and recourse against the arbitrary exercise of power is necessary. We need yet to learn why law is an appropriate and useful device for providing this protection and recourse.

To begin, consider three salient features of political communities. First, they are not spaces for intimate interaction. In political communities of any size, citizens do not and cannot relate to large numbers of others face to face. So, if the communities are to approximate the model of membership, the structure of mutual responsibilities and the modes of interaction and regard for equality and individual dignity in them must be embedded in practices and institutions defined by positive norms addressed to the community as a whole.

Second, historical communities give shape to the rational agency of their members—to their capacity to act in ways that are meaningful over time. The temporally extended nature of these communities offers resources to members for giving practical coherence to their actions and lives over time.[39] "One's history as an agent," wrote philosopher Bernard Williams, "is a web in which anything that is the product of the will is surrounded and held up and partly formed by things that are not."[40] Among the things that are not products of one's will are features of the natural world around one, but also, importantly, features of one's social world. Our actions take place in and get much of their practical significance from a social space in which our actions encounter and interact with the actions of indefinitely many other agents. The interpersonal relationships in which we live form a large part of our individual histories. All this takes place in, and is made possible in part by, the temporally extended environment created and sustained by the communities in which we find ourselves. Thus, the framework of a community that seeks to follow the membership model must take account of and provide resources for the temporally extended coherence of the community and its role in providing the statuses and scripts used by its members as they navigate through their social world.

Third, membership communities are likely to be ideologically diverse. Although they seek to be a genuine membership community, and aspire to make it a just one, they are likely to disagree about what justice requires. Their commitment to each other and to the membership engages them in striving for justice, but they insist always on recognition of the dignity and peerhood of each in their striving. This calls on them to seek what legal philosopher Ronald Dworkin called *integrity* in the public practices and institutions that structure the membership.[41] That is, they demand that when authorities make decisions in the name of the community, they do so in a principled way, in a way that can be publicly justified in terms of principles that members can see are intelligible expressions of a commitment to justice and the ideals of the membership even when they regard them as mistaken. The principles must reflect an appreciation of and honor decisions and positions taken by the community in the past. The public arrangements that structure a membership community must be recognizable to each member as expressions of proper regard for each as an equal member of the community, or, if short of that, as *bona fide* attempts to give concrete shape to that aspiration. Respect for past practice, then, is not a categorical demand, but must always be seen as serving this more fundamental value. Hence, accompanying it must be a responsibly critical attitude, holding past practice and its implications for the present and future to this aspiration.

Our discussion of the distinctive tools of law in Chapter 2 suggests that the law can provide an especially useful, even uniquely appropriate, means of tempering power to meet the demands of membership and its component values in historical communities. The rule of law calls for a framework of law common to all, universally applied and uniformly enforced. As *subjects of* a common body of laws, rather than being *subject to* the unaccountable power of others,[42] members enjoy the law's recognition and protection of their status as peers and their dignity as distinct and valued members of the community. By constituting the polity according to broad, public principles that embrace all members, the law—if it meets the demands of the rule of law—defines a domain of social life in which all are regarded as equals, and whose status as such is protected. This framework of a common law articulates a structure of mutual responsibilities. In the polity, asymmetry of power, especially ruling power, is inevitable, but the rule of law protects members against its arbitrary exercise. According to the demands of the rule of law, ruling power is legitimately exercised only if it is ordained by law and exercised within limits that law defines. Moreover, those who exercise that power are held systematically to account for that exercise, through institutions in which those subject to that power are entitled actively to participate. Being subjects of the law, they are subject to officials of the law but only on the condition that those same officials are accountable and thus subject to them as well. Underwriting the system as a whole is an ethos of fidelity in which members take responsibility for holding each other accountable under the law.

In addition, law provides the resources with which to articulate the interests and needs of members and the community in terms of *rights* that empower members to make claims upon those who exercise power, rights that the law and its officials are duty-bound to honor. In this way, law provides a means of honoring publicly the dignity of each member. Likewise, by providing members access to formal processes by which the law is applied and enforced, members can demand that officials provide warrant for their decisions and actions and challenge the warrants offered. They are entitled to present evidence, make arguments from the law, and hold those who act in the name of the law to that same law.

Law provides the medium in which those who exercise political power must justify that exercise in terms that meet the normative demand of integrity. The special kind of consistency of principle demanded by integrity is, as Dworkin argued, an expression of the more fundamental requirement of treating all in the community as equals. It is the form that respect for peerhood takes in communities divided in interest and conviction, but bound together by institutions of law that persist over time and that record the community's patterns of treatment of its members. Law is the political memory of the community, the moral record of the common, public life of its members. By requiring that all exercises of ruling power be justified according to principles drawn from this record, the law (when it satisfies rule-of-law demands) sustains the coherence of the community as it recognizes and respects the moral dimensions of membership. It enables members of the community to keep faith with their past as a public way of keeping faith with each other as members of a temporally extended community. Each member owes this faithfulness not to the community, nor to the government, nor even to the law, but to *each other* as co-members of a community governed by a common body of laws and aspiring to realize the value of membership.

However, while the heritage of the law sustains the community, there is no guarantee that the heritage is above reproach, that its moral record is unspotted. Recognition of this fact lies at the very heart of the law's commitment to integrity and so to the viability and normative force of the rule of law. For the demand that integrity makes on principled decision-making, that builds an arch of principle from the community's past to its common future, is rooted in the recognition that even principled decisions might be, from some reasonable perspectives, mistaken, perhaps even deeply so. Principled deliberation and decision-making that is made in the guise of justice and the value of membership must be open to challenge by appeal to those values. It can never be uncritical of its own record. It must recognize the legitimacy of rethinking, revising, and rectifying decisions when a compelling case is made. Thus, the rule of law grounded in the value of membership cannot regard *settlement* of disputes about politically or morally contested matters as the sole or overriding aim of law. Decisions understood to be final and beyond any challenge can only be regarded by the rule of law as unilateral impositions of power, as commands, but not proper matters of law, because actions authorized by law are always subject to accountability and hence to responsible challenge.

Conclusion

The rule of law, we have argued, promises a distinctive kind of protection and recourse against arbitrary power, protection and recourse provided by the law. This general idea entails principles: law's sovereignty (and its component principles legality, reflexivity, and exclusivity), equality in the eyes of the law (embracing equal protection and recourse), and fidelity. This brace of values and principles, we have argued further, articulates a mode of governance and a mode of association that are worthy of our allegiance because it serves the more fundamental value of membership. Membership puts individual *dignity*, *equality*, and *freedom* from subordination to the will of another in close internal, mutually qualifying connections. They find their home and best expression as elements of an especially valuable kind of community. Membership stands resolutely opposed to subordination of some in the community to others, and hence is opposed to subjection of some to the arbitrary power of others. Moreover, because the ideal of membership seeks coherence over time for communities and for their members, it calls on law to provide the needed protection against such subordination. Law, as we have seen, is more than a convenient means for protection against subordination; it provides protection in a way that lends integrity and coherence to the community of equals that it serves.

The rule of law is worthy of our allegiance because it serves a value with a proper place alongside our best understanding of other core values of political morality specifically justice, respect for human rights, and democracy. We are now in a position to explore the structure and depth of the relations among these values.

5
Democracy, Rights, and Justice

Fulke Greville (1554–1628), poet and dramatist, served Elizabeth I and James I in various important offices. In 1621, James I made him a peer of the realm. He knew law and power from the inside and, at least in the privacy of his poetry, did not deny the capacity of power to corrupt law and turn it to its own ends. He wrote:

> For though perhaps at first sight laws appear
> Like prisons unto tyrants' soveraign might;
> Yet are they secrets, which Pow'r should hold dear
> Since envyless they make her infinite,
>   And set so fair a gloss upon her will
>   As under this veil Pow'r cannot do ill.[1]

Long before Karl Marx, Greville recognized the capacity of law to mask power rather than constrain it, to cover with a cloak of legitimacy designs of the powerful to serve their own interests.

Legally Entrenched Injustice

No one doubts that laws can *go* wrong or *do* wrong. Law and justice can pull apart. Laws, we all know, can serve injustice and enable people to violate the moral rights of others. The fact that some practice or policy is enshrined in law is no guarantee that it is just, even if that law is duly enacted and appropriately enforced. We may seek "law and order," but we know from history, and sometimes from our own experience, that the order that law enforces can be gravely unjust. Law, all too frequently, entrenches appalling injustice.

If all this is undeniable, it appears that the rule of law has chosen a deeply flawed instrument for its campaign against arbitrary power. Cannot the rule of law itself be co-opted to sanction injustice, to give it a cloak of legitimacy? Of course, the fact that some laws do, or facilitate, injustice does not imply that the rule of law sanctions or approves of such laws. Laws do not automatically satisfy rule-of-law standards merely by being laws. The rule of law does not sanction every act or enactment of ruling power that passes itself off as legal. For example,

Law's Rule. Gerald J. Postema, Oxford University Press. © Oxford University Press 2022.
DOI: 10.1093/oso/9780190645342.003.0005

in the United States, the Fugitive Slave Act of 1854 established a procedure by which slaves who had escaped to the North could be hunted down, captured, and returned to their masters in the South by private bounty hunters. The process by which apprehended persons were certified as runaway slaves offered them no right to speak in their own behalf, and the law doubled the magistrate's fee if he accepted the allegation of the bounty hunters that the persons were runaways.[2] This act not only shored up the appallingly unjust system of slavery in the American South, but it also violated fundamental standards of due process that lie at the heart of the rule of law.

Similarly, as we will see in Chapter 6, retroactive laws violate a key rule-of-law canon; laws passed in secret violate the requirement of publicity; laws denying some citizens access to courts of law violate the requirement of recourse against official power. Moreover, there is no guarantee that governing power, scrupulously following the standards of the rule of law, will always do what is right and just, or respect fundamental moral rights. We cannot count on law always to serve just ends justly. We must allow for the possibility that the rule of law will not stand in the way of the governing power's successfully pursuing unjust ends.

If that is so, why think the rule of law is worthy of our allegiance? Legal philosopher David Lyons insisted that the law does not get respect for free; it has to earn it.[3] How can law earn the respect that the rule of law accords it if law can be used for decidedly unjust ends? Here's one reason, suggested by our reflections near the end of the preceding chapter. One might argue that the virtue of law, and the rule of law that recommends that we deploy it to temper ruling power, lies precisely in the fact that law does not easily bend with the changing winds of our judgments of justice. The possible gap between law and justice is a welcome feature in a political community that is committed to justice but recognizes that there are deep disagreements about what justice requires of the community. If we were to allow justice alone to govern governing power, we would not be protected when the justice that we seek departs from the justice that others in our community demand. We opt for law, on this view, just because we are not able to agree consistently over time on what justice requires of us. Law provides the publicly available constitution of our corporate lives despite our disagreements about justice. Likewise, the value of the rule of law, on this view, lies not in the guarantee it gives of just laws and the just administration of them, but in the reasonable hope of fully public accountability of all those who exercise ruling power to public standards.

The preceding paragraph articulates an attractive thought, but its attraction weakens, critics argue, when the injustices become serious. The problem of the rule of law's sanctioning injustice lies not in the rule-of-law ideal itself, they maintain, but in our all-too-narrow understanding of it. The standards typically associated with the rule of law are too modest and insubstantial, too thin and "legalistic." That ideal, to be worthy of our allegiance, must embrace fundamental rights, principles of democracy, and maybe other important principles of political morality.

Following these thoughts, however, we wander into the thicket of interminable debate between so-called "thin" and "thick" (formal and substantive) conceptions of the rule of law that we viewed from a distance already in Chapter 1. Legal philosopher Joseph Raz argued for limiting the rule of law to formal and procedural standards. Laws must be general, prospective, publicly accessible, consistent, intelligible, and the like, he insisted; and official administration and enforcement of laws must be impartial, congruent with the publicly available laws, and subject to review, and courts must be accessible to all and guarantee fair and impartial proceedings.[4] Yet he argued that, as demanding as these standards may be, a political regime meeting these demands might still erect and sustain an economic order based on slavery. "Law may . . . institute slavery without violating the rule of law,"[5] he conceded. Against this, Tom Bingham, eminent British judge and Law Lord, wrote:

> A state which savagely represses or persecutes sections of its people cannot in my view be regarded as observing the rule of law, even if the transport of the persecuted minority to the concentration camp or the compulsory exposure of female children on the mountainside is the subject of detailed laws duly enacted and scrupulously observed.[6]

The rule-of-law ideal itself embraces a number of fundamental human rights, he maintained. Among them he included the right to life, the right to liberty and bodily security, the right against torture, the right against slavery and forced labor, the right to a fair trial, the right to marry, the right to education, protection of property, and a number of other rights. All of these are enshrined in the European Convention on Human Rights or the UN Declaration of Human Rights. The World Justice Project's Rule of Law Index (2021) expresses a similar view. "A system of positive law that fails to respect core human rights established under international law is at best 'rule by law,' and does not deserve to be called a rule of law system."[7] Others argue that the rule of law is best understood as the rule of justice, freedom, and equality.

Although this line of thought expresses genuine moral discomfort with a purely formal or "legalistic" understanding of the rule of law, it does not yet offer sound *reasons* for incorporating substantive moral principles, or a set of human rights, into our conception of the ideal. Neither does it indicate how they are related to other rule-of-law standards. These standards, we have seen, are bold and demanding, but they do not encompass all the demands that political morality might justifiably make on a community and its government. To identify the rule of law with all the good we demand of a political community, to incorporate all standards of justice and rights into the ideal, obscures the rule of law's distinctive contribution to ordering of a decent society. As Martin Krygier reminds us, "some values are at the same time modest in scope, but precious all the same. If you ignore their modesty, you debase their worth."[8]

Complexity of the Rule-of-Law Ideal

For many, this debate is frustrating, leading some to conclude not only that the rule-of-law ideal is essentially contestable, as Jeremy Waldron has argued,[9] but pointlessly so. The problem, however, is not that arguing about the component principles of the ideal is pointless, far from it; the problem, rather, is that participants in the debate have not fully appreciated the complexity of the ideal. As a result, they often talk past each other. Moreover, if we should add to our conception principles beyond those we defended in Chapter 3 (sovereignty, equality, fidelity), we need arguments that link our core understanding of the rule of law and its grounding moral value with some of these additional concerns.

As we noted in Chapter 1, the rule of law is a middle-level value of political morality with a distinctive normative task: tempering power by means of law. A polity in which power is tempered is a good, admirable, and even perhaps just polity in that respect, but it is not a good, admirable, and just polity in all respects. We have also acknowledged that the ideal has implications for the kind of standards, institutions, arrangements, and practices needed adequately to establish it in particular political communities. These will be to some degree contingent and variable, since the institutions that best serve reflexivity or equality in the eyes of the law, for example, may vary across political communities depending on their histories and their material and cultural resources. Much debate over the components of the rule-of-law conception actually concerns these "downstream" implications. We will address them in that context in Chapter 7.

The rule-of-law ideal embraces important moral considerations at several different points. The core aim is directly concerned with protection of persons against domination, and hence expresses a concern for freedom of a certain kind. This concern, we argued in Chapter 4, serves the more fundamental value of membership, which blends concerns of community, dignity, and treatments as an equal. Arguably, this fundamental value may also call for arrangements of distributive or economic justice that require access to income, wealth, education, and opportunities for meaningful work that approximate equality. It may also have important implications for immigration policy and environment policy and call for political institutions and arrangements that approximate a robust democratic ideal. The rule of law has an important place in this model of the good society, making a distinctive contribution to its realization.

While the rule of law is designed to serve this more fundamental value, it is not likely to serve it by putting a ceiling on economic inequalities, securing quality education for every child, or providing universal health care. That is not its task in an ordered scheme of principles of political morality. It is *conceivable*, then, that the rule of law could exist in a political community that, nevertheless, allows serious economic or educational inequality or inadequate health care. Could it also, consistent with its core aim, founding values, and distinctive mode of legal ordering, allow torture, slavery, or denial of legal personality to some members? Must it embrace rights protecting speech and assembly and rights to form labor unions along with due process rights in criminal adjudication? If so, why? Where do they fit in our rule-of-law conception? Can we find them among the immediately subordinate principles alongside reflexivity and equality and fidelity? Or must we look downstream for such rights as key components in the best institutional realization of the ideal? Or are they welcome but contingent consequences of a polity's robust and stable commitment to the rule of law? In the course of this chapter and the next, we will address some of these questions. In this chapter, we will focus on the relationship between the rule of law and two other fundamental concerns of political morality: democracy and respect for fundamental human rights.

Does the Rule of Law Protect Fundamental Rights?

The issue of the relation between the rule of law and important rights is not settled by acknowledging the modest scope and project of the rule-of-law ideal, for there are reasons to think that the ambitions of that ideal include embracing at least some such rights either downstream or even closer to its heart. Two lines of argument articulate these reasons. One traces *consequences* we can reasonably expect from the robust realization of the rule of law in a polity; the other explores principled *grounds for including* some such rights within our conception of the (still somewhat limited) scope and project of the rule of law itself.

Fellow Travelers

Some defenders of the "thin" or formal conception of the rule of law concede that, although it is *conceivable* that a polity enjoying a robust rule of law may fall beneath minimal standards of justice and moral decency, nevertheless this is *unlikely*. The rule of law and basic justice and respect for fundamental rights, they argue, tend to travel together.

Their argument is not just that when a regime uses law to govern we can expect some degree of justice. After all, we have already seen that regimes of all kinds, even very repressive ones, find it useful to deploy law from time to time. Recall from Chapter 3 Ernest Fraenkel's characterization of the Nazi "dual state." The argument for convergence of the rule of law and basic justice is that where the rule of law is *established and robust* in a polity, there we are likely to find justice, or at least not radical injustice.

The argument goes something like the following. Because the rule of law makes heavy demands on those who wield power, it is unlikely that they will submit to those demands unless they are committed to its distinctive mode of governance on principled grounds. Those grounds also support recognition of at least certain fundamental rights. Consequently, power wielders are likely to be committed to respecting those rights as well. Philosopher John Tasioulas takes this line. He writes that, since the rule of law embodies "one strand of respect for human dignity," we might reasonably think that "a state attuned to that form of respect would be more likely to uphold its demands in other ways, like respecting rights rooted also in human dignity, even when more expedient means of achieving its goals are available."[10]

Similarly, legal philosopher John Finnis argues, "A tyranny devoted to pernicious ends has no self-sufficient *reason* to submit itself to the discipline of operating consistently through the demanding processes of law," since "the rational point of such self-discipline is the very value of reciprocity, fairness, and respect for persons which the tyrant, *ex hypothesi*, holds in contempt."[11] That is, the rule of law imposes a demanding discipline on those who exercise ruling power; they would not have sufficient reason to submit to this discipline without acknowledging and appreciating the more fundamental principles it seeks to serve. Since certain fundamental rights are grounded in the same principles, we can reasonably expect, that where the rule of law has taken hold, rulers will seek to avoid the most serious and manifest violations of those rights, for that would make their inconsistency obvious and undermine their legitimacy.

We must keep in mind that this argument does not attempt to show that following the core principles of the rule of law is necessary for effective government. We know all too well that rule by repression is not uncommon. We saw in Chapter 3 that unpredictability of government intrusion in the lives of citizens could serve the purposes of some wielders of political power. Those who are known to act entirely upon whim can force people to curtail their own freedom of action, and especially their willingness to express opposition to those with power over them.[12] It is only a matter of shrewd political calculation whether to govern by predictability or by unpredictability, and these calculations can change depending on the ruler's goals, resources, and perceived enemies. The ability to facilitate social coordination may be important for a healthy society, but coordinated opposition can represent a serious threat to a regime, and the regime may try to secure its political survival by dividing people, engendering distrust among them.

But the rule of law does not merely prescribe effective government; it defines a morally ideal mode of governance. The argument we are considering here is that when *that* mode of governance is truly established, it is *likely* that certain basic outlines of social and political justice will also find a secure home. At least, where a regime undertakes to rule in accord with the demands of the rule of law, its pursuit of injustice will be significantly curtailed. In this way we might reasonably hope that rule of law and certain fundamental principles of justice and respect for rights travel together.

One might wonder why a regime would undertake to govern in the rule-of-law way. Machiavelli argued that the strategy of rule by manifest repression and unpredictability is counterproductive;[13] however, whether the strategy succeeds depends on circumstances that can change over time. The above argument assumes, rather, that regimes will have reason to make this principled undertaking. But, we might ask, should we give political rulers the benefit of this doubt? Should we expect them to care much if anything about the principled foundations of the rule of law which they feel compelled (to be seen) to honor? Couldn't they simply be interested in getting, keeping, and enhancing their power, and regard being *seen* as complying with the rule of law's demands as a convenient way to do so? Why think *principled* consistency plays any significant role in their ruling strategy?

Lon Fuller suggested an argument to answer this kind of skepticism.[14] He argued that governing in the rule-of-law mode requires that rulers comply with the various formal and procedural standards of legality. Doing so forces into the public eye governmental policies and the legal instruments that rulers use to implement them. It is difficult, he argued, for regimes to pursue brutal, grossly unjust, fundamental-rights-violating policies in full publicity. After all, "tyrants don't like too much light."[15] This is, in part, because the government depends for success on the regime's perceived justice or legitimacy among its citizens and in the world beyond its borders. Moreover, it is important to those who exercise power that they appear legitimate in their own eyes. To achieve and retain legitimacy in the eyes of the public and of the rulers themselves, their exercise of power must meet conditions laid down in the rule of law and certain basic demands of justice and respect for rights. Thus, on Fuller's argument, regimes that largely comply with rule-of-law principles are unlikely to engage in manifest and fundamental injustice.

We may not find this argument entirely convincing, because this connection between the rule of law and justice is merely contingent. But that in itself is not reason to reject it, for Fuller and the others are upfront about the contingent nature of this connection. They argue that a contingent, but nevertheless significant, connection between the two obtains. Adherence to rule-of-law standards does not *guarantee* fundamental justice and respect for rights, but it cannot be dismissed for that reason. They travel together, although they do not do so necessarily or all the time. Moreover, if we accord accountability a central role in securing law's rule, as I have argued, then we cannot dismiss the efficacy of public challenges to the legitimacy of a regime's endeavors. We might conclude that, if the general direction of Fuller's argument is plausible, robust networks of accountability will not only promote adherence to law and formal and procedural standards of the rule of law but also contribute to adherence in the polity to wider principles of justice and respect for rights. However, Fuller's argument is only as strong as his key assumptions are true, namely, the assumptions that rulers are driven by a need to be seen to be legitimate in their own eyes and the eyes of observers and those observers (especially, other nations) are motivated to hold them to their professions. A survey of the behavior of contemporary governments suggests that the contingent connection is weak.

Legal scholar Paul Gowder takes a somewhat different tack, arguing for a contingent but considerable connection between the rule of law and certain other justice principles. He casts his argument in two different versions. First, he begins with the observation that laws that may not appear to be discriminatory considered in the abstract may be harmfully and invidiously discriminatory in the actual circumstances in which they are applied. Such laws, he argues, violate two core rule-of-law canons, one of which he calls "generality"—requiring that laws be expressed in broadly general, nondiscriminatory terms—the other "publicity"—requiring that laws be defensible in terms of public reasons. These are key canons of the rule of law, he argues, because the rule of law requires that the law treats members of the political community as equals (recall our requirement of "equality in the eyes of the law"). Concerning laws that are not discriminatory in the abstract but harmfully so in actual circumstances, governments face a dilemma: they must either change the laws or change the circumstances. If there are strong reasons to keep the law, then governments must work to change the circumstances that result in distortions that violate the rule of law. Thus, the rule of law exerts pressure to correct substantive injustice in the form of invidious discrimination.[16]

Gowder's second version explores what he calls "the rule of law's teleology of equality."[17] The rule of law can persist in a community, Gowder argues, only if its members have sufficient reason to commit to coordinated enforcement of the law against the powerful and thereby hold them accountable. Of course,

holding officials accountable is costly to citizens, so they need reason to participate, and especially, since accountability-holding requires a coordinated effort
among citizens, reason to believe that at least a sufficient number of others will
join them. Laws and official actions that fail the generality test treat citizens with
contempt, Gowder argues; they fail to treat them as equals. These mistreated citizens will not have reason to participate in accountability-holding efforts, and
that will likely weaken the confidence of others that their fellow citizens will join
them. Thus, the rule of law can be robust, and public officials will be held accountable for their exercise of ruling power, only when the political community
meets conditions for community-wide participation in accountability-holding
practices. Key among these conditions is law-enabled social and economic
institutions that publicly treat citizens as equals. Thus, Gowder concludes, the
rule of law's own "teleology" creates pressure to push social, economic, and political conditions in the direction of greater substantive equality.

Gowder's arguments have merit, but the second in particular is not entirely
compelling. After all, there are many ways to co-opt the support of a gullible populace. Massive egalitarian programs are not the only or even the most promising
ways of doing so. Indeed, a sincere and concerted attempt to reduce social and
economic inequalities is likely to alienate other substantial portions of the populace that are invested in the existing inequalities. Hence, there may be equally
good ("rule-of-law teleology") reasons not to pursue such egalitarian programs.

But even if we find Gowder's and Fuller's arguments plausible, showing that
the rule of law may support justice *in consequence* of its being established in a
polity, we may still think that these arguments do not capture fully the relationship between the rule-of-law ideal and fundamental rights. More can be said,
perhaps, or at least more aspects of this relationship remain to be explored.

Interdependence and Implementation

The Venice Commission of the Council of Europe maintained that the rule of
law joins democracy and respect for human rights as "three intertwined and
partly overlapping core principles."[18] This commitment of the Council of Europe
reflects not just a parochial ideal but also a universal truth about the relationship
between these values. I will deal with the relationship between democracy and
the rule of law presently, but first we should continue to explore the relationship between the rule of law and certain fundamental human rights. The Venice
Commission highlights two kinds of relationship between them—*intertwining*
and *overlapping*. Let's unpack these two metaphors.

First, the suggestion is that these two major values of political morality,
while in important respects distinct, nevertheless are linked. The relationship is

symbiotic. The two are interdependent, each having its own nature and function, as it were, but depending on the other to fulfill that function adequately. In this case, the functions of the two parties to this relationship are serving the more fundamental moral values in which they are grounded. Briefly, certain fundamental rights can adequately serve certain vital interests of human beings only with the assistance of law; and the law and its administration, conforming to the demands of the rule of law, serve their grounding values only when the law adequately recognizes and protects these fundamental rights.

This claim is limited. It is not that this symbiosis obtains between the rule of law and all moral rights plausibly regarded as universal human rights as codified, for example, in the UN Declaration of Human Rights or the various regional conventions that do the same (for example, the African Charter on Human and Peoples' Rights or the European Convention on Human Rights). The moral rights articulated and codified in these conventions may rest on a number of different moral grounds; they may serve a number of different important moral interests or human goods.[19] Some of these rights, however, exist in symbiotic relationship with the rule of law.

Interdependency has two sides. Consider first the dependence of certain rights on the rule of law. Claims of right have a distinctive structure. Recall our discussion of rights in Chapter 2. First, rights are not things one possesses, but rather morally inflected relationships. To say that Joan has a right to freedom of speech or a fair trial is to say that John (or some official of Joan's government) has an obligation to respect, provide, or refrain from interfering with Joan's enjoyment of these things. That is, a right is a morally charged three-way relationship between (1) a right bearer, (2) an object, and (3) a right respecter, bound by an obligation to the bearer. The right bearer is, at least for our purposes, a person (or group), the right respecter is some person or institution, and the object is something of value to the bearer. It may be an opportunity, an activity (e.g., speaking freely), a complex institutional process (e.g., fair trial), or a condition (e.g., the absence of interference in the possession and use of some material object). The right respecter *owes* the obligation *to* the right bearer—we might say this obligation is specifically *directed to* the bearer, who not only benefits from the respecter's fulfilling the obligation but is also the focus of attention, as it were, of the obligation. The respecter performs the obligated activities *in behalf of* the right bearer. In addition, the right bearers enjoy certain powers—in particular, the power to claim or demand that the respecter honor the obligation owed to them and a further claim on others to back up their demand. Often this takes the form of a secondary right of the bearer to recourse against the respecter who fails to fulfill the obligation.

Second, moral rights *exist* when the relationship of this kind is *justified* by compelling moral reasons. So, for example, Joan's right to physical security exists (presumably a right she shares with human beings universally) when her claim is supported by compelling moral reasons. These reasons must be sufficient to assign the right and its associated powers to Joan (everyone) and to assign the obligation to protect Joan's (everyone's) possession and enjoyment of physical security to some other agent *as owed to* Joan (everyone). The moral reasons that will do the job typically flow from certain important interests of Joan (everyone) or constituents of her (their) good. In addition, something about the right bearer calls for serving her particular interests or goods in the specific way that rights seek to do, namely, by assigning a weighty obligation to another agent, which is directly owed to the bearer over which she exercises some significant control. For some defenders of human rights, this special feature is the *dignity* of the right bearers—something about bearers of the rights that not only accords the benefits to them but also requires that others publicly acknowledge and respect their *status* as persons.

Moral rights, however, are often indeterminate in several respects. This indeterminacy may be significant for rights bearers, rights respecters, and third parties who may be called upon to endorse and enforce the bearer's legitimate demands. The objects of the right—the things or activities that must be provided or honored—may be vaguely or generically articulated; the identity of the bearers and especially of the respecters and supporting agents may be unclear; and the normative weight of the obligation relative to the costs of fulfilling it may be hard to determine from the moral case for the rights alone. It is at this point that law plays an indispensable role. "Law is often needed to fill in such gaps left by pure moral reasoning about human rights," John Tasioulas observes, "specifying the content of human rights duties and allocating them to duty-bearers in an effective and morally defensible way." Moreover, such laws and their enforcement must adhere to the standards of the rule of law; after all, "there is little point in enshrining human rights in law . . . if legal officials regularly fail to apply those laws impartially according to their true meaning."[20] In our world, our best hope that human rights will be respected and enjoyed lies in their being enshrined in legal institutions that meet the demands of the rule of law. Thus, human rights depend for their viability on the law.

Similarly, the rule of law depends on its symbiotic partner, certain fundamental human rights. The rule of law, we have learned, sets its face against the abuse of power over people, not only abuse by governmental actors but also by nongovernmental actors, and it seeks through law to provide protection and recourse for those who are vulnerable to abuse. Some of the most morally appalling forms of abuse and domination are singled out for condemnation by universally acknowledged human rights, among them torture, slavery, servitude, arbitrary arrest and detention, manipulation of thought, and systematic invidious discrimination on the basis of race, religion, ethnic origin, gender, and sexual orientation. Deploying all the resources of law may not be the only way to combat these abuses, but law is well equipped for this purpose. The rule of law's focused campaign with law's tools to protect against the abuse of power would be incomplete and defective if it did not include a concerted effort to name and protect these fundamental rights and provide effective recourse against their violation. The moral necessity of respect for such rights may rest on other grounds as well, but recognition of them by law lies at the heart of the motivating ambition of the rule of law. A polity cannot adequately serve the rule of law if the legal institutions it calls upon can be used systematically to abuse of power, as, for example, laws protecting the institution of slavery did in the American South.

Strictly speaking, of course, a legal system can meet rule-of-law principles and standards and yet fail to protect against systematic violation of certain basic human rights. However, the commitment to the values served by the rule of law would be hollow, conflicted in a fundamental way. Without unequivocal condemnation and concentrated efforts to root out violations of such rights, the moral core of the rule of law's ambition would be compromised. It is possible for a legal order to meet the formal and procedural conditions of the rule of law—generality, prospectivity, publicity, procedural due process, and the like—and yet systematically violate such rights. However, in doing so, the principled commitment to maintaining such an order would be undermined, shown to be false.

Moreover, the formal dimensions of law, supposedly protecting the dignity of persons by, for example, recognizing their capacity for rational self-direction, themselves could be corrupted to serve the ends of subordination and domination. Legal theorist Julian Sempill reminds us that "recognition of the capacity for self-control is compatible with degradation and humiliation. Indeed, certain Nazi—and Jim Crow—laws called for self-control of a most degrading kind."[21] Committed to supporting and respecting the dignity and status of each person as an equal qua member of the polity with the full resources of the law (as we argued in Chapter 4), rule-of-law designed formal institutions are vulnerable to corruption of this very mission if the law fails to recognize and enforce substantive rights protecting against such abuse. The moral integrity of the formal institutions and procedures of law requires recognition of this range of human rights. A legal order that allowed systematic violations of human rights to go unacknowledged and uncondemned would appear hideously deformed when judged by the rule of law's deepest commitments.

Thus, the rule of law and this range of human rights—those whose primary ground is protection against radical forms of abuse of power—are thickly interwoven and morally inextricable. Still, we must accept that this argument does not extend to all human rights claims or all dimensions of justice. So, it is possible for a polity to enjoy a robust rule of law and yet fall short on some measures of justice and fail to protect against violations of some rights. However, while some failures may compromise the integrity of the very the rule-of-law ideal, some mark the limits of its ambition and resources. Concern for the latter is in the remit of other important principles of political morality and devices for realizing them.

The rule of law and respect for human rights are distinct values, although they are complementary and intertwined. This is what the Venice Commission claimed. It added that they also partly *overlap*. I am not sure what exactly the Commission had in mind, but one way to unpack this idea is to explore the ways in which broad principles of the rule of law are institutionalized in historical political communities. We will discuss at greater length in the next chapter the institutions and components of the legal order that are likely best to realize the rule of law's basic principles, so I will only make a gesture here in the direction of arguments that will be developed further there.

The rule of law is robust in a political community when there are strong institutions for the adjudication of disputes and the just and impartial application and enforcement of the law. Institutions required for this purpose must be independent, accessible, fair, and impartial. To ensure that such institutions function properly and that they protect and provide recourse for individual citizens, a variety of rights of procedural due process must be enshrined in law. These include, for example, one's right to representation by counsel, to present evidence in one's behalf and make legal arguments about the bearing of the evidence and the legal norms on one's case, to confront witnesses, to hear reasons from the court for its decisions, reasons that are responsive to the evidence and arguments presented before it.[22] Many of these rights are defensible on independent moral grounds as important human rights, but we can also see them as critical to the implementation of general principles of the rule of law. In this way, the rule of law and human rights overlap.

Similarly, the rule of law is robust in a political community when networks of mutual accountability operate through effective institutions. As I will argue later, these may include judicial review of administrative decisions and formal ombudsman institutions. Legal recognition and enforcement of certain rights are critical for the effective functioning of these institutions of review and accountability. Included among these rights are, for example, rights of access to the institutions, rights protecting whistleblowers, and rights to competent professional assistance. Effective accountability, we will see, also depends on wide public participation, and for this purpose, institutions of government must be transparent and information must be available to the public in understandable forms. Several civil liberties are critical for the effective functioning of these institutions including protections for freedom of speech, assembly, and peaceful protest. These civil liberties, of course, lie at the heart of liberal democracy, but they are defensible on the ground that they are necessary for the effective functioning of institutions that implement the rule of law. Again, rights serving the rule of law overlap with rights and liberties recognized as key human rights and again with critical commitments of democracy. This leads us to the final question for this chapter: What is the relationship between the rule of law and democracy? How does law's rule relate to rule of the *demos*?

Democracy and the Rule of Law

The rule of law is intimately bound up with democracy, but the connection is somewhat different from its link to human rights. Again, we start with the thought that these concepts and the values they capture are distinct and play different roles in our political morality. We might say, that while democracy addresses the question "*who* govern me?" answering "we the people," the rule of law asks, "*how* am I governed?" or better, "*how* is power exercised over me?"[23] But this way of putting the question does not quite capture the difference. The notion of popular sovereignty answers the initial version of the question "who govern me?" On this doctrine, the people (*demos*), members of the polity regarded as a collective unit, is the ultimate constitut*ing* power. This body establishes the institutions of government, the constitut*ed* power. More accurately, on this view, the *demos* is the ultimate *source* of authority of the institutions of government. However, this does not tell us anything yet about the nature or structure of the government. Think of John Locke's political theory.[24] Locke, one of founders of modern-day liberalism, argued that the authority of government rests on the consent of the governed as expressed in voluntary participation in a founding "social contract." However, on Locke's account, consent empowers a commission to construct the frame of government, and this frame might not take the shape of a democracy or even a republic.

Aristotle taught that democracy is a *species* of *politeiēs* (*constitution*, using that term in its generic, lowercase sense). The *democratic* constitution (*politeia*) defines a certain mode of governance, a set of institutions by which power is constituted, exercised, and constrained. It, like the rule of law, is concerned with how power is exercised. The key feature of the democratic constitution is that power is constituted to realize in its institutions the root idea of *popular self*-government. In contrast, the rule of law tempers or qualifies *all* forms of sovereignty, including popular sovereignty. The speaker of the Polish parliament got it just wrong when a few years ago he said, "[I]t is the will of the people, not the law that matters, and the will of the people always tramples the law."[25] Democratic constitutions seek to make governmental power accountable to the *demos* through election of its representatives and its officials, who act as the agents of the people. However, the rule of law insists that the people, too, must be accountable to the law. Democratic self-governance must be structured according to the principles of the rule of law.

At the same time, democracy depends crucially on law. Democratic government enables *rule* of *the people*. But a *people* can exist as a coherent social unit only insofar as it is constituted by law, and it can *rule* only if its will is articulated in law. Democratically exercised governing power is deliberate and deliberative. Consequently, democratic governing power must be exercised through law and subject to law's rule. Thus, democracy depends crucially on the rule of law's promise to provide protection and recourse against the arbitrary exercise of power through the distinctive instrumentalities of the law. As political scientists Larry Diamond and Leonardo Morlino observe:

> [T]he rule of law is the base upon which every other dimension of democratic quality rests. When the rule of law is weak, participation of the poor and marginalized is suppressed; individual freedoms are tenuous and fleeting; civic groups may be unable to organize and advocate; the resourceful and well connected have vastly more access to justice and power; corruption and abuse of power run rampant as agencies of horizontal accountability are unable to function properly; political competition is distorted and unfair; voters have a hard time holding rulers to account; and thus, linkages vital to securing democratic responsiveness are disrupted and severed.[26]

Although the rule of law may exist in a political community that is not constituted as a democracy—it did so for centuries before the modern emergence of full-fledged democracies—democracies cannot function well without a robust rule-of-law foundation.

The relationship between the two modes of governance is even closer than this suggests. Democracy serves in its distinctive way values that overlap with those served by the rule of law. Democracy is the mode of governance best suited for citizens who seek a just community that they can share with other citizens on a footing of equality, and who acknowledge the inescapable fact that in their polity there is a diversity of perspectives on matters of justice and the common good. It is not possible faithfully to respect the fundamental equality of all members of the polity while seeking unilaterally to enact just one of the competing conceptions of justice. Unilateral determinations of the social order are by that fact alone unjust. Treating members as peers demands a *politeia* in which diverse perspectives on justice can be uttered, heard, and respected, and the views of members incorporated in some meaningful way into the structure of the polity. Mutual respect demands that members of a polity accord each other a comparable and substantial role in determining the social and political order, shaping its policies, and monitoring their execution.

In its distinctive way, the rule of law also protects and structures public recognition of the dignity, liberty, and equality of members of the democratic polity;

and it enables the effective pursuit of public goals of the polity by tempering the power of those entrusted with authority to act in the name of the polity. The ideals of the rule of law and of democracy are conceptually distinct but functionally intertwined. Rule-of-law mechanisms for holding elected officials accountable to the law and to democratic ideals are vital to democratic structures of governance. These mechanisms structure "horizontal accountability"—mutually constraining institutions within government—and "vertical accountability"— formal and informal arrangements by which a democratic public constrains the day-to-day exercise of power by public officials.

That is to say, democracy and the rule of law join their distinct forces and institutions to serve the same masters. The *rule of law is the infrastructure of democracy*, and *democracy is the natural completion of the ambitions that motivate the rule of law*. Democracy and the rule of law exist in a unique relationship of *interdependence*, of symbiosis.

Moreover, their respective institutionalizations also *overlap*. This, again, will be more apparent as we explore in Chapter 6 the implementation of rule-of-law principles, so just a few brief examples should suffice here. As the rule of law requires the transparency of government activities and widespread access to accurate information about them, and opportunities to challenge them, so democratic self-rule requires that its educated populace has access to information about the activities of government and about the evidence and opinion that shape public policies. Both require robust institutions enabling and protecting free public media. As effective public accountability of governmental action depends on institutions of a vibrant civil society, so too does democratic self-government. Both require support and protection of freedoms of speech, association, and assembly, and robust and independent institutions of education, universities, nongovernmental organizations, and the like. Thus, it is true that, although at the heart of each principle is a different focus on power, such that the specific structure of power concerns democracy but the effective tempering of that power concerns the rule of law, nevertheless, as we think about how best to realize and institutionalize these different concerns our proposals will often overlap.

Thus, to conclude this chapter, we must not confuse these three important pillars of political morality: democracy, human rights, and the rule of law. They make uniquely different contributions to a good, decent, and just political community. A proper understanding of their respective contributions is critical to our ability accurately to evaluate our own societies and effectively to marshal our efforts to bring them up to standard. Yet those same tasks require that we understand the deep and pervasive interdependency, and broad range of overlap, that exists among them. A fuller understanding of the rule of law depends less on policing the boundaries of the concept and more on exploring synergies between these symbiotes.

6

Realizing Law's Rule

The rule of law is a complex ideal, and its complexity has made understanding it difficult and especially contentious. In the preceding chapters, we have elaborated a conception of the rule of law that seeks to clarify contentious issues and introduce some order among its elements.

Recall that the conception consists of rule of law's *core aim* and immediately implied *principles*, and the deeper *values* that the aim and principles serve. The aim is to provide protection and recourse against the arbitrary exercise of power through the law. This aim is articulated in three principles: law's sovereignty, equality in the eyes of the law, and fidelity. This aim and its principles serve the value of membership, which brings together in complementary relationships freedom, dignity, equality, and community. There is one further important feature of the ideal: it exists only insofar as it is realized and articulated in the institutions and practices—governmental and extragovernmental, formal and informal—of historical political communities. The rule of law, like democracy, is by its nature an *institutionally realized ideal*. As a musical composition is realized in performance, and a thought is expressed in a particular language, so the ideal of the rule of law is realized in concrete institutions located in historically situated political communities.

The Task

Some moral ideals do not require institutional realization. Compare the virtue of generosity and the value of individual freedom. Generosity is expressed in attitudes, dispositions, and actions of individuals—in certain habits of the heart. Individuals enjoy freedom (in one sense of that ideal) when they can participate in a wide range of activities without interference from others. In contrast, consider David Hume's understanding of justice. He argued that just actions relate to each other like stones in a Gothic arch. Each action serves justice when they join a coordinated structure of just actions; without the support of the others, a given just-like action cannot serve its purpose; the action will not be just. In a similar way, activities aimed at constraining or containing abuses of power serve this end only when they fit into a structure of institutions and practices designed to enable, facilitate, and discipline them, orienting them toward realization of the rule

Law's Rule. Gerald J. Postema, Oxford University Press. © Oxford University Press 2022.
DOI: 10.1093/oso/9780190645342.003.0006

of law. These institutions are not mere "applications" of the ideal or implications of a general principle; rather, they are like a building constructed according to an architect's plan: the building realizes the architect's ideal. To understand the rule-of-law ideal we must look to the "buildings" that realize it.

It is common in discussions of the rule of law to identify the ideal with a set of familiar institutions, for example, separation of powers, judicial independence, limits on official discretion, and the formal requirements laws must meet. However, as Martin Krygier reminds us, this "confuses an abiding, precious, state of affairs, the rule of law, with particular and contingent means thought appropriate to achieve it."[1] The previous chapters of this work have tried to put the elements of an articulated conception of the rule of law in their proper places. Having explored the core aim and immediately implied principles, and the grounding value of the rule of law, we can now carefully consider the institutional realization of this ideal. An adequate understanding of the rule of law is realized in a structured set of institutions, practices, dispositions, and expectations in a particular political community that seek to realize the core aim and its principles, in service of and always informed by its underlying values.

This chapter proceeds mindful of two caveats. First, just as the same thought can be expressed in different languages such that translation always is to some degree interpretation, so too the same aim and values will likely be realized differently in different social and cultural circumstances. Designing appropriate and effective institutions involves a careful triangulation among the core aim, its principles, and grounding values, on the one hand, and the social, cultural, and political circumstances of particular political communities, on the other. In this chapter, we will explore important design principles for this institutional realization and illustrate them with institutions and practices that offer serious promise of achieving the design in what for most readers will be familiar social and cultural circumstances. In the next chapter, we will consider ways in which this initial sketch of the machinery of the rule of law may need to be modified where background circumstances vary significantly.

The second caveat is that we must recognize at the outset that no set of institutions and practices, no matter how well designed, can hope to defeat those who are singularly intent upon twisting them into tools to expand their own power, when they can do so with the approval or indifference of a substantial portion of the populace. The institutional machinery of the rule of law cannot guarantee a robust rule-of-law polity. An essential constituent element of robust rule of law is communities of officials and lay members who are committed to its realization. Put not your faith in princes, the rule of law counsels, but also, put not (all of) your faith in institutions. The conscience, commitments and integrity of the community, and of its individual members, provide the indispensable life-breath of the institutions.

A Model of Law's Rule Realized

Design Framework

The rule of law subjects the exercise of ruling power to law. Law disciplines ruling power: state authorities must rule only through or by law ("legality"); the laws must apply to governors just as they do to the governed ("reflexivity"); moreover, no state action is legitimate unless authorized by law ("exclusivity"). Law achieves this form of sovereignty through the essential underwriting support of networks of accountability. These networks, we learn in this chapter, must be found within the structures of government itself ("horizontal accountability") and outside government in the associations, institutions, and practices of civil society ("vertical accountability"). Law disciplines power by tethering its exercise to public norms. These norms direct conduct, and provide a deliberative framework for practical reasoning: the rule of law seeks to establish a rule of reason, or rather of reasons, addressed to those who exercise ruling power and to those subject to it. This requires that officials *have* legitimate public, law-grounded reasons for their actions, and are required regularly to *give* those reasons to the public; and those who are subject to ruling power are entitled to demand reasons, and adequate remedies for official violations of law, in forums created for that purpose. When institutions and practices implement these principles, the rule of law offers members of the political community protection against the arbitrary exercise of power and recourse against authorities when there are reasons to suspect them of arbitrarily exercising their power.

It does so through constituting, constraining, and sanctioning exercises of power; through enabling and empowering, as well as drawing and enforcing boundaries. It does its work *ex ante*, *ex post*, and *in medias res*. Some institutions work prospectively, creating structures and instruments of power, articulating norms and rules governing its exercise, and training persons in the discipline of its exercise. Other institutions work retrospectively demanding justification and accounting of the activities, assessing the activities and accounts given of them, and providing remedies where they are indicated and sanctions where they are needed. Other institutions and practices work *in medias res* to monitor, advise, and guide those who exercise ruling power.

Design Principles

This sketch provides a broad framework for thinking about how to give effective institutional expression to the ideal. The rule of law makes specific demands

(1) of the law itself, (2) of the application and enforcement of the law, and (3) of the constitution of ruling power generally.

First, the rule of law disciplines the laws themselves—or rather the practice of law-making.[2] It is nearly universally agreed that the rule of law requires that the laws through which governing power is exercised must be *general* in form (applying to classes of persons and circumstances); *accessible* and *intelligible* to the public; *prospective, consistent,* and *possible* (within the capacity of its addressees to comply); and reasonably *stable*. In addition, they must issue from a duly authorized process by duly authorized lawmakers according to recognized criteria of validity. These are, broadly speaking, formal conditions on laws; conditions that specify broadly the form laws should take.[3] We may still regard enactments that violate one or more of these criteria as laws for some purposes, but, from the point of view of the rule of law, they are deeply defective. They fail minimal standards of the rule of law. This is also true for laws that embed, authorize, or encourage patterns of invidious discrimination, because they violate the core rule-of-law principle that all who are subject to law's requirements are entitled to law's protection (equality in the eyes of the law).

Second, the rule of law disciplines the application and enforcement of law by governing authorities. Again, it is nearly universally agreed that official implementation of law must be congruent with and guided by the publicly articulated norms of law, and subject to public processes of official review and accountability, where law-based reasons for official actions can be demanded. The reflexivity and recourse principles require judicial review of official actions and effective procedures for challenging them and demanding remedies for violations of law and rule-of-law standards. In addition, enforcement of the law through courts must comply strictly with fundamental principles of due process, fairness, and impartiality. All who are subject to law must have guaranteed access to courts for both criminal and civil matters, unimpeded by legal, social, or financial barriers. Those who are drawn into law's orbit must be heard and respected in a court designed according to the above principles, and the court must base its decisions only on law and the evidence and arguments presented to it. Thus, the independence of the courts and of prosecutorial offices from external influence and pressure, especially from other departments of government, must be guaranteed.

Third, the exclusivity principle requires that law must authorize all governing power. The rule of law calls for articulated governance. The aim is not to disable government, but to *temper* it. Tempering essentially involves both constituting and constraining ruling power; enabling it to function, providing vehicles or recipes (legally constituted powers) for its exercise, as well as rules to guide and direct that exercise. For many countries, this has taken the form of principles of constitutional separation of powers. The basic tasks of governance—legislative, executive, and judicial—are distinguished and allocated to different departments, so that those who make the law do not also determine how and to whom they are applied in particular cases and those who adjudicate particular cases are free from pressure from the executive branches to pursue its policies or political needs.

For rule-of-law purposes, it is not enough that functions of government are separated and balanced in a variety of ways; the separate departments must also have responsibility to check each other. Assuring effective accountability, the indispensable tool of rule-of-law governance, is a key task of articulated governance. Governing power must be articulated to establish and enable a network of mutual (horizontal) accountability. Constitutional allocation of powers must provide publicly visible ways to keep those doing the public's business operating within and according to the public's law. An unavoidable but fertile and positive tension holds the various parts of the design together in service to rule-of-law aims: modes of meaningful accountability must be devised that also respect and reinforce the autonomy of the counterpoised centers of power and recourse.

These principles sketch in broad outline a familiar model of governance. The model has been elaborated in a variety of ways in different political communities, with varying degrees of success in approximating the rule-of-law ideal. This model needs still further elaboration, because it does not take fully into account the vast complexity of the modern state. For one thing, effective rule of law depends on mechanisms of constraint and horizontal accountability *within* the separated functions and powers of government at least as much as *between* them. To realize law's rule in the modern state, a quasi-fractal separation of powers internal to the separated branches is needed.[4] In addition, to complement this elaboration of institutions of intragovernmental accountability, the rule of law calls for extragovernmental organizations and practices rooted in civil society and protected by law that provide necessary means of vertical accountability. Let us look in turn at institutions and practices that articulate more concretely the tasks of horizontal and vertical accountability.

Intragovernmental Arrangements— Horizontal Accountability

Over a decade ago, legal scholars Eric Posner and Adrian Vermeule published a provocative book entitled *The Executive Unbound.*[5] They argued that James Madison's constitutional strategy of securing effective legal constraint of executive power, pitting separated powers against each other, has failed miserably in the modern state. In the United States, the Administrative Procedure Act (1946) provides the backbone of the modern American administrative state. It purports to constrain governmental power, but, they argue, it is virtually powerless; it creates vast areas in which administrative power is exempt from ordinary legal requirements.[6] Indeed, they insist that law *cannot* bind the modern executive; the only effective constraint is "politics."

They conclude that this failure of law entails the failure of the rule of law. The rule of politics, they argue, must replace the rule of law. Posner and Vermeule pose a serious challenge to the rule of law; however, at most, the analysis highlights challenges *for* the rule of law, problems that defenders of the rule of law must take seriously and address responsibly.

This analysis of the failures of law and of formal constitutional means of legally constraining power rests on a crude conceptual framework that cannot support it. Their definition of "law" recognizes only formally enacted, fixed rules enforced by courts empowered to impose powerful sanctions. All the rest is "politics," which the authors represent as working entirely outside and without the assistance of law. However, we have argued from the outset of this study that law rules just when there is a framework of mutual accountability and an ethos of mutual commitments that nourishes and sustains it. Formal institutions cannot do their necessary work without informal institutions and practices, planted in rich soil of mutual commitments. This informal infrastructure is not extralegal "politics" but elements of the rule of law that work in partnership with the more formal, visible, legalistic elements. The sober conclusion to draw from Posner and Vermeule's analysis of the weaknesses of "law" and formal constitutional institutions is recognition of the need to pay closer attention to the partnership, the intricate dance, between formal and informal, intragovernmental and extragovernmental components of the rule of law that must be realized in the modern state. The rule of law need not be abandoned, but it must be thoughtfully articulated.

We begin this process of articulation considering intragovernmental institutions and practices. I have argued that the ethos of fidelity gives life to formal or informal institutions, and that the attitudes, commitments, and practices of this ethos take shape in conventions and informal norms. Before looking at the quasi-fractal structure of the needed intragovernmental separation of powers, we must consider the essential role that the rule of law assigns to constitutional norms.

Constitutional Norms

Formal constitutions structure, vest, and temper political power. Designers of constitutions might like to think that they can accomplish this task through the careful creation and diligent maintenance of a written text and the formal institutions established by it. However, keen observers of the law at work in political communities remind us that effective functioning of a constitution that respects the rule of law depends on a complex combination of informal norms and practices, to which responsible participants hold themselves and others accountable.

Constitutional norms or conventions (I will use these terms interchangeably) are informal, practiced norms of the governmental community. They are a special case of *social norms*. They differ from rules of ordinary morality, from deeper principles of political morality, and from principles implicit in the text or jurisprudence of a country's constitution. *Moral norms* bind moral agents by virtue of their grounding in fundamental moral values and principles; thus, they need not be practiced to obligate those to whom they apply. Unlike moral norms, social norms depend for their content and normative force in part on the extent to which they are actually embedded in social practice. They are sometime said to be "arbitrary," but they are arbitrary not in the sense of being capricious, pointless, or practically empty, but rather in the sense that other norms might have played a similar role had they attracted a sufficient degree of commitment and compliance.

Constitutional norms are informal rules; only rarely do courts enforce them. We find them embedded in the temporally extended practices of officials and political leaders; they articulate the commitments undertaken by government officials. Governmental norms are a part of what some constitutional scholars call "the unwritten constitution":[7] conventions that are implicit in the practices that underwrite the constitution, rather than in the text or jurisprudence of the formal constitution. Although they do not fix the meaning of the text, they often determine the boundaries of appropriate or required behavior within its four corners. Constitutional norms typically supplement the text and sometimes even circumvent it.

Consider a few examples from the US context. Conventions prohibit the president from interfering in the regular operations of law enforcement (the Department of Justice) and intelligence agencies (CIA). Some protect the tenure of officers of key administrative agencies (the Federal Reserve and the Securities and Exchange Commission) from presidential interference by making them dismissible only for cause.[8] Inspectors general (IGs) hold several agencies accountable to existing law and norms; norms protect IGs from presidential interference. Norms prohibit presidential self-dealing and require the president to put his or her assets in a blind trust;[9] they also shape and limit executive pardoning power.

A network of norms also structures legislative business and interactions. The US Constitution gives various significant powers to Congress, but imposes few explicit duties on its members and explicitly defines few procedures for exercising these powers. Congressional folkways fill them out. Concrete norms of comity and reciprocity articulate general norms of mutual tolerance, forbearance, and truth-telling that control the daily interactions of lawmakers.[10] Some norms give powers to minorities to slow down legislative activity of the majority party; this gives time for more deliberate consideration of the merits of legislation and constrain attempts of the majority to entrench its power. Norms also limit attempts to use such devices in ways that can poison the legislative environment and throw the government into gridlock.

One cannot locate these norms in the text of the US Constitution or case law interpreting it. "Law is not enough," writes one scholar.[11] Formal constitutions tend to be quite general and incomplete. Constitutional and intrabranch conventions render the indeterminate, often very abstract, constitutional text more determinate, fill in gaps, and define, direct, and limit the discretion that the constitution grants or leaves entirely unspecified. They lend content and meaning to broad mandates and allocations of power. In addition, they integrate and coordinate the operations of intersecting governmental institutions.[12]

Government conventions limit the exercise of powers formally granted to various branches of government, powers which if exercised to their lawful extreme would bring the government to the point of collapse.[13] Other conventions keep partisanship within bounds so that government can function while remaining faithful to democratic and rule-of-law values. Self-limiting conventions do not eliminate or even greatly reduce partisanship, but they can do much to democratize it. They provide behavioral scripts that enable partisans to communicate their respect for each other in ways that underwrite mutual trust. They give public shape to democratic and rule-of-law commitments of political leaders and the polity they lead. Serving a democratic constitution, these conventions work to realize democratic values over the medium and long term, softening stark majoritarian elements of the formal institutions, and giving minorities some voice or influence in governance and a stake in the ongoing success of the democratic process. In circumstances of intense competition and conflict, where the stakes are very high, they structure practices of mutual recognition, and make trust and trust-worthiness visible. In the service of the rule of law, they provide mechanisms for tempering the exercise power, giving focus and force to efforts to hold accountable those who exercise it.

Of course, constitutional norms serve only imperfectly the institutions and the deeper values of democracy and the rule of law they seek to realize. Moreover, informal norms and practices can be hostile to the formal constitution and its fundamental aims. Norms, like the established formal institutions they serve, are subject to criticism and require constant maintenance, and sometimes members of the community must challenge them in order to bring about necessary reforms. (In Chapter 8, we will distinguish between natural evolution, intentional reform, and active sabotage of these norms and appropriate responses to these challenges.)

American constitutional scholar, Lawrence Tribe, characterized constitutional norms and conventions as "dark matter," that, unseen, exert enormous force on "ordinary matter" of constitutional law.[14] This metaphor is unfortunate, since it is crucial to the proper functioning of constitutional norms that they are relatively visible in the public discursive activities of participants. Nonetheless, the metaphor captures the important fact that formal and informal constitutional norms and institutions are interdependent in important ways. Informal constitutional norms operate in the environment of, and take their focus and meaning from, the network of formal constitutional norms and values they purport to serve. Likewise, formal constitutions depend on the thick networks of informal conventions for effective functioning. They can do the work for which they are designed only when complemented by compatible informal practices that more or less effectively serve underlying rule of law values to which the constitution is dedicated.

This interaction is dynamic; changes in one can prompt or retard changes in the other. This interdependence gives the Constitution and its unwritten norms significant strength. However, it also makes them vulnerable to exploitation by those who seek to hollow out the constitution. Political scientist Kim Lane Scheppele has drawn attention to a strategy common among autocrats of using good features of democratic constitutions to bad effect by ignoring the supporting features that compensate for or mitigate bad effects in other constitutions after which they are modeled.[15] Such efforts can usher in an autocratic "Frankenstate."[16]

Institutions of the Internal Separation of Powers

In the modern state, law can hope to rule only if familiar checks and balances among the three major branches of government are replicated *within* branches, especially the executive branch. The broad constitutional structure dividing powers and separating governmental functions must be further articulated in a distributed network of agencies, subagencies, and oversight offices both inside and outside the distinct branches.[17] In line with the fundamental rule-of-law notion of mutual accountability, this network must consist of interlocking circles of accountability; no one agency or office may stand above all the others, accountable to none (an "unaccountable accountability holder").

Within the US government, such institutions include Inspector General Offices of the Central Intelligence Agency and of the Departments of Justice, Defense, and Homeland Security.[18] Inspector General Offices—"junkyard dogs"—can be effective in exposing hidden illegal or otherwise inappropriate governmental activities.[19] Again in the United States, the Office of Governmental

Ethics was designed to play such a role. The White House's Office of Legal Counsel could and perhaps should do likewise, although its current structure awkwardly combines both legal policy advising and an expectation that its lawyers will speak law to power when necessary. In many Western governments, ombudsman offices play a critical role not only overseeing government activity but also providing a point of contact, and in some cases recourse, for citizens and organizations outside of government. Internal audits and legal recognition and protection of whistleblowers and similar channels of dissent make a less formal but important contribution to internal accountability-holding.

Legal scholar Margo Schlanger reported a few years ago on the use of what she calls "offices of goodness" within federal agencies of the United States.[20] Legislators establishing or overseeing a federal agency sometimes create such offices within the agency to encourage the agency to pay attention to values and concerns that do not fall strictly within the agency's mission. For example, when Congress created the Office of Homeland Security in 2002, it created the Office for Civil Rights and Civil Liberties to "oversee [the Department's] compliance with constitutional, statutory, regulatory, policy, and other requirements relating to the civil rights and civil liberties of individuals affected by the programs and activities of the Department."[21]

Such offices have various tools at their disposal. In addition to offering technical assistance and analysis, they monitor activity of agency officials for compliance with formal law and with informal norms and best practices. They gather and mandate disclosure of important information and develop channels for bringing the information to the public. They may also be empowered to challenge agency decisions or policies and in some cases to provide necessary approval or clearance. Like ombudsman offices, these institutions may provide a point of contact between the agency and the public generally, giving members of the public and various organizations of civil society access to the decision-making processes of the agency. To operate effectively these offices must have a significant degree of autonomy within the agency, while nevertheless being subject to accountability. Having a foot outside the agency may provide some protection for autonomy, while subjecting its own activities to review by another agency (or agencies) can provide necessary accountability. Professional associations may also hold occupants of these offices to professional standards.

Conventions and norms underwrite these formal and informal institutions that articulate, fractal-like, the intra-agency separations of powers; they enforce the autonomy of the agencies while defining modes and limits of accountability. Neither formal institutions nor informal norms can do their assigned tasks in upholding law's rule without the contributions of their partners. However, even this partnership alone may not be sufficient to secure law's rule. The rule of law also enlists resources of a robust civil society to sustain and enrich needed modes of recourse and accountability.

Civil Society and the Practice of Fidelity— Vertical Accountability

Two more components of the infrastructure of accountability are essential to its effective service of the rule of law; they draw on and implicate important institutions of civil society. (At the end of this chapter, we will discuss a third: a vigorous, independent, and rule-of-law committed legal profession.) One is a structure of mandates and processes to ensure that government activities are fully transparent, supplemented by a legally protected, vigorous free press that is known to be independent of control by government or other major centers of power. Publicity is the soul of justice—so Jeremy Bentham argued in the eighteenth century.[22] Translated into the language of this study: publicity provides the life-blood of fidelity to law. The other key components on which the various oversight offices internal to government depend are nongovernmental organizations, policy institutes, and the like. The effectiveness of horizontal institutions and practices depends on partnership with a network of institutions and practices of civil society.

Bentham brought these two dimensions together in his scheme of what he called "securities against misrule"—institutions of governmental accountability, we might call them. First among these institutions was what he called the Public Opinion Tribunal (POT). Modeled on the jury in the English criminal law system, Bentham charged the POT not only to monitor government activities but also to render a public verdict and act on it—to assess, challenge, and, where necessary, resist government action. A free government, he argued, must not just tolerate dissent; it must encourage and enable it: "Of a government that is not despotic, it is therefore the essential character to *cherish* the disposition to eventual resistance."[23] Bentham thought of the POT as a single, albeit complex, society-wide institution; however, what is needed, rather, is a distributed network of actors, institutions, and practices at multiple levels within civil society. Fidelity must animate and sustain this network, and law, in turn, must protect and support ("cherish") it.

Institutional Support for Fidelity

Chapter 3 articulated a vision of a political community in which the rule of law is richly realized; I called it "law's commonwealth." Fidelity is the animating spirit of law's commonwealth—a community in which all of its members, and not merely the legal or ruling elite, take responsibility for holding each other, and especially law's officials, to account under the law. This ethos involves not only reciprocal compliance but also mutual accountability. Law is capable of ruling only where members of the community—officials of all ranks and citizens alike—submit to and participate in a network of mutual accountability.

While one individual may hold another individual accountable, fidelity engages a wider responsibility: citizens participate in efforts to hold governing officials accountable to the law. Upholding law's rule is a large, socially cooperative endeavor. One's own efforts can contribute to that endeavor, but their success will depend on the efforts of many others as well. They, in turn, depend on the practices, structures, and organizations that gather, focus, and coordinate those collective efforts. The rule of law depends on a robust institutional infrastructure—multiple layers of permanently constituted institutions and practices of civil society.

These institutions and organizations perform three key fidelity-sustaining tasks. First, they promote, encourage, and nurture the ethos of fidelity. Educational institutions—schools, universities, civic associations, and professional organizations—are needed to provide citizenship training for member of the polity and professional training for judges, lawyers, and government officials. Second, they empower, enable, and facilitate accountability. Organizations inform and associations mobilize, organize, and direct the community's vertical accountability efforts. They provide platforms for launching interventions into internal governmental offices and agencies, influencing officials and taking advantage of the modes of recourse that constitutional and subconstitutional law provides. Third, the institutions and practices of civil society discipline individual and community accountability-holding efforts: they educate, focus, coordinate, restrain, and economize efforts and provide facilities for articulating grievances and grounds for them.

The law plays a crucial role in empowering, sustaining, and protecting these institutions and practices. For example, the law must protect individuals and civil society organizations from intrusive surveillance and other forms of government harassment. A key rule-of-law protection is the right against unreasonable searches and seizures embedded in the Fourth Amendment of the US Constitution. Another example is the protection of rights of free speech and association in a polity's fundamental law. We often defend them as key protections of the democratic polity, but they sink their roots equally deeply in the soil of the rule of law.

The law must also do what is feasible to protect the public sphere from disinformation and the degradation of public discourse. This, of course, is an especially delicate matter, but it is no less important for being difficult and fraught.

There are few bright lines to divide legitimate, but highly contested, speech from willful distortions of facts and information. Nevertheless, legal intervention may be necessary to preserve the integrity of discourse and people's trust in each other's participation in it. In Chapter 8 and again in Chapter 13, we will discuss this threat to the rule of law in some detail.

A Complex Scaffolding of Restraint

"A textured and connected society," writes Martin Krygier, "is a bar to the intrusions of state power."[24] Many organizations and institutions of civil society play a critical role in fidelity's institutional infrastructure.[25] They include vigilance committees (familiar in Bolivia) and citizen review boards (as in Mumbai); human rights organizations like Amnesty International, Human Rights Watch, and the Anti-defamation League; nongovernmental organizations (NGOs) focused on the environment, policing and criminal justice, and consumer protection; specially created informal ombudsman and watchdog agencies; and cultural organizations, business groups, trade unions, churches, and religious organizations. Professional associations—for example, medical, legal, social work organizations—educate and discipline their members and provide platforms for political action. As mentioned earlier, universities provide a critical perspective on, and an important counterweight to, information originating from government agencies. They provide crucial resources for information, analysis, and, with the critical help of a free and independent press, public fact-checking and policy-checking.

In Chapter 3, we discussion one example of citizen-initiated accountability-holding that occurred in 2004 in Greensboro, North Carolina.[26] In like manner, environmental watchdog NGOs, the Environmental Defense Fund, for example, actively work to goad government agencies to do their proper regulatory jobs. These citizen-initiated, privately funded efforts illustrate how a community's sense of responsibility to hold officials accountable, even twenty-five years after the fact, can take concrete form. Accountability seeks to construct a full public record and shared narrative of problematic events in an effort to rebuild norms of appropriate behavior.[27]

One important function of such organizations is to enable individual citizens and citizen groups to initiate claims in existing government oversight offices. Two Latin American scholars offer an example.[28] The body of a high school student was found on the outskirts of an Argentine city in a province in which political corruption, nepotism, and clientelism were widespread. Police and city officials ignored the case, but people in the city were outraged and organized a large number of silent demonstrations—*marchas de silencio*—to demand an investigation and a speedy trial. The protest engaged the local media, and as national media took up the case, marches took place in other cities around the country. These efforts eventually forced officials to investigate and bring the case to trial. The murdered child's father worked with others to establish a "Commission for Justice and Truth" consisting of nuns, human rights activists, trade unionists, teachers, neighbors, and others. This commission kept watch over the police investigation and trial. During the trial, the judges repeatedly made decisions systematically favoring the defense, compromising the impartiality of the court. The commission and national media kept the spotlight on the proceedings, and, after massive demonstrations, the trial was suspended and a new trial convened some months later. In this case, individuals, social organizations, ad hoc institutions, and eventually formal institutions of law worked together to hold individuals and public authorities accountable.

Advances in digital technology, despite their dangers (see Chapter 13), have aided in this endeavor of vertical accountability. One example should suffice. The World Justice Project sponsored a competition in 2021 entitled, "Advancing the Rule of Law in a Time of Crisis," the crisis being the COVID-19 pandemic. The winner in the "accountable governance" division was a documentation app called "Tella."[29] This app enables journalists, civil society groups, and human rights organizations to record and document with relative safety human rights violations, corruption, electoral fraud, and other abuses of power. Its objective is to "empower individuals and groups to easily, quickly, and effectively collect data and produce high quality documentation that can be used for research, advocacy or transitional justice." Launched in 2019, it has been used in Cuba to track gender-based violence, in Myanmar and West Papua to document human rights violations, and in Brazil to collect data on attacks on indigenous defenders in Brazil.

Lawyers and Law's Rule

We must recognize one further institution that is indispensable to the realization of the rule of law in both horizontal and vertical dimensions, the legal profession. Some think that the rule of law is the special responsibility of judges. "Judges," writes legal scholar Brian Tamanaha, "are the ones whose specific task is to insure that other government officials are held to the law. The ultimate responsibility for maintaining a rule of law system therefore rests with the judiciary."[30] However, Tamanaha locates this responsibility too narrowly; the legal profession generally bears this responsibility, and especially lawyers who do not wear judicial robes.

Essential for the realization of the rule of law in any given polity is a robust legal profession that understands and is deeply committed to the rule of law. (Of course, being trained in law is no guarantee of commitment to the rule of law. Victor Orbán, authoritarian leader of Hungary, and US Senator Josh Hawley and presidential advisor Rudi Giuliani, who led the charge to overturn the results of the American presidential election in 2020, after over sixty courts rejected every argument supporting the effort, are all trained lawyers.) Law can function effectively—it can offer normative guidance to those addressed by law, officials and lay people alike—only with the active assistance of lawyers. Lawyers are guardians and conservators of the rule of law. Due to their specialized knowledge, social status, and legal powers and opportunities, lawyers are uniquely situated to sustain (but also to undermine) law's rule. Lawyers' practice over time does as much as, perhaps even more than, that of judges to shape the contours of law. They are conservators of the law and guardians of its integrity and the public's trust in the law.

Lawyers for private clients play a critical role in enforcing key legislation. This is true in the United States where the civil rights acts of the 1960s rely on lawyers to enforce the rights against both private and government violators of the rights, and holding government officials accountable to the law they are sworn to uphold.

Lawyers are also essential intermediaries between law, citizens, and the institutions and officials of government. As Thelma, an acute observer of law, once said to her sidekick Louise: "[L]aw is some tricky shit." Ordinary citizens must be aware of and understand the law in order to guide their own actions, determine and defend their entitlements, and hold officials accountable. But the law is vast and complex, inevitably obscure and contested. It is the object of specialized study and apprenticeship. Bentham's ideal of "every man his own lawyer" was naïve in his day and much more so today. People need lawyers. Lawyers enable people to exercise and protect their rights and legal powers. Lawyers are translational agents and mediators.[31] They bring the law to the people and accompany people when they approach the forums of law. They make broad popular access to the courts of justice possible. Lawyers mediate between the citizen and the law, and between the citizen and government. Perhaps the lion's share of ordinary lawyers' activities takes place outside the courtroom and not even in its shadow. As Lon Fuller insisted, lawyers are architects of social structure.[32]

In addition, crucial to law's rule, lawyers bring law to government officials—speak law to power. They play a crucial role in tempering ruling power. They are authorized, and in many cases under professional obligation, to speak law to their power-wielding clients. Lawyers are "an important countervailing power to the state; tempering state power with fussy legal formalities."[33] It is not surprising that Dick the Butcher's counsel to "first, kill all the lawyers"[34] tempts political leaders. However, lawyers' unique intermediary role also makes them useful tools for modern authoritarians or power wielders who are indifferent to the rule of law, for they are capable, if so minded, of bending the law's language to suit those who have only contempt for law and law's rule.

The lawyer is one skilled in circumventing the law, according to Ambrose Bierce's cynical definition.[35] Yet, cynicism aside, lawyers, especially government lawyers, find themselves constantly navigating the margins of legality, advising and facilitating actions of their bosses in the inevitable gray areas of law. The law is complex and often does not offer bright lines. Lawyers must use careful, informed, and responsible judgment to determine what the law actually permits, authorizes, or requires.

According to a common understanding of their professional role, lawyers are bound to client loyalty (pursuing the client's interests—within the law) and by client control. Moreover, it is widely thought that ordinary citizens are entitled to a lawyer's aid to press any seriously colorable legal claim within the gray area, because, for citizens, "whatever is not prohibited is permitted." This is arguably consistent with a sound understanding of law's sovereignty. But it is important to keep in mind that the obligations of lawyers for private clients differ from those of government lawyers. The position of the government lawyer is different in three important respects.

First, the lawyer's "client" is the government agency, or its head, but only as office holder, not as a person. The government official is due the lawyer's efforts just insofar as the official seeks to act within the law that defines and constrains that office. Second, what is lawful for officials is not limited to what courts can enforce, because some important activities of, for example, the executive branch are not reviewable by the court due to rules of deference and justiciability. We have observed repeatedly, especially when it comes to activities of government, that the law is not limited to that which courts are likely to enforce. Moreover, as we have seen, in addition to explicit law, the norms and practices of the "unwritten constitution" guide and direct government officials. Third, there is a critical difference between the positions of government officials and citizens regarding activities in the gray areas of law. This is due in part to the fact that the government lawyers' opinions on matters of law are usually secret and insulated from challenge as to their soundness and legal integrity. Also, government officials are not entitled to free movement in the gray area. As we argued in Chapter 3, the principle, whatever is not prohibited is permitted, is inconsistent with the rule of law's principle of exclusivity. Government activities are legitimate only when and to the extent that they are clearly legally authorized. There is no law-free zone for those who exercise ruling power.

Thus, the proper model for the activity of the government lawyer is not client-interest-driven *advocacy*, which it typical for private, nongovernmental lawyers, but rather independent, fidelity-driven *advising*. The government lawyer's first responsibility is not to the person of the official, or the official's policies, but to the law, the constitution, and fundamentally to the rule of law. More than judges, the lawyer is *la bouche de droit* (the mouth of the law) when speaking in the halls of ruling power. And the lawyers' words mark out the guardrails, not the secret paths around them. Lawyers must articulate the law as it constitutes and constrains the exercise of government power; thus, even when matters are contested, they must give, and officials are entitled to, the best, rather than a merely plausible, colorable, policy- or politics-promoting, interpretation of the law. Government lawyers are key conservators of the integrity of law and key players in the system of accountability. Here accountability operates *ex ante*.

Finally, while lawyers are essential guardians of law, they must also have guardians. Playing an essential role of holding government officials accountable, they must be governed themselves by professional and other modes of public accountability. Only when such modes of accountability are in place can we hope to avoid reducing the rule of law to the rule of lawyers. Sometimes, of course, these mechanisms of accountability fail. Arguably, they failed to hold accountable the lawyers who provided specious legal cover for the George W. Bush administration's campaign of torture that, in a broad consensus of America lawyers, violated national and international law. These lawyers now hold secure positions in a major American law school and on the federal appellate bench.

Here we encounter yet again the hard reality: even well-designed institutions and practices of horizontal and vertical accountability cannot guarantee that law will effectively rule. In the end, as legal scholar Aziz Huq recently argued, "the robustness of democratic institutions [and practices] under the rule of law cannot be disentangled from the character and motivations of those elected or appointed to high office."[36] His observation applies to participants in networks of accountability beyond those holding high, elected office and for modes of accountability both horizontal and vertical. No set of institutions or well-designed practices can wholly eliminate the risk of a powerful person or party, indifferent to or contemptuous of them, working to reduce them to an empty shell. Well-designed institutions may be unable "to arrest the erosion of democracy and the rule of law by strongly determined and socially popular autocrats."[37] So writes Polish constitutional scholar Wojciech Sadurski, a keen observer of the erosion of his own country's commitment to the rule of law. Human institutions can enable the best of human nature; but they are also vulnerable to the worst. Ultimately, law's rule cannot be established or sustained unless a community and a lion's share of its members are willing to act with integrity from a principled commitment, in Adam Ferguson's words, to "make the terms" of the rule of law "be observed."[38]

These concluding reflections bring vividly to mind the limits of the rule of law. Similarly, our earlier reflections on the contingent factors that may spell the difference between effective and faltering institutional realizations of the rule of law bring to mind the dependence of the rule of law on the material, social, and cultural conditions of particular political communities. The task of the next chapter is to take a closer look at the limits of the rule of law and conditions under which it alone can thrive.

7

Conditions and Limits

The previous chapter argued that the rule of law is a necessarily realized ideal, that we can adequately understand this ideal and its implications for our conduct only after we have a clear view of the configuration of institutions, practices, subsidiary norms, and personal and collective dispositions of a particular political community in which it is realized. The rule-of-law ideal is like the architect's sketch or a composer's score that is realized in a building or performance. This way of thinking about the rule of law immediately alerts us to the possibility of variability in the realization of the ideal.

Varieties of Variability

For one thing, we should ask not whether the rule of law *exists* in a particular political community but rather how *robust* or vital it is. The ideal can be more or less adequately realized in a political community; rarely is it fully realized. The rule of law is everywhere to some degree a work in progress—or retreat. There are several dimensions of robustness. (1) The design of the rule of law's institutional machinery (the institutions, practices, norms, etc.) can to varying degrees be fit for the task of realizing the ideal. (2) The machinery can function better or worse. The design might be adequate, but for a variety of reasons, the institutions just do not work well. Among the reasons might be (3) the realizing institutions and its norms, or the principles of the ideal itself, can be honored and respected by power holders or by the larger community to varying degrees. Let's call these three dimensions of *robustness variability*.

Our analogy of the architect's plan suggests that realization of the rule of law can also vary along another axis. To construct the house according to the plan, the builder must take into account the available building materials, the particular conditions of the building site, and the skills of the available workforce, and, with these in mind, make adjustments accordingly. Similarly, the rule of law's institutional design must take into account the local circumstances, conditions, and resources of the political community in which it is to be realized. Consequently, the institutional machinery of the rule of law may vary with the local social, cultural, moral, and environmental conditions and resources available for its construction

Law's Rule. Gerald J. Postema, Oxford University Press. © Oxford University Press 2022.
DOI: 10.1093/oso/9780190645342.003.0007

and effective operation. Let's call this *cultural variability* (taking "cultural" in a wide sense).

The institutions and norms that realize the rule of law in a particular community tend to include a complex set of instructions for conduct; the various principles and norms work together, coordinated and balanced, as a system. What they require of conduct will depend in part on the actual circumstances of action and the options available to actors. Moreover, the principles and norms tend to be designed for what we might think of as "normal" circumstances, while actors and their communities may face circumstances that fall outside the normal range. Actors, seeking to honor the fundamental demands of the rule of law, may have reason to reconsider the balance among the institutional principles or norms or consider infringing a key principle in the interest of better serving the rule-of-law ideal overall. Let's call this *circumstantial variability*.

This rule of law is also subject to *normative* limits. Historical circumstances can affect its normative or practical force. It is also subject to another normative limit. In particular, as one moral-political ideal among others, the rule of law may call for conduct that is inconsistent with answering the demands of a different ideal or principle. For example, respect for the rule of law may counsel actions that justice or promotion of economic prosperity might frown on. It is possible that in some such cases, the rule of law should prevail, but in others, competing moral considerations may outweigh it. We must allow for the possibility that there are normative limits to its demands. In addition, there may be domains of social or personal life that, for good moral-political reasons, are off limits to the law, and hence to the demands of the rule of law. We will consider these normative limits of the rule of law in the second half of this chapter. However, first, we will take up the previous three forms of variability of the rule of law.

Contexts, Conditions, and Circumstances

Rule-of-law principles take on concrete meaning, institutional shape, and practical force in specific social, cultural, and political settings. In some such settings, the familiar rule-of-law machinery surveyed in the previous chapter can thrive; in others, their effectiveness or value may be compromised or even undermined. They may be relatively robust in some, weaker or compromised in others. "Can papyrus grow where there is no marsh? Can reeds flourish where there is no water?" (Job 8.11). Is it possible to identify social or cultural *preconditions* of the rule of law?

It is also possible that the rule of law's foundational aims and principles will be ill served by familiar institutional means, but served reasonably well by other, unfamiliar means. Social-cultural conditions may be unfavorable for establishing effective rule-of-law machinery—the reeds may not flourish in the absence of the needed water—or conditions favor different institutional machinery to serve the same fundamental ends. We take up, first, the issue of cultural variability, and then address the question of whether there are cultural preconditions of viable rule-of-law realization.

Cultural Variability

A story is told of a development project in Kenya. Firewood was running out due to deforestation, and wood smoke was polluting the air, so, in an effort to improve the local economy and environment, aid workers supplied the villagers with solar cookers. However, open-air cookers proved useless to them because of a strong taboo among villagers against cooking food in the open.[1] Similar stories can be told about attempts to build stable and effective rule-of-law institutions and practices in developing and post-conflict societies.

Scholars who have studied extensive efforts to transplant rule-of-law institutions and practices over the past several decades observe only modest success. They single out several causes of these results, chief among them are unrealistic objectives and a lack of deep contextual knowledge.[2] Awareness of distinctive modes of exercising power, sources of arbitrariness, and available resources to counter them are essential for successful realization of rule-of-law principles. Broad social practices and shared understandings affect the impact of institutions designed to reign in ruling power. "Institutions and practices of sorts not known in the homes of rule-of-law exporters [often] perform adequately in their own homes, even if they look quite strange to visitors."[3] Whether these institutions adequately do the work of the rule of law, Martin Krygier counsels, is not a question answered by appeal to definition or to a preferred list of familiar institutions, but rather by looking at how they actually work.

A political society that lacks robust versions of familiar rule-of-law institutions may not fail to meet rule-of-law standards by that fact alone. For example, access to courts, governed by legally defined procedures and guarantees of impartiality, is widely regarded as one of the requirements of the rule of law, but in some parts of the world, especially among rural populations, informal, customary modes of hearing and resolving disputes, not incorporated in the state legal structure, are widely available. They offer a kind of ordering of power in the language of the people involved, according to rules widely known and practiced in the community, with decisions made by people trusted in the community. Traditional, customary arrangements of this kind may not be perfect, but they may offer access to justice that is more timely and effective, less costly and less subject to corruption, than formal systems offered by the state. Although nonstate justice systems may not meet familiar standards of the rule of law, they may satisfy rule-of-law functions.[4] They serve the aim of more familiar institutions of the rule of law by other means. "There is usually no single right answer to the question how the rule of law requirement must be implemented" in a political community and its legal system.[5]

Cultural context is important, but sensitivity to the legal context is equally important. Comparative law scholars argue that it is often difficult to transplant legal procedures and norms from developed to developing societies because legal procedures and norms take their meaning in good part from their relationship to other norms in the legal system. The general nature of the system—civil-law or common-law traditions, for example—influence the meaning and force of specific procedures and practices, as does the nature and shape of the specific system.[6] Thus, institutions or practices that serve rule-of-law aims in one legal context, working in concert with other elements, can work against it when combined with other elements not friendly to the rule of law or in the absence of necessary supporting elements. As we noted in the previous chapter, political scientist Kim Lane Scheppele has called attention to an especially troubling consequence of this dependency. Political leaders seeking to mask their efforts to subvert rule-of-law constraints find it convenient to lift up their commitment to certain institutional elements, while undermining others.[7] In Chapter 8, we will explore in detail ways in which political leaders who seek to throw off the yoke of the rule of law turn its core institutions against it.

Robustness Variability: Preconditions of the Rule of Law

Rule-of-law institutions depend on the moral, cultural, and legal conditions in which they operate, so we might reasonably ask whether there are certain conditions that must be in place if any of the possible variations on rule-of-law machinery are to be viable or robust in any given political community. That is, are there *preconditions* of rule-of-law viability?

David Hume thought justice had such preconditions. He argued that following the demands of justice makes practical sense only in some circumstances.[8] Only when these conditions obtain can justice claim our moral and practical allegiance. He argued as follows: the practice of justice—respecting the possessions of others with the expectation that others will respect one's own—is costly but beneficial if one takes the long view. However, this practice *loses its point*—it makes no practical claim on us—in certain circumstances. This happens when, for example, all the material things we need and desire are as prevalent as the air and sea; or when some of us are so radically and unalterably dependent on the good will of others that, as he put it, we could not make the effects of our resentment felt; or when one falls into the hands of a gang of radically self-oriented and practically myopic ruffians. Moderate scarcity of goods and a substantial degree of interdependence among people ("objective" or material circumstances), along with a capacity to consider the long run and limited tendency to regard strangers benevolently ("subjective" or psychological circumstances), Hume argued, are among the most important preconditions of justice.

Similarly, there are preconditions that must obtain if seeking to install and then respect institutions and practices of the rule of law have a practical point. There would be no need for its protections if, for example, there were no significant inequalities of power such that some persons were vulnerable to domination by others; or if there were no benefit to be reaped from authorizing governing power; or if human nature were such that we could count on those who exercise power to do so only according to principles of public good and no one would occupy a position of dominance over others. In these circumstances, elaborate and costly rule-of-law constraints would lose their practical point. This is obviously true, but, for all practical purposes, it is of no interest, because these circumstances are fanciful, far from the human social realities we must contend with. The question becomes more interesting and challenging when we consider other cultural (subjective or intersubjective) and economic, social, or political (objective) circumstances.

Recall Martin Krygier's important point that "the rule of law requires that law *counts*, which in turn requires that it be widely expected and assumed to count."[9] Law counts when people in the community regard law as an important normative resource; it counts when they use law to plot the trajectories of their interactions with each other and with the authorities, and as a basis for assessing the conduct of others, especially officials. In some communities, law just doesn't count. Krygier retells a Bulgarian proverb: law is like a door in an open field; you can walk through it, but what's the point? Where this sentiment is widespread, law does not count. The rule of law cannot take root and flourish in these waters.

However, it is useful to look for the cause of the apathy and alienation expressed in the proverb. The civic culture itself may be the cause: it may be utterly anarchic, or rather anti-nomic. Such an attitude may grip subcommunities of a polity, if not the whole. Especially among the economically or politically powerful, the attitude may take hold that to follow the law voluntarily is something only morons do and that to be subject to the law is a sure signal of weakness.[10] However, in these circumstances, the rule of law has not lost its point; rather, it has failed, dramatically. The fault lies not in the rule of law or even in its institutional realization but in the moral culture needed to sustain it. (As we will see in Chapter 8, one of the deep threats to the rule of law is a society-wide coarsened conscience.) Here again we observe that the robustness of the rule of law in a political community is a function of the moral robustness of that community and the integrity of its members.

It is instructive to heed the objection that Thomas Reid, Hume's most trenchant critic on this matter, made to Hume's argument. Hume argued that in times of great scarcity, as in circumstances of extreme abundance, justice loses its point. On the contrary, Reid argued, it is precisely in circumstances of extreme scarcity that the spirit of justice must still prevail, although we may have to adjust the means by which we serve justice. Thus, when the need is great and stores of food are limited, responsible persons may legitimately breach the usual rules of property, but they must still follow an orderly and equitable mode of distribution.[11] Similarly, we must argue that, in morally barren circumstances, the point of rule-of-law protections remains; the need for them may be greater than ever.

Another cause of alienation may be that the law itself has failed to take root in the community, or it may provide little opportunity or resources for ordinary people to engage with it and use it in their daily interactions. As we observed in Chapter 3, this is likely when the legal system is weak and incapable of restraining corruption and domination by those in positions of social, economic, or political power, or when ordinary citizens lack the resources make themselves heard. Law may not count in the lives of ordinary citizens, not due to a moral failing in them, but to a failing of the law. The lesson we learn from this failing is not that in such circumstances efforts to build and sustain the rule of law are pointless, but that work is needed to build the legal institutional infrastructure needed to realize its aim.

The preconditions identified thus far do not meet the model of Hume's circumstances of justice, because seeking rule-of-law constraints in these circumstances has not lost its point. Perhaps we can think of other circumstances that more plausibly fit his model. I have argued, for example, that the rule of law is robust only when political elites and large segments of the polity in general take responsibility for holding each other publicly accountable. This implies that, as political theorist Stephen Holmes put it, "an active and even boisterous citizenship is essential for the rule of law." It calls for "a degree of initiative from ordinary citizens beyond willingness to stand in line on election day."[12] One is likely to develop the motivation and courage needed to hold the government to account only in certain cultures. Moreover, there must be public spaces in which persons can interact as autonomous individuals, entitled and encouraged to think for themselves, and motivated when necessary to speak out and challenge those in power. Cass Sunstein reports that, in some cultures, encouraging wide-ranging discussions in heterogeneous groups is often difficult due to obstacles with deep cultural roots. One woman, when asked why she did not contribute to the discussion in her group, replied, "In China, we are taught that to speak out is not beautiful."[13] This reluctance to speak out reflects broad patterns of social stratification, gender-based, as in this case, but often class- or race-based. Authoritarian, strongly hierarchical, or especially vindictive modes of social and political power can intensify pressures to remain silent or deny certain portions of society the means for such activity.

However, we must take some care as we assess this line of thinking about the limits of the rule of law. The "circumstances" in such contexts are "objective" in the sense that they are deeply embedded in the fabric of the society and not merely reflective of individual reluctance, but they are no less "subjective." They define the horizons of the practical lives and deliberation of individual members. It is true that in these circumstances, activities that I have argued are essential to robust rule of law in a polity may be viewed, at least by some members, not as pointless but as unavailable because unthinkable. In other circumstances, social arrangements and practices put an especially high personal price on speaking out; resistance and criticism of those in power is thinkable, but far too costly to move from thought to action. It would be as unreasonable to blame the Chinese woman for her reluctance to speak, as it would be to blame individuals alienated from corrupted and ineffectual legal systems.

Yet there is room for blame, or rather criticism, of the authoritarian social structures, rigid class or racial stratification, radical inequalities of economic and political power, and vicious vindictiveness that encourage and enforce silence. The "circumstances" are not, as in Hume's discussion, due to broad and enduring features of human nature or natural material and environmental conditions. They are due to human social arrangements; arrangements that make it difficult for robust institutions and practices to take root, but not circumstances that make the deep values served by the rule of law normatively irrelevant or out of place. On the contrary, the difficulty of mobilizing the social resources needed for society-wide fidelity is reason to condemn such social relations for their perpetuation of dispiriting forms of human domination. The social structures that make it difficult to maintain robust protections against the arbitrary exercise of power are themselves centers of domination and arbitrary power. The modes of association they represent stand opposed, not orthogonal, to the valued mode of association that I argued in Chapter 4 underwrites the practical force of the rule of law. These political communities are sites of the failure of the rule of law, not alternatives to it.

We can take this argument one step further. I argued in Chapter 3 that equality in the eyes of the law and fidelity are two key principles that lie close to the core of the rule-of-law ideal. If a radically unequal distribution of economic and political power threatens both the principles of the rule of law and the deeper values that underwrite them, then we have reason from within the rule-of-law ideal itself to condemn these inequalities and seek a more equitable distribution, or rather a distribution that does not uphold widespread structures of domination. That is to say, the rule of law has important normative implications for not only the structure, institutions, and practices of law itself but also the distribution of power within society and its economy.[14] The rule of law, I argued in Chapter 5, does not promise a fully just or decent political community. Justice and the rule of law are distinct principles of political morality; nevertheless, their prescriptions for a good and decent society may overlap and reinforce each other. This should not surprise us, since the deeper value that the rule of law serves—membership—while it does not prescribe equality of resources or position, does prescribe social and political arrangements, and a mode of social ordering and association, characterized by mutuality and a place for each member to stand recognized as a peer. Where social and economic conditions undermine the possibility of being equal in the eyes of the law, entitled to access to institutions for recourse against the arbitrary exercise of power, and to participating in networks of mutual accountability, those conditions stand condemned not only by egalitarian principles of justice but by the demanding rule-of-law ideal as well.

Circumstantial Variability

The rule of law may exert normative pressure on us to work to improve circumstances in which it must operate. However, unusual historical circumstances can also shape the demands that the rule of law makes on conduct that seeks to honor it. This is, perhaps, most evident in times of national emergency. Institutions and practices that in ordinary times robustly serve the ends of the rule of law may face special challenges in times of crisis. In times of emergency, war, and severe civil unrest, political leaders chafe under strict legal rules and demanding legal procedures. During the American Civil War, President Abraham Lincoln suspended *habeas corpus*—the constitutional protection of speedy hearings to make public the reason for detaining persons. Similarly, in response to terrorist threats, political leaders find it especially difficult to respect international and national laws prohibiting torture or restrictions on search and seizure.

In times of crisis, government officials tend to see ordinary procedures as threats to speedy and effective government action; after all, many argue, the rule of law is not a suicide pact.[15] Yet, others argue, it is precisely in times of crisis that we most need legal protocols, practices, and procedures to ensure deliberate, responsible, and effective action. In Chapter 12, we will explore these arguments about the scope, force, and limits of the rule of law in times of crisis.

Political conditions can be unstable in another respect that puts recognized rule-of-law principles under strain. A stark example of this is the situation facing the world community and those acting in its behalf after the defeat of Nazi Germany. Robert Jackson, Chief Prosecutor for the Nuremberg war-crimes tribunal, argued that Allied powers must prosecute, condemn, and punish high Nazi officials for war crimes and crimes against humanity. However, in many cases, the actions of the Nazi officials were consistent with laws of the Reich at the time and, some argued, international criminal law at the time was silent regarding them. Yet the principles *nulla crimen sine lege/ nulla poena sine lege* (no crime/no punishment without a law established and promulgated prior to the act) had an honored pedigree as a fundamental principle of criminal justice and exemplar of rule-of-law constraints on ruling power. Jackson argued that prosecution and punishment of Nazi officials was justified on rule-of-law grounds, despite its possible infringement of a fundamental rule-of-law maxim. Against those who demanded swift, summary, and manifest retributive justice, he insisted on following processes prescribed by the rule of law. It was necessary to bring these heinous acts and their perpetrators to legal justice, he argued, ensuring that charges be publicly argued according to the highest standards of due process, as a demonstration of, and foundation for rebuilding, the rule of law in a nation and a world order in which it had been seriously threatened.[16] Trials would "demonstrate . . . the supremacy of law over such lawless and catastrophic forces as war and persecutions . . . and implement the law for the practical task of doing justice to offenders."[17] In his view, we serve the rule of law best by reordering the balance among its realizing principles. While at the time some charged that this was nothing more than "victors justice," many around the world found Jackson's argument compelling.

Nascent democracies in transition from totalitarian rule are sometimes thought to present similar challenges to the rule of law, justifying suspension or outright violation of core demands of the rule of law in hopes of preserving or promoting greater commitment to the ideal and its institutional realization in the long run. Acting strictly in accord with one of its principles may not be the best way to build robust institutions that serve them.[18] If we accept Jackson's argument, we must recognize that events may sometimes pit some rule-of-law principles against other such principles; in specific historical circumstances, the rule of law may limit itself.

This highlights the fact that when the rule of law is realized in particular institutions and practices that properly serve its foundational principles and underlying values, our work is not done. Historical events demand of us responsible and nuanced practical judgment as we live out our commitment to the ideal. It also alerts us to the possibility that the rule of law may have normative limits.

Normative Limits of the Rule of Law

When you listen to defenders of the rule of law—indeed, if you read earlier chapters of this book—you might get the impression that this political ideal is rather full of itself. After all, it insists on law's *sovereignty*, and this sounds worrisomely imperialistic, an unwelcome intruder into every corner of our lives. However, it is time to put this suspicion to rest by admitting that this profoundly important moral-political ideal has its limits. The province of the rule of law is large, but it does not encompass the entire universe of political, social, and personal life and the moral values and principles that we hope are respected there. There are boundaries beyond which rule-of-law concerns may not tread. The rule of law is only one concern of political morality among others. Its place in the web of moral concerns fixes the boundaries of its proper scope.

We can distinguish two kinds of such boundaries. One kind stems from the recognition that there are limits to the proper reach of the law and of the distinctive means by which its sovereignty is secured. Beyond these limits, law and rule-of-law concerns may not go; beyond them, law and demands for public accountability are not only unwelcome but also inappropriate—for example, choosing a career or voting in a presidential election. These are areas in which law, and the rule of law, are *off limits*. The other kind of boundary is more porous. In these areas, rule-of-law demands are not strictly out of place, but competing concerns of political morality override or seriously qualify them. The first we might think of as the normative limits of *law* (and hence of the rule of law); the second limitations of the rule of law's *value*.

Limits of the Rule of Law's Value

We live in a morally pluralist world. People in different cultures and subcultures within them embrace widely differing personal values and comprehensive views of what is good and right. More fundamentally, the universe of the right and the good on which there are such widely differing perspectives is populated by a variety of fundamental values and principles. The moral universe is plural, not just people's views about it.

The rule-of-law ideal has a place in this universe, planted firmly in the yet more fundamental value we called "membership." In this universe we find values like security, freedom, justice, general welfare, and prosperity. Some of them, like membership, are internally complex. Justice, for example, concerns itself with the adequacy and distribution of basic material and social resources (distributive justice), but also with proper grounds for and kinds of punishment (retributive justice), and guarantees of access to goods necessary for a decent life (human rights). It is a matter of some dispute among philosophers whether the coherence of the moral universe requires that there is a fixed ordering of moral values and the principles internal to them, such that some are systematically subordinate to others and that one chief value rules that universe.

The best money, however, is on the view that the moral universe is not structured a priori to eliminate all potential conflicts. Thus, moral agents may face circumstances in which, for example, one rule-of-law principle conflicts with another, or justice and the rule of law conflict, and these agents must find a way responsibly to resolve the conflict. They must exercise responsible deliberative judgment to determine which of the conflicting values or principles takes precedence in the circumstances. In these cases, each of the values may be valid and of serious moral concern, but the demand on action of one of them overrides the competing value.

Typically, we think of this mode of practical deliberation as a matter of "balancing" one value against the others in the very specific circumstances in which the conflict arises, and the outcome is seen as limited to that particular set of circumstances. However, this model does not accurately represent the deliberative process when responsible moral agents engage in it. At least two features complicate this picture. First, it does not acknowledge that the competing values often have a rich texture and the differing textures influence the deliberations. For example, the rule of law is a fundamentally institutional value. It has its normative eye on the long game. It counsels that immediate or short-term gains, in terms of the well-being or rights-protection of individuals, may be difficult to sustain over a longer term. Similarly, it encourages deliberators to consider systemic effects of their decisions, or structural features of their circumstances, which they might overlook if immediate gains and losses are exclusively in view. Such long-game and systemic considerations may not be decisive, but they give shape and direction to what may be difficult deliberations.

Second, some values that we think of as potentially in opposition may be more closely interrelated. They may be interdependent and mutually limiting. This is arguably the case for justice and mercy. These values are distinct; they view offenders through different moral lenses. Nevertheless, one might argue that mercy must not displace justice, nor justice mercy; that, rather, they must work together in some way. Mercy qualifies and perhaps complements justice. It may also complement the rule of law. We will explore this complex relationship in detail in Chapter 11.

We learned in Chapter 5 that the relationships between the rule of law and democracy and between the rule of law and certain fundamental human rights are especially close. The rule of law provides the necessary infrastructure of democracy; as a consequence, activities that violate rule-of-law principles may also pose a serious threat to democracy. Similarly, legal policies and practices that violate or weaken protections of certain fundamental human rights threaten the legitimacy of the law and weaken its support in the community's commitment to the rule of law.

Government officials, and especially judges and lawyers, who bear a special responsibility for respecting and upholding the rule of law, may feel most acutely conflicts that arise between the rule of law and other dimensions of political morality. For example, consider the judge under legal mandate to impose what she holds to be an unjustifiably harsh sentence on a young person convicted of drug possession or a life sentence for a convicted minor. Or consider the prosecutor who comes to believe after long and serious struggle that the criminal justice process is systematically biased against men of color; or the lawyer in apartheid South Africa, who believes that his regular professional activities contributes to the oppression of black South Africans.[19] In such cases, the moral price of maintaining fidelity to law may be very high. The judge, prosecutor, or lawyer may conclude that it is too high, that serving the rule of justice takes precedence over serving the rule of law. The value of the rule of law has its limits.

This may have been the case when, as the American Civil War raged, President Lincoln issued the Emancipation Proclamation (1863) declaring an end to slavery in the Southern states. Lincoln may have believed that he had the legal power to do so as an exercise of his war powers under the Constitution, but this argument was shaky, and, more fundamentally, it completely undid the fragile compromise among the states on which the original Constitution of 1787 was based. Legal scholar Noah Feldman argues that Lincoln's act "broke our Constitution"; Lincoln "consciously . . . violated core elements of that Constitution as they had been understood by nearly all Americans of the time, himself included."[20] Lincoln's deliberations were complex, slow, and agonizing. His commitment to the law was deep, but he also came to see that the compromise Constitution could not be reconciled with the more fundamental principles of freedom and equality embedded in his understanding of democracy and that of the Constitution. To be sure, war-related strategic considerations also must have played a large role in his decision—moral dilemmas do not always have sharp outlines. However, we can imagine that his struggle at its core was a struggle between his commitment to law's rule and a moral imperative to use his power to change the law in a fundamental, but unconstitutional, way to protect enslaved members of his nation. Leaving aside the question of the accuracy of this sketch, Lincoln's dilemma illustrates our point that requirements of honoring the rule of law can conflict in fundamental ways with other important moral values that override them.

In thinking about these limits, we would do well to keep in mind philosopher Simone Weil's good counsel. She acknowledged that in some situations, two genuine obligations are incompatible and we have to sacrifice one of them. Nevertheless, she argued, "even in such a case a crime is committed if the obligation so sacrificed is not merely sacrificed in fact but its existence is denied into the bargain."[21] It is important for us to realize that the moral value of the rule of law remains even when we must sacrifice it for some other important value that, in the circumstances, is morally more compelling.

Yet, viewed in a different light, Lincoln's dilemma illustrates the moral complexity of the rule-of-law ideal itself. A closer look might reveal a way to resolve the conflict while still honoring the core moral concern of the rule of law. On our understanding of the moral foundations of the rule of law and its immediately implied principles, equality in the eyes of the law is an integral component of the ideal. Slavery manifestly violated this core concern for equality. The dilemma, seen in this light, concerned how best to honor the rule of law: by complying with fundamental law that itself fails to respect rule-of-law principles and its moral core, or violating it and taking steps to better orient that law toward this moral core.

In such troubling cases, careful and responsible discernment is of utmost importance. Some argue that lawyers and especially judges are duty bound to defer to the law in all cases and not allow their personal values or policy preferences to override their legal and professional duty, a duty funded by the rule of law itself. However, this analysis is flawed, and the argument distorts the moral situation facing lawyers or judges. True, the rule of law requires that lawyers and judges regard themselves as acting in the name of the community as a whole, and not in their own behalf. But it does not require—it could not require—that they check their moral judgment and the burden of moral responsibility at the courthouse or legal office door. Such conflicts arise between sound principles of public political morality, not personal preferences or scruples—principles that are binding upon the community as a whole, in whose name judges and lawyers must act. Moral agents are not off the hook of moral responsibility when they don the livery of law.

The upshot of these reflections is that, while the normative demands of the rule of law carry great weight, they do not always determine the right thing to do. The rule of law demands that moral agents exercise responsible, prudent judgment. Alongside the virtue of fidelity, the rule of law depends vitally on integrity.[22]

Off Limits

The rule of law, we have often said, looks to the law to protect against the arbitrary exercise of power. The law defines public rules of conduct for officials, associations, and citizens. The rule of law also authorizes and requires us to hold officials and citizens publicly accountable for conduct governed by law. Yet there are significant areas of social and personal life where we regard as unwelcome the intervention of the state through the long arm of the law and regard attempts to hold individuals accountable entirely out of place. Some "arbitrary" decisions are not objectionable, and freedom to make them is desirable. One need not publicly defend one's choice of restaurant for dinner with friends, for example, even less one's choice of hobby, career, employer, or mate, not to mention one's decision to stop cancer treatment. Much of our domestic lives we think is or should be off limits to the law.

So, too, are some economic interactions. The law leaves performance of some provisions of business contracts to the sole and absolute discretion of one of the parties. The law may recognize an implied covenant of good faith and fair dealing in some situations, but in other situations the party may act for any reason or no reason at all.[23] Many employment contracts entitle the employer to change at will the terms of employee benefit packages, and often to hire and fire. Some such activities attract the rule of law's concern, as we noticed in Chapter 2; others arguably may be beyond law's proper control.

In the public domain, prosecutors enjoy wide discretion, and heads of government often have similar discretion in granting pardons. Likewise, in democracies, voters have a civic duty to vote thoughtfully and responsibly, but officials may not demand of any individual citizen a public justification of her vote, and it would be inappropriate for other citizens to call for it. Indeed, law and social norms carefully protect the secrecy of the ballot.

Of course, identifying extreme cases is relatively easy; drawing lines and making decisions in threshold situations is more difficult. Still, we can sketch a framework for drawing some lines and offer a few principles to guide our decisions. To begin, we should ask two related questions. (1) Is deployment of the law necessary or rationally indicated in order to serve the rule of law's core aim, its immediate principles, or principles or norms of the machinery that seek to realize it? And (2) is it appropriate, in light of general principles of political morality, to deploy law to regulate the governmental action or aspect of social or economic life under consideration?

Regarding the first of these questions, we can readily agree that not all arbitrary decisions involve in a critical way the exercise of power over others, or do so in relationships in which the power is significantly unequal or asymmetric. This suggests the *first* principle to guide our decision-making: activities of legitimate rule-of-law concern are those that involve considerable power of one party over others, the relationship is one in which the power is significantly unequal and the stakes of the exercise of this power are high. In these conditions, the structure of unequal power enables the domination of one party by another. However, by this measure, situations involving one's choice of restaurant, career, or mate do not engage the concern of the rule of law. Indeed, since the aim of the rule of law is to protect persons from domination of others, one desired consequence of approximation to this aim is a protected domain of personal self-mastery. The rule of law limits itself, prohibiting the intrusion of law (also perhaps nongovernmental actors) in many aspects of ordinary life.

Where the stakes are high and the asymmetry of power is great, the rule of law legitimately takes an interest. This is especially true of public governmental power. The rule of law's concern is serious enough, we argued in Chapter 3, to justify a manifest asymmetry between its demands on public ruling power and its demands on nonpublic actors. We learned there that the principle of exclusivity holds that exercises of public ruling power are justified only when explicitly authorized by law. For private actors, whatever the law does not prohibit is legally permitted; but the opposite maxim applies to government: whatever is not legally authorized is not permitted. The basic reason for this asymmetry is that governments tend to wield outsized power compared with ordinary citizens, civic associations, and many business entities.

Of course, we find major asymmetries of power in the nonpublic domain as well; and where this is true, the rule of law may legitimately make demands on power wielders. Hence, as I argued in Chapter 2, where the power of employers over their employees is very unequal and the stakes are high, the rule of law may legitimately seek to protect employees from the arbitrary exercise of employer power. The existence of this power may be enough to warrant the scrutiny of law.

Capacity and Costs

This, our first, principle marks out broad areas for the "legitimate concern" of the rule of law, but not (yet) the domain of justified legal intervention. Whether law's intervention is justified requires that we address the second of the questions we distinguished earlier—the question of when intervention is appropriate in view of competing moral concerns. Two kinds of considerations can inhibit our willingness to invite law to constrain activities that meet the criteria of our first principle: the *capacity* of law to provide protection against the arbitrary exercise of this power and the costs, primarily the *moral costs*, of doing so.

The capacity constraint suggests a *second* principle that we must follow to determine the limits of law. It requires that we consider carefully whether the law has tools effectively to protect against exercises of power that fall within the scope of the rule of law's legitimate concern. The law is, after all, a blunt tool.

We can more effectively address with informal means many problems raised by the exercise of power, because the problems require continuous attention and more nuanced judgment than law enforcement officials are equipped to provide. In some cases, this is true of governing the activities of professionals; sometimes self-disciplining within the profession is more effective and efficient. Here again, we need sensitive appreciation of the cultural resources of the community, especially the local community, to work out the scope and limits of the law's intervention.

Others have argued on similar grounds that, in certain circumstances, effective control of the decision-making of government executives is entirely beyond the capacity of law. Situations of national emergency, they say, lie beyond the capacity of law to govern. Law is a matter of norms, and norms assume or presuppose normal situations, but, they say, emergencies are, by definition, outside the normal; they are unique and unprecedented.[24] Moreover, emergencies demand swift, decisive, and unquestioned decision-making. The plodding processes of law cripple it. This argument, I believe, is seriously flawed. We will explore its defects in Chapter 12. Although the argument is flawed, the premise is correct: one limit of the law, from the point of view of the rule of law, lies in the limit of its capacity to provide the protection it promises.

In Chapter 2, we identified two other areas in which major concentrations of power create the possibility of its arbitrary exercise: the domain of international relations and the domain of the internet and so-called Big Data. Some have argued that the rule of law has no role to play in these domains, because *it can't*—it lacks the capacity to constrain the exercise of power in these domains. We will address these challenges in Chapters 13 and 15. In the remainder of this section, we will address the other pressing question regarding the limits of law, and thereby the limits of the rule of law's legitimate concern: the question of the moral costs of such intervention.

We can measure the *moral costs* of legal intervention in different terms. These include rights violated, important interests of individuals or welfare of the community disserved, national security jeopardized, and many others. Because the rule of law is just one value of political morality among others, any attempt to draw a limiting circle around the rule of law's legitimate concern about asymmetric relationships of power will engage careful consideration of the place of the rule of law in this constellation of values. Thus, for example, to determine the extent to which the law may intervene in the relationship between employers and employee on rule-of-law grounds, we must look to general political theory to locate the ground of rights of property, the value and limits of markets in labor, the possibility of fair bargaining among parties, and many other like issues. This is not the place for such exploration, but we can make two general observations about it. First, where the stakes are high and the asymmetry of power is great, the relationship between employers and employees will be an area of the rule of law's legitimate concern. The fact that employers do not exercise public governmental power, that their relationship with their employees is in that sense "private," is not enough to remove it from the scope of the rule of law's concern. Second, the fact that this power falls within this scope does not settle the question of when intervention is justified and when it is off limits.

Although this chapter will not engage in detailed line drawing, we can identify two broad kinds of moral costs that this enterprise must keep in mind: costs of *distortion* and costs of *intrusion*. Regarding costs of distortion, the thought is that introducing law to solve problems does not always improve social-political relations. More law is not always better. In fact, proliferation of law in a political community can distort rather than enhance life in and of the community.[25] Neither liberty, security, nor dignity is enhanced where law governs every aspect of life down to its particular details. Regarding costs of intrusion, it is important to recognize there must be areas of life, relationships, and physical spaces in which individuals need not, or must not, be made answerable to the state or to the larger community. Concerns of privacy and autonomy urge that the law respects and protects domains of self-mastery.

These concerns play out in important ways when we consider asymmetries of power in domestic relationships. Undoubtedly, asymmetries exist between spouses or partners and between parents and children, and stakes can sometimes be very high. Yet close surveillance of these relationships and demands for public accountability for decisions within them are often arguably unjustified; intrusion of the law and even, perhaps, the intrusion of neighbors, are off limits. Even if domination within the relationship is possible, policing the mere possession of unexercised power or power exercised largely in the interests of the relationship and its individual members comes at a high moral cost. Intimacy, love, caring, and long-term commitment give these relationships great personal and social value. Law and public accountability-holding in this domain are not just unwelcome, they can distort and damage the relationship. Thus, we might agree that intervention is justified only after the exercises of power within the relationship reach levels of serious abuse or neglect. Respect for the fragile value of domestic and other interpersonal relationships requires that legal intervention be limited; but a general level of vigilance may also be required because legitimate hierarchies of power can degenerate into illicit domains of domination.[26] Of course, again, where the precise limits are to be drawn is a matter of careful, responsible, and nuanced judgment.

In addition to limits on the legitimate intervention of law in affairs and relationships, there are also limits to fidelity and accountability-holding. We may reasonably wonder whether fidelity opens the door for a tyranny of the scold. Breaking a conspiracy of silence in police ranks is arguably an appropriate exercise of the responsibility, but demanding public justification of a neighbor's vote in a contested election clearly falls beyond the pale of appropriate accountability-holding. Again, drawing lines between appropriate and inappropriate exercise of this responsibility calls for careful and nuanced judgment.

Fidelity provides scaffolding for a valuable mode of association. The rule of law, we learned, is not only a bulwark and bridle but also a bond. However, exercising the responsibility of mutual accountability in some areas of community life, or pursued in some ways, can weaken and even tear asunder that bond, creating a climate of suspicion and distrust rather than one of solidarity and mutual commitment. Too vigorous or too intensely pursued accountability-holding can incur heavy costs of intrusion and distortion. Decency requires that we pay sensitive attention to the time, place, and especially the manner in which a fellow member is called to account. Motivation is also important. Accountability-holding is vulnerable to certain characteristic deformations of motivation. The woman who denounced her husband to Nazi authorities after learning that he was having an affair,[27] is a notorious example. Self-righteous meddling is another. Accountability is an expression of a commitment to that which binds the community together; when people use it for other purposes, especially for purposes that weaken that bond, they exceed its normative limit.

Considerations of mercy, or compassionate grace, as I shall call it in Chapter 11, also limit fidelity. Holding others accountable is an exercise of a certain kind of authority, subject to norms of decent citizenship. Mercy is among these norms. The exercise of this authority must always be "seasoned" with mercy, partly to counter the deformation of motivation to which this informal authority is otherwise prone.

Legal scholar Barak Richman tells a fascinating story of New York City diamond merchants in the last century.[28] Most of the dealers were members of the ultra-Orthodox Jewish community and quite poor; at the same time they handled and traded vast quantities of high-value diamonds. These "diamond-studded paupers" were bound by a strict code of honesty and fair dealing, backed by religious norms and tight relationships of their religious community. Sanctions, imposed by elder merchants, were severe. Yet the elders showed remarkable leniency, motivated by compassion as much as profit, when they sometimes rescued an individual who failed to pay his debts, entering into an agreement with a delinquent trader to allow him to recover and rebuild his reputation. The practice, writes Richman, "reflects the balance between the serious need to deter cheating with the compassionate recognition that individuals have human frailties."[29]

Conclusion

In this chapter, we explored the conditions and limits of the rule of law. We acknowledged that the rule-of-law ideal has its normative limits. Because the rule of law is one value in a constellation of important values of political morality, it is not always possible to serve it fully when doing so may compromise other values. It is possible, for example, that in some circumstances the rule of law must give way to more pressing demands of justice. In addition, sometimes the rule of law is limited because proper reach of the law, the means by which we are protected against the arbitrary exercise of power, is limited. In some contexts law is off limits, its intrusion is too costly.

We also acknowledged that the institutions and practices that realize the rule of law depend for their meaning and efficacy on the specific material, cultural, and legal conditions of those communities. Because these conditions are variable, rule-of-law institutions must be modified to take advantage of distinctive resources and answer the distinctive challenges that this variability offers. The problems posed are problems of institutional translation, as it were. However, sometimes the weakness of rule-of-law institutions lies not in their design, but in the underlying conditions and the appropriate response is to address the conditions rather than adjust the institutions. In such circumstances, the rule of law is not out of place, lacking its point and value, but rather the need for rule-of-law protections remains great, and the task is to build the infrastructure necessary to sustain them. Because of their dependence on background practices and culture, rule-of-law institutions are vulnerable to serious threats.

8

Threats to Law's Rule

We observed in the introduction to this book that the rule of law is currently under grave threat, not only in authoritarian regimes and fledgling democracies but also in established democracies with strong reputations for commitment to the ideal. The recent World Justice Project's annual report referred to in Chapter 1 documents the decay.

This chapter concludes work over seven chapters to articulate and defend a conception of the rule of law, identifying its core aim, fundamental principles, varieties of institutional realization, and circumstantial and normative limits. The task of this chapter is to call attention to salient threats to the rule of law. The aim is not to demonstrate or chronicle current threats to law's rule. We must leave that to journalists, political scientists, and historians. Rather, the task is to identify the *kinds* of threats to which the rule of law is most vulnerable. We will explore the ways that the rule of law can falter and fail, not only falling short of its ideal but also falling away from it. It seeks to identify threats to achieving or maintaining a robust presence of the rule of law in our political communities.

Weakness

We can gather salient threats to the rule of law under three broad heads: weakness, subversion, and erosion. *Subversion* collects threats arising from active efforts of persons, parties, groups, and movements. *Erosion* collects threats due to decay of the ethos that provides the vital lifeblood of the rule of law. We will find that subversion and erosion sometimes interact—erosion of the rule of law's ethos enabling subversion and subversion instigating and hastening erosion. First, however, we will mention briefly a third category of threat, *weakness*, especially weakness of the institutional realization of the rule of law.

There are, of course, many ways that the design of rule-of-law institutions can fall short of what is needed in particular political communities to realize effective constraints on governing power. Two kinds of institutional weakness deserve mention here because they pose serious threats to the viability of the rule of law.

One such weakness is inadequate institutions for policing corruption among political elites and reducing the influence of wealth and economic power in government. Weakness of institutional limits on corruption and the role of wealth

Law's Rule. Gerald J. Postema, Oxford University Press. © Oxford University Press 2022.
DOI: 10.1093/oso/9780190645342.003.0008

in government threatens the viability of constitutional and other legal means of controlling governing power, hollowing them out and turning them into masks on the actual sources and exercises of power.

A second signal weakness is institutional rigidity. Institutional stability is both a condition and a product of robust rule-of-law governance. However, institutions designed for a polity's social, economic, and political circumstances at a particular point in time may fail to do an effective job when local or global conditions change substantially. The vitality of the rule of law in a polity is under threat if its constitution and auxiliary institutions and norms erect especially high barriers to efforts to adjust the legal framework to substantially changed circumstances. Some observers have argued that this is the case in the United States, where its Constitution makes amendment very difficult compared to other mature democracies.[1] Rigidity poses a threat to the rule of law because frustrated reformers may be tempted to achieve their goals through extra-constitutional means. It is, of course, a difficult challenge to design a constitutional system that ensures stability while avoiding rigidity and stagnation that can threaten that very stability.

Weakness may also lie not in a polity's institutions but in its culture. A political community in which law just does not count suffers from this weakness. It is more apparent in the legal profession. H.R. Khanna, Justice of India's Supreme Court, observed that among the marks of decay of the rule of law are "a docile bar and a subservient judiciary."[2] Rule-of-law institutions cannot operate effectively or even long survive where lawyers and judges—essential guardians of the rule of law—are not vigilant and prepared to act when the need for defense of the rule of law arises. Similarly, in modern polities dominated by organized political parties, constitutional checks and balances cannot operate effectively with feckless or unprincipled parties, parties that value party loyalty and long-term dominance over commitment to the rule of law. As one political scientist remarked, "[P]ower corrupts and the prospect of losing power corrupts absolutely."[3] We will say more about these cultural weaknesses when we address the threats arising from erosion. These weaknesses represent especially great threats to the rule of law when they are exploited by political players intent on subversion or combined with other forces of erosion.

Subversion

One major source of such threats lies in efforts actively to subvert or sabotage core institutional checks on the exercise of governing power. Subversion is a many-headed monster, but we must not confuse it with mere violations of law or of institutions and norms serving the rule of law. When it is adequately realized, the rule of law is a homeostatic system. Violations may temporarily disturb the system's equilibrium, but not destroy or greatly weaken it. Adequate accountability mechanisms supply a major equilibrating force. We should measure the strength of the homeostatic system not by the likelihood of violations but by the vitality and resilience of its accountability mechanisms. It is not surprising that power wielders, wishing to be free of law's bridle, will target accountability mechanisms, especially the judiciary and public media. Hungary and Poland, observers argue, have been following this recipe for several years.[4]

Other subversion agents, however, may not be as systematic or methodical. They may simply wish to game the system, exploit its weaknesses for short-term political or personal gain. Their threats arise more from indifference to rule-of-law principles than ideological vision, more from chafing against on this or that bridle on their power than from commitment to a program of wholesale destruction of constitutional checks. Some subversion agents, once encouraged by initial successes of piecemeal subversion, go for larger game. For purposes of charting salient varieties of threats to the rule of law, we should not focus entirely on the hardline systematic saboteurs. Both kinds, the serious saboteurs and the accidental ones, may have devastating effects on the vitality or viability of the rule of law in political communities unlucky enough to have such leaders.

Factors other than the intention of the actors may be more important in determining the scope or seriousness of the threat. These factors include whether the attacks are episodic or persistent, specific or systematic, publicly defiant or quietly dissident. Publicly defiant departures often show contempt for the law and institutions serving the rule of law; they not only cause alarm, but also, if especially brazen, can set an example and encourage violations among others whose commitment to law's rule is shallow or unstable. This is especially true when the defiant violations are persistent and affect a wide range of laws or informal norms.

The choice of targets of subversion also makes a difference. We can isolate two targets for special attention: constitutional *scaffolding* and institutional *soft matter*.[5] The former comprises the formal institutional economy of accountability defined by the constitutional and legal system—the structure of institutions, processes, and procedures that articulate formal checks on power. These, we learned in Chapter 6, include both constitutional-legal government institutions and a variety of structures that empower organizations and associations of civil society to engage in regularly holding power wielders accountable. Rule-of-law soft matter comprises the informal constitutional, intragovernmental and civil-society norms and practices that, as we also learned in Chapter 6, give life and meaning to the formal institutions of accountability.

Scaffolding

"No tyranny is more cruel," wrote Montesquieu, "than the one practiced in the shadow of the laws and under the color of justice—when, so to speak, one proceeds to drown the unfortunate on the very plank by which they had saved themselves."[6] Contemporary leaders, seeking to subvert the rule of law, use subtle means rather than mount frontal assaults on the constitution. Such "stealth authoritarians"[7] aim to degrade the power of significant sources of opposing power, in government and in civil society, by legal or quasi-legal means, turning the law and its guardians against the rule of law and the people that cling to it for protection.

They use the law against the law. "Duly enacted law has become the primary method of [aspiring authoritarians' efforts at] consolidating power."[8] They use times of emergency, like the recent COVID-19 pandemic, to carve out areas in which they can exercise power without legal constraint or systematic accountability (so-called legal "black holes").[9] They introduce changes in the constitution, sometimes by explicit amendment, but more often by weakening the norms and practices on which the constitution rests, thereby hollowing out constitutional constraints on their power. They use criminal and civil law and intragovernment operational regulations to disable or weaken key centers of oppositional power: especially the courts and media, but also internal accountability institutions like inspectors general and ombudsmen offices. They pack courts and accountability offices with loyalists, enlist occupants of government offices and the courts by corruption or co-optation and subject holdouts to "discipline." They also enlist lawyers to weaponize the law. They gain governing power "not with a phalanx of soldiers, but with a phalanx of lawyers,"[10] and use the language of the rule of law to disguise their attacks.

The breakdown of the rule of law in Poland illustrates some of these techniques. Since it came into power in 2015, the Law and Justice Party (PiS) has carried out a sustained assault on Poland's core constitutional institutions, especially the independence of its judiciary.[11] The PiS-dominated Polish government has paralyzed the Constitutional Tribunal and put the National Council of the Judiciary (responsible for making judicial appointments) under Party control, making all its members appointable by Parliament. It also greatly weakened the Supreme Court, purging it of established members and creating a Disciplinary Chamber to muzzle judges and prosecutors. Judges seeking to apply EU law and other constitutional constraints on the Polish government have been threatened with abusive criminal charges and other coercive measures.[12] In January 2020, the Parliamentary Assembly of the Council of Europe voted to open a formal monitoring procedure for Poland, declaring that Poland's recent laws "severely damaged the independence of the judiciary and the rule of law."[13]

Soft Matter

In the words of constitutional scholar Wojciech Sadurski, PiS turned

the law against itself: acting within the literal meaning of the rules or within an apparent legal gap, but disregarding the norms of conduct necessary to accomplish the original purposes for specific legal provision. In other words, even when a particular PiS action was not a breach of the law, textually speaking, it was corroding the norms that are a necessary support for the law if it is to perform its functions.[14]

Subversion of supporting norms, the soft matter of law, was key to the Party's strategy.

Critics of the Trump administration highlighted similar attacks by the president on constitutional soft matter. For example, they called attention to his attack on the independence of the Department of Justice, his firing of inspectors general without cause, his abuse of executive pardon power, his filling of high-level government positions with acting appointees thereby avoiding constitutionally mandated Senate approval, not to mention his defiance of the norm of accepting the results of a presidential election.[15]

The impact of subversion of the soft matter may be subtler and only gradual, compared to outright attacks on the constitutional scaffolding, but it can be devastating if it is not swiftly and publicly challenged. Forceful responses that publicly condemn violations and violators can re-establish the equilibrium of the homeostatic system, especially when those who have special responsibility for accountability-holding respond effectively. However, maintenance of informal norms and resistance to their subversion, while vital to the economy of rule-of-law accountability, nevertheless, calls for subtle judgment and a special kind of vigilance. To understand this subtlety, we must take a short detour to explain the nature of informal norms and the variety of departures from them.

The Nature of Norms

Salient features of social norms include the following.[16] First, constitutional and other informal norms and conventions are normative standards for members of the governing community or the polity more generally; they exist insofar as practiced in that community. They are observable in the norm-responsive conduct and attitudes of members. Norm-responsive behavior includes not only conduct that is compliant with the norm but also conduct widely regarded as deviant, and a range of responses to perceived compliant or deviant conduct, including behavior assessing, affirming, or challenging it. Conventions are not private rules followed by individuals; they are relatively stable nodes in a network of common norm-responsive activity.

Second, general convergence of community conduct around the norm is a critical condition of its existence. Each member counts on most of the others to comply, and their reasons for complying weaken as general compliance appears to slip. Still, members do not merely observe whether others comply; they regard each other as participants in a common practice, so they care about the norm-responsive behavior of other members.

Third, norms are informal, that is, members enact and enforce them rather than formal institutions. However, that does not make them fragile or soft. They can be resilient and resistant to deviations, because their existence and content depend on the responses of the norm community to departures and compliance. Reasonably robust social norms can survive departures, and may even become stronger, as the norm community challenges deviations and holds the violator to account for deviating.

Fourth, conventions tend to be internally connected—they hunt in packs—and their meaning depends on the relationships that exist among norms in the pack. This is especially true for constitutional norms, which exist in a complex network of informal and formal norms, informal practices, and formal institutions. Network dependence can be both a source of strength and resilience and a source of weakness. Departures from norms in the network can have very different effects depending on the nature and circumstances of the departures and the role that the norms play in the network. If a relatively minor norm is violated, and the norm community responds adequately either to contain or to justify it, the equilibrium may not be disturbed at all. If the departure is more serious, but the network is relatively strong, the departure may destabilize the network somewhat but members can restore the equilibrium with only small changes. However, departures from load-bearing norms—especially when repeated frequently, publicly, and with manifest disregard for the values they purport to serve—can have a serious destabilizing effect, on the particular norm and possibly on the network in general.

Finally, informal norms require actors to behave in certain ways; they mark conduct as *to be done*. Norms may be arbitrary in the limited sense that they are path-dependent and could have been otherwise, but they are not necessarily pointless. Their normative force depends a trio of factors: the extent of publicly available compliance with the norm in the practice community, the compelling nature of the values that the norms purport to serve, and the effectiveness of their service to those values. Of course, some norms *are* arbitrary and pointless, or have become so when the circumstances in which they had been useful change. Moreover, some norms are simply morally bad. This may be because the values that they purport to serve are unsupportable, or the collateral moral costs of complying with them are usually too high. Members of the community may still comply with the norms, and they may retain vestigial practical force due to community expectations, but the reasons they offer may be easily defeated.

Some norms may be suboptimal, in the sense that some other norm might better serve their values, but still retain their normative force. Conventions have the distinct virtue of being generally followed: conduct, deliberation, and accountability within the norm community are oriented to them and by them. They retain their normative force, if no better arrangement can secure enough conviction and compliance to do the work of serving adequately their underlying values. Of course, this does not preclude reform of the conventions; and the need for reform may be great. Yet any successful reform effort must get the norm community to coalesce around a new or revised norm.

The effect of departures from norms, then, depends on the seriousness with which participants take responsibility for their practice. In particular, it depends on (1) the extent to which others engage in the deviant conduct, (2) the nature and extent of the responses of other participants, (3) the nature and plausibility to other participants of the claims that deviators make in defense of their conduct, and (4) the values to which participants appeal when holding deviators accountable for their conduct. Departures from norms, even highly public departures, do not themselves subvert the norms or the rule of law they serve. However, once practices are corrupted, violations are harder to address and to repair.

Norm Departures, Norm Challenges, and Responses

Social norms are mortal: they emerge, mature, grow stronger or weaker, change their character or orientation, and may eventually wither away, all in the course of people using them and adjusting them to their social, political, and physical circumstances. Whether conduct is convention-conforming, convention-deviating, or convention-changing depends less on the intentions of actors and more on how that conduct it taken up, less on actors' ambitions and more on the community's response to it. Only some departures represent genuine challenges to the norms. In order better to tailor responsible reactions to departures, we should distinguish several varieties of them.

Three types of deliberate deviations from existing social norms directly challenge the norms: departures that infringe a norm, deviations that seek to reform it, and actions that defiantly flout it. Norm *infringers* depart from the norm, but do not intentionally challenge it; rather, they seek to justify the departure by appeal to a competing but overriding norm or principle. Norm *entrepreneurs* challenge the norm in hopes of reforming or replacing it. Norm *saboteurs* seek to deal a deathblow either to the norm or to the system of which it is a part—I will call them *breakers*. Other saboteurs seek to game the system, turn it to their own purposes, indifferent to the norm's continued existence—I will call them *gamers.*[17] Norm saboteurs of either kind may target only select norms on a largely ad hoc basis, although aspiring autocrats typically attack the framework of constitutional norms wholesale. The entire system chafes them because it seeks to temper their power. They may follow a master plan of sabotage, or their sabotage may be opportunistic, diffuse, and indiscriminate. The different kinds of norm challenges call for different responses from defenders of constitutional norms and the values they serve.

Norm infringers, mindful that their conduct breaches a norm, seek to justify their breach by appeal to concerns that, in their view, override compliance with the norm in the specific circumstances that they face. Since norms rarely command unconditional adherence, the behavior of norm infringers is not likely to threaten the violated norm fundamentally, although it may change the norm community's understanding of its practical force. The norm community, in its quotidian activity of holding co-members accountable, will assess the infringer's challenge. It may ultimately accept or reject it, but it need not reassess the standing, meaning, or scope of the norm.

Norm entrepreneurs pose a different set of challenges. Norms emerge through practice over time; they are rarely created from whole cloth. Some actors may violate a norm in the hope of replacing it with a better model. *Ex iniuria non ius oritur* (right does *not speak*, is not established, through violation of right) is sometimes said to be a principle of international law.[18] Norm entrepreneurs, in effect, rely on its contrary: *ex iniuria ius oritur* (right *speaks* through the violation). Although the violation itself may not change the conventional "*ius*," it may initiate a process of change. The success of the entrepreneur's action depends on the discursive uptake of other members of the norm community. As we have seen, deviant behavior does not itself unravel the convention, let alone usher in a replacement. Whether it does so depends on the response of other members of the community.

How should defenders of the rule of law respond to norm entrepreneurs? Responsible members recognize that existing rule-of-law institutions and the practices that underwrite them are imperfect, often gravely so. Fidelity to the rule of law and its institutions and values does not require uncritical submission to them or automatic sanctioning of perceived violations; rather, it requires critical engagement. Committed to faithful participation in the practices, defenders may reasonably see the entrepreneur's challenge as creating opportunities for renegotiating imperfect constitutional norms.

However, it is difficult to determine in real time when changes are likely to result in genuine reform of imperfect practices and norms. Not every change that appears to be an improvement moves the practice toward its ideal; neither does every apparent movement away from the ideal actually weaken the practice.[19] Fidelity to the rule of law demands of defenders a subtle understanding of the practice, of the value of the rule of law, and of available effective means to serve them. In addition, norm entrepreneurs and their supporters must also be mindful of the need to rally the norm community around an alternative norm that promises to serve these values more faithfully. Undermining an existing norm without a viable alternative in the wings threatens the values entrepreneurs seek ultimately to serve.

Defenders must also recognize that informal norms hunt in packs. Norms work because they work together, and they fail when they work against each other. In some respects, this gives constitutional norms tensile strength; however, conversely, challenges to one such norm can reverberate throughout the system, causing unexpected and potentially unwelcome adjustments. Reform-minded challenges to constitutional norms that fail to give serious attention to replacing them with revised norms can open the door to practices poisonous to the rule of law. The calculus is complex; the constructive project is difficult; both are vital to success of the norm entrepreneur's project.

Norm saboteurs pose the most serious challenge to those who seek to defend the rule of law and the institutions and norms on which it depends. The class of norm saboteurs includes those who engage in what legal scholar Mark Tushnet called "constitutional hardball."[20] They deliberately violate constitutional norms for political advantage. They may defiantly violate norms because they oppose democratic or rule-of-law constraints on their power, or simply because they sense an opportunity to achieve partisan political goals, even if doing so hollows out key democratic institutions. Typically, such saboteurs are gamers, playing the norms for the political advantage they can get out of them, ignoring them when they stand in the way of their goals. They may deploy the rhetoric of democracy or the rule of law, but their behavior reveals no commitment to them.

Norm saboteurs threaten rule-of-law institutions, but they also threaten the broader polity. They not only disrespect constitutional norms, the laws, or constitution they underwrite; they also parade in bright colors their disrespect for members of the immediate norm community. They treat with contempt those who work together to produce and reproduce the infrastructure of democratic constitutional and rule-of-law values. They scoff at the trust the norms enable and express. In this way, they also express contempt for the commitments of the polity in general and contribute to their erosion.

How is a defender to respond to the saboteur's challenge? The stakes in this interaction are often high, because constitutional norms shape democratic processes by which important policies, hence winners and losers, are determined. The temptation to respond to "constitutional hardball" with equally rash, norm-defying measures may be strong. Because constitutional norms are effective and binding only if participants can reasonably expect a degree of mutual compliance, taking the high road come what may will not be a compelling tactic. In their private lives, individuals do not wish to be "cullies of their own integrity," as David Hume put it.[21] Even more so, in the public domain, playing by the rules can look like a sucker's strategy.

Under these circumstances, it is tempting for defenders of constitutional norms to play reactive hardball, arguing that their opponents did it first or worse, and that they mean only to restore a level playing field. These are playground strategies, transparent to opponents and supporters alike, and more likely to escalate the conflict than to motivate saboteurs to reassess soberly their defiance. To play reactive hardball is to play the norm saboteur's game, hastening the saboteur's objective.

The proper questions to ask are not who started the norm violations, or who is the worst offender—that is a game that no one can win—but rather why the norms are important and how to repair or reform them. There is no algorithm to guide resistance against norm saboteurs; however, the following considerations must shape the deliberations of participants in democratic rule-of-law practices.

Two general principles head the list. The guiding star must be fidelity to underlying democratic and rule-of-law values, especially the commitment to constituting and nurturing a community of equals. This requires that defenders resist short-term partisan gains when they threaten to weaken rule-of-law institutions. Tit-for-tat hardball responses may sometimes increase the costs to saboteurs enough to encourage future compliance; however, retaliation is more likely to further erode constitutional norms and weaken public trust in the ability of governmental institutions to live up to its underlying values.

Second, embattled opponents of norm saboteurs must keep in mind the interdependence of informal norms. They should include in the range of their responses attempts to strengthen supporting norms that are not explicitly under attack. Combined with a more general effort to engage opponents in incremental trust-building measures, this strategy may prove an effective democracy- and rule-of-law-sustaining response to opposition hardball.

Subversion may be overt or stealthy, attacking the visible constitution and its institutions or the soft matter of norms and practices of the unwritten constitution. In whatever form, its threat to law's rule is there for many, if not everyone, to see. A less visible, and perhaps more profound, threat lies beneath the surface of political practice in the moral culture of the political community.

Erosion

A strong ethos of fidelity among officials and in the public generally animates and maintains the rule of law in a political community. That ethos is a constituent of, and sustained by, the community's larger moral climate or conscience—its attitudes, practices, and modes of thinking of, relating to, and caring for each other. This environment is vulnerable to erosion; and erosion can, in turn, weaken the foundations of fidelity. Erosion of a community's conscience is another source of threat to law's rule. As Justice Khanna reminded us, a signal mark of rule-of-law decay is "a choked and coarsened conscience."[22]

Coarsened Conscience

Conscience needs education, models, support, correction, and reinforcement. The moral climate of a political community is a kind of commons from which personal conscience must draw. People add to, sustain, or weaken the commons through their activities, interactions, practices, and engagements with other members of the community. The personal conscience and commitments of individuals live and breathe in the moral environment of their political community. When toxins invade that environment from without, or breed within it, conscience is likely to become choked and coarsened.

The moral norms of a community can decay from within through inattention due to indifference or distraction. "Whether conduct counts as unethical [in a community] depends on what conduct is on people's view screens," writes legal scholar Cass Sunstein.[23] As conduct becomes more common, what once met opprobrium comes to seem ethical. Wrongdoing greeted with silence tends to define deviancy down.[24] To maintain its vitality, a community must exercise its conscience by doing, and celebrating doing, the right thing, and by calling out wrongdoing. Apathy generates atrophy.

External forces, also, can initiate erosion or accelerate a process already under way. For example, the corrosive effects of digital technology on our social and political lives are all around us. In Chapter 13, we will discuss the threat to law's rule posed by digital domination. Of present concern, following on our discussion in the previous section, are actions of political leaders that sabotage constitutional norms and broader norms of fairness and decency. The erosion of conscience among leaders and the broader community enables and emboldens deviation, and violations, in turn, accelerate erosion, especially when they are barefaced and unashamed, performed publicly by major public figures. "A petty thief that evades prosecution has virtually no impact on the rule of law, but a CEO that evades prosecution is an advertisement."[25] Leaders who show contempt for ordinary values look attractive to those whose allegiance to them is weak; they offer precedent, permission, and encouragement to engage in similar behavior.

A coarsened conscience may be evident in a community in three dimensions that bear on the vitality of the rule of law's ethos: the shallow depth of its convictions, the narrow horizon of its concern, and the corruption of its public discourse.

Shallow Convictions

Public conscience is choked when individuals and groups, whether officials, parties, or movements are heedless of or indifferent to the long-range consequences of their actions, especially when they use or abuse law, institutions, or norms to game the system for short-term personal or political gain. This attitude signals a deeper corruption: the lack of a sense of responsibility to and for the values that law and the community's norms serve. Gamers regard law as either an arbitrary imposition or a resource they can manipulate; compliance is for those who are not smart enough to make law work for them or too weak to resist its demands. To gamers, concern for fairness is a sign of weakness, and self-restraint born of mutual respect is a sucker's strategy. Indifferent to the law, they are indifferent to the damage that their actions may bring to the values it serves.

Law, of course, is not self-justifying, and informal norms may go badly wrong. Sometimes other demands of political morality overshadow the demands of law and call into question allegiance to conventional scruples. However, those who conscientiously challenge the law, or infringe norms, acknowledge that law counts, and that the values it, perhaps imperfectly, serves should be honored even when the law is disobeyed or important norms are compromised. Gamers lack such commitments. Their convictions are shallow. The likely long-term effect of their actions, unlike the actions of those who seek to reform the law or temporarily infringe governing norms, is to sever law and norms from the values they aspire to serve.

Paradoxically, the ultimate danger of the erosion of this dimension of conscience is not anarchy but autocracy. Incapable of attachment to values deeper than personal gain or narrow party loyalty, they retain the ability to attach to salient leaders, especially when those leaders also manifest contempt for law and the norms on which it rests. Commitment to a framework of reciprocal, multi-leveled obligations that are owed to each other is transformed into unidimensional loyalty to the leader. It is not surprising, then, that aspiring autocrats are the ultimate gamers.

Narrow Horizons of Concern

Conscience with shallow roots is a major source of threat to the rule of law, especially when the toxin spreads through the polity. A second source lies in the narrowing of people's horizon of mutual concern. Where solidarity is weak or limited to one's circle or tribe, fidelity cannot thrive. This coarsening is evident in the disheartening difficulties that local authorities in many countries have faced when trying to mobilize an effective community response to the COVID-19 pandemic. On the streets and in the public buildings of cities and towns around the United States, the desire to go without a face covering took shape in the minds of many as a fight for a fundamental individual right, and any attempt to infringe upon that right was seen as reason to man the barricades in full out revolt. One might be inclined to regard this as typical American rugged individualism run amok, egged on by politicians who sought to gain from the movement. However, I think it signals a deeper lack: an inability of people to entertain, or even conceive of, the possibility of a challenge that is common and that calls for common, collective effort. Indeed, even simply representing something as a common concern generates unqualified distrust and hostility.

The inability to conceive let alone sustain common purpose also entails an inability to recognize mutual obligations. People find it hard to conceive of obligations that arise from interdependence and common needs and that we owe to each other. When this toxin invades a political community, the idea that honoring a common bond expresses respect for each other and recognition of common membership is unavailable. This represents a serious threat to the rule of law because the ethos of fidelity leans heavily on the capacity to recognize common needs and commitment to honor mutual obligations.

Corruption of Public Discourse

Nowhere in contemporary society is the coarsening of public conscience more evident than in the domain of public discourse. Presidential adviser Kellyanne Conway, defended then President Trump's notorious public mendacity, saying, "People realize that no one on TV is under oath."[26] What does it say about public discourse when people believe that speaking truly is optional unless one faces a prison sentence for lying? Of course, misinformation, spinning the facts, and ordinary lies are commonplace in politics. In the past, active, aware, and critical citizens, with the help of a responsible press, were usually able to recognize spinners and sellers of snake oil, and to separate the lies from underlying realities distorted by them. However, recent technological and political developments have made this task far more difficult. Big media platforms reward rage and sensationalism and relegate rational assessments to positions far down the page. Likes not logic, emotion rather than evidence, determine the spread of opinions.

The Power of Power Lies

In addition, some leaders in word and deed express utter distain for responsible discourse and some of their lies have become legendary. The Big Lie is a political tool known to practitioners and theorists of politics from its earliest days. In Plato's *Republic*, the lie may have had "noble" motivations, but lie it was.[27]

However, in recent years we have seen the perfection of what journalist Masha Gessen called the "power lie." The political Big Lie was big, but not brazen; its effectiveness depended on the fact that its departure from reality was not immediately obvious to the public. However, those who deal in power lies defy the reality staring them and their hearers in the face. The power lie, Gessen writes, "is the lie of the bigger kid who took your hat and is wearing it—while denying that he took it. . . . [T]he point of the lie is to assert power." It not only creates "alternative facts" in front of one's eyes, but it forces hearers to "choose between your experience and the bully's demands."[28]

Ordinary lies are politically destructive; they loosen the ground beneath trust in government and each other. Brazen lies, especially lies of a powerful leader that revel in liberation from the bondage of truth, in turn liberate others and enable them to reap the benefits. Such lying, in addition, shakes the foundations of public accountability, freeing those who exercise power from scrutiny by painting all challenges appealing to shared reality as partisan "fakes." The power lie, by conjuring its grim myths, threatens to drive all appeals to a self- or group-transcending reality into the realm of myth, liberating those who exercise power from accountability. Lying on the scale of power lies poses a fundamental threat to law's rule.

Moreover, such mendacity expresses contempt for those who take their epistemic responsibilities seriously, and it delights in domination of its hearers—a domination that is no less damnable for its warm welcome by the faithful. Indeed, it invites hearers to abandon personal responsibility for their convictions and transfer loyalty to the liar. The emergence of mendacity on this scale threatens not only the integrity of the process of public deliberation but also the integrity of citizens themselves. In the midst of World War II, French philosopher and activist Simone Weil wrote, "[T]he need for truth . . . calls for protection against error and lies . . . [and] public health measures against poisons in the domain of thought."[29] The poison is no less destructive of the public domain, calling for even more vigorous moral public health measures. "The steady degradation of the public sphere" represents one of the most serious threats to the rule of law.[30]

Shrinking Public Space

The 2021 Rule of Law Report of the European Commission wrote, "An enabling framework for civil society allows for debate and scrutiny of those in power; and when their space to operate shrinks, it is a sign that the rule of law is at risk."[31] The degradation of public discourse stems not only from disinformation and power lies but also from the shrinkage of public space, of public *place* and public *practice*.

Public discourse, the essential medium of accountability, needs a public place. Public place is not merely the physical plot in which it occurs, but a necessary condition of its occurring and vitality. In it, we share information and join argument. Even more fundamentally, in public places people, regardless of assigned identities—"of every walk of life," we used to say—*encounter* each other and experience together, if only for a few moments, their immediate environment, its beauties and pleasures, its odors and inconveniences. There they exchange greetings, nod in recognition, and share a passing observation. This is the rich, loamy soil of public life—of the life of a public—in which seeds of a generalized trust, or at least absence of distrust, can grow, a willingness to engage with people not intimately known to us. (See Chapter 10 for a discussion of modes of social trust and distrust.) Where this space and place are not available to individual citizens, it is very difficult for openness to engagement to take root, for such trust is *inter*personal even when it is not intimately *personal*. It is interpersonal in the sense that it can take place only when the trustor recognizes, or is willing to bet on, the trust responsiveness of another. That takes a kind of sense, or sensitivity (Hume called it "sympathy"), that is distinctively inter*personal*, engaging persons even when they are not intimates.

In this soil, more carefully cultivated exchanges of views, arguments, deliberations, and debates can take root. Public discourse is encouraged and nourished where there is place for extra-partisan engagement, where people with different needs, interests, and aspirations, different stories and frames of reference, share a common physical and social environment. Participation in this space must be protected formally by law and informally by mutual commitments. Participants must be protected against assault on their status as equals, but not from challenge, discomfort, or disagreement. Where public spaces of this kind are rare, it will be difficult for the ethos of fidelity to take root; where they are shrinking, it will be difficult for it to thrive.

Public place is not enough. Public discourse flourishes when members of the political community have acquired to some degree the dispositions and discipline of its *practice*. Among the necessary dispositions are an openness to encounter others and a willingness to engage with them and a willingness to pay due attention to others, when the aim is not to agree on a principle or a program, nor to settle disputes, but rather to heed and hearken to each other, to deepen understanding and pave the way for recognition of common problems and challenges—also, a willingness to bear the burdens of conviction.

The Burdens of Conviction

> From the place where we are right
> flowers will never grow
> in the spring.

> The place where we are right
> is hard and trampled
> like a yard.[32]

So writes Israeli poet Yehudi Amichai. This hard and trampled place is the place of conviction springing from a sense of comfortable certainty. No new or challenging seed can penetrate its rock-hard surface; from it no new life or growth can spring. However, the problem lies not in the convictions themselves, but in the irresponsible manner in which they are held. A deep threat to law's rule lies in a widespread unwillingness to shoulder the burdens of conviction.

In *On Liberty*, John Stuart Mill wrote eloquently of these burdens.[33] Opinions and judgments, he argued, are not private possessions; they have an unavoidable public dimension. A sense of certainty nurtured in one's private self is not sufficient; on the contrary, it reveals a hubristic assumption of infallibility. Human beings are worthy of respect as intellectual and moral beings because "[their] errors are corrigible," that is, human beings "are capable of rectifying [their] mistakes, by discussion and experience." Experience alone is not enough, he argued; discussion is also necessary. Through discussion with others, one can interpret and test experience and consider contrary experience and arguments. For beings "with human faculties" and frailties, the only basis for "any rational assurance of being right," the only possible "approach to knowing," is submission to challenge from others, seeking "for objections and difficulties, instead of avoiding them . . . and [shutting] out no light which can be thrown upon the subject from any quarter." "The beliefs which we have most warrant for have no safeguard to rest on, but a standing invitation to the whole world to prove them unfounded." Only thus, he argued, does truth have a chance of reaching us. This warranted assurance stems from a steady habit of issuing a standing invitation to the world to assess one's judgments, thus "hearing what can be said about [them] by persons of every variety of opinion and studying all modes in which it can be looked at by every character of mind." Mill's wise counsel deserves elaboration.

Convictions regarding matters of empirical fact or normative principle necessarily point beyond themselves and their possessors to a potentially common or public world. Convictions are more than mere thoughts entertained in the mind or utterances made in the presence of others. If we expect others to take our thoughts seriously and use them as grounds for our actions, we must accept two responsibilities. One is the burden of *commitment*. Commitment points beyond the person who holds them to reasons, evidence, or grounds that warrant her holding it. "Because I say so" (or "because it is *mine (ours)*") is never a sufficient warrant for opinions held as convictions. Convictions point beyond the holder's sincerity and sense of "certainty," and rest on matters accessible and assessable by others. The second burden is responsibility to recognize the *corrigibility* of convictions and the *standing of others* to assess them. This requires openness to evidence and reasons that may contradict or challenge the reasons we take to warrant our convictions, and openness to assessment of those reasons by others. Sometimes people say that the *facts* or *truth* binds us, but this is not literally correct. Facts (and principles) bind us just in the sense that *others* hold us accountable to a reality that transcends our private reality. Moreover, pressing our opinions on others with nothing more than sincerity to warrant them is groundless exceptionalism, a loyalty to self. It is often a barely disguised exercise of power.

Thus, the burdens of conviction entail obligations: (1) to locate the ground of the conviction in considerations that transcend the self and are potentially accessible to others; (2) to accept the entitlement of others to assess the adequacy of those considerations to ground the conviction uttered; and (3) to participate in a process by which one's convictions, but also the assertions, judgments, and convictions of others, are considered, weighed, perhaps debated. This is not a matter of subjugation to an external authority, because the obligations entailed by conviction are mutual and balanced. The source of the convictions in the commitment of the speaker obligates hearers to respect the speaker by focusing their responses on the self-transcending grounds said to warrant the convictions. Rules of mutual accountability define the process of deliberation.

The process to which convictions are oriented is public in several respects. It ordinarily takes place in the presence of others, and it regards considerations that are reasonably taken to be (at least potentially) accessible to them; the process is interactive, a process of asking for, exchanging, and assessing reasons. Also, as Mill's sketch made clear, the scope of the relevant "public" is not rigidly limited; in principle, "persons of every variety of opinion and . . . every character of mind" are legitimate members, provided, of course, that they also accept the burdens of conviction. In practice, this implies that we must make an honest effort to enlist participation from beyond one's circle and that any practical boundary of the relevant public is itself corrigible, vulnerable to challenge.

Public discourse flourishes when participants accept these burdens of conviction. Where they do not, public discourse is destabilized, accountability is enfeebled, and law cannot rule effectively.

In sum, law's rule is threatened in a political community when its institutions are weak and rigid, unable to respond flexibly to changes in domestic and global circumstances; when political actors seek to subvert the formal institutions that realize the rule of law or the norms and practices that animate them; when responses to attempts at subversion lack vigor and conviction; and when the moral culture in which the ethos of fidelity thrives is corrupted and public spaces in which accountability can flourish shrink. However, these threats need not succeed; threats can be addressed, attempts at subversion can be answered, public spaces can be restored, and even erosion of a nation's moral culture can be reversed. Ultimately, the rule of law thrives in a polity when its members, committed to it and the vision of community that it serves, are, in the words of Adam Ferguson, "determined, by their vigilance and spirit, to make these terms be observed."[34]

PART I: CONCLUSION

Part I of this work is likely to leave careful readers uncomfortable. It defends a bold thesis: law alone must rule; yet the rule of law is subject to limits and conditions. The rule of law is not the sole or sovereign political value; neither does it demand that law is ubiquitous in the life of a political community. However, even limited in this way, doesn't the rule of law claim too much? It promises protection and recourse against wayward power. Can it possibly perform as promised? Isn't it just out of its element in the international domain and doesn't it lead to national suicide in times of emergency? Doesn't it prevent us from achieving a decent mode of governance by obstructing the exercise of discretion needed for mercy and equitable judgment? Is there not a risk that fidelity, the rule of law's underwriting ethos of community-wide mutual accountability, actually will drive out the very trust on which decent and just governance fundamentally relies?

The conception of the rule of law articulated and defended in these chapters faces serious challenges, which, if they succeed, would drive the ideal, its bold colors muted, into a small and tidy corner of political morality. The aim of the chapters of Part II is to show why these challenges do not succeed.

PART II
CHALLENGES

9

A Dialectic of Deference and Dissent

Law is sovereign—this is the bold thesis defended in Part I. This chapter begins an effort in this second part to answer a series of serious challenges to this bold thesis. Perhaps the most salient such challenge is implicit in the recitation of facts opening the previous chapter. There we observed the marked decline of the rule of law in many countries around the world and learned of concerted efforts, by ruling authorities and rogue bands of citizens, to defy and subvert the law. The rule of law condemns subversion and defiance of law. Yet the rule of law relies on robust practices of accountability; it encourages protest, resistance, whistle-blowing, even defiance of those who illegitimately speak in the name of law. It appears, then, that fidelity is on a collision course with finality.

Fidelity demands that *law alone* is the final arbiter, not the understanding of any individual, official, or institution. "The ultimate touchstone of constitutionality," Justice Frankfurter insisted, "is the Constitution itself and not what we have said about it."[1] Law rules in and through the practical reasoning of officials and citizens, but the meaning and force of law is often contested. Thus, inevitably, what the *law says* is always what some person or institutional *spokesperson says* it says. We always receive law in translation, as it were. But, if univocal law is to rule, and not any (or every) person, there must be some one person or institution that speaks law authoritatively and uniquely. Put it another way. Law vests legitimate governing power in individuals, and defines and authorizes institutions and modes of exercising this power, but, then, it seems that law can rule only if legal subjects regard as final the directives of legally authorized individuals and the institutions through which they work.

If that is the case, then finality displaces fidelity: fidelity insists on accountability, but finality evades it. However, if accountability-holding involves active challenge, dissent, and even protest, refusing to accept as final the decisions of legal authorities, then the challengers have the last word. The mantle of finality falls on their shoulders. Everyone is a judge in his own eyes. Fidelity drives out finality. The rule-of-law snake eats its tail.

This antinomy threatens to undermine the intelligibility of the ideal of law's sovereignty. We cannot proceed with our discussion of the variety of challenges facing our conception of the rule of law until we answer this pressing challenge. This chapter will not explain away the tension between finality and fidelity by rejecting one or the other. Rather it will seek to manage the delicate dialectic

Law's Rule. Gerald J. Postema, Oxford University Press. © Oxford University Press 2022.
DOI: 10.1093/oso/9780190645342.003.0009

between them—more precisely, between deference and dissent—that lies at the heart of the rule of law.

We begin our answer to this challenge by filing some of the sharp edges off the opposing positions we have just considered.

Finality is the idea that political order and constraint of political power are possible only if law is settled, and it is commonly thought that law can be settled only if some person or institution has final say about the law. However, a reasonable doctrine of finality allows appeals to and challenges to authoritative decisions. It recognizes the value of a hierarchical structure of decision-making, and insists that challenges go through a regulated hierarchical process and that they must stop with the decisions made at the apex of the hierarchy. Legal scholars Henry Hart and Albert Sacks, for example, argued that "decisions which are the duly arrived at result of duly established procedures . . . ought to be accepted as binding upon the whole society unless and until they are duly changed."[2] Authority at the apex of a hierarchy settles two things: what *the law says* and what *we should do* given what the authority says that the law says.

Fidelity also recognizes complexity. Law fails to rule, we have argued, if those who speak for the law—or, rather, speak *the law*—escape accountability, but it also fails if everyone is a judge in his or her own eyes. For then we have simply shifted unaccountability from the One to the Many. Fidelity recognizes that law is an *institutionalized* discipline of public practical reasoning. That is, the norms of law have meaning and force because they are embedded in a disciplined practice of practical reasoning, and that practice is realized in a complex web of institutions. Thus, fidelity tethers accountability to substantive rules and principles of law, and to its institutional structures and processes. Fidelity informs our inquiries concerning what law says and what we may or must do when those in power speak in the name of law.

These considerations do not eliminate the tension between finality and fidelity, but they give it a sharper focus and bring two key questions clearly into view: Who says? and So what? The first recognizes that we always receive the law in translation, through what someone says the law says. The second recognizes that law acts through those who act in its name. The first concerns where responsibility for saying what the law says should lie; the second concerns how others should act with respect to those who speak and act in its name. The dialectic between deference and dissent pervades answers to each of these questions.

Who Says?

The law guides, directs, constrains, and enables through its role in the deliberations of those who are its subjects, including those who speak and act in its name. Inevitably, law is contested, so the sometimes impertinent question, who says? becomes pertinent and pressing. At the same time, our commitment to law's sovereignty rules out certain answers to the question. No person, party, or institution can say beyond all challenge what the law is. We can never mean by "settling" the law that someone's saying it *makes it so*. Furthermore, in view of the essentially discursive character of law, the authority of a claim regarding what the law says rests entirely on the weight of the reasons, evidence, and arguments that can be marshaled in its favor; and these reasons and arguments are always open in principle to further assessment. We can only establish the truth of a claim discursively, by further argument. It is never a matter of someone's saying so.

However, we must balance that fact with the fact that the law allocates power to decide the law to certain institutions and their incumbents. We must weigh claims made by authorized deciders in light of their *competence* and their *credentials*. Through training and experience in law's discipline of reasoning, certain persons acquire competence that gives epistemic authority to their determinations. Further, the law structures their deliberations and decision-making with procedures that focus their attention on the reasons, evidence, and arguments that fix the law. If these institutions and procedures follow rule-of-law principles, they select persons who have acquired competence in the law through training and experience, who are committed to law's rule, and who enjoy protections to some degree from influences outside the law.

Thus, in determining what the law says—what it requires of us, or permits us or enables us to do—we must give full consideration to the weight of the law's reasons and arguments, as we best can judge them. In addition, we must give due weight to the competence and credentials of those to whom the law has allocated decision-making power. However, to give their decision-making authority due weight does not require that we simply give in. No decisions settled by authority of the decider are absolutely beyond all dispute; all decisions are in principle corrigible and settled matters are vulnerable to being unsettled. These considerations instruct the dialectic of deference and dissent at work in the task of determining what the law says.

Critics argue that the institutional arrangement in which the courts, culminating in decisions of a single supreme court, are final arbiters of what the law says ("judicial supremacy") amounts to rule by judges, rather than rule of law. They advocate, instead, some version of "departmentalism," according to which each major branch of government is assigned coequal interpretive authority.[3] On this model, officials in each department are entitled to act on their own reading of the law and constitution. However, from the point of view of the rule of law, this model is no improvement over rule by judges, since it entitles each branch to proceed as judges in their own eyes, unaccountable to any other. Interpretive authority is scattered.

The rule of law seeks a middle way, in which the branches share responsibility for interpretation of the law. A partnership arrangement distinguishes and co-ordinates roles and defines the kinds and scope of mutual deference. Principles of deference mark out lines of respect for institutional competence and constitutional credentials. In this view, when it comes to matters of constructing the meaning and application of constitutional provisions and legislation, courts are due wide (but not absolute) deference. The reasons for this deference are clear: the judiciary is specially trained and experienced in the discipline of law; the appeal structure provides multiple opportunities for hearing and rehearing controversial issues; and court procedures favor publicity of deliberation and public articulation of reasons for decision. Yet such competence does not extend, for example, to assessments of the wisdom, justice, or political support for matters of public policy. In well-designed constitutions, the distinctive roles and functions of the various branches of government are determined in part according to competence and related considerations. For example, the legislature in a democratic polity is likely to reflect better the will of the people than an unelected court. Similarly, courts are better equipped to identify and articulate the legal and constitutional boundaries of the power of the other branches, rather than leaving the matter for each branch to determine for itself.

Finally, in a system of shared but differentiated interpretive authority, "settlement" is not a matter of saying making it so, but rather a product of collaboration over time, a matter of achieving a deliberative equilibrium. A competent branch may temporarily settle contested issues by decision, but opportunities for reconsidering it and upsetting the settled result must be available. Constitutional scholars who favor some form of shared interpretive authority sometimes talk of "dialogue" among the interpretation partners.[4] However, this pitches expectations for departmental interactions rather too high.[5] We might more reasonably hope for iterative and discursively responsive interaction and settlement over time.

Several democracies in the West have tried various means of structuring shared responsibility for constitutional interpretation among branches of government.[6] Consider a few examples, focusing on assessment of the constitutionality of legislation. First, consider arrangements for assessment of legislation before enactment. Several countries assign responsibility for assessing draft legislation to sub-branches of the executive branch or the legislature or independent (or quasi-independent) chancellors of justice. For example, in the Netherlands, the law prohibits courts from striking down legislation on constitutional grounds (although they can review legislation for conformity with human rights treaties).[7] The quasi-independent *Raad van Staat* advises on all legislation. When it raises serious objections to proposed legislation, the government must debate the bill within the Council of Ministers and respond to the objections of the *Raad van Staat* in notes accompanying the bill sent to Parliament.[8]

One can find several different models of postenactment constitutional review of legislation in constitutional systems around the world. In some systems, nonjudicial bodies play a key role. However, most arrangements for postenactment review involve the courts. They do so in a variety of ways.[9] Some courts follow an interpretive principle of presumption. They presume that parliament intended the legislation to be compatible with the constitution and stretch the legislation's language to fit this presumption. Parliament has the power to enact legislation that makes its will clearer, even if that is inconsistent with the constitution as the courts read it. Other courts have power to declare the legislation incompatible with the constitution, but cannot invalidate it (so-called "weak review"). Others can invalidate legislation, but suspend this effect to give the legislature time to respond. This leaves it open to the legislature to correct the offending legislation or reinstate it notwithstanding the court's declaration.[10]

None of these models fully institutionalizes the aim of shared responsibility, but they approximate it to varying degrees. In them, deference plays a role, but so does something like dissent. For example, if one of the partners in this shared-responsibility arrangement judges that the weight of reasons and argument and considerations of competence and credentials of decision makers compels the conclusion that the temporarily settled decision must be challenged, it may make its challenge known in whatever way the institutions enable.

In the United States, many constitutional scholars agree that the Constitution assigns ultimate interpretative responsibility exclusively to the courts. But even in this "strong review" arrangement, modifications that move toward wider sharing responsibility within the judiciary are possible. In the recent debate over court reform, some American constitutional scholars have proposed a sweeping rearrangement of the personnel and duties of the federal judiciary.[11] According to this scheme, the Supreme Court would sit in panels of nine justices selected at random from the ranks of the (850) judges in the federal court system. No panel would have more than five justices from a single party. Each panel would sit for a limited period (a few weeks or months), after which the judges would return to their lower court assignments; the sitting panel would select cases for future panels. As is currently the case, judges would be nominated and confirmed by elected officials, but would have life tenure and so would be protected from undue external influence. A code of ethics and mechanisms for enforcement of the code would apply to all judges.

With respect to the operation of the Court, this reform would decrease the ideological partisanship of each decision and remove the opportunity and incentive for individual judges to develop personal ideological agendas over a lifetime tenure.[12] It also would greatly reduce the potential of the Court establishing, by a single vote margin, highly contested decisions that are then difficult to challenge. The system would motivate judges to work in common to maintain the coherence and integrity of the law over time. Since new justices would cycle on and off the Court frequently, later panels would have opportunities to challenge, reformulate, limit, or overturn previous decisions. This would force judges to cast their decisions and rationales for them in terms that could command support from their colleagues in the wider judiciary. No single decision would enjoy absolute finality, although the panels would still honor the principle of *res judicata*. It is likely that decisions would settle into strong precedent over time, gradually gaining strength, through the collective efforts of the judiciary. This arrangement still approximates rule by judiciary, but takes a decisive step away from rule by individual judges (or a small number of them, appointed for life). Its rule-of-law credentials would be enhanced further if the independence of the judiciary from political pressures coming from the executive and legislative branches is secured by the legal profession, and especially its judicial branch, holding its members to high professional and rule-of-law standards.

This is not the place to debate the individual merits of these proposals. They are offered here to illustrate what constitutional arrangements of shared interpretive authority might look like and to spur further thinking about how we might give institutional shape to the dialectic between deference and disagreement or dissent.

So What?

Law's rule is robust in a political community, we have argued, only when there is a robust, community-wide network of mechanisms and practices of accountability. Accountability involves not only making and publicly expressing judgments that disagree with the decisions of authorities but also demanding the authorities' reasons for their decisions and actions, assessing those reasons, and acting on those assessments. Accountability-holding sometimes takes the form of protest, resistance, or even defiance of authorities. Even more than the question, who says?, the tension between finality and fidelity forces us to face the question, so what? When does the accountability on which robust rule of law depends fundamentally call for actions contrary to the orders of authorities? We cannot be happy with the answer that we must always obey authorities even when wrong; but neither can we be entirely happy with the answer that dissent and defiance are required whenever, in one's judgment, the authorities are wrong. Law's rule can be effective only when there is wide scope for accountability and, consequently, room for civil dissent; but even dissent that claims legal warrant can threaten the rule of law. Unconditional deference to authorities would eviscerate fidelity; unlimited protest would undermine the protection that the rule of law promises. Again, this question entangles us in the dialectic between deference and dissent.

Because this issue is complex, we will proceed carefully, keeping several important distinctions in view. First, we should distinguish two groups of dissenters, because the actions available to them and the rules that apply to them are likely to be different. One group includes *officials*. Their dissenting actions may involve, for example, noncompliance with the orders of their superiors or other government departments, or leaking information that other officials would like to keep under wraps. The other group includes *nongovernment actors*, including individuals and organizations of civil society.

Second, we must distinguish civil dissent from the more familiar form of protest, civil disobedience. *Civil disobedience* involves violation of law in an effort to bring some wrong or injustice to public attention. *Civil dissent* is law-focused protest or resistance. Its aim is to hold officials accountable to the law, acting in name of the law, not against it. Such accountability-holding protest may involve defiance of the orders of the authorities, as a way of challenging their actions or decisions, or their claims to act with legal warrant. Civil dissenters act on their judgment that the authorities got the law wrong. Inevitably, conscientious civil dissent pits the officials' view of the law with that of dissenters.

Civilian Resistance

One more distinction. With respect to the activities of civilians, dissent may follow regular channels or move outside such channels. *Regular channels* include, for example, the courts, offices of ombudsmen, public meetings confronting elected officials, and various uses of public media. As we have seen in previous chapters, protests and challenges made through these regular channels are major weapons in the rule of law's accountability arsenal. To authoritarian (or authoritarian-leaning) governments, they represent threats and are major targets of government attempts to disable checks on their power. If the rule of law is to be robust in a political community, its law must provide and protect wide civilian access to these channels. Moreover, civilians' rights to participate without penalty must not depend on the correctness of their views of the law. The authorities bear the onus of demonstrating good faith and sound warrant for their activities.

The potentially more controversial channels of protest are *irregular*, among them defiance, demonstration, and disruption. Even in the best-case scenario, where there is a robust array of regular channels for civil dissent, the rule of law recognizes the legitimacy of some modes of irregular dissent. This is because regular channels are expensive, available only to those with resources to make use of them, and usually limited to individuals or small groups. Irregular modes of dissent engage a wider public that can give voice to collective grievances. They make public the necessary involvement of the community in the continuing task of demanding accountability of those who exercise governing power. In less than ideal conditions, where regular channels are few, weak, compromised, or unavailable to wide sectors of the community, irregular channels may be the only means for achieving some degree of accountability of government power wielders.

Defiance

Recall our discussion in Chapter 2 of Mrs. Marsh's challenge to the town regulation that prohibited solicitation without a permit. Authorities of Chickasaw, Alabama, denied her request for a permit to distribute religious literature in front of the town's post office. She refused to comply, defied the town's order, and was arrested and convicted of the crime of remaining on premises after she was ordered to leave. Mrs. Marsh challenged the town's regulation and her conviction, arguing that they violated her constitutional rights to freedom of religion and freedom of expression. The state of Alabama supported the town's prohibition and its action against Mrs. Marsh. The case eventually went to the US Supreme Court.[13] The state argued that the corporate owner of the town had a right to control the inhabitants of Chickasaw just as homeowners are entitled to regulate guests on their property. Mrs. Marsh challenged that argument, and the Court agreed with her. It argued that since Chickasaw performed the functions of a municipality and the corporation took on the role of government, it was subject to constitutional limits on the exercise of governmental power.

Mrs. Marsh's defiance of the orders of town authorities initiated a challenge to its exercise of power that was ultimately successful. Town officials were duly authorized agents of government, but their orders lacked legal warrant and, on that ground, Mrs. Marsh defied them. When the Supreme Court affirmed her challenge, it vacated her conviction for defying the order. In effect, the Court recognized the act as legally innocent. This is in accord with the rule of law; it recognizes that there are limits to required deference to the orders of authorities. This thought is familiar. Even the military recognizes such limits. Soldiers are obligated to refuse to obey manifestly illegal orders. Mrs. Marsh refused to comply with the orders of town officials; she did not refuse to obey the law. Her defiance challenged the legal standing of the order, not its morality or justice. Defiance of authorities is not necessarily disobedience of the law.

The rule of law allocates different responsibilities to dissenters and authorities regarding the judgment of the legality of the authorities' order. Dissenters are responsible for exercising their best judgment regarding the law. Challengers must consider both the weight of substantive arguments for and against the legality of the order and the weight of authoritative determinations of the matter of the order's legality. Thus, challengers considering defiance may conclude that on their best judgment they must defer to the authority's determination, even if they judge that the determination is mistaken, because the weight of all these reasons taken together makes defiance unjustified. On the other hand, reasons for deference may be defeated, when matters have not been fully and fairly determined and strong arguments compel the judgment that the orders lack legal warrant, provided that the costs to the community of defiance are not excessive.

Authorities also bear responsibilities. They must respect the right of noncompliance, and the law must recognize a defense against prosecution for violation, when the dissenter's judgment is sincere, considered, not a manifestly unreasonable reading of the law, and, again, the costs to the community are not excessive. To put any greater burden on dissent—requiring, for example, that the judgment of the authorities' legal warrant be correct such that dissenters act at their peril— would put dissent beyond most ordinary citizens, reserving it only for those with sophisticated knowledge of the law or with financial resources sufficient to engage a skilled lawyer.

The rule of law depends on community-wide participation in accountability-holding. Law must provide opportunities for and protection of challenges to law and legal authorities that are essential parts of this accountability-holding. Law must recognize a qualified right of conscientious defiance of legal orders, a right that allocates responsibility for its exercise to both authorities and dissenters.

Demonstration, Disruption, and Spillover Disobedience

Some noncompliance is quiet, but dissent is often public and noisy. Demonstrations of opposition to authorities and their judgments and orders may involve loud denunciations. The rule of law does not demand decorum; it requires respect, and willingness to listen and engage in public discourse, but it does not require silence or submission. Demonstrations typically are disruptive; they inevitably cause public inconvenience and discomfort. They especially make authorities uncomfortable—that is often their aim. The legitimacy of dissent in the view of the rule of law depends on dissenters acting on their best judgment of the law (considering both substantive reasons and reasons of authority) and costs to the community; disruption, inconvenience, and discomfort are often not sufficient to defeat the legitimacy of dissent. Here, again, the rule of law recognizes the delicate dialectic of deference and dissent.

The extremes are easy to identify. If causing any inconvenience or disturbance could defeat the legitimacy of dissent, a valuable mode of public accountability-holding would be silenced. On the other hand, violence against the lives or personal security of persons is beyond the pale of rule-of-law legitimacy, as is violation of reasonable criminal laws. In cases that fall between these extremes, authorities and dissenters must exercise nuanced judgment. Authorities must weigh protection of the community against the need for effective means of community involvement in holding authorities accountable and the need for recourse against the arbitrary exercise of power. In view of the importance of accountability-holding dissent, authorities should lean toward tolerance of noisy and disruptive activities. They must also recognize that challenges to their authority are likely to elicit in them a response inconsistent with their commitment to the law. They are likely to confuse a challenge to their orders with a threat to law-based order. Dissenters, in turn, must recognize that the premise of legitimacy of their protest is their commitment to the law and the demand that authorities comply with it. This requires adherence to law and especially to respecting the rights of persons and property protected by the law. They must also recognize that the psychology of collective action can easily cloud and compromise their judgment.

People who engage in demonstrations or defiance are rarely single-minded; grievances with different sources are likely to motivate and complicate their actions. Civil dissent can spill over into civil disobedience. Disruption may involve not only defiance of legally questionable orders but also violation of clearly valid laws. Such actions are likely to fall beyond limits recognized by the rule of law. We may still welcome such actions as legitimate exercises of democratic rights of protest, but their justification will have to come from a theory of the grounds and limits of civil disobedience, not rule-of-law-inspired civil dissent. Justified civil disobedience may go beyond the limits of justified civil dissent.

With these considerations clearly in mind, it is possible to sort some troubling cases of protest. In April 1963, the Southern Christian Leadership Conference (SCLC) planned a march in Birmingham, Alabama, to protest the injustices of racial segregation. The city prohibited demonstrations without a permit and granted authorities nearly unlimited discretion to grant or deny such permits. The SCLC requested a permit, but city authorities made clear that under no circumstances would it grant the permit. An orderly march took place over Easter weekend as planned, defying city authorities. Marchers acted on the judgment that the city ordinance and refusal of city officials to permit the march unconstitutionally denied the marchers their rights to protest peacefully. Fred Shuttlesworth and several other marchers were arrested and convicted of violating the city's ordinance. Six years later, the US Supreme Court declared the ordinance unconstitutionally broad and reversed the convictions. The Court wrote, "[A] person faced with such an unconstitutional licensing law may ignore it and engage with impunity in the exercise of the right of free expression for which the law purports to require a license."[14]

Shuttlesworth and his colleagues fall clearly within the legitimating conditions we have just laid out. The Court in this case agreed.[15] However, the same cannot be said for those who engaged in the demonstration at the US Capitol on January

6, 2021. These demonstrators also acted in defiance of authorities. Their aim was to challenge the results of the 2020 presidential election, which they loudly charged was "stolen." At the time of this writing, the full story of what happened on that day has not yet reached the public, but the following is clear. Some of those who participated believed (or at least said) that they were acting in defense of the Constitution, but their views were manifestly without merit and declared to be so, after full hearings in over sixty courts. Moreover, the protesters did not merely defy orders of authorities, they bludgeoned police officers and journalists, smashed windows and doors of the Capitol, trashed offices in the building, stole items from offices of members of Congress, seriously threatened the security and lives of members of Congress and their staffs, and violently interfered with the Senate's attempts to carry out its constitutional responsibilities. This was not a case of legitimate civil dissent; it was a demonstration that erupted into violent violations of some of the most fundamental laws of the land. Despite their professed "love" of the Constitution,[16] the actions of these protesters trashed it and the fundamental principles of the rule of law that it serves.

Official Resistance and Noncompliance

Fidelity requires action not only from civilians against government officials but also from officials within government regarding the decisions and orders of their own superiors or of other departments of government. However, recognition of the legitimacy of civil dissent among government officials against authoritative determinations of the law appears inconsistent with the fundamental aim of the rule of law to protect against the arbitrary exercise of governing power. For example, in 1958, Governor Faubus of Arkansas defied a federal court order, backed by the US Supreme Court, to desegregate the Little Rock schools. Isn't this a paradigm case of infidelity and defiance of the rule of law?

Also, government agencies sometimes refuse to accept the effect of court rulings beyond the parties to the litigation (the practice of "non-acquiescence").[17] For example, the US Secretary of Health and Human Services disagreed with Supreme Court decisions regarding the eligibility of certain disabled persons for federal benefits and announced she would not follow the Court's holdings.[18] This defiance of the courts again looks like a paradigm case of infidelity. Recall *US v. Lee*: "No officer of the law may set that law at defiance with impunity. All the officers of the government, from the highest to the lowest, are creatures of the law and are bound to obey it."[19]

However, on this matter, the rule of law again is complex. For it seems to permit, even applaud, some unauthorized leaks of sensitive government information and other forms of intragovernmental defiance. For example, in early

2017, Acting Attorney General Sally Yates refused to defend then President Trump's executive order prohibiting entry into the United States to refugees and citizens of seven majority-Muslim countries. In a letter to Department of Justice lawyers, Yates wrote, "My responsibility is to ensure that the position of the Department of Justice is not only legally defensible, but is informed by our best view of what the law is. . . . At present I am not convinced that the defense of the Executive Order is consistent with these responsibilities nor am I convinced that the Executive Order is lawful."[20]

The cases are different, of course. Governor Faubus and Secretary Heckler refused to comply with decisions of the courts, while Acting Attorney General Yates refused to defend a presidential executive order. Do these differences make a difference in the view of the rule of law? Aren't they all public officers? *Lee* reminded us that there is an asymmetry between the rule-of-law duties of civilians and those of government officials. The officials, unlike civilians, are "creatures of the law." Formal and informal norms of law sharply limit the scope of their legitimate actions. Still, even within the government, and between departments of government, compliance with authoritative decisions is not always required. Here, too, we must acknowledge a dialectic between deference and dissent.

Yet, as in the case of civilian dissent, the movement of the dialectic is sensitive to certain general considerations. First, the overarching aim of the rule of law is to provide protection against the arbitrary exercise of power, recognizing that the most fertile source of such abuse lies in vast inequalities of power, like those between government officials and agencies, on the one hand, and nongovernmental entities, especially individual citizens, on the other. Thus, because officials generally wield far more power than civilians do, and are exclusively creatures of the law, the balance of reasons leans heavily in favor of official compliance with the law and with authoritative determinations of the law. In general, the more ruling power officials wield, the greater deference they must pay to authoritative decisions, even when they are, in the officials' judgment, mistaken.

Second, considerations of relative legal competence and the allocation of decision-making power among departments of government, give weight to determinations by courts, especially courts at the apex of an appeal process. This, of course, may vary to some degree according to the structure of shared responsibility of interpreting the law fixed by the constitution and its underwriting norms. Add to this the fact that the greater the power wielded by officials or departments of government the more likely will its exercise of power on its own, possibly idiosyncratic, understanding of the law appear arbitrary. Thus, the executive, especially lawyers for the executive, must be most deferential to the courts' interpretations of executive power and avoid the appearance of manipulating the indeterminacy of law for purposes of political advantage, security of political power. In this domain, the maxim, no one should be a judge in their own cause, applies with greatest force. Similarly, the more the constitution allocates responsibility for interpreting the law to a department, for example, to the judiciary, the more keenly must it keep its eye impartially on the law and resist influences on decision-making from beyond it.

Finally, the greater the power of the official or the department of government, the greater is the demand for transparency of judgment, when the official acts against the best judgment of law of other departments, especially the judgment of the courts. For, ultimately, law can rule only when there is a robust practice of accountability within the government and the wider political community.

Conclusion

The rule-of-law ideal demands that law alone rules. Law rules when there is a complex network of reciprocal accountability-holding within the political community, with a freestanding body of law supplying the standard to which all exercises of power are held. *Law* rules governing power by equipping *people* with the means effectively to hold that power to account. Law rules, not any individual's or institution's understanding of it; hence, any exercise of power, including authoritative determination of what the law says, is in principle open to challenge, disagreement, and dissent. Responsibility for interpreting the law must not lie in the hands of any single department of government, but rather should be shared among departments according to competence. The law allocates power to various officials of government to direct the actions of those who are subjects of law. The rule of law recognizes the need and appropriateness of deference to these authorities. However, their decisions are also subject to challenge and dissent. If accountability of power wielders is to be meaningful and robust, there must be wide room for civil dissent. The rule of law also acknowledges that deference may be obligatory and civil dissent in some cases may be illegitimate. The ideal of the rule of law itself calls for a delicate balance of the needs for dissent and for deference.

10
The Trust Challenge

The Neoplatonist Iamblichus included in his own *Exhortation to Philosophy* a long passage from a work by an early Sophist whom we know only as "Anonymous Iamblichi." We encountered an important argument of his in Chapter 1. He argued that living together in a condition of lawlessness (*anomia*) is worse than living alone, but necessity drives human beings to live together. Thus, necessity drove human beings to "make law their king," adding that "the first result of lawfulness [*eunomia*] is trust."[1] Our author here ties together three notions—law, lawfulness, and trust—and from this family of notions springs a robust and attractive understanding of the rule of law. Or so I have argued. However, like all families, this one is not without its tensions. For lawfulness—fidelity, as I have defended it in these pages—takes accountability-holding as its core. However, it is widely believed that the demand for accountability stems from distrust, and consequently drives out trust. But if accountability is at the heart of *eunomia* and distrust is the condition and consequence of accountability, we must conclude that our anonymous Sophist has led us astray.

A Strategy of Distrust

In the eighteenth century, it was a commonplace of political thinkers that constitutions must be built on a solid foundation of distrust of those who wield power. "Political writers have established it as a maxim," David Hume observed, "that, in contriving any system of government, and fixing the several checks and controuls of the constitution, every man ought to be supposed to be a *knave*, and to have no other end, in all his actions, than private interest."[2] In the same vein, Thomas Jefferson wrote, "In questions of power, then, let no more be heard of confidence in man, but bind him down from mischief by the chains of the Constitution." For, he explained, "free government is founded in jealousy, and not in confidence; it is jealousy and not confidence which prescribes limited constitutions, to bind down those whom we are obliged to trust with power."[3]

Jefferson speaks of "confidence" versus "jealousy"; others, more typically, speak of trust versus distrust. Jeremy Bentham, writing about the same time, made distrust central to his strategy of constitutional design. He proposed a carefully engineered system of "securities against misrule" to counteract the

Law's Rule. Gerald J. Postema, Oxford University Press. © Oxford University Press 2022.
DOI: 10.1093/oso/9780190645342.003.0010

pervasive threat of abuse of power by officials. Security against misrule, he insisted, requires maximal "responsibility" of government officials. "For security against breach of trust, the sole apt remedy is . . . constant responsibility." For this, the primary and most effective tool is "on every occasion and at all times, the strictest and most absolute dependence" on the public.[4] "Publicity is the very soul of justice," he argued. "It is through publicity alone that justice becomes the mother of security."[5] Publicity entails both transparency and vigorous, vigilant public accountability-holding. Security "depends upon the spirit, the intelligence, the vigilance, the alertness, the intrepidity, the energy, the perseverance, of those of whose opinions Public Opinion is composed."[6] However, Bentham asked, isn't this system of *public responsibility* nothing more than "a system of *distrust*"? Yes, indeed, he replied, but "every good political institution is founded upon this base," for "whom ought we to distrust, if not those to whom is committed great authority, with great temptations to abuse it?"[7] This theme has remained strong in contemporary constitutional thinking.[8] Philip Pettit, echoing eighteenth-century republican theory, insists that eternal vigilance is the price of liberty, and that vigilance is a "sustained manifestation of distrust."[9]

Yet a serious tension lurks in this cold-sober embrace of the suspicion of power and those who wield it. The tension is evident at the margins of Bentham's thought; we see it also in Jefferson's: we are "obliged [i.e., we have no choice but] to trust government," he wrote. At least, it is widely thought that government, especially democratic government, cannot function well in civic soil poisoned by suspicion and distrust. These concerns bear on our understanding of the content and feasibility of the rule-of-law ideal. A necessary complement to institutional legality, we have argued, is a robust ethos of fidelity, according to which members of a political community, citizens and officials alike, take responsibility for holding each other accountable under the law. Trust also lies at the heart of law's ethos. Fidelity depends on a shared standing to hold each other accountable that involves entrusting to each other the authority to hold one to account. Fidelity in the vertical dimension, which *inter alia* involves people holding those who exercise political power accountable to the law, depends on the combined efforts of the people, which can be effective only if individual citizens can trust others to join them in the effort.

However, if Hume, Jefferson, Bentham, and hosts of constitution designers after them are to be believed, institutionalized structures of accountability enact and manifest distrust and suspicion. This assessment reflects an apparent aversion to accountability in interpersonal relations. "Being called to account for one's actions and claims," Jonathan Wolff observes, "gives the impression that one is not trusted, that one is an object of suspicion and hence is not being respected."[10] Close monitoring, it is thought, is poisonous to interpersonal relationships of value. This brings us face to face with I will call *the trust challenge*. We understand trust to be a key ingredient in effective governance as well as a necessary condition of effective efforts at holding power accountable. However, the challenge argues, accountability thrives on distrust and drives out trust. This tension, the challenge alleges, lies at the heart of the rule of law: the rule of law demands accountability; accountability depends on trust; yet accountability manifests distrust and drives out trust, thereby jeopardizing the rule of law.

The aim of this chapter is to answer the trust challenge. Vigorous accountability-holding, I will argue, is not a threat to political and civic trust but an important support for it. Both trust romantics and trust cynics uncritically adopt a particular form of personal trust as their paradigm and draw unwarranted inferences from this paradigm. To pull the sting from the trust challenge, we need a nuanced understanding of trust and distrust as they occur in civic and political contexts and the ways in which being held to account engages these attitudes. This chapter takes a careful look at the nature and various forms of trust and distrust, but first it recalls the understanding of accountability appropriate to its task of enabling law to rule that we set out in Chapter 2.

Accountability Fit for the Rule of Law

We learned in Chapter 2 that accountability-holding is an interpersonal, normatively structured, discursive activity. The accountability holder calls on the giver to provide an account of the giver's activity, and the holder assesses that account. The account seeks to explain or justify the giver's actions; and the holder assesses the giver's actions in light of the giver's reasons. The holder is entitled to call for the account from the giver; and the giver owes an obligation to the holder to provide it. The holder is also subject to norms of the relationship and is liable to be held accountable for its activity.

Accountability fit for the rule of law is a public activity—the account is given *in* public, regarding public matters, and given to officers of the public or to the public generally. The norms defining the relationship and the domain of the giver's activity are the laws of the political community, and the reasons to be given are determined by the discipline of law. According to the fidelity thesis, each party subject to law submits to and participates in a network of mutual accountability. Although each occasion of accountability-holding is asymmetrical between the holder and the giver, on other occasions the holder is liable to give an account to some other holder, perhaps for his calling the initial giver to account. These connections form a network, rather than a hierarchical chain.

In this model of accountability, sanctions lie in the background. There is nothing defective or incomplete about an accountability mechanism that does not explicitly build in sanctions to enforce the judgments of accountability holders. The holder's power to call the giver to account is normative, not physical, and it is not necessary that enforcement other than issuing the judgment itself is ready to hand. Liability to critical assessment does not necessarily carry with it liability to *punishment*. Sanctions are auxiliaries, assisting but not essential to the demanding and assessing of accounts.

The call for those in power to provide reasons relies on an appeal to common norms of law and to the presumed commitment of the giver and the holder to make these norms effective. Consequently, the holder appeals to the giver's integrity, or at least the giver's concern for the esteem or good offices of the holder or the public. These motivations connect with the giver's presumed commitment to law. The giver may find the holder's adverse and public judgment painful and unwelcome, but that is because the giver takes seriously her commitment to the law and the holder's judgment implicates this commitment and may cast unfavorable light on it. Accountability that focuses solely on providing external incentives (especially coercive incentives) for compliance leaves out of the picture the crucial discursive element of law and fails to appreciate and make use of the full range of the offices of the law. The incentives involved in rule-of-law accountability are meant to be internal to the norms to which parties are held accountable or to their mutual commitments to fidelity.

Accountability fit for the rule of law is a distinctive kind of accountability, reflecting distinctive features of law and the aims and values of fidelity. The question now for us to consider is whether it is rooted in distrust and drives out trust. To answer this question, we should take a closer look at trust.

Trust—Contexts and Contraries

Trust, paradigmatically, concerns a kind of relationship.[11] The nature of this relationship will vary as the contexts in which it thrives vary. Different contexts bring some features to the foreground and move others to the background. The trust challenge concerns the effect of widespread practices of accountability on trust in political and civic contexts. So, to assess the challenge, we need to understand political and civic trust. However, our understanding of trust is shaped by our experience of trust in interpersonal relations. We will begin with this paradigm and then adjust our understanding to fit trust in political and civic contexts, which are rather different. We must avoid taking trust in thick interpersonal relations as our model, but we must also take care not to exaggerate the differences between trust in personal and political contexts. The key to answering the trust challenge lies in a careful assessment of both.

Interpersonal Trust

Trust involves a stance—a complex combination of attitudes and dispositions to act—of one party toward another. To bring interpersonal trust into focus we should distinguish it from reliance and prediction, stances that approximate, but do not fully realize, trust.

Proto-Trust: Reliance and Prediction

Trust involves a person's reliance on some other party. Reliance is a confident belief issuing in a readiness to act. Proto-trust, we might call it, is an asymmetrical relation between two parties: one party (a) is vulnerable to actions of another that could affect something that the first party values or cares about, and (b) relies on the other, at a minimum, not to damage the valued item, but (c) believes there is some risk that other party, not being under the party's control, will not act as predicted.

Proto-trust falls short of trust. This is because one could take this attitude toward animate or even inanimate parties—toward nature, for example, or toward one's bicycle—that lack agency. Trust, however, involves parties who are capable of agency. First, trust involves, to some degree, an exercise of agency by the trusting party. Consider Alice and Ben. If Alice trusts Ben to take care of her house while she is traveling, she makes herself vulnerable, or willingly accepts her vulnerability, to Ben's dealing with the house. If Alice literally has no choice but to rely on Ben, for example, if by legal arrangements all of Alice's assets are under Ben's control, then there is no need—there is no room—for Alice to trust Ben. Indeed, Alice may actively distrust Ben, and may seek any way she can to avoid relying on him, and yet have no choice but to rely on him.

Second, Ben must be a free agent, acting on his own, not coerced or compelled to act in ways that affect Alice's valued item.[12] There is no need or room for Alice to trust Ben, if someone else credibly threatens Ben to watch the house or else. If trust has room to work, Ben must be free to act competently and have some discretion regarding the exercise of that competence. Ben is free within limits to decide how to act in response to Alice's trust.

Another reason why Alice's reliance on Ben might fall short of trust is that it lacks a critical interpersonal dimension. If Alice bases her reliance only on predictions of what she knows of Ben's competence and motivation, then, again, her stance only approximates trust. The relation between Alice and Ben is not necessarily personal; it is not substantially different from the relation Alice has to her bike, only the bases of Alice's predictions are different. However, trust proper is an interpersonal relation. Missing from predictive reliance is an interactive, recognitional dimension. Alice trusts Ben when she relies on him because of *how he stands to her*, not merely because of (what she knows about) how he stands to something that she values,[13] and when both parties recognize that fact.

Robust Recognitional Trust

Interpersonal trust has a complex recognitional dimension. The difference is signaled by the fact that when Ben does not act as Alice expected—does not perform as trusted—Alice is not merely disappointed. She feels that Ben has failed her; she feels betrayed. Alice's expectations may be defeated, but they are based on assumptions about how Ben ought to behave, not on how he is likely to behave. Alice expected Ben *to* behave in a certain way; she did not merely expect *that* he would. Responsibility of the trusted party is a salient feature of this interpersonal dimension. The trust stance is a stance taken by a person engaging another person, recognizing his key moral features and the moral dimensions of their relationship.

We can identify the following features of this robust mode of trust. (We will see presently that ordinary cases of trust may shade off from this robust, all-in case.) First, trust has distinctive normative or moral dimensions. As we have just seen, the trusting party's expectations are normative in nature, not merely predictive. Moreover, what Alice expects Ben to do in caring for something she values may vary with the circumstances and moral considerations that emerge in them. Thus, Ben's actions will be properly responsive to the trust placed in him if his conduct is good enough, even if not optimal. Indeed, Ben may fail to act as Alice trusts him to act and yet not betray her trust; for his acting as Alice expects might, in the circumstances, involve doing a greater wrong to another person or may require Ben to shoulder burdens far greater than Alice can reasonably ask him to bear. Ben does not show himself to be untrustworthy if he does not act as trusted. He does not fail her, even if her expectations are defeated. Similarly, Alice's trusting is subject to moral norms. Her trusting involves, within limits, acknowledging that Ben must exercise discretion, that his conduct is not entirely within her control. Accordingly, Alice will not engage in close monitoring.[14] And she must recognize that there are moral limits to properly trust-responsive behavior. She should be willing to understand or even forgive Ben's failing to live up to her expectations.[15]

Second, the recognitional dimension of robust trust is critically important. The trusting party not only expects certain behavior but she invites the trusted party to accept her trust and actively engages his agency. Philosopher Philip Pettit's notion of *trust responsiveness* helps us explain this dimension of the trusting relationship.[16] Ben is responsive to trust placed in him if he takes the fact Alice manifestly trusts him to do something in her behalf as itself a salient reason for acting as trusted. Responsiveness to trust is different from sensitively responding to another's need or even to a person's dependency on one. A trust-responsive person responds appropriately to another person's *manifestly* counting on them.

The recognitional dimension of trusting also moves in the reverse direction. In some circumstances at least, trusting behavior should itself be responsive to manifested *trustworthiness*. Alice may trust Ben based solely on his general reputation as trustworthy, but if he signals his trustworthiness, if he gives her some token of assurance of it, Alice (other things equal) should respond to this invitation with trust in Ben. The responsive dimension of this phenomenon is evident in the fact that, in some circumstances, Ben, having signaled his trustworthiness, might take Alice's refusal to trust him as an affront. He may reasonably judge her refusal as a kind of moral failing on her part. She falls short of what he has some moral reason to hope for.

Robust trust involves mutual recognition of a morally interesting sort. Alice manifestly counts on Ben, hoping or intending that her doing so will trigger his motivation. His recognition of this manifested trust engages his antecedent reasons for fulfilling her trust. Alice's trust manifests her recognition of Ben as potentially responsive to her trust and hence trustworthy. Her trust invites Ben's recognition of Alice's vulnerability, and of the valued thing she put in his care. Alice's trust also engages Ben's commitments, his sense of integrity and his sense of himself as trustworthy.

A typical motivation for trust responsiveness is esteem—for example, Ben's desire to be regarded as trustworthy by Alice and perhaps others who observe his conduct. He may desire this, either, because he values or seeks their good opinion or because he wishes to draw on their good offices in future. We will return to this motivation when we consider political trust. Other motivations are also familiar. Ben may wish to build or maintain a strong relationship with Alice that he values for its own sake or he may care about Alice and wish to enable her to make use of his competence. What is critical for robust trust is only the trusted party's responsiveness to trust—his taking the manifested fact that the trusting party counts on him as a salient and significant reason to act as trusted.

Third, interpersonal trust has a characteristic cognitive dimension. Trust inevitably affects the way the trusting party evaluates evidence.[17] "The world looks different when viewed with trust from how it looks when viewed with distrust or neutrality," writes philosopher Karen Jones. "Trust is a lens that changes how agents understand their situation and the reasons it affords."[18] The trusting party is inclined, within some limit, to view evidence in a light favorable to the trusted party. This is not, as some have argued either irrational or pre-rational.[19] On the contrary, it is typical of the cognitive attitudes that people take toward their personal attachments, their valued relationships and the people involved in them. The evidence of the risk that the other party will not prove trustworthy is bracketed not because other evidence outweighs it but rather because the very act of weighing it does not fit comfortably with wholeheartedly inhabiting the relationship that the trusting party has and values, or seeks to establish.[20] This is especially true of trust that is embedded in rich interpersonal relationships. Those attachments would not have the intrinsic value they have for us, and could not survive, without to some extent holding calculation based on careful evaluation of it at a deliberative distance.

Proleptic Trust

One may entrust something of value to another person without fully trusting the recipient. I will call some such entrustings *proleptic trust*. I should explain.

While trusting is a stance involving a kind of attitude and a disposition that a person takes toward another person, entrusting is a mode of conduct that has an important communicative dimension; it involves actions that signal or enact trust. It is possible for a person to *entrust* something of value to another without fully *trusting* that person. In that case, one party communicates trust to the other party, but she does not (fully) trust him, *yet*. This is possible because entrusting draws on certain public meanings, meanings available in the environment of the parties involved.

Our understanding of robust recognitional trust brings trusting and entrusting close together, because the trusting party means to engage in conduct that is visible to the other party and is intended to trigger behavior that fulfills that trust. However, in some cases, one may entrust something of value to the care of another while not entirely *trusting* that person, that is, without fully believing in advance that the other party is fully trustworthy. One may do so hoping that the other party will take the opportunity to show himself responsive to the trust.[21] Conduct may *communicate* trust by virtue of the public meaning such conduct typically has, although the agent does not yet *harbor* that trust. This is anticipatory trust, or, as I like to call it, *proleptic* trust—*pro-leptic* because it *takes* something *before* something else. I entrust something to you, communicate trust, not merely anticipating but in hopes of *prompting* a trust-appropriate response in you. There is nothing sinister, manipulative, or insincere about this entrusting. Entrusting something of value to another *invites* a certain kind of mutual recognition and interaction rooted in it. Proleptic trust is an invitation to, an entrée into, a trust relationship. Proleptic trust depends on ordinary, public understandings of behavior expressive of trust.

Proleptic trust, and perhaps robust trust more generally, can work only if the environment in which the parties interact supports it. First, Alice's conduct must communicate her trust to Ben and perhaps others. Consequently, it must have the public significance of signaling her reliance and vulnerability and her normative expectation of his trust responsiveness. Consequently, the meaning of Alice's action *as entrusting* and Ben's action *as trust responsive* must be available to each other and some relevant range of third parties. Similarly, Ben will be able effectively to signal his *trustworthiness* only if his actions or words convey his sincere invitation to be trusted. For these communications to take place, there must be enough entrusting, trust-fulfilling, and trust-inviting conduct in the social environment in which Alice and Ben interact that their actions can reasonably be understood as entrusting, inviting trust and fulfilling trust. In social climates poisoned by cynicism or a pervasive assumption that everyone is out only for his or her own private good, proleptic trust and robust trust will be difficult to achieve.

Second, proleptic trust is not likely to succeed where there are sharp divisions between the trusted party and the trusting party, or in the social environment in which they interact. Where sharp divisions obtain, Ben may not care about Alice's opinion of his trustworthiness, or may not care about the opinions of others like Alice. Moreover, for proleptic trust to elicit trust-responsive behavior, the relationship between Alice and Ben must not give Ben reason to think Alice's reliance on him is motivated by something other than his potential trust responsiveness—for example, if Ben were forced by some third party to act on Alice's behalf. This is so because, in that case, her reliance would not be viewed as entrusting conduct. Similarly, the relationship must not be such that there is a significant and obvious inequality of power between the parties. If Alice holds Ben in her power, his action will look ingratiating, mere sycophancy, rather than being responsive to her trust; or Alice's conduct will look hypocritical, rather than trusting. Similarly, if Ben holds Alice in his power, her reliance and vulnerability will lack the necessary dimension of voluntariness, and she will lack the opportunity to engage his trust-responsive behavior. Her reliance will look like acquiescence not trust. Thus, the manifest presence of strong sanctions for Ben's behavior and manifest inequalities of power between the two parties can make entrusting impossible and can turn otherwise trust-responsive behavior into mere compliance.

In sum, the social context of behavior potentially relevant to trust, and the social meanings available in that context, can materially affect the possibilities for entrusting, trusting, and trust-responsive conduct.

Varieties of Nontrust

The discussion just completed provides some of the resources that we will need to answer the trust challenge to the rule of law. However, we need to transpose this understanding to the civil and political context and explore the operation and options for trust in that context. But first we must look more carefully at the opposite of trust, *distrust*, for the trust challenge argues that the demand for accountability at the heart of the rule-of-law ideal stems from a strategy of distrust that is corrosive of trust.

To begin, we must recognize that trust and distrust define a spectrum.[22] Along this spectrum fall clear, all-in cases of trust at one end, and full-fledged cases of distrust at the other end, with mistrust occupying a band between them. Moreover, some garden variety cases of trust may share only some features of clear cases of trust or share them to the robust degree of all-in cases. For example, one's trust in another may be limited in scope (one may trust another in some matters but not in other matters) or in intensity (one may be willing to forgo monitoring generally but not completely). Trust may shade into mistrust and mistrust may shade into distrust. Those who put the trust challenge tend to assume that all the space beyond all-in trust lies the domain of distrust.

Distrust

Distrust stands at the opposite end of the spectrum of attitudes and dispositions characteristic of trust. Distrust involves more than a lack of reliance on another; it involves intentional *withholding* of reliance, a *refusal* to make oneself vulnerable to another person. Moreover, people who distrust may have no choice but to rely, but then their reliance will be unwilling, diffident, and possibly defiant. Whether they also manifest these attitudes will depend, in part, on the costs to them of their doing so. They may be disposed to withdraw reliance at the first safe opportunity, or take all feasible measures to protect themselves from the harm they fear may eventuate.

Distrusting persons base their withholding of reliance or diffidence on deep and active suspicion of the other party's competence or motivation. Alice distrusts Ben; she believes that Ben would (or does) treat with indifference, if not contempt, any attempt she makes to entrust something to him. She not only believes him to be unreliable but believes that, if given the chance, he is likely to act out of ill-will against her or with indifference to her interests. She believes that Ben will answer any trust that she might place in him by exploitation or domination. Moreover, distrust, like trust, colors Alice's interpretations of Ben's conduct, insofar as it bears on her interests. But the interpretations have a valence opposite that of trust. Alice is strongly inclined to see Ben's motivations as sinister even though others might find them entirely innocent. In this respect, the distrusting person tends to be resistant to and discounts evidence of the other party's cooperativeness or benign motivation.

Mistrust

Lying on the spectrum between trust and distrust are doubt and mistrust. Alice's trusting stance toward Ben can vary in two dimensions. On the one hand, Alice may have greater or less confidence in, or doubt about, Ben's competence, motivation, or trust-responsiveness. On the other hand, Alice, depending on her level of confidence or doubt, may adjust how much of what she values she is willing put in Ben's hands. At some indeterminate point, her less than full trust shades into a region of mistrust, characterized by some degree of doubt, which is still distinct from distrust.

If Alice mistrusts Ben, she may still be willing to rely on him to some extent, while still harboring doubt to some degree. Her reliance will be correspondingly cautious and tentative, perhaps taking some precautions against a worst-case scenario and taking care about what she puts in his hands. She may hedge her bets, without closing off opportunities for him to demonstrate his trustworthiness. The stance one takes toward another whom one mistrusts is still open to further evidence regarding the other party's trustworthiness and trust responsiveness. She may be willing to give Ben the benefit of the doubt she still harbors.[23]

Falling short of *mistrust*, one might harbor some doubts about the other party's trust responsiveness and yet *hope* that, by manifestly counting on him, she might engender trust-responsive behavior and plant a seed that could grow into trustworthiness. She may even be willing to *entrust* something of value to the care of the other person, trusting them *proleptically*.

Beyond the Interpersonal Paradigm

We also find trust in contexts less intimate than those we have had in view thus far. Impersonal contexts may be informal or to various degrees formally structured or institutionalized. In informal contexts, people may encounter other individuals, but their interactions with them are mediated and at a distance. The trust may be directed not at any particular individual but rather at unassignable members of a social group or occupants of a social role. In formally structured contexts, institutions can figure in trust relations in either of two ways.

First, the institution itself may be the trusted agent—people put trust *in* the institution. They trust the institution to perform as designed or advertised, believing that it is likely to be fair, to serve their interests, or to serve important values to which they are committed.[24] Call this *institutional trust*. People who have meaningful opportunities to participate in the institution may be more likely to trust it, but nonparticipants may also trust social or political institutions that they judge likely to serve their needs or interests. This trust may amount to little more than unforced reliance, but it might involve significant normative expectations. And people may genuinely feel betrayed when the institution does not meet their expectations.

Second, the institution may be the incubator or underwriter of trust, either robust interpersonal trust or the more distant impersonal trust of an individual occupying an institutional role. Call this *institution-dependent* trust. One's trust in another person is institution dependent when one trusts someone in an official position, in part based on what one knows about how the institution's processes and procedures underwrite the official's competence and motivations. On that basis, one counts on the official, within certain parameters, to act in one's interest, or at least to act fairly when it comes to matters of one's interests. This is roughly akin to personal trust, but it is more distant and mediated by the institution. One's trust in the official depends on one's confidence in the institution, but it may extend to something approximating personal trust in the other party when she acts in her official capacity.

Impersonal contexts differ from paradigm interpersonal contexts of trust in several respects. First, the trusted or distrusted party is not familiar to the trusting party. Cases of institutional trust look a lot like predictive reliance. People rely on the design of the structure, constitution, and procedures of the institution to produce outcomes that serve their interests or values. Where the trust is institution dependent, the individual trusted will be anonymous or a stranger to the trusting party, known only through the features, powers, and obligations of incumbents in that role.

Second, there is little opportunity for shared personal experience between the trusting and trusted parties. Personal encounters between individuals, if they occur, will be episodic and institutionally mediated. The parties will appear to each other as abstracted individuals, representatives of roles or offices, rather than concrete persons. Thus, the personal aspects of trust relations will be thinned out. The recognitional aspects of trust will be less concrete and depend heavily on background social conventions and practices known to the parties. While in interpersonal contexts, parties can customize background understandings and public meanings, recognitional resources in impersonal contexts will be generic and off the rack. Some political scientists maintain that trust is not possible among strangers, but they overlook the resources available in a community for understanding and interpreting the behavior of others in a widely shared culture. Broadly available social meanings of behavior, rather than meanings born in intimacy, will play a dominant role in institution-dependent trust encounters.

Third, in impersonal contexts, one may feel that it is reasonable to place trust in institutional agents that other members of the community trust. Public and general assurances of their trustworthiness replace more immediate sources of assurance. The climate in which people who are more or less strangers encounter each other takes on greater importance here. Similarly, the nature of the reliance is also likely to be different in impersonal contexts. The range of options open to the trusting party will be limited, narrowing the scope for the trusting party's voluntarily entrusting something of value to the care of another. Where trust is possible in these contexts, it may not involve a robust undertaking or entrusting, but rather some form of willing acceptance.

Fourth, in impersonal contexts, some form of nontrust may be the normal default, rather than trust, and this will shape the public meanings of trust-giving and trust-responsive conduct. A wary response to signaled trustworthiness might be viewed as more reasonable, less likely to strike one as offensive or a lack of respect, among strangers than between persons well known to each other. The same may be true regarding the extent to which monitoring of the trusted party by the trusting party is tolerated or regarded as reasonable. Similarly, if it is known that one's trust responsiveness is motivated by a desire for the esteem or good opinion of others, a close interpersonal relationship might be damaged, but the same motivation may be entirely appropriate in contexts of institution-dependent trust. Trust-fulfilling behavior may be important to an official be-cause it implicates his integrity or his commitment to certain principles, and the good opinion of others reflects back to him an assessment of his integrity or of the commitments he takes seriously.

Trust—Civic and Political

Mindful of the nature of robust interpersonal trust and of the effects that differences of context can have on the nature and dynamics of trust, we can pro-ceed to explore more directly civic and political trust.

Civic Trust

Civic trust is the form of trust that members of a political community have in other members or groups of members of their community, or in the associ-ations and institutions that structure their civic life. Civic trust is a species of impersonal trust. Trusting parties are participants in the political community, engaging regularly with other participants. Civic trust concerns public matters, but its modality is "horizontal"—looking to other members—rather than "ver-tical"—looking to public officials and representatives of government.

The scope of civic trust in a political community can extend just to a neighbor-hood, town, or region; but it can also encompass an entire national community. In the latter, community members may be quite diverse. Because the context for such trust is impersonal, the relationships in which trust is offered and accepted may be relatively thin and distant, mediated by institutions or formally struc-tured associations. So if one has trust in another person in this civic context, it is unlikely to be rooted in personal encounters, and one is unlikely to have any personal knowledge of the other party's character, commitments, loyalties, general cooperativeness, or trust responsiveness. Nevertheless, as we have seen, the personal, recognitional aspects are not necessarily eliminated; rather, they are likely to take a different form.

Climate of Trust

Civic trust thrives in a wider climate of trust in a political community. In some cases, members of the political community may consciously undertake to put trust in other members, but often trust functions in the background, as the climate of trust in which members of the political community interact.

Hume observed "a good natured man finds himself in an instant of the same humour with his company; and even the proudest and surliest take a tincture from their countrymen and acquaintance."[25] Confirming Hume's remark, recent social scientists have reported that a given individual's level of trust is often influenced by the trust levels of others around them.[26] People sense, without being able to describe accurately, the climate of trust in a community.

The climate of trust (or mistrust or distrust) in a community is a social rather than personal phenomenon. It has a public dimension that is not reducible to the attitudes and dispositions of individual members. The climate of trust in a community is a kind of "commons of the mind," in philosopher Annette Baier's useful phrase.[27] People draw on, add to, sustain, or weaken the commons through their trusting activities, interactions, practices, and engagements with other members of the community. These trust-related activities include not only trust-responsive conduct but also failures of trust, betrayals, and abandonments of trust, and challenges to, corrections of, and attempts to repair such failures. The trust commons may be articulated in informal norms. The trusting relationship and the attitudes and dispositions rooted in it are made concrete in these informal norms and expressed in conduct shaped by them. The norms offer scripts for the ongoing drama of civic trust. Generic trusting is simultaneously expressed and nourished, enacted and reproduced, through compliance with informal norms of self-restraint, mutual respect, fairness and decency, and challenges or corrections to perceived deviations from them. Public behaviors can nourish or poison the climate, enrich or impoverish the publicly available "language" of impersonal trust.

This climate is more sensed than observed by participants. Specific acts of trusting and entrusting (or mistrusting and distrusting) take shape in it. In this climate, from the implicit scripts, conduct gets its public meaning. Acts can be seen as giving or withholding trust, as fulfilling or betraying trust. In the absence of repertoires developed through direct, interpersonal interaction, individual members draw on this commons to anticipate and assess the conduct of non-intimate fellow members. They depend on it for the public meaning of their behavior. They also draw resources from this commons to reinforce social bonds within their circle and to extend trust to those beyond the limits of that circle. This commons is an important component of what social theorists call "social capital."[28]

This climate can be rich and robust or thin, incomplete, and fragile. It may be narrowly circumscribed, limited to small subgroups of a political community, or broad and community-wide, embracing many diverse subgroups of the polity. Depending on the scope of trusting, the climate in a political community can be simultaneously trusting and distrusting; trust within a subgroup, for example, can feed or respond to distrust of the wider community. Wide-scope trust is likely to encourage, enable, and support generalized trust in subcommunities. But breakdowns in the climate of trust in a political community as a whole can result in a rise of distrust of members of the community generally and, simultaneously, an intensification of trust in members of smaller subgroups that provide refuge from the larger political community.[29] Breakdown of civic trust often leads to fragmentation of the community and intense, sometimes destructive, small group trust and loyalty. Similarly, small group trust, especially among social or political elites, can create equally intense, but more widespread, civic and political distrust, if the elites ignore or alienate large portions of the wider community.

Political Trust

Political trust is the trust that those who are subject to political power place in those who exercise that power. It is trust in its vertical dimension. It may be institutional or institution-dependent, directed either toward governmental institutions or toward public officials. The political trust that citizens may have is typically mediated by civic associations or institutions. Consider, first, citizens' trust *in* government or its constituent institutions.

Citizens who trust in their government rely on its constitution, structure, procedures, and institutions. They take confidence in the design and real-time operation of government institutions. They regard the guiding principles and values of the institutions as benign and believe that they align generally with their own interests and values and that government institutions tend to function according to design. Good institutional design deploys mechanisms to provide citizens with dependable evidence of the performance of public officials and safeguards against abuses of public power. Their expectations are not merely predictive but also normative. Citizens who take an internal point of view with regard to the institutions of government see government not as an alien force but as an entity, perhaps even an agent, on which they can make normative demands. Citizens *expect* government and public officials *to* perform as required by the constitution and laws, which, they assume, broadly conform to the principles and values underlying them.

However, compared to trusted parties in personal contexts, government is a very different kind of trusted agent, and the trust that citizens put in it is decidedly impersonal. The kind of attitudes trusting citizens adopt are appropriate to the kind of agent that government is. Government institutions are formal entities, agents. The performance of governmental institutions is inevitably impersonal. Formality in this context is a virtue. Governmental institutions are trusted, in part, because we can expect them to function according to design, even though the people staffing them constantly change. Political theorists call this "the principle of substitutability."[30]

Trust in institutions does not entirely close off some form of quasi-personal trust in officials; on the contrary, trust in institutions enables quasi-personal trust and underwrites it. Citizen trust of officials is mediated by institutions; it is institution dependent. Citizen relations to individual public officials that occupy positions of authority are correspondingly formal. Parties to the trust relationship do not meet on a personal basis, but rather as occupants of institutionally defined roles or positions. Government institutions define and structure the encounters and secure competent and properly oriented performance. Such structures, procedures, and safeguards are not incidental to the operation of the institutions; rather, they are intrinsic to their design and proper functioning. Something approximating interpersonal trust is not impossible, but an impersonal, institution-mediated form of trust is more common.

Indeed, in the political domain, robust personal trust—or something that mimics it—in public officials can be very dangerous. Authoritarian leaders and certain forms of populism seek to generate a robustly personal relationship of trust between the leader and the people, unmediated by political institutions or civic associations. The formality and distance of the kind of political trust we have just considered is anathema. On this view, the people—or rather individuals *en masse*—must feel a direct, emotional connection with the leader. Of course, the elimination of distance is only imaginary, rooted in the feeling that the Leader is *like me* and reinforced by the sense that he is speaks directly *to me* and *for me*, unmediated by representative institutions. This form of trust—or fantasy trust—is especially useful for the Leader, because it sets him free from any genuine form of accountability. Leaders who seek this kind of trust are proper objects of our deepest suspicion and distrust; mechanisms that weaken this distorted kind of trust are not troubling to the rule of law.

Responses to the Trust Challenge

We have outlined salient features of interpersonal trust, emphasizing the critical normative and recognitional features of the relationship. We have placed trust and distrust on a spectrum from robust trust at one extreme and firm distrust at the other. Attitudes that move away from robust trust shade toward mistrust and mistrust can shade into distrust. Distrust, we learned, harbors a deep suspicion of the motivations and intentions of the distrusted party, a suspicion that darkens all evidence about those motivations and makes impossible reliance on what to other observers might look like trustworthiness. Mistrust, in contrast, while it is wary, is still to some degree open to positive construals of behavior and apparent motives of other persons. Those who do not fully trust, but are open to the possibility of trust-responsive behavior of another person, may entrust something of value to that person in the hope of prompting a trust response. "Proleptic trust," we called it.

We observed that the ability to engage in genuine trusting relationships depends on the existence of an environment in which persons can communicate their trust (even if only proleptic) and trust responsiveness. In interpersonal contexts, this environment will be built upon close personal encounters and repertoires of actions that take on appropriate meanings through them. In civic and political contexts, the nature of the trust relationship is different; it is less personal and direct, and it is mediated by institutions. In these contexts, the repertoire of actions available to communicate trust and trust responsiveness will be different and more limited. This communication will depend on scripts, broad public meanings, that are available in the community at large and dependent on a background climate of trust.

Political trust combines trust in governmental and legal institutions with institution-dependent trust. Civic trust, we have seen, is a kind of social trust that depends on a background climate of trust. Contraries of political and civic trust are also recognizable. Attitudes across the trust-distrust spectrum are possible, from robust trust to weaker forms of trust through the range of mistrusting attitudes and conduct to full and deep distrust. With this understanding of civic and political trust, mistrust, and distrust in their various dimensions, we are equipped to assess the strength of the trust challenge to the fidelity thesis that lies at the heart of the rule-of-law ideal.

Accountability and Civic Trust

Is accountability a threat to civic trust? Recall trust challengers argued that being called to account is often experienced as an interpersonal insult, expressing distrust and hence a failure of basic respect. By extension, they argue, accountability undermines the civic climate of trust. However, this objection is mistaken, I will argue. Mutual accountability in the context of interpersonal relations, on the contrary, presupposes and expresses trust, rather than distrust or even mistrust, and can build and reinforce trust. Moreover, this fact informs our less personal civic relations and the social meanings of actions available to us in our civic interactions.

Moral philosophers commonly regard mutual accountability as central to moral life and the moral community. In the first edition of *Theory of Moral Sentiments* (1759), Adam Smith wrote:

> A moral being is an accountable being . . . a being that must give an account of its actions to some other, and that consequently must regulate them according to the good-liking of this other. . . . But tho' he is, no doubt, principally accountable to God, in the order of time, he must necessarily conceive of himself as accountable to his fellow creatures.[31]

Echoing Smith, philosopher Stephen Darwall has argued that if actors fail to fulfill their obligations, they are liable to moral blame, and "moral blame comes with . . . an implicit demand for accountability and acknowledgment of the legitimacy of this demand." Likewise, guilt "is itself a form of holding oneself accountable." To hold others accountable for their actions is not to threaten or apply some incentive to conform to their obligations. It is, rather, to ask for an account of their actions and to encourage them to hold *themselves* accountable, to take responsibility for their actions.[32] Darwall characterizes all of morality in these terms; he calls it "morality as equal accountability."[33]

Far from insulting or denying respect, holding another accountable is an expression of respect, if it is reciprocal. "Holding someone responsible," Darwall observes, "commits the holder to the idea not just that he has an authority to hold the other responsible, but also that the other can hold himself and others responsible as well."[34] Morality so understood is not a matter of every person subjected to an externally imposed, impersonal code of norms, but rather as a norm-structured practice in which each person is and regards himself as accountable to others and they to him. To purport to hold another accountable, under these conditions, is not to exercise unilateral authority over the other person but to acknowledge common participation in the practice of mutual accountability to common governing norms.

In this practice, unlike in structures of bureaucratic or managerial accountability, trust plays a key role. For in holding another accountable, one acknowledges the authority of the other party to hold oneself accountable. One puts oneself in the hands of another person, makes oneself vulnerable to that person's freely exercised judgment, to the "good-liking of this other," as Smith put it. This entrusting is reciprocal.

Acts of holding accountable may have the properties trust challengers allege when the norms are externally imposed, or where there is no recognizable community between the holder and the giver, and especially where the accountability-holding is not mutual. In such circumstances, holding another person accountable amounts to subjecting that person to one's unilateral power or demonstrating to the subject the fact and burden of that subjection. However, the accountability at the center of fidelity is not like this. It is and must be mutual. Fidelity can fail, of course, but then trust is undermined not by fidelity but by the failure of fidelity.

Civic trust is a condition and a consequence of mutual accountability in the civic membership. Where each is the guardian of each, there is no reason for one to regard being called to account as an insult or the expression of distrust. Mutual accountability-holding can be a form of participation in a climate of civic trust. Moreover, it provides a means of publicly signaling one's trustworthiness. It can enhance, rather than threaten, trusting activity in the community. We may conclude that, as long as accountability at the civic level involves mutual submission to and mutual participation, the practice presupposes and expresses trust rather than threatening it.

Of course, social conditions can undermine or threaten this practice. In a culture otherwise dominated by distrust, it may not be possible for the morality of equal accountability to gain a foothold. In the absence of widely recognizable examples of mutual accountability-holding, where duties are impersonal and imposed from above and demands for compliance are unilateral, it may not be possible to read attempts to hold persons accountable as involving trust. If the soil of the community's civic culture is poisoned, mutual accountability characteristic of fidelity cannot thrive. We must concede, then, that, under some social conditions, accountability may be read as nothing more than the exercise of externally imposed power, but also in this climate, fidelity in general could not get a foothold, and, sadly, robust rule of law could not long exist. Under these conditions, law itself can survive, if at all, only by depending on the use of coercive force beyond levels few could regard as tolerable.

Accountability and Political Trust

A reply along these lines is also available to those who challenge accountability in the political domain. As we have seen, political trust and its contraries can attach either to the political institutions themselves—various agencies of government, or the regime as a whole—or to public officials. I will focus on the latter, institution-dependent, form of trust and the challenge to it allegedly posed by robust accountability of officials.

Recall, political theorists and constitution writers, following the lead of Hume, Jefferson, and Bentham often insist that those who exercise political power must be held to systematic accountability, institutionalized in "the chains of the Constitution" and other legal devices. They have called attention to two constant dangers of political life. One danger is the potential for abuse of power and corruption of human motivation that is an inevitable feature of putting great power in the hands of human beings. The other is the danger of citizens putting unconditional and unquestioning trust in officials. We recognized the wisdom in these worries when we highlighted the danger of putting trust in leaders modeled on intimate, relational trust. Acknowledging these dangers, clear-eyed institutional designers have proposed measures of control and accountability that they were happy to characterize as devices of *institutionalized distrust*.[35]

Trust challengers seize on this characterization. They argue that mechanisms of accountability are motivated by, publicly express, and effectively nurture political distrust; from this they conclude that accountability represents a threat to good government and the rule of law, rather than, as Bentham put it, means of securing against misrule. The technologies of distrust, rooted in a deep suspicion of those who exercise power, engender an expectation, resistant to counter evidence, that officials are irredeemable "knaves."

They argue that systematic accountability undermines effective government in three ways. First, mechanisms of accountability stifle reasonable judgment, and turn officials' decision-making rigid and inflexible.[36] This makes conferring trust unreasonable, they argue, since trust necessarily confers an important degree of discretion on the trusted party. Second, accountability demoralizes public officials because it weakens motivations in officials that we should nurture. Accountability mechanisms, if they are pervasive, make it difficult for officials to demonstrate their trustworthiness. Their actions will reasonably be seen as predictable, self-protective responses to sanctions, rather than responses to trust placed in them. Subjecting officials to external sanctions, critics argue, crowds out desirable internal motivations, including trust responsiveness and concern for the public good.[37] Third, they argue that frequent publicly visible uses of accountability mechanisms undermine the public's confidence in government institutions and public officials. Although general confidence of citizens in a regime and its institutions is enhanced by knowledge of the existence and availability of mechanisms of accountability, when these mechanisms are deployed, confidence in public officials tends to decline. Paradoxically, "the potential availability" of such controls, writes sociologist Piotr Sztompka, "must be matched by their very limited actualization."[38]

These concerns are important, and I agree that political distrust, if pervasive in the polity, is corrosive of good government and of robust rule of law. But a more careful assessment of political distrust and of the nature and consequences of mechanisms of accountability will allow us to pull the sting of the trust challenge. The lesson we should draw from observations of potential costs of deploying mechanisms of accountability is not to retreat from rule-of-law demands for effective accountability mechanisms, nor to concede that accountability and political trust are incompatible. Rather, we should conclude that we must design accountability mechanisms and practices to avoid or reduce to a minimum these potential effects.

To begin our response to the trust challenge, recall that distrust lies at one extreme end of the trust spectrum. It involves active withholding of reliance on the distrusted party, rooted in deep suspicion that the other party, given the opportunity, will treat one's interest with indifference or contempt. The distrustful person is closed to new evidence of the potential good will or trustworthiness of the other party and reads all evidence in a light unfavorable to that party. In the political context, distrust tends to produce in those who harbor it cynicism, alienation, and despair, with the further result that they disengage from political life, or radically oppose and may even seek to undermine its institutions. Distrust is, indeed, corrosive of political life. It represents the danger opposite to that of naïve political trust that motivated designers of the chains of the Constitution. However, mistrust takes a very different stand. While it acknowledges doubt, it is willing to engage, even perhaps to rely (with precautions), on the other party. A mistrustful party is open to evidence of the trustworthiness of others, willing to respond with trust to credible signals of trust-responsiveness. A sober assessment of political power and its institutionalization should lead us to avoid both naïve trust and deep distrust. An open, if somewhat wary, mistrust seems more reasonable. It also leaves open the option of proleptic trust.

Next, recall that the political trust in view here is institution dependent. Rarely do citizens address officials directly. Governmental institutions and civic associations of many kinds mediate their encounters. These associations themselves are organized in different ways for different kinds of accountability and for holding accountable different kinds and levels of governmental officials.

Thus, for the most part, political trust and its contraries take shape in impersonal contexts. The personal attitudes that individual citizens or officials take are not our main concern. Rather, we should focus on their conduct that is relevant to and expressive of trust—their entrusting conduct, their conduct-withholding reliance, and their trust-responsive conduct. Accordingly, we must consider the publicly recognized meanings of the conduct involved in public accountability-holding activities, meanings that are available in the civic climate and reasonable inferences from them. The expectations in these impersonal contexts are likely to be different from, and not plausibly modeled on, more intimate personal contexts. The questions we must consider, then, are (1) what attitudes and dispositions along the trust-distrust spectrum do accountability-holding activities signal or communicate, and (2) what effect these are likely to have on the conduct and motivations of government officials.

Starting with the first question, we can uncover the plausible public meanings of these activities by looking at their publicly acknowledged aims and presuppositions and the reasonable associations that people may make between these activities and others seen as similar in motivation and upshot. Accountability mechanisms are meant to make good the rule of law's promise of protection and recourse against the arbitrary exercise of power. They are meant to give shape in institutions and practice to the partnership between those who wield political power and those who are subject to it. This partnership involves mutual commitments to comply with the law, but more, it involves common commitments to hold each other accountable to its terms. Although the relations between individual officials and individual civilians will be perceived as unequal, there is still a publicly recognized mutuality or reciprocity between officials and the public, when the institutions are well designed. Accountability depends and thrives on mutuality.

Second, the assumption animating the design of accountability mechanisms is not that human beings are inherently malevolent or untrustworthy ("knaves"). Rather the assumption is that ordinary human beings are motivationally weakest in circumstances where they wield power over the lives and fortunes of other human beings and where the temptation to use that power for personal aggrandizement is great. The law regularly and reasonably makes concessions to predictable, all-too-human weaknesses. For example, the criminal law recognizes that ordinary people will succumb to duress, or other failures of judgment or will, which some persons might have the strength to resist. The rule of law does the same.

Third, we noted earlier that the public meaning of trust-relevant conduct takes shape against the background of certain default assumptions. In the more intimate, interpersonal contexts, some degree of trust or at least tempered circumspection is the default. Even so, this default assumption often is suspended in circumstances where the stakes of relying on another person are very high or typical temptations are very strong. They are also suspended when people engage in innocent competition, in games or sports, for example. We can expect the same to be true in impersonal, especially political, contexts.

With these considerations in mind, it is reasonable to think that the accountability-holding actions of citizens say publicly something like the following to officials.

We agreed to submit to the law and your execution of it on the condition that you also submit to law and regard it as the guide and judge of your actions and ours. Moreover, recognizing that concentrated governing power is in many respects far greater than the dispersed power of individuals and civic associations, we nevertheless entrusted this power to you, making ourselves vulnerable to your actions as free agents and to your judgments of us. We did so because you also submitted to the law and our judgment of your best efforts to comply with and enforce it. Our holding you accountable for actions in the domain of your power as defined by the law provides you opportunities to show your good faith in acting out your commitment in circumstances that otherwise might compromise that good faith. We do not expect that you will deceive us or abuse your power or act against our legally protected interests from malevolent motives. But we know that the temptations of power are significant. Routine calls for you to give account of your exercise of the powers entrusted to you protect you from those temptations and from interpretations people might otherwise give to your actions as taken in bad faith and inconsistent with your commitment.

If this is the prevailing message and coercive sanctions only lie in the background, then the appeal to the integrity and public spirit of officials, or at least to their interest in the good opinion of others, can move to the foreground. If demands for accountability are made on a routine basis and not personally directed, then they will look more like invitations to officials to hold themselves accountable and to connect the execution of their official duties to values and commitments important to them.

Accountability mechanisms thus characterized do not presuppose or express distrust in any significant way. They may be motivated by and may even express caution based on realism about the dynamics of power and its temptations. They may also express a willingness to take certain precautions to avoid worse-case scenarios. But this stance is one of moderate mistrust and maybe even a modest form of trust—wary perhaps, but open to evidence of the good faith and trust responsiveness of public officials. Moreover, this moderate mistrust or modest trust leaves open the option of genuine proleptic trust. Indeed, the participation in accountability mechanisms looks more like community exercises of proleptic political trust than resolute refusals to trust and withdrawals of reliance. They engage rather than constrain the exercise of judgment by public officials. They recognize publicly the autonomy and moral capacities of officials, and put in play the concerns of public good, justice, and law's substantive demands on which we want official judgment to focus.

Accordingly, we have good reason to think that accountability-holding activities will not drive out intrinsic motivations of integrity or concern for the public good. Rather, they are open to, and seek to encourage, trust-responsive behavior on the part of officials, behavior that not only publicly demonstrates officials' good faith but also allows officials to act in ways that maintain their own integrity. There is nothing essentially punitive about holding to account a person to whom great power is entrusted. Rather, accountability makes manifest that exercises of power are subject to the deliberative forces of law and provides a public forum for those deliberative forces to work.

Of course, the desire for esteem may lie behind trust-responsiveness,[39] but, as we have seen, trustworthiness is primarily about trust-responsive behavior, and not about the reasons that motivate it. In this respect, trust in impersonal contexts may differ from trust in more intimate settings. Esteem is often spoken of as a kind of sanction, added to social norms to enforce compliance, a kind of informal punishment. But, in fact, esteem has a rather different psychological profile. Abraham Lincoln, in a speech early in his political career, said, "Every man is said to have his peculiar ambition. I have no other so great as that of being truly esteemed by my fellow men by rendering myself worthy of their esteem."[40] Lincoln recognized that esteem has an inner as well as outer dimension, a dimension more closely aligned with a person's integrity than with a loss of an object of desire. Hume, one of philosophy's most penetrating observers of human motivation, wrote, "[T]o love the fame of laudable actions approaches so near the love of laudable actions for their own sakes, that these passions are more capable of mixture, than any other kinds of affections."[41] Hume's observation is sound, I think. Officials may find desire for esteem—for the good opinion of others regarding proper, just, equitable decision-making—indistinguishable from finding these considerations themselves intrinsically compelling.

We can conclude that well-designed mechanisms of accountability are not properly characterized as institutions of distrust but rather mechanisms of proleptic political trust, or at least of mitigated moderate mistrust. They represent institutions and practices of active and engaged vigilance, rather than sullen, alienated disengagement. We also can answer the argument that the visible use of such mechanisms have a depressing effect on trust. This effect can be mitigated by educating citizens' normative expectations of official behavior and their understanding of concessions to human weakness that are manifest in the mechanisms of accountability. It will be dampened even more through active engagement of citizens in the mechanisms of accountability.

However, we cannot leave this topic without a sober concession. We must concede that the public meaning just outlined may be unavailable in political communities characterized by a climate of pervasive cynicism about human motivations, especially the motivations of public officials. That is, rule-of-law accountability devices can express and support modest trust if they operate in a moderately healthy climate of civic trust. Where the only publicly salient examples of official conduct are actions manifestly insensitive to, or contemptuous of, norms of trust and trustworthiness, it will be difficult for people to read official conduct through any other than distrustful lenses. Yet again, the decay of the rule of law is signaled, as Justice H.R. Khanna put it, "a choked and coarsened conscience."

A special case of this poisoned climate of civic trust is evident in societies deeply polarized by partisan political, religious, racial, or ethnic differences. Where their fellows treat citizens with deep suspicion, distrust, or worse just because of their membership in rival groups, it will be difficult to sustain robust political trust, or even moderate mistrust, of political officials who will inevitably be associated with some such groups to the exclusion of others. Devices of accountability do not cause this problem, but it will undermine their effectiveness and jeopardize law's rule. Even worse, in this climate accountability mechanisms may be misused or even "weaponized" for partisan political purposes. The sad truth is that no devices, constitutional, legal, or civic, can guarantee their own purity or success in protecting against the arbitrary exercise of power.

Yet in a climate of moderately healthy civic trust, and when the accountability mechanisms are known to work reasonably well, and the institutional checks and balances are also doing their work, space is opened up for genuine if moderated institution-dependent political trust. Effective and publicly functioning accountability mechanisms enhance and support political trust. Well-calibrated accountability devices are not expressive of distrust and may in fact carry public meaning of trust (however proleptic) and promise to enhance rather than undermine political trust.

Conclusion

The fidelity thesis that we have explored in this chapter and book embraces James Madison's insight: "As there is a degree of depravity in mankind which requires a certain degree of circumspection and distrust, so there are other qualities in human nature which justify a certain portion of esteem and confidence."[42] Once we understand the kind of accountability invoked by the fidelity thesis, and the subtle dimensions of civic and political trust and their contraries, we can pull the sting from the trust challenge. It is not the case that a deep tension lies at the heart of the rule-of-law ideal. Vigorous efforts at accountability do not drive out trust of an important and valuable kind. Rather, such trust is a condition and reasonably hoped-for consequence of it. The rule-of-law ideal does not assume that all power holders are knaves, but it does recognize that even the best of us are at our weakest in conditions that allow or encourage arbitrary exercises of that power. Constraints on such exercises recognize and capitalize on the "other qualities in human nature" that inspire our confidence.

11

Dilemmas of Discretion

Equity and Mercy

The seventeenth-century English jurist, Sir Edward Coke, severely criticized a statute of Henry VII for granting justices of the peace unfettered discretion to define and punish a wide range of vaguely stated offences. He insisted that Parliament must "leave all causes to be measured by the golden and streight metwand of the law, and not to the incertain and crooked cord of discretion."[1] Coke took a side here (elsewhere modified, as we shall soon see) on a debate with ancient roots. Leading the opposing team in this debate was Socrates' pupil Xenophon. In his biography of Cyrus the Great, Xenophon insisted, "the good ruler is a living law with eyes that see."[2] Coke's team argued that laws of England are "streight," and "all men's causes are justly and evenly measured" by them. Xenophon's team judged laws to be lifeless, lacking the vision and judgment of the good ruler. This debate continues to challenge law's rule to this day.

Crooked Cord or Law with Eyes?

Plato's *Statesman* dramatized this debate.[3] The framing question was: What form of governance will secure a just and decent polity, being ruled by the best ruler or by the best law? The best ruler has full grasp of the principles of justice and the common good, possesses the practical skills needed to apply them properly to circumstances of daily life, and is motivated to use this expertise for the benefit of the polis. The best laws have the following properties: they are just and directed to the common good; simple, general, and understandable; fully public such that their authenticity and content is accessible to all; and inflexible and slow to change.

Both options are problematic. The problem with laws is that they can be blind to the variable circumstances of daily life and following them in some cases is irrational, undermining the very purposes they are meant to serve. Surely, if a trainer who prescribes a regime finds that his trainee is not getting stronger, or a doctor who prescribes a course of medicine finds her patient is not getting well, it would be irrational for them to say, "Well, that's the rule; we gotta stick by it." The problem may not be that the regimen or the course of medicine is generally

Law's Rule. Gerald J. Postema, Oxford University Press. © Oxford University Press 2022.
DOI: 10.1093/oso/9780190645342.003.0011

ill-conceived—they may be just right for most people in most circumstances most of the time. Similarly, the problem with laws may not be that they are unjust or wrong, but that laws, just by being laws, get it wrong in some particular cases. Thus, Plato initially sided with Xenophon. What we need, he argued, is "living law with eyes that see"; that is, good rulers with the freedom to use their good judgment to tailor prescriptions for the good of the polis to the individual circumstances and capacities of each member. That would be our best option, except for the fact that finding persons with the requisite expertise is extremely hard and entangles us in interminable disputes over what counts as a decent and just polis; and it is even harder to find persons with the requisite just dispositions. To entrust those who happen to find their way to power with the wide freedom to exercise it without laws to constrain it is to invite the tyrant to rule in hopes that he will resist turning that power to his own interest.

That risk is too great, Plato admitted, concluding that the only politically prudent, albeit distinctly second best, option is to embrace law's rule and forgo the benefits of discretion. Any attempt to mitigate its rigidity, allowing those who administer the law to take account of circumstances not countenanced in it, would corrupt its rule. The only protection against the caprice of rulers is law. Better to entrust the polis to rigid, inflexible, and general laws than to the caprice and inevitable corruption of venal men.

Aristotle found this solution unpalatable and insisted that a nuanced and carefully trained capacity of judgment could reconcile these opposing sides and bring discretion, properly educated, within the scope of law's rule.[4] Coke agreed. The mistake made by the Henrician statute was to create a legal black hole, granting power to magistrates without tethering it to law. He insisted that any grant of discretionary power must legally bridled. Discretion is the capacity "to discern between falsity and truth, between wrong and right, between shadows and substance, between equity and colourable glosses and pretences, and not to do according to their wills and private affections."[5] Discretion must be "limited and bound with the rule of reason and law." Discretion does not go *beyond* or *against* law, he argued; it is a matter of discernment *through law* of what is just.[6]

This debate sets the task of this chapter. Our task is to find, if we can, a role for discretion within law's rule. However, "discretion" is used to refer to phenomena that span a wide spectrum. At one extreme, it refers to decisions freed from law, entirely unguided by (positive) law, or the power to derogate from law or suspend it. At the other extreme, it refers to a power to decide some matter, where the decision engages to some extent the judgment of the decider. This is a limiting case of discretion, of course, because judgment is needed even where decisions are guided by well-articulated, reasonably precise rules. Between these extremes fall arrangements that vary in the scope they give to discretion guided in some way by law. Law, for example, may supply standards or more or less broadly expressed principles; they may direct the decision maker to take into account a range of factors but not precisely define their relative weights; or the decider might have to determine which of two competing rules or principles should prevail.

The sites of discretion properly occupying this middle ground are many. Within the public domain, discretion is often granted to officials managing the services or exercising the regulatory functions of the modern administrative state, especially those at the apex of the executive hierarchy. It is also a regular and inescapable part of adjudication. Sometimes law allocates discretionary power to nonpublic entities and private individuals. At these various sites, discretion plays different roles and poses different kinds of challenges for the rule of law. This chapter considers in detail two such challenges: *equity* as it arises in private law adjudication and *mercy* as it arises in criminal adjudication. Chapter 12 will consider decision-making in times of *emergency* in the exercise of *executive pardon* power.

Equity

The concern of this chapter is, in part, to explore the possibility of the rule of law accommodating, perhaps even welcoming, equity and mercy. For this purpose, the task is not to analyze these concepts, to map the terrain of their use in contemporary discourse, or to regiment that use, but to isolate certain moral and jural phenomena that appear to pose special challenges to law's rule and to explore ways to meet them.

Equity in Its Jural Habitat

The idea of equity that we shall focus on fits into a constellation of moral-political values that includes justice, mercy, equality, law, conscience, correction, and mitigation. In addition, we will focus on equity as a quality of judgments or persons in distinctively legal or jural contexts, rather than in more broadly political contexts. In contemporary political discourse, people think of equity as a species of equality, more nuanced than mere sameness of treatment. It takes into account, for example, different starting points or special disadvantages when assessing the impact of social programs. It is concerned with real or material, and not merely formal, equality of opportunity. This is a legitimate use of the term "equity," but this chapter is concerned with a different notion.

The jural notion of equity has a long history going back to Aristotle, and it played a large role in the development of English law.[7] We will consider here mainly the decisions and actions of judges and other legal officials. By extension, we might speak of a private person as behaving equitably. In Aristotle's view, one who acts inequitably—who is "a stickler for justice"[8]—insists on his legal rights despite the disproportionate costs to another party. A few examples may help fix this jural kind of equity in our view.

Equity scholar, Emily Sherwin offers two classic cases for our consideration. First, elderly Mr. Panco agreed to sell the house that he built with his own hands to Rogers. Because her husband was deaf, Rogers discussed the transaction with Mrs. Panco, who was not a native English speaker, and they prepared an agreement for the sale of the house at the price of $5,500, although in testimony Mr. Panco said he intended to ask for $12,500. Mr. Panco signed the agreement without reading it, but later refused to convey the property. Although the court found no evidence of fraud or undue influence in the transaction and concluded that Mr. Panco was in breach of the sales contract, it denied Rogers' claim for specific performance—actual transfer of the property. The court argued:

> [A]n application for specific performance is directed to the sound discretion of a court of equity. . . . [T]he court must be satisfied that the claim is fair, reasonable, and just, and in judging of its fairness, the court will look not only at the terms of the contract itself, but at all of the surrounding circumstances, including the relations of the parties. . . . Where the enforcement of a contract for the sale of land would be harsh, oppressive or manifestly unjust to one of the parties thereto, its specific performance will not be decreed, but the parties will be left to their remedy at law.[9]

In a second case, Mrs. Ali agreed to sell her house to Patel.[10] The transaction was fair, but closing was greatly delayed, though not due to any action of Patel or any legal fault of Mrs. Ali. During this delay, Mrs. Ali had two more children, was diagnosed with cancer, and one leg was amputated. At closing, she was entirely dependent on her sister and neighbors. Again, the court refused to order Mrs. Ali to convey the house to Patel, limiting his remedy to damages for loss of bargain.

Parties suing for nuisance often appeal to the equity jurisdiction of courts. In one such case,[11] the defendant was unhappy that his neighbor was breeding foxes on his property because the defendant thought it would make it difficult for him to develop his land into residential property. He had his son repeatedly fire a gun, succeeding in his hope to disrupt the foxes' breeding. The neighbor sued for damages and an injunction. The court awarded both, reasoning that, although the defendant was legally entitled to fire guns on his property, he did it with the intent of harming the neighbor, committing a wrongful nuisance.

In another case, Elmer Palmer killed his grandfather, Francis Palmer. The elder Palmer's daughters sued to prevent Elmer from claiming his inheritance as specified in the deceased's will, asserting that they were intended beneficiaries of a will that Francis had planned but was prevented from executing by Elmer's action. They did not claim that Francis's will was secured by fraud or that Francis was incompetent when the will was executed; rather they argued that Elmer's killing of his grandfather estopped Elmer from claiming what he was entitled to under law. The court, exercising their equitable judgment, agreed.[12]

As these cases suggest, equity involves the exercise of discretionary judgment that seeks to correct and mitigate the harshness of law. Over its history, equity has often been thought to be rooted in the moral conscience of the judge or ruler, transcending and standing in judgment of law itself. This, in turn, caused many to join John Selden, seventeenth-century polymath and raconteur, in thinking that equity is "roguish," measured only by the idiosyncratic and always-changing chancellor's foot.[13] However, Selden's dismissal is hasty. There is more to the story.

The notion of equity is shaped by its relations to the notions of justice, mercy, and law. Often, the harshness that equity is meant to correct is due to bad, cruel, or unjust laws. In that case, equity is thought to do justice where the existing law fails. We should not ignore this dimension of equity in our exploration here, but neither should we allow it to obscure the dimension that Plato, Xenophon, and Aristotle called to our attention, namely, that laws may be harsh or do injustice merely by virtue of their being laws. Equity is able to correct law because it "judgeth according to circumstances."[14] With justice in view, but realizing that laws cannot by their nature always do justice, the equitable judge seeks to do "particularized justice," paying sensitive and sympathetic attention to features not explicitly set out in the legal rules. Such justice, it is argued, is within the ambition of law but not within its reach. Equity does "what the law desires but cannot perform."[15] Equity, wrote the medieval English jurist St. German, is "ryghtwysenes that consideryth all pertyculer cyrcumstaunces," while "extreme ryghtwysenes is extreme wronge."[16]

This focus on sensitive attention to particulars, especially particulars of the parties in litigation, is often thought to bring equity within the orbit of mercy.[17] Sometimes, as in *Patel v. Ali*, the reason for mitigating the harsh consequences of straightforward application of the law may not be entirely clear. Nevertheless, it is useful to distinguish equity from mercy even though the difference in some instances is subtle. Equity is a *species* of justice, while mercy *tempers* justice with compassion (or so I will argue in the next section). Mercy is a matter of grace rather than duty, of compassion rather than respect for rights. Thus, while mercy seeks to temper justice within the frame of law, equity seeks to correct law to achieve particularized justice. A failure to judge equitably, like a failure to be merciful, may draw warranted moral criticism, but it is a different kind of fault. The concepts of equity and mercy are oriented toward law and justice in different ways. Equity does not stand outside of law, in pristine judgment of it, but rather is internal to law or its ambition and works together with it to achieve that ambition.

Of course, these thoughts do not yield a precise understanding of equity in the jural context, but they orient our exploration and raise important questions. How can equity work within law and yet correct it? How can discretion motivated by equity "work through law," as Coke insisted? More generally, is equity understood in this way compatible with the general ambition of the rule of law?

Obstacles to Understanding Equity

Standing in the way of our understanding how the rule of law might accommodate and even embrace equity is Plato's thought that discretionary judgment destroys law, or rather, equity destroys law's promise of certainty and protection against arbitrary exercise of power, because equity is as variable and singular as the will of the judge who purports to use it. Uncertainty and arbitrariness are the inevitable consequence of allowing equity to creep into adjudication. However, as we saw in Chapter 4, the quest for law's certainty is a fool's errand. Following legal rules requires judgment, so, if judgment entails uncertainty, then uncertainty is inescapable. The aim must not be to eliminate uncertainty but to manage it, keep it within bounds, and avoid its downside risks.

For this project, Aristotle offered a promising beginning. The circumstance-sensitive judgment of judges must be trained, subjected to a discipline of perception and reasoning. Law, we have repeatedly argued in this book, provides just such a discipline. In Chapter 3, we argued that law is a disciplined practice of public and publicly oriented practical reasoning. Critical to the practice is the focus of perception and reasoning on resources provided by the body of law as a whole. It is on these common and public resources, and their internal relations, that the capacity for judgment is trained. Equitable judgment, as Coke taught, is the product of the trained capacity of "discernment *through law* of what is just." Moreover, this discipline is common and public. It is common in that it is not an individual skill, but one practiced in and by a community of practitioners, held to standards by that community. It is public in that practitioners must display in public not only the product of its working, but also the process; its reasons and reasoning as well as its decisions. This engages the further, critical element of rule-of-law management, public accountability. Thus, equitable judgment may yield some uncertainty, but it is manageable; it is not arbitrary when it is set in an institutional context that secures adequate public accountability.

A second but subtler thought also inhibits our understanding of equity's role in a rule-of-law regime. On this view, law and equity are opposed values, locked in agonistic struggle; any gain for equity brings with it a regrettable loss of the value that law promises. We sometimes think about liberty and security this way, for example; so too the relation between loyalty to friends and responsible discharge of the public duties and the relation between freedom of choice and protection of public health. But some value pairs, while different, are related more intimately. They are internally related and interdependent. They are complementary because they are mutually limiting, each responding to and correcting limitations or potential defects of full implementation of the other. Well-intentioned and conscientious judgments that seek to do what is just and right in particular circumstances suffer from well-known deficiencies; they are subject to characteristic deformations.[18] The characteristic deformation of equity judgments is a kind of practical myopia. Focusing on the particular trees within its immediate field of vision, one risks failing to see the forest, its impact on one's field of vision, and, in turn, the impact of one's decisions on it. In addition, without some external points of reference and constraints, it is often difficult for one to distinguish sensitive perception from personal or partisan prejudice; and difficult to articulate in publicly accessible reasons the grounds of one's judgment. Judgment without law to guide and orient it is not "law with eyes" but not law at all; it loses its ability to do "particular justice" and thereby its publicly beneficial value. Equity, strictly speaking, is parasitic on law; "[a]t every point equity presuppose[s] the existence of common law.... Equity without common law would have been a castle in the air, an impossibility."[19]

Similarly, as we have seen, law without equitable judgment suffers from a complementary form of myopia. It is blind to the very conditions in which it seeks to realize its aims. Unable to anticipate in advance all the complex movements of life in the polity, it avoids practical absurdity only when it allows equity, suitably disciplined, to correct its focus. Laws proceed from an *ex ante* perspective; equity works *ex post* (typically, but not exclusively). Each brings benefits to the polity when they can work in partnership, each correcting the others, helping them avoid otherwise inevitable deformations. A legal system can achieve its ambition of promoting specific goals constituent of the public good in a way that respects justice only when it brings together and draws on these complementary and mutually limiting perspectives. Seeing these values as agonistic, as fundamentally in opposition, Plato felt forced to choose one over the other. Aristotle, sensing their complementarity, proposed a beneficial partnership. An intelligible public framework for governing the exercise of power must find a way to yoke law and equity institutionally and internally.

The Equity-Law Partnership

One model of this partnership arose in English law. For much of its history, the English legal system comprised both law and equity. Law was the domain and product of common-law courts; the Court of Chancery served equity. Boundaries between these courts were guarded jealously. The law administered by common-law courts consisted of islands of parliamentary statutes surrounded by a sea of doctrines, principles, and rules that emerged over time from judicial determination of particular cases, a process that was governed by a duty to follow precedent (*stare decisis*). Although the doctrine of precedent as practiced by the courts was flexible enough to allow for adjustment and correction, the courts' rules often grew rigid, and claimants sought equitable relief from Chancery courts. However, this institutional distinction, while it prevailed for centuries, became increasingly artificial. Inevitably, feeling the pressure to avoid the appearance of arbitrariness and often finding general solutions to problems that first emerged in the interstices of common-law rules, equity courts articulated doctrines that took on the nature of general, formal laws, allowing at some points a somewhat wider scope for judicial discretion. In the late nineteenth century, English, American, and Commonwealth jurisdictions merged common law and equity. The dual-court system was replaced by a single system in which courts administered both law and equity.

Yet equity was neither removed from the court's toolbox nor left to roam free to challenge the regular operation of law at the whim of the court. It was given a special institutional place as the complement of law-oriented adjudication. Legal scholar Henry E. Smith recently characterized this institutionalization of equity within the American legal system as "meta-law."[20] "Law's complement" might be a more accurate term, because, he argues, equity presupposes and serves law in a distinctive way. His model refines the Aristotelian notion that equity fills gaps inevitably left by law. It carefully defines the kinds of *problems* created by law's necessary generality that equity addresses and articulates the *principles* or *maxims* and *processes* that structure equitable discretion.

The boundaries of the domain of equity's proper operation, on Smith's model, are defined by failures of law due to complexity of the problems brought to the courts. He identifies three kinds of such problems.[21] (1) *Polycentricity*: polycentric tasks involve many people, objects, or activities and complex interdependencies among them. (2) *Conflicting rights*: equally valid rights often come into conflict—in nuisance cases, for example—but resolution of the conflict *ex ante* and in general may be especially difficult, requiring context-sensitive reasoning *ex post* to reach a satisfactory decision. (3) *Opportunism*: law's generality also provides opportunities for misuse of law or abuse of rights by those who are sophisticated and unscrupulous, opportunities that may be difficult to anticipate and legislatively prevent.

When problems arise in one of these areas, equity deliberation is triggered by one or more of the following patterns of facts:[22] customary practices are violated (signaling that a party may be acting opportunistically); a party acts with apparent bad faith or deception; one of the parties suffers or will suffer disproportionate hardship, or is especially vulnerable. Terms like "bad faith" or "disproportionate hardship" do not bring into play specific legal rules that mandate legal intervention; rather, they invite a different kind of evaluation within an equitable framework. This framework enables a closer look at the context of the interactions between the parties in light of considerations of fairness and justice and may invite a search beyond the four corners of the law for appropriate remedies.

Equity deliberation is contextual, requiring sensitive attention to facts at a greater level specificity, but also within a broader frame, than is normal for adjudication under laws. It also requires sensitive consideration and balancing of a number of different values, interests, and concerns. However, this reasoning is guided. Over the years, a number of principles and maxims have evolved to guide equitable decision-making.[23] Among them we find, for example, "equity regards substance rather than form"; "no one may profit from their own wrong"; "they who come into equity must come with clean hands"; "equity imputes intent to fulfill an obligation"; "equity aids the vigilant and diligent"; "equity suffers no wrong without remedy"; "the court will not be made an instrument of wrong." These maxims do not exhaust the guidance given to courts seeking to make equitable judgments, neither do they function like fixed rules, but they do give their reasoning shape and direction.

The institutional process of equity adjudication gives further definition to equity reasoning. Legal scholar Matthew Harding calls attention to several features of equity's institutional framework that contribute to this definition and direction.[24] First, such reasoning works with materials—facts, contexts, and considerations—that are presented in a public forensic process. The bipolar structure of private litigation limits the range of facts, doctrines, and remedy options that the court is authorized to consider. Also, parties to litigation are entitled to present evidence and substantiate their pleas for relief in a carefully regulated fashion; and judges are duty-bound to take seriously and weigh appropriately the evidence and arguments offered by the parties. Second, judges are bound to articulate their decisions in terms of reasons that can sit coherently within the body of law as a whole. Even as they exercise discretion, judges must seek to render decisions that are and can be seen to be sensible within a system of law that achieves integrity and coherence over time. Third, they are bound to articulate these reasons in and to the public, responding to the evidence and arguments offered by the parties and the demands of systemic integrity. This secures accountability of the courts' discretionary judgment.

Of course, existing mechanisms of public accountability may fall short of what is necessary to protect against the arbitrary exercise of judicial power, but the fault lies not in the rule-of-law ideal but in our attempts to realize it in our formal institutions and informal practices. Far from demanding that we purge equity jurisdiction from our legal systems, the rule of law urges a productive partnership between the two complementary ambitions of law and equity. When law protects its own integrity, the rule of law is served; it is compromised when law is turned against itself, as it is when latter-day authoritarians seek to preserve constitutional forms while "hollowing out" their substance and the constraints on power that they impose.[25] Similarly, the realization of the rule-of-law ideal must include mechanisms of self-correction. Recognizing the law-limiting, but ultimately law-enhancing, capacity of a robust partnership with equity is one such mechanism of self-correction. It also provides people with recourse against those who seek cover of the law to exploit or oppress them. We need law to protect and provide recourse against those who arbitrarily exercise power over them; however, where law itself provides the means of or cover for such power, the rule of law calls on equity to correct this abuse. Equity enables legal institutions to resist the use of its resources against the interests of those persons and values it seeks to serve. Thus, equity when yoked to law—and law refined and corrected by equity—is not an enemy of the rule of law but one of its key foot soldiers.

This suggests that the law-correcting function of equity-shaped discretion may serve not only to achieve particularized justice but also other important values. One such value is oversight of fiduciary activities in the area of trusts. Beyond the scope of the notion of equity, discretion plays another disputed role, this time in the domain of criminal law. Like equity, mercy seems to pose a challenge for the rule of law.

Mitigating Grace

If the rule of law is willing to accord equity a role in its normative ideal of governance, might it also find room for mercy? The two notions generate similar rule-of-law worries because both encourage officials, especially judges, to exercise discretion to mitigate the harshness of prevailing laws. Both may introduce uncertainty, partiality, and unfairness into the operation of law, critics argue, and thus challenge or compromise law's rule. But there are also important differences between these two values that prompt a closer look at mercy even after we have put these worries concerning equity to rest. While the primary legal habitat of equity is private law, we call upon mercy to season criminal justice. The two notions collect different key moral concerns: equity seeks particular justice, while mercy is mitigating grace,[26] motivated by unmerited compassion against undisputed demands of justice. We can get by with a little equity here and there, but mercy seems to pose a more potent challenge to law's rule.

Perhaps not everything that we might reasonably call mercy can be granted admission into a robust rule-of-law regime; still, there is a familiar and morally compelling form of mercy that is compatible with, and maybe even a necessary complement of, the rule of law. Our task here is, first, to sketch the profile of this form of mercy, and then to locate a proper role for it in a legal regime that meets the demands of the rule of law.

Power, Discretion, and Compassion

A victorious soldier spares the life of his captive foe. Some might say that the soldier showed mercy and the vanquished soldier was "at the mercy" of his enemy. However, others might think that the biblical story of the Good Samaritan (Luke 10.25–37) offers a better paradigm of mercy. A man on the road to Jericho stopped to aid the victim of a brutal mugging, bandaged his wounds, took him to an inn, and paid for the man's lodging as he departed. Despite his outsider status, the Samaritan proved to be the victim's true "neighbor," we are told, because he showed him mercy (*poiēsas eleos*—literally, *did* mercy). Mercy might also have been at work when a judge reduced the mandated sentence for manslaughter for a man who, driving while intoxicated, crashed his car and killed his daughter and wife, who were riding with him.

These stories illustrate some features of our richly textured ordinary notion of mercy. This notion has played a key role in theology, in secular moral thought and practice, and even in politics and law from ancient times to the present. We think of mercy in many different contexts, but for our purposes the dominant one is jural. Mercy finds its way into the halls of penal justice—at the sentencing phase of a trial, in the working of grand or petit juries, and when prosecutors determine what crimes to charge, what sentences to propose, whether to offer a plea bargain. Police, too, may find reasons of mercy influencing their decisions about what crimes to investigate or whom arrest; and it may influence the deliberations of parole boards. Perhaps the most public site of leniency is the chief executive's exercise of pardon, clemency, and commutation powers. In fact, executive pardon power raises unique questions for the rule of law, and we will postpone discussion of them to the next chapter and focus our attention on the other sites of judgment in the penal process.

Several conceptions of mercy have vied for primacy in moral and political thought. Despite their differences, they agree on the following core components: *mercy involves the authorized exercise of unexpected discretionary mitigation of harsh treatment intended to benefit the recipient.* Let's unpack this proposal. The treatment is discretionary in the sense that it is not strictly required by existing valid rules, but rather may be justified by considerations not encompassed by those rules. Merciful treatment is less harsh than expected or merited, and the recipient is its immediate beneficiary. Finally, due to their relationship with the recipient, the mercy givers are in a position, and in mercy's jural forms are authorized, either to exact the harsh treatment or mitigate it. This fact is often thought to imply two other features. First, the act is regarded as in some sense a gift—a matter of grace we sometimes say, but this does not imply that it is wanton or done without any reason. Second, the relationship between the giver and receiver of mercy is asymmetric, either due to the situation they find themselves in or to the normative framework of their relationship. The mercy giver has discretionary power over the beneficiary to impose harsh treatment or exercise mercy. The receiver is "at the mercy" of the other party. Thus, rule-of-law alarms sound for two reason: the "gift" is not rule-governed and is given against a valid mandate to the contrary; and this exercise of discretion takes place in the context of a manifest inequality of the parties.

Missing from this characterization is any consideration of the reasons for which leniency is granted. Is the good or welfare of the beneficiary the focal concern? Or is it meant to benefit some third party—another individual, the community at large, or the mercy giver? Do these reasons spring from compassion or public spirit? Or calculated self-interest? At this point, different traditions of understanding of mercy diverge.

One such tradition stems from ancient Greek and especially Roman-Stoic sources. Its point of departure is the thought that mercy is an expression of power, distinct from and in strict opposition to legal justice. It is the supreme expression of sovereignty: the sovereign holds life and death in his hands, entitled to set aside the law, for any reason or no reason at all. Yet, on this view, the wise sovereign wields this prerogative power carefully and prudently to achieve his ends and sustain the supremacy of his power.[27] Clearly, this understanding of mercy stands in stark opposition to law's rule. Clemency is a tool and a symbolic representation of the subordination of law to the ruler.

This understanding still lingers in the linguistic field of "mercy," but a better candidate for our exploration stems from religious traditions that link "mercy" to compassion, as in Hebrew (*rachum chanum*), Greek (*eleos*), and Latin (*misericordia*). Compassion-mercy is wider than mercy that operates in the context of law and judging—the Good Samaritan exercised compassion-mercy, but did not judge the conduct of the victim. Still, there may be room for compassion-mercy in the jural context, involving not only sympathy with the suffering or plight of another but also efforts to mitigate the suffering. Set in this context, mercy immediately brings justice into view, but "seasoned," as Shakespeare's Portia put it, by mercy. In the prophet Hosea's powerful image, God has every reason to be consumed with anger at Ephraim's injustice and infidelity; however,

> My heart churns within me,
>   My compassion altogether is stirred.
> I will not act in My blazing wrath,
>   I will no more destroy Ephraim.
> For I am God and not a man. (Hosea 11.8–9)

The God of Israel recoils from just judgment—the altogether human response—after reflection on His love for Israel and its inevitable suffering. According to the Talmud, when the shofar is blown before God, God gets up from the throne of judgment and moves to the throne of mercy.[28] Mercy and justice are distinct; they view the potential recipient of mercy through different moral lenses. But, according to this tradition, mercy must not displace justice, nor justice mercy; rather, they must work together in some way; and only in that way can the world endure.[29]

Mercy is not indifferent to justice or to the fault of the recipient; mercy "refuses . . . ever to let the person off the hook for that fault."[30] It does not condone, justify, or excuse wrongs done by the recipient. Rather than exonerating the wrongdoer, rescinding or regretting the condemnation of the wrong, it mitigates the *consequences* of that judgment. This explains why it is often thought that mercy is an appropriate response to sincere repentance, which entails a resolute turning from the wrong done. The wrongdoing is condemned, but because the wrongdoer turns his back on it, distances himself from it, it is appropriate to see him in a different light, one that takes into account a wider spectrum of his past and prospects for an altered future. The wrongdoer need not any longer be identified and hemmed in by the wrong done.

Mercy has its own moral focus and source of motivating reasons. It qualifies and perhaps complements justice; it is not owed to, or deserved by, the recipient. Yet it may be in certain circumstances something that *ought* to be extended, for which there are compelling reasons. To refuse to extend mercy in such cases, we might reasonably think, is a moral failure. This is true within the Stoic tradition as well. Seneca warned, "[I]t is a fault to punish a fault in full."[31]

Following this tradition, we may add to the features of mercy we surveyed earlier, two more features. (1) Mercy is motivated by compassion and so is focused on the particular features of the recipient. (2) At its best, mercy stems from and is nourished by self-reflection of the giver.

First, the driving motive of this form of mitigating grace is *compassion* for the suffering individual. Not only is she the immediate beneficiary but mercy is extended to her *for her sake*, in view of *her suffering* or the special hardship that punishment will impose on her. Thus, it focuses the decision maker on the history, circumstances, or specific condition of the recipient. Thus, we might call this form of mercy "compassionate mitigating grace." Leniency meant to heal divisions in the nation, to reward an offender's cooperation with the prosecution, or even to counter harshly unjust law, may be justified, but these reasons fall outside the kind of mitigating grace this tradition brings into view. However, the special suffering of the offender's family or dependents may sometimes motivate leniency. While its focus is not directly on the special circumstances of the offender, compassionate mitigating grace may also embrace such considerations.

A second thread runs through this tradition of reflection on mercy. This idea is given voice by Portia.

> Though justice be thy plea, consider this:
> That in the course of justice none of us
> Should see salvation. We do pray for mercy,
> And that same prayer doth teach us all to render
> The deeds of mercy.[32]

Think on this, Portia challenges Shylock: If you were to turn the demand of justice back on yourself, would you not seek mercy? Indeed, if justice were the only measure of our actions, none of us would enjoy salvation. Portia's rhetorical strategy draws on the view that we are moved to mercy through self-reflection, through reflection on the fact that not only are we all fallible but we are vulnerable to obstacles to our moral flourishing. While some of us are saved from temptation's force by our circumstances ("by the grace of God"); for some, the obstacles to flourishing may prove too great. Isabella in *Measure for Measure* makes the trope even more explicit. "Go to your bosom;/Knock there; and ask your heart what it doth know;/That's like my brother's fault."[33]

Sir Matthew Hale sat on the King's Bench judging criminal cases. In his diary, he echoed Portia's theme:

> It is the grace and goodness of God that I myself have not fallen into as great enormities as those upon which I give judgment. I have the same passions and lusts and corruptions that even those malefactors themselves have. . . . But even while the duty of my place requires justice and possibly severity in punishing

the offense, yet the sense of common humanity and human frailty should at the same time engage me to great compassion to the offender.[34]

Hale linked self-reflection to compassion and both of them to mercy. Reflection on common human frailty engenders compassion, which, in turn, counsels mercy.

Stoic philosophy also recognized self-reflection as the source of mercy; yet Seneca insisted that compassion must play no role in the exercise of merciful judgment. Hale's understanding of mercy as compassionate mitigating grace offers a better explanation of the role of self-reflection, I believe. For if compassion is disengaged, then self-reflection and reflections on the circumstances of the other party are as likely to yield indifference, not mercy. Compassion makes palpable the similarity of conditions, focusing on common vulnerabilities, shifting differences to the background, and bringing home to the judge the plight of the potential beneficiary. "The merciful narrative attitude is a way of acknowledging the humanity of the wrongdoer and doing justice to one's own."[35] Motivated by a keen sense of commonality, the exercise of power takes on a very different moral character. Rather than a threat to the dignity of the beneficiary, it affords officials an opportunity to affirm common humanity.

Thus, compassionate mitigating grace avoids the unwanted features of the Stoic tradition and offers a morally compelling form of mercy. But we still must ask, is there a place for mercy in a rule-of-law regime? In particular, can we combine it in a morally satisfactory way with other proper goals and principles of the criminal process and the responsibilities of officials, especially judges, to serve these goals and respect these principles?

Mercy in the Criminal Process

Do Justice and Leave Mercy to Heaven

Thwackum, Tom Jones's tutor, "was for doing justice, and leaving mercy to heaven."[36] Admittedly, he was a hypocrite, and he played favorites among his students; but he voiced a common sentiment, precisely appropriate, it is thought, for officials in the criminal justice system. Judges must check loyalty to friends and partiality to family at the courthouse door; they should do the same for mercy, not because mercy is not a moral virtue, worthy of esteem and emulation, but simply because there is no proper place for it in the criminal justice system. Two key features of mercy prompt this response: its motivational source and its mitigating effect. The mitigation of the otherwise expected and deserved harsh treatment prescribed by the law is the product of discretion motivated by compassion. It appears unruly—not governed by rules—and even lawless; and it undermines the work of justice. Moreover, compassion threatens the impartiality of judicial decisions and opens the courthouse doors to wayward emotions. Mercy's challenge to the rule of law seems obvious.

Critics often argue that mercy judgments are unreasoned and arbitrary.[37] However, mercy is not unreasoned; the reasons to which compassion alerts the judge are different from those of retributive justice, but they are no less reasons; and they function more like multifactor standards than fixed rules. If there is a reason for requiring officials to check mercy, along with loyalty and family partiality, at the courthouse door, this must be due to something about mercy reasons themselves and not merely the fact that they are different from reasons of desert or are not captured by straightforward legal rules.

The deeper problem, critics argue, is that mercy is a lottery; grants of mercy are determined by chance. Some persons are by nature or experience more compassionate than others, and this is true for judges as well. Whether offenders are treated with mercy or not depends on whether the mercy lottery assigns them to Judge Warm-Heart or Judge Rule-Bound. Two offenders guilty of the same crime, with the same substantial degree of culpability, doing the same legally recognized and morally condemnable wrong, may nevertheless be given significantly different sentences, because one judge tends to give mercy considerations weight in his deliberations, but the other keeps them at arm's length. This outcome is inevitable as long as officials in our criminal system are human, but it is arbitrary and treats offenders unfairly.

Yet not every chance-determined difference of sentences is unfair. A prosecutor may offer an offender the option of pleading guilty to a lesser offense, carrying a less harsh sentence, in exchange for valuable information he happens to have. Although the offender is guilty of a crime more serious than the one charged and is no less culpable than others who serve the prescribed sentence for that crime, he is given more lenient treatment for what in effect is the random fact that he has information that is useful to the prosecutor. We recognize that considerations other than desert may properly be weighed in determining the punishment to be imposed on an offender, and the availability of those considerations in particular cases may be random. The differential treatment is not unfair.

So are mercy-justified decisions similarly fair?[38] Normally, when we judge actions of the state unfair, we object to harm that it unfairly imposes or benefits that it unfairly denies, not just to the fact that the treatment is different. However, where mercy genuinely falls randomly, no harm is done to the offenders; for the beneficiary of the merciful treatment receives less punishment than is deserved and those treated more harshly are treated as they deserve. The offenders are treated differently, but strictly speaking, no harm is done to them. (Harm, or rather some form of injustice, may be done to victims if some offenders are granted merciful treatment, but that is a different concern. We will consider it presently.) Of course, harm might be done if the difference in treatment is not justified, but the shared assumption is that leniency is motivated by mercy-relevant, hence morally creditable, reasons.

Harm and wrong may be done if the benefits are allocated in a way that, although motivated by compassion, follows and reinforces patterns of social privilege or racial, gender, or other modes of invidious discrimination. But this serious objection is not directed to the differential treatment but to mercy when it tracks or reinforces existing social inequalities. Surely, it is a moral wrong, a general and condemnable injustice, if the state smiles with mercy only on those already privileged. Mercy that tracks or reinforces marked patterns of invidious discrimination is morally compromised, deformed.

Even if mercy is not entirely out of place in the criminal system, it can go wrong. Mercy is to a degree risky. Discretionary judgment can be ill-used; mercy can be ill-judged. Officials granting mercy must look not only to the specific circumstances of the offender before them but also to the wider context and impact of their judgments. If mercy is to have a chance of being consistent with the rule-of-law demands, it must not only temper or season justice, it must itself be tempered. (We will say a bit more about this shortly.)

However, critics argue, the root problem of giving mercy a place, even a modest one, in the criminal system is that mercy is motivated by compassion. Compassion has no proper place in legal reasoning and especially not in the reasoning of officials in the criminal system. Compassion has its seat in the heart, not the head—in the domain of the "beast," not of "reason"; hence, this not appropriate to the rule *of law*. The rule of law demands detached and impersonal judgment, but compassion is emotional and personal. It is dangerous, first, because it is nonrational and hence unpredictable, ungovernable; second, because it is liable to bias and partiality; third, because mercy laces benefit with contempt; mercy is degrading to the recipient. Let us consider these worries in turn.

The first worry rests on a common but inaccurate understanding of compassion. Philosopher Martha Nussbaum has persuasively argued that we sell compassion short if we think of it as an emotion that we experience passively— a "passion" outside of our agency that pushes or pulls us toward action. Compassion, rather, is a painful emotion occasioned by awareness of the serious misfortunes or suffering of other persons, but this emotion is not nonrational.[39] Rather, like other key emotions, it has a strong cognitive element, involving an evaluative judgment that appraises some object or experience as important for the other persons' well-being. This involves an assessment of the seriousness of the suffering and its impact on their experience and lives. It also involves reflection on the similarities between those suffering and the person feeling compassion. This reflection enables the compassionate person to make sense of the other person's experience as suffering—"estimat[ing] its meaning by thinking what it would mean to experience it oneself."[40]

This important cognitive element puts compassion in the domain of rational control, which is not to say, of course, that such control is always or adequately exercised. Indeed, it can be distracted or weakened by other factors. Human reason, we know, is subject to a range of biases and maladies. Compassion is too; in particular, it is subject to partiality. At first, this might seem puzzling, for if compassion is active in one's breast, one is directed away from oneself to the needs or well-being of another person. Moreover, since compassion involves taking up the perspective of the other person, relating it to one's own, and, in that way, making space for the person to be heard, it would seem that compassion would offer an enhancement of impartiality, not a threat to it.[41] However, imagination is vulnerable to bias. One's judgment of similar possibilities may be narrowly focused and uneven,[42] because of the conditions under which one learns of them. Trained under circumstances in which the scope of "like us" is narrow, or people are ranked in order of social worth, compassion-funding imagination may be limited, narrow, or distorted. Yet, by the same token, imagination and compassion can be trained to a more expansive scope, to correct for the distortion caused by narrowly focused attention. Thus, although the potential for partiality and bias is real, it is not a reason to regard mercy's motivation as inappropriate in the criminal system, but only a reason to be on our guard against sources of its deformation, and to find and fund correctives for them.

Finally, is it degrading to be the beneficiary of another's compassionate largess? This worry has two likely sources. One source is the view that one respects the dignity of others just when one respects their moral autonomy, the exercise of their moral capacities,[43] and to attend to the physical or psychological needs or deficiencies of others is to look after matters other than what makes them worthy of respect. It demeans them. Add to this that mercy is always is exercised in a context of inequality, and it is easy to see why responding to another's neediness would be seen to be condescending. Nietzsche gave painful expression to this understanding of compassion. He wrote:

[I]t is the essence of the feeling of compassion that it *strips* the suffering of what is truly personal: our "benefactors" diminish our worth and our will more than our enemies do. In most cases of beneficence toward those in distress there is something offensive in the intellectual frivolity with which the one who feels compassion plays the role of fate: he knows nothing of the whole inner sequence and interconnection that spells misfortune for *me* or for *you*![44]

In contemporary English usage, this is the clear overtone of our word "pity." Responding to the needs of others with pity is, we think, inevitably condescending.

(Kant called it "an insulting kind of benevolence."[45]) "There but for the grace of God go I" is not an expression of humility, but of self-congratulatory privilege.

However, it is a mistake to think that human dignity resides only in the rarified domain of moral autonomy. Human persons are embodied moral agents with human needs who depend on the world and other persons around them for their flourishing, and for their ability to exercise their moral autonomy. To recognize moral agency as if it were detachable form all the rest that makes us persons is to fail to recognize the dignity of persons.[46] Moreover, pity in its modern usage is different from the compassion that properly motivates mitigating grace. Pity looks to need and deficiency, while compassion looks to *the person in need*—to the needs as they affect, afflict, and potentially disable the person. Nietzsche had pity in mind, not compassion. To bring another's misfortune home, compassion draws on one's recognition of common humanity, on that which binds us together, common vulnerabilities as well as common capabilities. Compassion properly focused is not condescending, but rather affirming commonality. Pity, we might say, is a morally deficient form, a deformation, compassion.

Yet we must recognize that the deformation of compassion into pity is more likely in contexts of manifest inequality of power between the compassionate person and the object of her compassion. This is the case when mitigating grace is motivated by compassion, especially in the criminal process. Thus, while mercy in the criminal system is not necessarily condescending or demeaning, it can be. Merciful judgments can recognize and affirm the dignity of offenders. But we see again that, in the criminal system, mercy is vulnerable to distortion or deformation, and we must find ways to minimize the risk of such distortion occurring. Mercy, like justice, must be tempered.

The Place of Justice and Mercy in the Criminal Process

Legal philosopher Anthony Duff has argued that mercy has no place in a morally justified criminal process.[47] Mercy, he concedes, is an important moral value not only in interpersonal relations but also as a constituent element of a good and decent political community. Nevertheless, it is extraneous to the core goals of the criminal justice system. The proper justifying aim of criminal punishment, he argues, is the forceful communication of the polity's condemnation of the wrongs and injuries suffered by victims that is clearly and publicly articulated in its schedule of crimes. Punishment is justified because and only when it is deserved. Seen in this light, mercy is an *intrusion* into a system directed to this goal. It is a moral-political value entirely independent of the proper retributive justice goal of the system and, consequently, cannot be integrated into that system. In some instances, judges who extend compassionate mitigating grace to a condemned person may be justified on moral grounds, but they perform such acts of mercy as moral agents *outside of and against* their responsibilities as officials of the state. If the court properly concludes that the accused is indeed guilty of the crime charged, the judge is duty bound to sentence the condemned to the legally prescribed punishment. Judicial mercy is a moral oxymoron.

Duff's argument is sophisticated, but it depends on a limited understanding of the complex moral shape of the institution of criminal punishment, and it lacks an appreciation of the close relationship between mercy and justice as components of the justification of that institution. Retributive justice and mercy are distinct values; they may endorse different official decisions. In some such cases, mercy must prevail. Mercy "seasons" or tempers justice, but this tempering is internal to the criminal process. Philosopher John Tasioulas offers a way of thinking of mercy as an integral part of a morally justified institution of punishment.[48] (Note that the task is to articulate conditions an institution of criminal punishment must meet if it is to be morally justified. It is a separate question whether the institution of punishment in any political community meets these conditions.)

To begin, we can agree that punishment involves the deliberate infliction of hard treatment or serious loss on a wrongdoer because of the wrongness of the conduct by an official of the state who is authorized to inflict it for that reason.[49] But intentionally inflicting suffering on another is usually and correctly condemned as a grave moral wrong. So punishment needs compelling reasons in its favor to counter serious moral opposition to it. It is not possible to offer here a full defense of punishment, but it is reasonable to join Tasioulas in thinking that at its core the general justifying aim of punishment is to communicate condemnation of the wrongdoing to the wrongdoer, the victim(s), and the community at large. To wrongdoers, punishment demonstrates in strong terms that the conduct is unacceptable and holds them accountable for their responsible acts. To victims, the punishment publicly vindicates their rights and restores victims to their rightful place in the community, the place denied them by the wrongdoer. To the community, it declares that the law takes its standards of behavior seriously and assures members that they can expect their fellow members to comply with those standards.

To this broad aim, we must add other key values. First, the institution must ensure that, throughout the process, the rights and dignity of those who are accused and possibly condemned are fully and publicly respected. Thus, punishment may be inflicted only on those who truly deserve it and only to the extent deserved: punishment must be calibrated to fit the gravity of the wrong done and the culpability of the wrongdoer. (This is the *retributive*, desert-oriented dimension of punishment.) In addition, these key components must be demonstrated publicly in a fair and impartial judicial process in which those who are accused have a full opportunity to contest the charges and give evidence of their innocence, and judicial determinations of guilt are to be based on the evidence presented. Moreover, the punishment inflicted must scrupulously respect the rights and dignity of the wrongdoer. (This is a stronger requirement than merely that the punishment must not be "cruel" or "unusual.")

Second, other important values complement this central justifying aim, for example, the general aims of crime prevention and restorative justice (seeking reconciliation of offender, victim, and the broader community).[50] The criminal law must give fair notice to the community of the precise nature of actions condemned and liable to punishment. Also, the criminal law must meet the formal conditions of legality: they must be public, general, prospective, consistent, and not impossible to follow. Moreover, courts may be required to enforce constraints on police behavior to ensure that the criminal process is not abused. (In the American context, think here of so-called Miranda warnings given to arrested persons informing them of their rights.) Into this mix, Tasioulas argues, we must also introduce mercy. The institution of punishment in a given political community is morally justified only if it approximates the demands of these various values, combined in due proportion. The overarching aim of public condemnation and the other component values informs and constrains the retributive, desert-oriented dimension of punishment. Mercy enables the institution "to communicate its censure in a more nuanced and humane vocabulary."[51]

This framework is helpful, but mercy and justice are more intimately related than it recognizes, and mercy is integral to the criminal process at a deeper level. It is not just one moral value among others in an optimal mix; it is deeply implicated in the general justifying aim of communicating condemnation.

Mercy and desert-oriented justice are not only distinct moral values that may push responsible deliberation in conflicting directions but they are complementary and interdependent. For Micah, the prophet of Judah, those who seek justice *and* love mercy are not constantly conflicted but in proper righteous balance (Micah 6.8). William Shakespeare, the prophet of Elizabethan England, describes vividly in *Measure for Measure* the high social and personal costs of leniency without justice and of rigid justice untamed by mercy. The Duke's leniency made Vienna's laws a scarecrow, "more mocked than feared." Liberty, thus loosened, "pluck[ed] justice by the nose."[52] Yet Angelo's strict, "precise," and inhumane regime of justice proved too much even for him, letting loose both self-righteous condemnations and hypocritical self-exceptions. The message of Shakespeare's play, even if formally comedic, is tragic. We come to see that neither justice nor mercy can stand alone, but their combination is difficult to realize. Moreover, both mercy and justice, or their appearance, are vulnerable to misunderstanding, abuse, and manipulation by those granted the authority to act in the name of the community. Mindful of the Bard's lessons, we should nevertheless seek a more hopeful, if not easier, reconciliation. We can begin with a second look at the general justifying aim that Tasioulas proposed for the institution of criminal punishment.

Punishment, we have seen, is intentionally inflicted harsh treatment that is justified only when it gives effective public expression to the community's condemnation of the wrongdoers for their wrongful deeds, and only when and just to the extent that such condemnation is deserved. Public condemnation, we can agree, may be justified, but why may it take the form of inflicting harsh treatment, suffering, and loss on the wrongdoer? The ancient Athenian playwright Aeschylus puts us on the track of an answer. In the last play of his trilogy, the *Oresteia*, the "Furies" relentlessly pursue and torment Orestes for killing his mother. The goddess Athena intervenes, puts Orestes on trial, and ultimately acquits him. The Furies are furious. However, Athena convinces them to submit to the judgment of law and renames them in their new role "Eumenides"—the gracious ones. The moral of the story, of course, and one key thesis of the rule of law, is that the powerful and potentially destructive emotions of anger, resentment, and indignation that explode into revenge must be subjected to the forces and processes of law. But, as Martha Nussbaum notes, "the Furies are not banished from the city: instead they are civilized, and made part of Athena's judicial system."[53] The disapproval expressed by officially imposed punishment is not merely a cool judgment of the adjudicated fact of moral or legal wrongdoing; it expresses, in a suitably civilized mode, the righteous pain and anger of resentment and indignation of a wronged victim and a wronged community.

Thus, condemnation necessarily gives expression to a *judgment* that is meant to convey in articulate and public form the emotions that naturally accompany it. Harsh treatment is never sufficient; it is a necessary auxiliary of the judgment. Words are rarely sufficient to convey condemnation fully and effectively. Condemnation has an essential behavioral component. Just as in interpersonal relationships, various forms of behavior both naturally and conventionally make the resentment against wrongdoing felt, so in this more public context words naturally and conventionally signal the authenticity and the seriousness of the judgment. I say "naturally and conventionally" because part of the aim of expressing resentment in the interpersonal context is to communicate the victim's pain caused by the injury—both the moral *insult* and the *loss suffered*. Such communication succeeds when something of that pain is actually felt by the wrongdoer. Communication of pain is a natural concomitant of expressed resentment. There is, then, a natural link between the condemnation expressed and some sort of pain or loss suffered by the person blamed.

In the political domain, the relationship between wrongdoing and pain is natural and conventional. The association of wrongdoing with suffering and loss, primarily that of the victim, is natural enough, but its public expression is likely to take different forms, depending on the means of expression available and their ability to bring the suffering home to the wrongdoer. Harsh treatment, following on just determination of responsibility for the wrongdoing and the offender's culpability, has a good chance of bringing home not only the authenticity and sincerity of the community's judgment but also the moral pain and the loss suffered by the victim.

Criminal justice, understood in this way, is anchored in law and thus in judgment that is shaped, articulated, and grounded in reasons. When it is fitted to its moral purpose, it gives effective expression not only to judgments of disapproval and blame but also to the personal and communal emotions that naturally and appropriately accompany them. The criminal process speaks the refined language of law, but it gives expression and meaning to interpersonal and communal relationships in the polity. It must be based on an understanding of its members as complex beings—each person uniting rational capacities and moral autonomy, emotional depth that funds meaningful relationships with others, and physical and psychological needs, strengths, and vulnerabilities that differ in details but converge into recognizable patterns of commonality.

With this in mind, we can begin to understand the ways in which the distinct values of justice and mercy might play complementary roles in the criminal process. We found this dynamic at work in the relation between law and equity; it is at work again in the relation between justice and mercy. Mercy and justice focus on different aspects of the process, each value addressing its own concerns. Pursued separately and single-mindedly, each is vulnerable to certain characteristic deformations that may weaken or even undermine its normative force. *Fiat justitia ruat caelum*—do justice and let the heavens fall—is the motto of the zealot who has lost hold of the beating heart of justice. Only a simulacrum of justice counsels the ruin of the heavens. Mercy, too, may lose its moral charm when its pursuit threatens to bring down the heavens. The key thought for our purposes is twofold. First, some of the limits of these values are not merely incidental and occasional, but are consequences of their distinctive features that can be anticipated and prepared for. And, second, the complement of each offers a necessary, if not always sufficient, corrective.

First, consider desert-focused justice. The *Oresteia* tells the story of law civilizing vengeful passions. When it does its job well, law provides space for the expression of important reactive moral emotions like resentment, but it keeps them under wraps. Yet both the controls and the residual passions, which are essential to the strategy and hence to justice in the criminal process, are subject to deformations. The controls depend on a strategy of abstraction, focusing attention on the right and on the rights and dignity of victims and wrongdoers. This funds a valuable egalitarian dimension of criminal justice. (Many familiar criminal systems, of course, manifestly and tragically fall far short of these conditions of justification.) The criminal law and the process of criminal adjudication tend to focus exclusively on the offenses, on the offenders' culpability, states of mind, and general conditions of responsibility, and on the victims' injury as the measure of the moral wrong done to them. They abstract from the whole person of the offender (and sometimes of the victim). The law, especially the criminal law, is meant to be "no respecter of persons." Or rather, it must respect all persons and each person, but not differences among them other than those that are manifest in their choices and the actions that issue from them. Our familiar iconography represents *Justice* as blindfolded, with sword in her right hand and scales in her left. The blindfold excludes bias and prejudice, partiality and undue influence, and features of the accused's life or situation, from just judgment, allowing *Justice* to focus on arguments of law and evidence carefully screened for relevance to the limited matter of right. However, Chesterton writes,

> the horrible thing about all legal officials, even the best, about all judges, magistrates, barristers, detectives, and policemen, is not that they are wicked (some of them are good), not that they are stupid (several of them are quite intelligent), it is simply that they have got used to it. Strictly they do not see the prisoner in the dock; all they see is the usual man in the usual place. They do not see the awful court of judgment; they only see their own workshop.[54]

And their workshop is one that trains an attitude of abstraction in order to achieve a desired degree of impersonal judgment. Legal judgment is meant to be, and (some argue) is required by the rule of law to be, impersonal. Yet its weakness or vulnerability lies in just this impersonal nature. The potential result, the risk, is that those who exercise judgment fail to see the prisoner in the dock.

This abstraction and impersonalism risk two further deformations. First, they blind officials to the experience of the harsh treatment inflicted. Philosopher Jean Hampton offered a view of the communicative function of punishment that differs in one important respect from the view we articulated above. She begins with the idea that *wrongdoing* is communicative. Through his action, the wrongdoer sends the message to the victim: "You are less than me, subordinate to me, and I don't have to regard your interests or rights or well-being as any particular concern of mine." He also sends to the community this message: "I am an exception to your rules; I am not bound by them. I am above them and above the rest of you." The point of punishment, on Hampton's account, is to take the wrongdoer down a peg; to diminish him and thereby restore the victim's dignity in the eyes of the community.[55] As a description of the actual operation of punishment in our society, this strikes me both tragically accurate and deeply morally troubling. It is accurate in that it describes a serious risk that is always in play when a person in a position of power over others intentionally inflicts pain, suffering, and loss on them. The message of punishment, meant to express effectively the authenticity and force of the condemnation of the wrongdoing and the wrong-doer, risks demeaning the wrongdoer. It is morally troubling because it demeans another, especially those subject to our power over them. It is inconsistent with treating those who are accused and convicted with the dignity that is always and everywhere their right and our duty.

Second, criminal justice, if not tempered, can motivate an intolerable self-righteousness on the part of those who exercise and enforce judgments of condemnation and the community that seconds them. The culpable wrongdoing of the prisoner in the dock or cell bespeaks a weakness worthy of condemnation, a weakness to which I am not susceptible, says the self-righteous official to himself. It is also evident in the contempt that ordinary people among us have for those with criminal records and our willingness to accept without protest demeaning modes of punishment and condone demeaning modes of treatment of convicted persons after they have served their sentences. I thank God, we say silently to ourselves, that I am not like such people.

Our practices of punishment are vulnerable to other deformations, but these will do to indicate a role for mercy in the criminal process. Mercy is able to respond to the offender's repentance, which indicates that the offender has taken up the communication of the condemnation and the victim's suffering and in-dignity. Mitigation of the punishment, in such a case, does not signal that the wrongdoing is condoned or overlooked, but rather follows on and is a fitting response to the change of heart and life of the offender. Beyond this, mercy provides those who sit in judgment with a wider view of the offender, refusing to identify the person with the wrong done. In his Inferno, Dante represents the sinners, Francesca da Rimini and her lover Paolo, as a flock of birds alighting for a brief moment only to fly off to another spot and then another and another, endlessly.[56] Their sin was undisciplined and willful desire. In Dante's hell, unre-pentant sinners are condemned to engage eternally in only those activities most closely associated with their sins. They become the sins they once freely chose. Hell, Dante suggests, is becoming one with one's wrongdoings. And the first task of sinners in purgatory, he suggests, is "to uncover their own beauty,"[57] to see themselves and their moral beauty beneath the stain of their wrongs.

Criminal justice, abstracting from the person and focusing only on the wrong and the offender's culpability, risks deformation that identifies the person solely with the deed. It condemns the wrongdoer, the victim, and their community to a kind of hell: the victim sees the offender only as the-one-who-violated-me, and herself only as victim. The community only sees the offender as the-one-who-wronged-her-and-defied-our-law. The offender, seeing himself through the eyes of the victim, sees only the one-who-violated-her. And sees himself in the eyes of the community as outlaw and outcast. Mercy provides an opportunity to break this hellish distortion. It allows officials, the victim, and the community to see the offender as a person beneath the persona of the offense. Mercy will not allow the sinner to perish with the sin.

Mercy is capable of doing this because it depends on the decision makers' capacity for self-reflection and recognition of common vulnerability. American Federal Appeals Court judge Alex Kozinski considered the sentence he should give to a young woman convicted of a drug-related offense. She had no criminal record, but stupidly agreed to arrange a drug deal with someone who turned out to be an undercover drug-enforcement agent. As the judge was thinking about her sentence—his options ranged from probation to life in prison—he remembered an incident of a week earlier.

> I had been at home absorbed in work when I heard the doorbell ring. When I went to the front door, I found it wide open, and a young couple was standing there holding a toddler—my young son Clayton. I was a little surprised, as I thought Clayton was playing in the house. [The couple had been] driving down my street . . . and found the child sitting in the middle of the road. Apparently, I forgot to close the door, and Clayton [. . .] made his way outside and into traffic.

I came to see that the young woman was "not the only one in the courtroom who had made a big mistake," he wrote. That enabled him to, as he put it, "err on the side of forgiveness."[58] Self-reflection allowed Kozinski to see beyond the offender to the person and to extend compassionate mitigating grace to her. Mercy enables a different form of egalitarian recognition than that provided by law's focus on desert, recognition of common vulnerability rather than common moral capabilities. In a political community, one that seeks to bind whole persons together in a meaningful membership, this form is no less important than that which sees only moral agents and their responsible or irresponsible choices.

However, mitigating grace, even when motivated by compassion, is in like fashion vulnerable to deformations that are not merely incidental. They spring from facts about the nature and typical contexts of the exercise of this grace. We encounter one such deformation in Shakespeare's description in *Measure for Measure* of Vienna under the Duke's administration. Lucio confesses that from the bawd "Mistress Mitigation," he "purchased many diseases under her roof" (Act I, Scene 2). The Duke's "strict statutes and most biting laws" were "to themselves dead" because "dead to infliction" (Act I, Scene 3). Of course, mercy does not condone wrongdoing; it is a response to the person duly and publicly condemned, compassionately mitigating a just and deserved punishment. However, untempered by justice and without the structure of the criminal process, leniency is likely to encourage contempt for the law and, in turn, contempt for those justly protected by it. This is not mercy properly understood, but a perversion, a deformation of it. In the absence of condemnation, mercy loses its moral appeal. In this respect, mercy depends on just law, fair criminal processes, and dignity-respecting institutions of punishment to prevent its perversion.

Again, mercy is mitigation moved by compassion, and compassion springs from imagination, but this imagination, we have seen, is itself subject to limitations. Imagination alerts one to otherwise unperceived ways in which the other party is "like me," or I am "like her." This, David Hume recognized, is the root of what he called "sympathy."[59] Yet, he observed, we are more likely to recognize such similarities among those in our circle than in persons beyond it. Imagination, and hence sympathy and compassion, are inevitably limited, but not irredeemably so. And, thus, compassion, while capable of alerting us to surprising points of commonality with others, is vulnerable to bias and partiality.

In O. Henry's story "Law and Order," a teenage boy arrives in a Texas town flaunting his cowboy duds and pearl-handled pistol. Pedro Johnson laughs at the boy and threatens him, and the boy shoots Pedro in response and returns immediately to New York City. The sheriff follows him, bribes a judge to give him an extradition order, and prepares to return him to Texas to face stern justice. The sheriff's deputy notices a scar on the boy's face and recognizes him as the sheriff's long estranged son. The sheriff immediately decides to take the boy back to Texas and teach him all he knows about ranching, abandoning all intention to bring the boy to justice. When the deputy reminds the sheriff of his duty to take the boy into criminal custody for shooting a respectable citizen, the sheriff replies, "Oh hell. That don't amount to anything. That fellow was half Mexican, anyhow."[60] Partiality and prejudice combined to corrupt the sheriff's leniency.

Structures of the criminal process and its pursuit of justice within it provide a needed corrective to this tendency. Focusing on the moral agency of the offender to the exclusion of factors that might otherwise cloud our judgment encourages a kind of egalitarian attitude that enables one to look beyond the limits of family and circle, to expand the scope of those "like me." There are no guarantees, of course. Prejudice, bias, and partiality are constant threats to judgment, whether of justice or mercy, but as complements, their respective strengths help to counter their effects of their respective weaknesses.

The fact that mercy is always exercised in the context of a relationship of asymmetric power also makes it vulnerable to corruption, as we have seen. Since the potential beneficiary of the mitigation is "at the mercy" of the mercy giver, and is not in a position to demand merciful treatment as a matter of right but depends on the giver's discretion and grace, leniency publicly and grandly given can convey a message of condescension. Unless carefully tempered, merciful gestures and acts can communicate and reinforce the recipient's and observers' perceptions of the recipient's subordinate status and unequal worth. Compassionate mitigation, we have seen, can be degrading. Mercy deformed looks only at the need and is blind to the person in need. Again, leniency shown by those in positions of power but not constrained by justice is not mercy, but a deformation of it, all the more troubling for stemming from or encouraged by features endemic to mercy. Just as law and justice need mercy to steer it away from their deformations, so mercy depends on a secure framework of legal justice to protect it from its limitations.

Thus, justice and mercy are distinct but complementary values, combined to sustain a decent and humane criminal system by tempering each other at the points at which they, on their own, would lose their normative force and evaluative appeal. But they can do so only when the institutions that seek to realize them are structured in such a way as also to give effect to their complementarity. The details of such wise institutional design are beyond the scope of this chapter and the abilities of its author, but a few broad principles of construction recommend themselves.

First, legislation should make room in criminal laws and the adjudication process for constrained mercy. This may involve avoiding strict schedules of mandatory sentences, replacing them with broad standards and outer bounds to guide judgment and steering it away from predictable sources of bias, prejudice, and distortion.

Second, consideration of the demands of justice and the counsels of mercy should be ordered in sequence.[61] Determination of guilt and punishment deserved in view of the gravity of the crime and culpability of the offender should be made in a process that publicly recognizes and respects the dignity of the accused and gives due consideration to the injuries and losses of victims. Only then should judges take up discretionary consideration of the offender's story, and only within the guidelines and subject to the protections that mercy-minded legislation puts in place. Mercy does not supplant public condemnation of wrongdoing or of wrongdoer; rather, when it is appropriate, it takes up the further matter of what form this condemnation will take.

Third, although the decisions are for judges or other officials to make in exercise of their guided discretion, it must be clear to offender, victim, and the community at large that the officials act in the name of the community as a whole. They do so not only when they pronounce their verdicts but also when they extend mercy in determining the sentence to be served. Thus, officials must make and justify merciful judgments publicly, in mercy-relevant terms that are publicly accessible and assessable. In addition, those who make them must be subject to mechanisms by which they are held accountable for those judgments. Guidelines for exercise of mitigating grace and a process by which officials are held to those guidelines are important if mercy is to be accorded a proper place in the criminal justice process.[62]

Seen in this way, mercy, like equity, does not represent a challenge *to* the rule of law. Rather, the challenge *for* us committed to the rule of law is to design institutions that adequately combine these values and realize their complementarity.

Mercy in the Polity

We saw in Chapters 1 and 3 that the rule of law not only prescribes a distinctive mode of governance but also models a morally desirable mode of association. We might ask, then, whether mercy is exclusively a virtue of formal legal institutions, or is it also welcome in the polity at large. The answer is that it is important in the polity as well. Although lay members of the political community are not authorized to impose or mitigate punishment, their essential role in the exercise of fidelity, their obligation to participate in networks of mutual accountability, puts them in positions of temporary authority vis-à-vis each other, and equips them with sanctions of blame and shame to back up their demands for accountability. Exercising these responsibilities without compassionate grace can inflict deep damage on the association and the shared status it seeks to nurture and sustain. Mercy can encourage in others complementary trust and compassion. Properly moderated, it can help build structures in which justice is best realized and expressed.

This thought has deep roots both religious and secular. Rabbis, in their midrash on biblical story of creation, imagine God saying at the moment of creation, "If I create the world with mercy [alone] sin will abound [and the world will not survive]. If I create it with justice [alone], how can the world exist? Therefore, I will create it with both mercy and justice and it may thus endure."[63] Seneca, writing in the first century CE, urged the emperor Nero to "consider how great would be the loneliness and desolation if none should be left but those whom a strict judge would acquit."[64] This question is not just for the Neros of this world but also for us who must live in the world that we seek to make habitable. The twelfth-century compilation of English law, *Leges Henrici Primi*, seems to have grasped this truth. It declared that "it is a rule of law that a person who unwittingly commits a wrong shall consciously make amends." But it adds immediately, "he ought however to be the more accorded mercy and compassion at the hands of the dead man's relatives the more we understand that the human race grows sick with the harshnesses of a cruel fortune and with the melancholy and wretched lamentation of all."[65]

Law, we have learned, can rule only if its formal norms and institutions are planted in the rich soil of fidelity, the animating soul of the rule-of-law ideal. The rule of law is robust in a polity just when its members, and not merely the legal or ruling elite, take responsibility for holding each other and especially law's officials to account under the law. Fidelity nurtures and gives public expression to an association that treats laws as the political framework of mutual recognition of each as co-members of the community. Participating responsibly in the community's networks of accountability is key to that mode of recognition. But this mode of association and its quotidian activities are vulnerable to deformation. Although the networks of accountability are meant to be mutual, in each instance of accountability-holding one member stands in a relation of temporary authority with respect to another. That relation is vulnerable to abuse. Opportunities for demanding accountability of another can be used not to affirm common bonds, reminding each other of common responsibilities, but rather as occasions for publicly upbraiding others or self-righteous meddling in another's affairs. Especially troubling are those who inform on or denounce neighbors to authorities, knowing that those authorities will themselves abuse the ruling power entrusted to them. The informer who denounces his neighbor, like the "stickler for justice" who insists on his rights despite the fact that the burden of compliance will fall heavily and unfairly on the other party, abuses his rights and the power those rights accord to him. These deformations of accountability turn practices meant to control the abuse of power into instruments of abuse.

Mercy in the exercise of accountability, in contrast, contributes to the strength of the community. Recall the story told in Chapter 7 of the "diamond-studded paupers" of New York. The diamond dealers were generally poor but handled vast amounts of high-value gems and took on large amounts of debt. Strict norms of fair dealing and honoring debts were severely enforced by the ultra-Orthodox community in which the dealers lived. Nevertheless, elders showed remarkable leniency at times—compassionate grace—allowing a fallen dealer to recover and rebuild his reputation. They understood "the temptations of ambitious deals, the difficulties of managing liquidity constraints, and the costs of inexperience." The practice reflected the recognition among the elders of the community of the need to temper their aim to deter cheating with compassion for human frailties. "The remarkable features of these community enforcement mechanisms," Richman adds, "is that they are intimately woven into the natural community fabric."[66]

Mercy and equity moderate and temper the exercise of accountability and thus are important constituent elements of the ethos of fidelity. Mercy does not counsel abandoning efforts at accountability, let alone condoning abuses of power in violation of the law, but it constrains the time, place, and especially the manner in which accountability is demanded and assessed. Without mercy and the compassion that moves it, a rigorous practice of accountability can weaken mutual trust and poison the special kind of solidarity characteristic of valued membership, the mode of association fostered and protected by the rule of law. But mercy is sensitive to differences among cases. For example, persons holding positions of public trust are properly held to higher standards of compliance, commensurate with the more potent means of power at their disposal. We may reasonably be reluctant to deal mercifully with the wrongs they do or threaten. Also mercy in nonjudicial contexts, as in judicial ones, must extend its compassion not only to wrongdoers but also to victims. Mercy blind to victims is also mercy deformed.

Equity and mercy pose two challenges for the rule of law. A third, perhaps even more pressing, is the challenge of necessary executive discretion in times of crisis. With our understanding of adequate answers to the challenges posed by equity and mercy, we can take up this further dilemma of discretion.

12

Executive Power Leashed

Crisis and Pardon

Two principles stand at the foundations of the rule of law: that the law by which rulers govern must also govern the rulers (reflexivity) and that all ruling power must be legally ordained (exclusivity). Law is sovereign; ruling power, especially that exercised by chief executives, is subject to law's sovereignty. Even where fixed legal rules must yield to some form of discretionary judgment, law must prevail; it must structure and guide the exercise of discretionary judgment and hold it accountable.

These fundamental principles of the rule of law are subjected to extraordinary strain in two kinds of circumstances: when the nation is in peril and when the chief executive sets aside the law to pardon individuals convicted of crimes. War, civil unrest, natural disasters, and pandemics push hard against these two core principles. In emergencies, the stakes are extremely high, and the complexity of the crisis can be overwhelming. The well-being and even survival of the people demand swift, decisive action; however, many argue, law is an impediment to urgently necessary action. *Necessity knows no law*, according to the old Roman Law maxim. The law should authorize crisis decision makers and then stand aside, letting them get on with their necessary work without constraint. The force of this line of thought has been compelling for centuries. Times of crisis pose a fundamental challenge to law's rule.

Seen against this background, unconstrained executive pardon power seems far less perilous: a few criminals don't serve or serve out their justly imposed sentences. However, it too is a form of lawful lawlessness.[1] In the late 1990s, a Federal Appeals Court understood the US Constitution's grant of pardon power in this way. It maintained that "the very nature of clemency is that it is granted solely in the will of the dispenser of clemency. He need give no reasons for granting it or denying it."[2] This power, is "absolute," former president Trump used to boast. The decisions, he said, are exclusively his, and his critics will have to live with them.[3]

The rule of law is imperiled in both instances because a person at the apex of governing power exercises power outside of and often against the law. The prince or the president is sovereign, not the law. In both cases, fundamental principles of the rule of law are challenged. This chapter addresses these two challenges. It

Law's Rule. Gerald J. Postema, Oxford University Press. © Oxford University Press 2022.
DOI: 10.1093/oso/9780190645342.003.0012

argues that executive pardon powers and emergency powers can and must be leashed by law.

Executive Pardon

Cesare Beccaria, eighteenth-century theorist of criminal law, wrote of executive clemency and pardon, "Happy the nation in which they will be considered as dangerous." Immanuel Kant worried that pardon power is "the slipperiest" of all the rights exercised by the sovereign. And Montesquieu argued that pardon power, a remnant of monarchy, is unsuitable for a republic.[4] And even in monarchies, the pardon power was often limited. In the seventeenth century, Matthew Hale argued that according to English common law, royal pardons must only be used "for the public good" and not for crimes against individual members of the public. The king could only "pardon those offenses of the highest nature, as against his own suit."[5]

However, the framers of the US Constitution granted near unlimited pardon power to the president.[6] Florida's supreme court wrote that executive pardons may be given "for good reasons or bad, or for any reason at all," adding that the

> act is final and irrevocable. Even for the grossest abuse of this discretionary power the law affords no remedy; the courts have no concern with the reasons which actuated the executive. The constitution clothes him with the power to grant pardons, and this power is beyond the control, or even the legitimate criticism, of the judiciary.[7]

This may overstate even the Constitution's broad grant of pardon power, since the Constitution explicitly prohibits pardoning "in cases of impeachment," for example. Nevertheless, many in the legal community, and especially those who advise chief executives, understand the pardon power in these very broad terms.

The power is said to be lawless—intentionally placed beyond law's governance—but still lawful by virtue of the fact that law authorizes it. It is "legally uncontrollable arbitrariness," duly recognized, conferred, and protected by law.[8] It is astonishing that even courts, sober legal scholars, and practicing lawyers who are not directly employed by the chief executive are willing to talk about executive pardon power in such extreme terms. For it is utterly clear that, understood in this way, executive pardon power is not only exercised beyond and even against the law but also is in direct and irreconcilable opposition to the rule of law. It is defended as a valuable corrective to law and legal processes gone wrong, as "a half-blind groping response to [justice that] cannot be articulated or bound in law";[9] however, the remedy is worse than the disease. It does not just incidentally permit but actively invites and even celebrates abuse. So conceived, pardon power seems to be the residual cancer of absolutism that we thought was long ago surgically removed by democratic institutions deeply rooted in the rule of law.

Of course, even theorists of absolutism recognized that those who legitimately exercise absolute power are conscience-bound to do so for the public good— in the name of the *salus populi*, as they put it. And, likewise, when defenders of executive pardon power are careful about their language, they concede that the power is used properly only when pardons are granted for reasons of mercy, to secure peace or political reconciliation, to remedy miscarriages of justice, or similar reasons. They also concede that it is abused when the president grants pardons for personal or political gain, to enrich his family, or is motivated by racial or other forms of prejudice. The problem is not that there are no uses of the pardon power that all agree are inappropriate, but rather that, in the words of the US Department of Justice, "in the exercise of the pardoning power, the president is amenable only to the dictates of his own conscience, unhampered and uncontrolled by any person or branch of government."[10] That is to say, although we have a pretty good idea how the power should be exercised—or at least how it must not be exercised—no person or institution in government is or should be entitled to challenge it. It is discretionary, and hence ruleless; and it is entirely beyond the legitimate role of legally devised processes to hold the exerciser of the power accountable. However, this only slightly more modest understanding of the pardon power is also inconsistent with the core rule-of-law principles because it is thought to be beyond all means of accountability. It is a form of arbitrary power, no less when exercised admirably than when abused.

If we imagine that we are designers of the constitution and laws of our political community seeking to do the best we can to realize a robust rule of law, we have two options. One is to follow Montesquieu's recommendation and exclude pardon power from our constitution. The other is to include a suitably bridled form of the power, circumscribed to reduce the risk of abuse but leaving it enough room to do the good its defenders promise. Let's explore the second option.

First, to say that pardon power, because it is necessarily discretionary and strictly not rule-bound, is "ungovernable" by law, a "ruleless groping," is irresponsible hyperbole. Thinking about the matter soberly, we must acknowledge that it is possible to identify in meaningful standards the range of considerations that provide legitimate grounds for granting pardons and, even more importantly, provide rules that define clearly improper grounds. Of course, gray areas may still appear in the interstices of these two groups of standards, but we must not exaggerate the size of this gray area or the complexity of dealing with it. We can articulate in law standards that are not hopelessly vague. Although applying such standards requires mature and responsible judgment, the standards can still guide judgment in a meaningful way and signal to the public that the discretionary power granted to the executive has been exercised responsibly. Likewise, we have lots of experience identifying forms of invidious discrimination, enough for us to recognize with a reasonable expectation of wide agreement when prejudice is the driving motivation or effect. Similarly, prohibition of pardons for personal financial or partisan political gain, to obstruct justice, to benefit family or close friends, or to reward or secure political loyalty are not all that difficult to understand and apply. The law deals with difficult matters of motivation and effect all the time. The exercise of this power does not fall beyond its capacity to govern.

Second, the rule of law insists on full publicity of all pardon decisions and their rationales. They must be defended in public, to the public, and to other branches of government, especially the legislative branch. The decision may be the president's, but that implies that the president bears responsibility for it, and responsibility entails public accountability. Courts may also be involved, especially where clear boundaries of the power have been defined.

Third, it is possible to write legislation to make it a crime for the executive to sell or offer to sell pardons for personal financial gain, in exchange for political campaign contributions, or benefit to his or her family, or to use pardon, or the promise of pardons, in a corrupt scheme to obstruct judicial proceedings. Sanctions for violations of such laws could include criminal penalties after the executive has left office and impeachment while still in office. Laws could also deprive the executive of the power to pardon persons before they have been charged, tried, and convicted. Courts may then have to act to invalidate the pardons if granted contrary to such laws. This power of the courts could be extended to invalidating pardons secured by fraud, bribery, or other corrupt exchange of benefits.

Further, the rule of law would recommend processes that could reduce the risk of abuse of the pardon power. Currently, in the United States a separate office of the Department of Justice handles all petitions for pardon and advises the president. This process is vulnerable to manipulation by the executive and to internal conflicts of interest, since the Office of the Pardon Attorney is staffed largely by prosecutors.[11] An alternative, suggested by several participants in the 2020 Democratic presidential primaries, was to create a bipartisan board, adequately staffed with experts in rehabilitation, re-entry, and the like, to advise the president. This board could refine broad legislative guidelines for granting pardons. Making these standards public would add transparency to the process and subject the executive to political pressure to exercise the pardon power in a way consistent with its rationale.

Executive pardon power, then, is not ungovernable, although in some legal systems it may be ungoverned. The task for partisans of the rule of law is not to work to extirpate the power from the law, but creatively to devise standards and processes by which the power can be stripped of its arbitrary features and turned to its use as a valuable corrective for law and legal processes that have gone wrong.

Pardon power is not ungovernable, but many argue that executive power needed to address emergencies decisively is. This we are often told, not only by writers wearing the livery of the latest ruler but also by sober scholars and constitution writers. Extraordinary times call for extralegal powers. This thinking poses a challenge that goes to the very heart of the rule-of-law ideal.

Crisis

Problems posed by law's necessary generality and the complexity of ordinary life are familiar enough. We explored some of these in Chapter 11. Also, in the doctrine of self-defense (and third-party defense), the law itself recognizes that actions usually prohibited by law are sometimes justified—not merely *morally* justified but justified in the sight of the law itself. Necessity makes lawful what is otherwise unlawful, it is said. But the necessity doctrine does not cut action loose from the law; law still supplies the grounds and guides for the action. Self-defense is legally justified, for example, only when the threat is truly serious, immanent, and itself unjustified, and the violent defensive response is the only option reasonably available and is proportional in its potential harm to that which is threatened unjustly. The law's doctrine of necessity recognizes a *legal justification* of actions that in other circumstances would be serious crimes.

Defenders of executive emergency powers go further: *necessity knows no law*, they say. They stretch Cicero's slogan, *inter arma enim silent leges*: the law goes silent, they argue, not only in war (*inter arma*) but in all times of crisis. It runs out. It is as irrelevant as fencing rules in a rugby match or on the battlefield. In emergency, the rule of law has no force, no voice, no point, because law is impotent. Law is not sovereign because it cannot rule. These critics argue that, unlike equity and mercy, emergencies pose a fundamental *challenge to* law's rule, not merely a *challenge for* the rule of law to manage. Emergencies lie beyond the province of law's rule.

However, this chapter argues that it is not national crises that threaten the rule of law, but this way of thinking about law in times of crisis. The challenge can be met. Justice Sutherland wrote, "If the provisions of the Constitution be not upheld when they pinch, as well as when they comfort, they may as well be abandoned."[12] Rule-of-law demands pinch hard in times of genuine crisis, but it is in such times that we need the rule of law and it needs to be strengthened.[13] Our guide here, as in Chapter 11, is Sir Edward Coke in *Keighley's Case*: when discretion is granted by law, it must be "limited and bound with the rule of reason and law,"[14] even in emergencies.

The Challenge Refined

To take the critics' challenge seriously, we must first ask two questions: What do critics mean by "emergency"? and What does it mean to say law does not apply to it such that it falls silent in times of crisis? Consider the second question first.

When critics say law falls silent in times of crisis, they tend to run together three different arguments. (1) Sometimes they argue that law is by *conceptual* necessity out of place in emergencies. Concepts presuppose certain conditions for their proper application. As loyalty is out of place among business competitors and fair play is out of place among rogues, so law is out of place in emergencies. Certain conditions must obtain for laws to offer guidance or protection, but these conditions are absent in times of crisis. Laws are norms; they function only in normal circumstances. (2) The *psychological* argument looks similar at first, but it is different. The argument is that in emergencies laws cannot get a foothold in the deliberative psychologies of decision makers. Perceptions of the urgency and scale of the peril push legal considerations beyond their horizon of consideration. (3) According to the *normative* argument, we *ought not* legally constrain executive decisions in emergencies. The costs of doing so are prohibitive; after all, critics argue, the law is not a suicide pact.

To test these arguments responsibly, we need to understand better what emergencies are and why they should be thought to generate law-silencing crises. Emergencies are circumstances of great peril and complexity that urgently demand a decisive response. The crises that challenge the rule of law typically are situations in which the nation, or some significant portion of it, faces a high risk of very serious harm, and a response to avert or minimize the harm is urgently needed. Extraordinary circumstances demand an extraordinary response; however, determining the most effective response is very difficult because emergency situations are extraordinarily complex and available options are limited. The stakes are very high, and the factors in play are many and intertwined. When combined, these factors tend to compound the problems posed by each separately.[15] Urgency tends to limit the information available, or it is available to only certain people, and may limit options or opportunities for effective response. Critics of the rule of law typically assume that these features bring with them two other salient features. Emergency circumstances are not only complex but also novel, so we can't anticipate them or provide for them in advance; and they demand utmost secrecy. *Extreme peril, complexity, urgency, beyond our capacity to anticipate*, and demanding *secrecy*—these factors taken together are thought to define emergency situations.

However, emergencies and crises come in a variety of types, and they may vary widely in seriousness, scope, urgency, novelty, and the need for secrecy; and these factors also come in degrees. Consider the various *types* of emergencies or crises a nation may face: threats to national security—within national borders (violent public disorder, or domestic terrorism) or from beyond the borders (war or foreign terrorism)—natural disasters (episodic like floods and hurricanes, or systemic like climate change), catastrophic events (nuclear plant explosions or large-scale industrial accidents), financial collapse, and pandemics.[16] Each of these presents enormous challenges to responsible governments because they are beyond the routine situations (and exceptional situations) that law regularly deals with.

Yet even this rough typology makes clear that beyond normal situations there is a spectrum of extranormal situations. It extends from those that are not especially troubling, through those that are seriously troubling, through those that are truly severe, to the most extreme. Some natural disasters come fast, others are predictable enough that authorities can prepare for them to some extent. Some, like the 2008 worldwide financial crisis, are unpredicted but not entirely unpredictable. For some the onset is fast, for others onset is slower. Some are of limited duration, like hurricanes; some endure, like pandemics. Secrecy may be necessary for some, like some threats of attack by foreign adversaries; for others, like natural disasters, financial crises, and pandemics, the widest possible access to information is critical. Thus, in analyzing law's capacity to aid in response to emergencies, we must take care to avoid thinking in terms of categorical differences between normal and non-normal.

Law Can't Function

Consider, first, the conceptual and psychological arguments. Both conclude that law *cannot* function in emergency.

The Inevitable Silence of Law

The basic argument for the inevitable silence of law in times of crisis starts from the familiar premise that we explored at length in Chapter 11; circumstances can outrun legal rules that are necessarily general. American Founder and Federalist Alexander Hamilton put this premise in crisis register and drew the critics' conclusion. "It is impossible to foresee or to define the extent and variety of national emergencies, and the correspondent extent and variety of the means which may be necessary to satisfy them. The circumstances that endanger the safety of nations are infinite." So "no constitutional shackles can wisely be imposed on the power to which the care of it is committed."[17]

Emergency circumstances not only threaten extreme peril, their occurrence cannot be anticipated, neither can we devise *ex ante* effective means of dealing with them, neither can we determine *ex post* credible standards for assessing responses to them. "Every general norm demands a normal, everyday frame of life to which it can be factually applied and which is subjected to its regulations." However, "there exists no norm that is applicable to chaos," wrote Carl Schmitt, the early twentieth-century German legal theorist.[18] The universe of emergencies is radically particular, complex, and unruly, but law is a regime of norms, oriented to the past, incapable of nuance and complexity, and slow in grasping and adjusting to nonroutine situations.[19] Norms can operate in normal circumstances, but emergencies are by definition abnormal and not susceptible to management by norms. Therefore, *necessarily*, law cannot guide officials to respond to emergencies, prepare for them in advance, or even grasp exactly when they have begun. With regard to all such matters, law is necessarily silent. Law is reduced to one simple task: to designate the person who is to determine when an emergency exists and how to respond. The law determines who the decider is but is powerless to determine, or even guide, the decider's decisions.

Some critics of the rule of law take this argument in more radical directions. They argue that the weakness of law to guide executive action extends beyond manifest crises. Legal scholars Eric Posner and Adrian Vermeule, for example, argue that crises are just the limiting case of extremely rapid change in the policy environment in general. The same problems created by emergencies

> also work to undermine legalistic constraints on the executive. The complexity of policy problems, especially in economic domains, the need for secrecy in many matters of security and foreign affairs, and the sheer speed of policy response necessary in crises combine to make meaningful legislative and judicial oversight of delegated authority difficult in the best of circumstances.[20]

Former US vice president Dick Chaney uttered a sentiment common in important circles of American politics. "Given the world that we live in," he was quoted as saying, "the president needs to have unimpaired executive authority to meet the demands of modern governance."[21]

Inspired by Carl Schmitt, others push this thought even further. They argue that in our fundamentally disordered and violent world, the abnormal and chaotic lies behind a thin veil likely to burst through at any moment in political history. The normal is temporary and unstable, while the very real potential for chaos and evil is permanent. Thus, the law cannot rule, because at any moment the decider must be free to identify the emergency and act accordingly. Power to act swiftly and decisively must be in the hands of one capable of responding to the demands of the moment, beyond all challenge and resistance. The one who decides the exception is sovereign, Schmitt famously concluded,[22] for the one who decides the exception decides whether law is in play or not. Law cannot be sovereign when the decider determines whether law rules.

Political theorist Michael Walzer warned that "emergency" and "crisis" are "cant words used to prepare our minds for acts of brutality."[23] Walzer's words ring true for this argument. The radical extensions of the conceptual argument suffer from exaggerations that reduce the argument to absurdity. The argument indulges in two forms of exaggeration. First, it exaggerates the blindness of law to the complexity of concrete circumstances to which they are meant to apply. This is partly due to critics' failure to recognize resources in the law beyond the most rigidly determined and simply defined legal rules. We have reviewed several times in this book the capacities of law to guide without fully determining decisions, guidance which then enables reasonable and reasonably effective accountability-holding by parties other than those making the decisions. Second, the radical argument also exaggerates the chaos in the world and our inability to anticipate extreme emergencies and devise adequate responses to them. Our rehearsal of the range of types of crises and the spectrum of intensity of such crises brings a degree of realism to the discussion of the role of law in emergencies that is entirely missing from this radical approach.

In addition, the radical argument proves too much. For if the need for responsible and prudent judgment is the sign that law must fail, then it fails not only in emergencies but across the board. Law is impossible at all points, not only when the executive must make decisions. Furthermore, not only is law impossible, so too is *any* rule-following, any normatively guided action. Unless critics refine their analysis of the problem of the indeterminacy of legal norms, their argument proves that pickup basketball, choral singing, appreciation of jazz, and communication through language are impossible, or utterly miraculous.

It proves too much in another way. If the generality of legal norms incapacitates law, then moral assessment is equally undermined, for morality is, at least in part, a matter of norms. We are left only with decision and power, beyond good and evil. Some radical critics, following Schmitt, embrace this conclusion. Emergencies transcend norms—moral as well as legal—they argue. Morality, like law, is defeated by chaos. However, this argument cannot give us a *reason* to opt for a lawless decider, for a reason is itself a general consideration. So we have *no reason* to abandon law, and certainly no reason to put in its place a Sovereign to whom we are bound to obey. Hence, the radical argument destroys itself.

The moderate version of the conceptual argument also fails due to exaggeration, but it also indulges in equivocation. It equivocates over the notion of "normal." Normal is that which is part of the ordinary, everyday, more or less expected and routine aspects of life; normal is also that which is, as we might say, "norm-apt," capable of being encompassed within a norm. It is a mistake to think that what is extraordinary, outside our ordinary experience and so is not routine, is necessarily not norm-apt, utterly beyond our capacity to consider it in terms of laws, norms, and reasons. And even when it may not be possible to precisely fix a *rule* in advance to fit a nonroutine situation, we often can identify broad features of situations and circumstances that will call for responses of certain recognizable kinds. A natural disaster, for example, may hit a community unaware, but the community may have in place protocols and resources to respond when it does. Herein, again, exaggeration lies at the heart of this argument. While it may not be possible to anticipate every possible detail of a crisis situation, and prudently weigh all the relevant but competing considerations, nevertheless, proven protocols and broad principles can narrow the indeterminacy and give guidance to those who must make crucial decisions. Utterly unique, ultra-perilous, absolute secrecy-demanding situations—emergencies at the extreme end of the spectrum—may arise. However, it is a grave mistake to treat all crises as extreme in this way, and irresponsible to create a constitutional order that can be set aside whenever the chief executive sees a cloud rising over the nation—or his political future (which he is not likely to see as different).

The Incurable Weakness of Law

Sometimes, critics argue that the weakness of law lies not in the laws themselves but in the psychology of decision makers who face the urgent demands of emergencies. The argument deploys a version of the maxim, necessity knows no law, but in this case the claim is that necessity incapacitates official decision makers. Alexander Hamilton wrote, "It is in vain to oppose constitutional barriers to the impulse of self-preservation."[24] The law's job is to guide the deliberation and decisions of officials; however, in crisis, legal norms that ordinarily guide their decisions and actions do not—they cannot—do the job. The intense pressure of emergency situations shifts laws into deliberation neutral.

A crude version of the argument suggests that deliberation is short-circuited and decision makers simply respond to the immediate threat, heedless of the law. But that is an implausible characterization of executive decision-making under pressure. Hamilton offered a more plausible assessment. Necessity overcomes the usual force of law in official deliberation, he suggests. The "necessity" here is the overriding importance of national self-preservation—the well-being, security, even survival of the people. To understand this claim, recall that legal rules cannot exercise practical constraint or direction on their own; they depend on decision makers regarding them as binding and integrating them into their deliberative economy. This is reinforced often by their appreciation of the fact that others will learn of their decisions and hold them accountable. The argument, then, is that in emergency situations, where the peril is great and urgent, considerations other than that peril are eclipsed; the noise of the crisis drowns them out. The claim is not that the reasons for urgent action against the law override competing considerations, and that decision makers, heeding the overriding normative force of these considerations, find the reasons compelling. That is the premise of the *normative* argument. We will consider it presently. This *psychological* argument focuses on the effect of the peril and urgency on the salience of legal reasons in the deliberative psychology of decision makers.

Of course, the rule of law is fully aware that even under ordinary circumstances, laws themselves may not be sufficient to motivate compliance with their terms when other goals or interests might incline officials toward abusing their power. Accountability-holding networks play a crucial role as law's auxiliaries, as the infrastructure of law's rule. The psychological argument addresses this dimension of the rule of law as well. In emergencies, it is argued, other branches of government, charged with constraining the executive in a system of checks and balances, are more than willing to delegate untrammeled decision-making power to the executive. Recognizing the overwhelming demand for swift and decisive action, the pervasive uncertainty of the situation and their awareness of their own ignorance, legislators and courts see no option but to give wide and unconditional scope to executive power.[25] It is of little moment whether what drives this deference is a rational assessment of relative competencies of the branches of government or a failure of political nerve. The fact is, critics argue, necessity again undercuts and obviates law. Executive oversight by other branches of government is pragmatically infeasible—the constitution cannot do its work. These are "palliatives that have proven largely ineffective."[26]

For several reasons, this line of argument is no more persuasive than the more radical conceptual argument. Consider, first, the argument as applied to primary executive decision makers. Here again, exaggeration reigns. It is implausible to think that, across the range of types and intensities of emergency situations, *only* concerns of response to the immediate crisis *can* enter the deliberative economy of decision makers, that panic eclipses deliberation of *all* decision makers regardless of their experience and maturity. Indeed, the gravity and complexity of the situation calls for deliberative capacities to function at full strength, with wide vision and emotional maturity. Our elected officials may not always be equipped with such capacities and maturity, but this is not a problem for the rule of law but for our methods of installing decision makers in positions of power. It is precisely in such circumstances that we need practices and protocols that enable decision makers to approach complex situations with their deliberative capacities at their sharpest. Rather than inspire confidence in government officials, this argument, if we were to take it seriously, should warn us about putting enormous power in the hands of persons so likely to be overwhelmed by situational panic. The facts brought to our attention by this argument, if they are facts, alert us to challenges any regime seeking to realize the rule of law must take seriously and address responsibly. They do not, however, demonstrate that law is incapable of working to channel and constrain, as well as enable, the exercise of power in times of crisis.

Similarly, the argument as applied to other departments of government is also unconvincing. Critics like Posner and Vermeule document failures of the American system, where time and again legislative and judicial actors have stepped back from their responsibilities to check executive overreach in times of crisis. But such failures only imply *insufficiency* of the constitutional order, not *incapacity*—failures of responsibility of government officials, not failures of the rule of law. "It doesn't work and hasn't worked" does not entail "nothing like it can work." Again, failures alert us to problems the rule of law must solve, challenges the rule of law must meet, not the emptiness of the ideal. Moreover, respected legal scholars have pointed out the critics' exaggeration of cases of failure of legislative and judicial oversight of executive action. They have provided empirical evidence that national constitutions, statutes, and courts have proven to be able to constrain government actors.[27] This is true even in emergency situations. Tom Ginsburg and Mila Versteeg have argued, for example, that during the COVID-19 pandemic courts, legislatures and subnational governments have played an important role in constraining national executives.[28] That is, law and constitutional arrangements *can* check and sometimes *have* checked executive action.

Should Law Constrain Executive Action in Crises?

The psychological argument fails the plausibility test. It should not confused be with the different, *normative* argument. Critics argue that, even if, sometimes, law can do its work to constrain executive action in emergencies, bolstered by oversight activities by other government branches, relying on them to play a role in crisis decision-making is a mistake.

The Argument for Law's Silence
Such arrangements are practically infeasible, according to critics, because other branches lack the institutional competence to act swiftly, decisively, and with the degree of secrecy necessary for effective responses to emergencies (and the modern policy environment more generally).[29] "Decision, activity, secrecy, and dispatch will generally characterise the proceedings of one man, in a much more eminent degree, than the proceedings of any greater number," Hamilton argued.[30] Moreover, it is argued, only the executive has access to the information needed for decisive action in times of crisis.

This is clearly a normative argument. It does not show that law *cannot* constrain officials; on the contrary, it assumes that it *can*, and argues that it *should not be allowed* to do so, that the best constitutional arrangement puts wide powers in times of crisis in the hands of the executive. This is the most plausible construal of the critics' argument. The conceptual and psychological arguments disguise a normative claim about the best way to equip decision makers for emergencies.

According to the normative argument, when it comes to constitutional arrangements for dealing with inevitable emergencies, the kind of constraints usually required by the rule of law are simply too costly. The price for protections against abuse of power that they exact is too high when survival depends on speed, secrecy, and decisiveness. It turns the constitution into a suicide pact. Necessity, it is argued, justifies suspension of ordinary constitutional-legal constraints; more precisely, necessity justifies a legal-constitutional arrangement that accords exclusive and untrammeled power to the supreme executive in emergencies. This normative argument is the argument we must address if the rule of law is to sustain its bold claim that law is sovereign.

However, we must emphasize that a full-throated defense of law's sovereignty can nevertheless recognize that in some circumstances the executive may be *morally* justified in acting outside or even against the law. Such actions would be illegitimate in the eyes of the law, and inconsistent with the rule of law, but we might still be grateful for them and even regard them as morally justified, all things considered. This is conceivable, because, although the rule of law makes normatively weighty demands on individuals and on the polity in general, these demands may not always override competing moral considerations. As we have argued in Chapter 7, law claims sovereignty over all those who exercise power over others, but it does not claim sovereignty over all other principles of political morality. The issue for us now is whether the legal order should be structured in such a way as to recognize and authorize legally unguided and unbridled exercises of power—that is, whether it should recognize "lawful lawlessness" contrary to the demands of the rule of law. I believe the answer must be no.

Law Must Speak in Emergencies

There are several important reasons why we should not accede to the normative argument's challenge to the rule of law. Simply put, the argument ignores very significant costs of legally recognizing lawless power, even if limited to times of crisis, while it, again, exaggerates the costs of constraint on such power by taking the most extreme cases of emergency as the paradigm for all emergencies. It is simply not true, for example, that secrecy is necessary in all kinds of crises. On the contrary, gathering information from the widest possible sources can be critical to effective management of a crisis. This is certainly true of pandemics, but also true of emergencies due to natural disaster, industrial accidents, and even civil disturbances. Likewise, as events after the 9/11 attack demonstrated, initial efforts to prevent further attacks may have been driven by urgency, but the long-term responses to terrorism (however problematic) were driven by a sense of the gravity of the peril, but not by the need for urgent swift action.[31] Moreover, not all novel situations demand urgent responses, and not all urgent situations are novel. Of course, some emergencies combine extreme peril, genuine novelty, radical urgency, and a need for utmost secrecy. But many do not, and it distorts our thinking to put all emergencies into the basket with the most extreme.

More importantly, we need a more balanced understanding of the costs of legal arrangements for dealing with emergencies, not only costs of constraints on executive power but also the costs of lifting all constraints from it. Among such costs we must weigh the following.

First, Justice Robert Jackson reminded us that emergency powers, unless adequately guided and monitored, "tend to kindle emergencies"; they "afford a ready pretext for usurpation."[32] Unless tied to reasonable standards, those who exercise emergency powers are likely to see emergencies and the necessities they bring with them when detached observers would not. Stephen Holmes reminds us that "emergency conditions do not suspend the laws of human fallibility."[33] He adds that a system of unmonitored executive discretion

> exposes itself to the danger that the executive officials who happen to be in power at the time [during a crisis] will feel that inaction is psychologically intolerable or will . . . have a bias toward aggressive action that, while psychologically satisfying (not to mention electorally advantageous) in no way corresponds to the requirements of the situation.[34]

Second, Stephen Holmes has persuasively argued that it is precisely in times of crisis when stress levels are high that decision rules and protocols are most valuable.[35] He invites us into the emergency department of a hospital. Emergency department personnel are keenly aware that the stakes are high, risks of delay are great, as is need for swift and decisive action. Nevertheless, to minimize the risk of fatal but avoidable mistakes, they follow protocols they have practiced in advance. "Emergency response personnel follow pre-established protocols precisely because they understand the dangers they face," dangers of relying on gut reactions and immediate responses to the situations they face.

Paradoxically, rather than precluding adherence to appropriately designed protocols, extreme urgency requires it.[36] In the absence of protocols, decision makers are not more deliberatively flexible, but significantly less so. Protocols free decision makers from psychological compulsions, biases, behavioral rigidities, false certainties, and cognitive deficiencies like confirmation bias and aversion to self-critical thinking. "Constraints can be empowering,"[37] Stephen

Holmes reminds us. They focus one's aim, and remind one of longer-term object-ives and other dangers or important considerations that are likely otherwise to be drowned out by the immediate demands of the crisis. Training, discipline, co-ordination, and practice do not cripple improvisation; they free it up.

Of course, such protocols, to be useful, must themselves be designed carefully, and thus must be based on prior experience. Opponents argue that emergencies are necessarily novel and so cannot be anticipated, but the protocols Holmes has in mind do not themselves determine the particular decisions that must be made in the emergency situations. Rather, they structure the emergency deliberative and decision-making process, forcing decision makers to take proven steps to keep deliberation open to information and opportunities, offering heuristics to block obstacles to clear thinking, and requiring that decision makers rely on de-liberation partners. Of course, protocols can be poorly designed and corrupt or disable good decision-making, but the solution is to design better ones rather than to cut off decision-making from them.

Third, critics argue that legal rules tie deliberation to rigid, strictly past-oriented strictures when what is most needed is the ability to read clearly the complexity of the pressing circumstances. However, deliberation unconstrained by or freed from the influence of established rules is often no less a prisoner of the past. The prison is the individual decision maker's own past. Rule-free de-liberation is not free-range deliberation; it must draw on the decision maker's personal experience. It is a dangerous myth that when decision makers are freed from rules and strictures they can see particular situations in all their naked and extraordinary complexity. We attend to that which we are habituated to recog-nize, and we systematically overlook other features of our situation. We can train our attention to focus on other considerations, of course, as a skilled painter will see in a landscape much that an untrained eye would miss. But training is a form of habituation. Decision makers are not freed from the past, nor suddenly able to see the particularities of the emergency situation that are obscured by rules; rather, they remove one lens only to put on another, without recognizing they have done so.

Finally, in the absence of a requirement to justify one's judgments to other de-liberation partners, decision makers are more likely to make bad or ill-considered decisions. The rule of law requires transparency. The requirement on deci-sion makers to give reasons publicly tends to improve the reasons. Adversarial processes—institutional structures that force consideration of contrasting or competing accounts of facts and relevant principles and values—can compen-sate for personal or ideological rigidities of decision makers. "To reject the rule of law," Stephen Holmes argued, "is reckless because it frees the government from the need to give reasons for its actions before a tribunal that does not depend on spoon-fed disinformation and is capable of pushing back. . . . A government that is not compelled to give reasons for its actions may soon have no plausible reasons for its actions."[38]

It is easy, therefore, to exaggerate the costs of legal constraints on decision-making in times of crisis and ignore the significant costs of legally unconstrained decision-making. The challenge is to construct the decision environment in times of crisis to optimize good decisions and effective responses while minimizing the risk of abuse of governing power. The rule of law has a role to play in designing this environment.

Managing Chaos: Emergency within a Legal Framework

Emergencies are real. Crises can threaten mortal peril. "Emergency does not create power," Chief Justice Hughes once said, but it "may furnish the occasion for the exercise of [extraordinary] power."[39] The challenge for the rule of law and for constitution writers concerned to uphold the rule of law is to enable and manage this power. "Crisis does not suspend all laws or abrogate every fundamental right," the International Commission of Jurists declared; "rather, the state of emergency exists within a legal framework."[40] The previous pages of this chapter argued that this task is not impossible or pointless, but there is no denying that it is difficult. Nevertheless, since World War II nations around the world have sought to define a legal framework of emergency powers in their constitutions. Ginsburg and Versteeg report that "over 90 percent of all constitutions today include clauses allowing for the declaration of a state of emergency."[41] The idea of a state of emergency has found its way into constitutional thinking,[42] although it was once an extraconstitutional or contraconstitutional idea. The question is how to accommodate emergency powers in a constitution consistent with and guided by fundamental principles of the rule of law.

The aim of the rule of law, we have argued throughout this book, is not to emasculate ruling power but rather to temper it. Tempering is a multilevel project. It seeks to empower, enable, prepare, constrain, oversee, and learn from the exercise of power in times of crisis. Tempering involves both enabling and bridling that power. Enabling involves defining and allocating powers, disciplining its practice, providing resources to guide their exercise, and opportunities and mechanisms for learning from experience of managing crises. Bridling involves both directing and constraining this exercise, and defining mechanisms for holding it accountable to the law's guidance and, after the fact, learning how to do it better the next time.

Tempering focuses on three points in time relative to emergencies: before the crisis hits, during the crisis, and after it has passed. It must provide resources, guidance, and discipline prior to the emergence of the crisis, determine powers and constraints on them at the inception of the crisis and during it, and provide for its termination, and structure opportunities for review and accountability after the crisis has passed. The key powers that must be defined and allocated include powers to determine (a) powers to decide on the existence and onset of the crisis and its termination (when), (b) powers to decide the entities that will bear primary responsibility for responding to the crisis (who), (c) powers to determine broadly the shape and limits of those responsibilities (how), and (d) powers to assess the exercise of those powers (how well).

National experience and the experience of other countries can guide this effort to outline in broad terms the kinds of crises that can threaten the nation and the risks of abuse to which emergency powers are vulnerable. These abuses include, for example, enhanced opportunities for corruption and for adoption of measures unrelated to the emergency, especially those that might enhance the political security of those in power and permanently compromise fundamental rights. There is also the risk that those who exercise ruling power might try to hang on to these expanded powers beyond the termination of the crisis by altering the constitution to make the emergency powers permanent or making emergency decrees into permanent laws. These and other risks of abuse that we can learn from the past must be addressed and minimized in the legal framework designed for emergencies. The experience of nations over time can yield a repertoire of best practices from which legal-framework designers can draw.

The legal framework must start with explicit constitutional provisions underwritten by implicit principles, but it can also include regular statutory or common-law instruments and principles. It must also look beyond the executive branch of government to consider means for involving the legislative and judicial branches, auxiliary governmental institutions—ad hoc tribunals and regular oversight bodies—and civil society institutions. Rule-of-law respecting efforts seek partnership rather than exclusive control, carefully orchestrated coordination of power rather than its concentration.

The difficulty of constructing this legal framework is great, but its importance is greater. I cannot offer detailed proposals here, but some general principles can be suggested to guide wiser minds that must be enlisted for the project. (The following list of principles is based on a survey of modern constitutions, especially those of Germany and South Africa, which have served as models for many contemporary attempts to build emergency powers into national constitutions.)[43]

First, consideration must be given to the determination of the occurrence of emergencies and hence the occasion for the exercise of emergency powers. Because crises fall along a spectrum of intensity, gravity of the harm or peril, scope, urgency, and need for secrecy, attention must be given to distinguishing in broad terms the kinds of emergency situations that the framework seeks to address. With this in place, attention must be given to determining the onset and termination of the various kinds of emergency contemplated. Regarding the onset of a crisis, declaration of emergency must be made only by officials duly authorized to make it, with participation of parties in government beyond those who will exercise the emergency powers. The declaration must not be retrospective and must be public. Both the declaration and its rationale must be widely promulgated and must meet conditions of previously articulated legal standards. The declaration must be reviewable by appropriate agencies other than the agency declaring the emergency. Courts may be the appropriate agency for this purpose because they are usually best equipped to assess evidence, judge compliance of the declaration with legal standards, and make public any violation of the standard should it occur. Also, states of emergency should be temporally limited and mechanisms for extension must involve participation of government agencies other than the executive.

Second, the scope of emergency powers and measures must be carefully defined. Actions beyond normal legal or constitutional provisions may be authorized, even in derogation of certain rights, but protocols for exercising these powers and procedures for engaging other parties in deliberation should be established in order to discipline the deliberation and counter characteristic modes of cognitive myopia. In addition, some measures must be put off limits from the outset: (a) certain fundamental rights (e.g., torture) should be designated as "non-derogable"; (b) the constitutional order must be protected against constitutional amendment during the crisis and emergency decrees should not become permanent laws. And (c) emergency legal provisions must not include a power to dissolve parliament or seriously impair the operation of the courts.

Third, derogable rights may be suspended only as a last resort, only when strictly necessary and proportional to the potential harm to be averted, and only for a limited time.[44] This applies especially to restrictions on the press and on rights of dissent. Both the necessity and the proportionality must be determined by "objective" standards; that is, facts must fully support the judgments; sincere belief on the part of those who exercise the emergency powers is not sufficient to warrant suspension. Also, suspension must be entirely free of legally proscribed forms of discrimination both in intent and effect. Persons detained by authorities in exercise of emergency powers must have legally secured rights to challenge the detention, and reasons for their detention must be publicly available.

Fourth, transparency of governmental decision-making is very important.[45] Institutions must be established for public assessment and accountability of governmental actions, through the courts where feasible or by other tribunals or informal or ad hoc institutions, when they might be expected to do an effective job in their place.

Fifth, the legal framework should provide resources, opportunities, and incentives for self-evaluation and self-correction by those who exercise emergency powers and others charged with their oversight. These opportunities and mechanisms should be available during the crisis as well as after the fact.

These five broad principles call for partnership between agencies of the executive branch of government and other government branches and informal political mechanisms. Collaboration provides the best chance for good decisions in emergency situations, mitigating the weaknesses of decision makers and building a strong sense of common purpose. The legislative branch can play a critical role in shaping emergency powers and providing oversight of their exercise. It should help in determining the onset of an emergency and assessing whether conditions warrant a declaration of emergency. It should also help in determining whether the state of emergency should be extended or terminated. At crucial points *in medias res*, it may also offer valuable advice, counsel, and critical assessment of efforts to address the crisis. New Zealand's early management of the COVID pandemic offers an impressive example of such partnership.[46] Early on in the crisis, the New Zealand government took strong measures to combat the spreading virus. It combined them with robust transparency and accountability. It regularly published the legal basis for its extraordinary measures. In addition, it established a parliamentary Epidemic Response Committee, with an opposition majority and led by the opposition, to monitor, to advise, and to scrutinize government actions. The Committee was charged to report to Parliament on any matter relating to the government's management of the epidemic.

Courts and informal tribunals can also play a critical role. These institutions are best equipped to assess government action according to existing standards regarding the onset of states of emergency and continuing need for emergency powers, and to scrutinize the scope, necessity, and proportionality of measures adopted to address the crises. They may be empowered at some points to invalidate government measures, but more likely and more reasonably they can publicly underscore the appropriateness or inadequacy of the measures and their consistency with deep principles of the law. They can act *in medias res* as "weathermen," alerting the public to rule-of-law threatening storm clouds.[47] After the fact, when popular anxiety has subsided, court assessment of government actions can uncover lessons for the future and provide a public record as a base for teaching those lessons. Courts are well-equipped for this task because they have the capacity to set specific cases in a wider legal and political context.[48]

However, we have learned earlier in this book that laws and legal institutions alone are never sufficient to constrain the exercise of power. This is true in normal times and even more so in times of crisis. The emergency-power tempering partnership must include institutions of civil society as well. Legal scholar Aziz Huq has argued that legal chains are weak and require political will to prevail. It is equally true that political forces taken alone are weak because they lack adequate information and are likely to be plagued by coordination problems. But these impediments can be mitigated through the law. "Executive constraint . . . is coproduced by the operation of both legal and political forces working as complements."[49] Law aids the operation of these political forces of civil society by providing legal standards, which, even if they are broad, provide focal points for organizing cooperative activity. It also aids by requiring transparency of government actions and providing strong protections against interfering with freedom of the press and rights of protest. In addition, it can assist *ex ante* by enabling and nurturing strong institutions of civil society that can organize the dissemination of information to the public during the crisis and coordinate political action based on that information.

Conclusion

Law can exercise sovereign rule only if it is wise enough to recognize and acknowledge, and supple enough to respond, to challenges to its rule. No challenge is more serious than that posed by times of mortal threat to a nation and its people. Yet even in such circumstances the rule of law is not silenced; indeed, the need for systematic and effective protection against the arbitrary exercise of power is never greater. This fundamental political ideal requires for its realization in times of crisis our wisest judgment, our most skillful efforts at design, and our most serious commitment to keep the ideal alive. If we fail, the essential infrastructure of all that is just, decent, and good in our polity will crumble.

13

Digital Domination

Taming the New Leviathans

Our daily lives, the way we live, work, and play, are in the process of digital trans-formation. Every aspect of our lives—in public, at work and leisure, at home in the kitchen, the living room, the nursery, the bedroom—is rendered into data, transmitted to data consolidators, analyzed, sent to data brokers, and exploited for economic, political, and sometimes for criminal purposes. This global data-sphere is growing at a pace beyond the comprehension of most of us. The devices plugged into this data-driven world are "always on, always tracking, always monitoring, always listening, and always watching"; they are always learning.[1] Most of this is going on without our knowledge. Kazuo Ishiguro's recent novel describes a near future world, but it is not a world where robots increasingly re-semble human beings, but where human beings increasingly resemble machines animated by artificial intelligence (AI).[2]

This is dizzying and disorienting, as any radical transformation that challenges fundamental steadying points of our lives would be. It has already provided enor-mous benefits. It has spurred advances in medical research, delivery of health care, and improvement of safety on the streets, and lifted the burden of labor from our shoulders. However, the digitization of our world is, in the words of the Norwegian Consumer Council, "out of control."[3] The speed, scope, and designed-in opacity of the process has far outpaced and made obsolete ordinary social and legal processes of control. What is more, just in two decades, command of the global data-sphere and the digitization of our lives have been concentrated in very large part in the hands of a few dominant digital companies ("Big Tech"), in-cluding Meta/Facebook, Alphabet/Google, Amazon, Apple, Microsoft, Twitter, and a few others. These digital platforms are the new Leviathans, the centers of a new form of ruling power.

The power wielded by the new Leviathans rests not on the power of the sword or control of material resources, but rather on control of data and the technol-ogies that produce, collect, process, package, and distribute it. This power is immaterial, ephemeral, yet its ability to penetrate our lives and manipulate our behavior dwarfs that of more familiar forms of power. It would have been the envy of every ancient potentate and renaissance absolute ruler. Digital platforms

Law's Rule. Gerald J. Postema, Oxford University Press. © Oxford University Press 2022.
DOI: 10.1093/oso/9780190645342.003.0013

are, in the estimation of the Stigler Committee on Digital Platforms, "the most powerful political agents of our time."[4]

This power is immaterial in another sense: it is not territorial. As it defies borders of the self and the personal, so it ignores, transcends, and defies conventional national borders. Its scope, in ambition and in reality, is global. Largely and intentionally hidden from view, it appears impersonal—the product of algorithms and artificial intelligence, untouched by human hands. What is more, we have willingly, albeit unwittingly, invited it into our lives, embracing it as the unseen condition of nearly costless conveniences.[5]

These new forms of concentrated power have largely escaped control and accountability. They are free to exercise it arbitrarily. Moreover, they have proposed to articulate for us standards for their proper exercise and have asked us to trust them to adhere to these self-defined standards. Their concentrated power is, in the words of Stanford's interdisciplinary working group, "like a loaded weapon sitting on the table in front of us." "No liberal democracy," they argue, "is content to entrust concentrated political power to individuals based on assumptions about their good intentions or on the merits of their business models."[6] The extent of the intrusion of digital technologies into our lives may cause unease for many reasons, but the concern falls within the scope of the rule of law when digital agents exercise power over us individually or collectively. The devil is not, strictly speaking, in the data,[7] but in the concentration of mass data power in the hands of corporate entities, and the small number of people who direct them.

The task of this chapter is to detail the nature of this power and the nature and consequences of digital domination exercised by the new Leviathans, and to explore measures we might collectively take at the national and international levels to tame them. The first section describes in some detail the nature and sources of digital power. The second explains that AI technologies represent a potent form of *power over* people and their communities, a form of domination that is the proper concern of the rule of law. The third section considers a variety of ways in which we can use law to protect and provide recourse against the arbitrary exercise of this power.

Digital Power

From the beginning of recorded history, some people have exercised power over other people. For most of this time, the source of this power was physical and material, deriving from control over the natural world and the bodies and allegiance of others. In the modern era, advances in technology (for example, the development of steam power and electricity, and devices driven by them) greatly increased this power. In the digital age, advances in technology created a new and radically different form of power.

The Power of Mass Data and Artificial Intelligence

This power lies in knowledge—not the ideas or information embedded in the content submitted to and communicated among computers, but rather information about the users and their uses of computers and other devices. Computers and computerized devices, simply by their ordinary modes of operation, produce enormous amounts of data. This data is collected, cooked, and consumed: it is extracted, aggregated, connected, and analyzed, then it is packaged in useful new products and sold on ever-expanding markets. Technology companies discovered the enormous economic value of what at first seemed merely to be the "exhaust" of computer processing and connecting via the internet. They monetized it, packaged it, and sold it, mainly to other companies interested in advertising their products, and to other end users who found many valuable uses for the surveillance it enabled.

Some of this data is directly tied to persons—names, phone numbers, Social Security numbers, addresses; some is less direct—location information, "likes" and "clicks," biometric information, products purchased, and websites visited. In addition, there is a vast amount of data *about* this data, so-called "metadata." This is information about the context of the primary level data. For example, the text of an email is data, its metadata includes the subject, from/to names, date and time sent, sending and receiving server names and IPs, format, and anti-spam software details. Similarly, a photo is data, while metadata includes its date and time, filename, camera settings, and geolocation.

The root assets of the digital economy, unlike more familiar industrial and material assets, enabled the industry and its power to grow exponentially, a recent *Brookings* study observes.[8] These assets are inexhaustible (data can be used repeatedly without diminishing), incrementally inexpensive (computers can calculate and networks can distribute the results at very low incremental cost), iterative (use of data creates new data and new products), and nonrivalrous (the use by one party does not preclude use by another). These features are enhanced, Tom Wheeler points out, by network effects—the value of the service or product increases as it engages more people—and the extremely low marginal cost of distribution. This data now fuels an industry that produces hundreds of billions of dollars every year. (Apple's profits for the second quarter of 2021 were $21.7 billion, nearly twice the annual profits of the five largest US airlines in 2019 before the pandemic.[9] On February 3, 2022, Facebook stock lost more than one-quarter of its value—$232 billion.)

The basic tools of this industry include end-user computers of all kinds, the internet that connects them, and a vast array of AI technologies that process and analyze the data. The industry got a huge boost when miniaturization of computers made it possible to put computers in a wide range of devices for everyday use. AI processing produces more data, and more devices produce more data to feed into this processing. "At the heart of machine learning and artificial intelligence . . . is an unquenchable demand for more data," Wheeler observes. "That demand is met by digital perpetual motion where data use begets data products that beget more data and beget more products."

The main activities of digital technologies include data collection (for example, internet scraping, location data gathering), data storage, access and sharing or transferring of data, correlation of data across data sets, and processing and analyzing data. The core technologies, referred to loosely as "artificial intelligence," combine data, algorithms, and machine learning. Algorithms clean, prioritize, and filter data and find associations and notice relations and patterns among entities. Having been "trained" on a mass of data, algorithms autonomously produce new algorithms that yield predictions, directions, and, inevitably, masses of new data. In this way, computers "learn" to act without being explicitly programmed; they act "autonomously" in the sense that they can respond to their environments without being steered by a developer. Nevertheless, human actors define and constrain the "learning," determine the sets of data from which machines learn, and fix the goals and articulate the principles to guide the learning. Human actors also engineer the products in which the prediction capabilities are installed and decide how they are distributed to the public.

Because the appetite for data is insatiable, a crucial task of digital power wielders is to engage users and keep them engaged, thus generating more and more data. This involves stimulating and enlarging users' need to stay connected to, and actively engaged with, their devices and creating ever-new products to satisfy (but not too much) that need.

Internet-connected computers already pervade our public and our private lives: our phones, iPads, and laptops; "smart devices" of many sorts, including TVs, light bulbs, refrigerators and other appliances, kitchen devices, home security cameras, thermostats, and toys (now referred to collectively as the "internet of things"); devices that track and monitor our bodies; ours cars; bank ATMs and grocery store cash registers; GPS devices of all sorts; and the list could go on. As Bruce Schneier puts it, we no longer have things with computers in them, but now we have computers with things attached.[10] Digital platforms that manage the data coming from all these sources aim to be "the operating system[s] of our lives."[11]

An industry of companies, dominated by the large digital platforms but including other data brokers and marketers, has sprung up to use this vast amount of personal information. "Everything from our preferences, movement, habits, physical attributes, and a vast amount of seemingly inconsequential information about our devices is being logged when we browse the internet, use our phones, make transactions, and move around the physical world."[12] From the data stored and analyzed, such companies know what we buy, what we want to buy, what we prefer, what we value, what we possess, where we live and work and like to eat, who our friends and associates are, what our gender identity is, and much more. With very little work, they can predict with remarkable accuracy what we are likely to do in many situations.[13] We are secretly assigned unique identifiers and vast amounts of personal information is attached to them.[14] Digital platforms typically maintain that this personal data is anonymous, but with very little effort, the anonymity barrier can be breached.[15] Moreover, this data is hidden from our view behind an "algorithmic veil."[16]

The power of digital platforms and other wielders of mass data is also in part constituted and sustained by the legal environments, national and international, in which they operate. Digital platforms, for example, claim a kind of ownership of personal data extracted from computers, scraped from the web, and siphoned off of phone location records. In many countries, individuals have no systematic rights of control over this data. Moreover, digital platforms have been able to fend off access to the data and the products of their processing of it by claiming the protection of trade secrets and nondisclosure agreements. These legal shields prevent independent researchers as well as government regulators from access. In addition, in the United States, much of the work of digital platforms has been given constitutional protection under the First Amendment (protecting "freedom of speech") and statutory protection under Section 230 of the Communications Decency Act (1996).[17]

The Power in Aggregation

We can gain some insight into the nature and scope of digital power if we look more closely at the structure of mass data processing. Digital power arises from aggregation of information and from operations of AI technologies on aggregated information. To understand digital power, we must replace a one-to-one model of power with an aggregation model.

We intuitively think of power in the following way: Alice acquires something from Bert (some material possession, labor, information) or controls something that Bert depends on, and Alice uses it to get Bert to do, think, or feel something. One party exercises power over another party; the power relationship is one-to-one, mediated by something Bert wants or depends on and Alice can manipulate. Of course, the parties may be corporate or institutional entities. In fact, an intuitive understanding of politics typical of liberals casts the power-wielding government as an institutionalized corporate entity and the power subject as an individual citizen. The political power relationship is thus conceived as one-to-one: government is one party related individually to each citizen. This, of course, does not accurately reflect political realities in most polities, including liberal democracies. In these polities, the relationship between individual citizens and their national governments is bridged by a complex network of intermediate communities and associations, some formally defined, others informally constituted.

The one-to-one model is an even worse fit for the relationship between the most important wielders of digital power and those who are subject to it. It is not as if some digital platform company sends a digital agent to my house, talks his way in, notices my Social Security number on my computer screen, and then uses it to gain access to my bank account. The lack of fit is due to the deep structure of private digital power, which is a product of both the technology and the economic and legal framework in which wielders control and use the technology. For them, the value and the power lie not in discrete bits of information but in the aggregation of masses of such information. Moreover, strong network effects, strong economies of scale and scope, high and increasing returns to use of data, and low distribution costs together put dominant economic players in a position to close the market to all comers, thereby securing for them a monopoly or near-monopoly position.[18] Much of this, again, is due to or aided by the dynamics of aggregation of data and control of technologies to analyze and exploit it. Power-generating aggregation plays a role in the collection and the analysis of data, and it shapes the scope and direction of its use.

First, consider the collection of data. Only an exceedingly small amount of data from persons is what we would ordinarily think of as "personal information" within one's control—for example, name, address, Social Security number, bank account number, prescriptions, and medical diagnoses. Most of it is or comes from traces of the actions, thoughts, attitudes, and preferences that are extracted from personal use of devices, in and through interactions with other persons or entities (and contextual information about them). Such traces—clicks, likes, searches, views, purchases, location data, metadata from them and from photos, conversations, and exchanges—are generated by interactions among users of computers and devices at home or out of doors, and by a large variety of interactions in public or semi-public spaces while using public infrastructure. The parties to one's interactions may be other persons, groups, organizations or associations, commercial entities, or government officials.

The information is in some sense "about" individual persons, participants in the interactions. However, it is not discretely personal, and it is very rarely within one's control. At the limit, the information collected is an aggregate to which each party to the interactions contributes, but which through collection, collation, and processing takes on properties beyond those brought to it by each contributor. For many such interactions, the meaning and character of one's own behavior are decisively shaped by the fact that they take place with or in the meaningful presence of others. For other interactions, the meaning of one's behavior is a product of a kind of joint activity, in which one is both active and passive, as an agent and recipient. Frequently, such interactions are layered. Beyond immediate participants are secondary ones listening or "cc'd"; beyond them are subsequent or indirect participants linked through sharing, "tagging," or "retweeting" and through third-party bundling and channeling.

The value of such interactions to individual users is due to and greatly increased by network effects. The aggregate or mass reach of the interactions is what attracts people to participate. Friendships are, in one sense, "cheap"—easy to make and maintain.[19] The media are pervasive and increasingly difficult (for many psychologically impossible) to escape in good part due to their aggregate character. Digital platforms and purveyors of digital devices and services exploit the pervasive and intricate embedding in social interactions and social relations to generate more data by attracting more people and more engaged activity from them.

Second, consider the processing and analysis of information. Here, especially, aggregation is key to the value of the data to digital actors and the power it accords them. The data is initially amassed through continuous processes of extraction and collection. This data is collated, and data sets are correlated and prepared for use by algorithms and especially for machine-learning training. The data is structured and classified, elements are associated and aligned, patterns are discovered, and from these processes, predictions are made, directions are articulated, adjustments to environments are made, and from this activity more data is produced. The beat goes on, at a pace and scale we could not predict a few decades ago. "Almost nothing short of a biological virus, can scale as quickly, efficiently, or aggressively as these technology platforms," former CEO of Google Eric Schmidt observed. "This makes the people who build, control, and use them powerful too."[20]

Because the more data that a system works with, the greater the accuracy and precision of its predictions and directions, the importance or value of discrete bits of information and the personal source of them is vanishingly small. Most of the data cannot be meaningfully disaggregated, although algorithms can use this data to predict with near pinpoint precision the choices and identify the thoughts, preferences, or moods of individuals. Aggregation makes this possible. Bruce Schneier notes that with enough metadata we do not need data to tell us everything we want to know about a person's life.[21]

Digital Power Wielders

We argued in Chapter 2 that the rule of law is concerned with the power of *agents*, especially when the relationship between parties is characterized by inequality and dependency. Recall the exchange in Steinbeck's *Grapes of Wrath* between bank representative and Dust Bowl farmers thrown off their farms during the Depression. The bank representatives argued that it was The Bank, not any person, and certainly not they, who demanded their land. This, of course, was nonsense. It is no less nonsense when said of the wielders of digital power. Actors at various levels—coders, engineers, computer scientists, data controllers and processors, data brokers and marketers, and ultimately corporation leaders—are all agents capable of bearing moral and legal responsibility. If, for purposes of the rule of law, governments and their officials are proper bearers of responsibility, so too are the wielders of digital power. We can distinguish four groups of digital power wielders.

The rule of law is especially concerned when this power is concentrated in the hands of a few entities. This concentration is evident in the first group of digital power wielders: national governments and government officials (intelligence and law enforcement officers, regulatory agents, and the like), and increasingly in global governance institutions. Governments, of course, look to digital power to enhance and expand their capacity for surveillance. The second group includes the small number of digital platforms, large telecom companies, and internet providers. Digital power is especially concentrated in the Big Tech companies: Alphabet/Google, Amazon, Apple, Meta/Facebook, Microsoft, and Twitter. These mammoth digital platforms dominate their markets and, in consequence, wield enormous social and political power.[22]

The third group, mid-level designers and users, includes a wide array of analytics vendors, providers of mobile apps, and marketers (retailers, device makers, car dealers, travel agencies, etc.).[23] Especially noteworthy are data brokers who buy, repackage, and sell personal data, and "sensing nets"—entities that collect, collate, and classify data traces from devices and apps.[24] The fourth group, call them "opportunists," includes, on the one hand, legitimate groups and organizations of civil society, and on the other, rogue users, hackers, cyber criminals, and disinformation peddlers. I will focus in this chapter on the "big fish" that wield concentrated digital power and, to a lesser extent, middle-level digital actors. Since earlier chapters discussed rule-of-law constraints on governments, we can focus our attention here on nongovernmental digital actors, the new Leviathans.

Digital Domination

Control of mass data and the technologies that analyze it give controllers power to do a large and expanding range of things, some of which are greatly beneficial, some of which are fearsomely harmful to individuals and communities.[25] Aided by such information, police can locate missing persons and track down crime suspects; social media companies can link us to potential friends and business associates and inform us about important social and political issues; AI-enabled technologies can help us distribute medical supplies where they are needed most and manage traffic and transportation. An auto insurance company, equipped with the right information, can tailor insurance policies to people's driving habits, but it can also influence their behavior by disabling their vehicles when they try to drive after a night out drinking. Those who control information about persons through collection and analysis of data gain power over persons to influence their behavior, experiences, and relationships.

In the digital domain, domination of ordinary individuals and communities by wielders of digital power is an ever-present possibility, and often a potent reality. Domination, we learned in Chapter 2, involves power over another in conditions of inequality or asymmetry of power and the possibility of wielders exercising it arbitrarily. Both asymmetry and potential for its arbitrary exercise characterize digital power, especially where it is concentrated in the hands of digital platforms.

In the digital economy, knowledge is the coin of the realm, and digital platforms enjoy a massive asymmetry of power over knowledge. This asymmetry is due in part to the very nature of the technologies of artificial intelligence. Telephone, computer, and internet users know little or nothing about the data that is extracted from their activity, or even that such data is being collected; they know even less about the uses to which that data is put and about the entities to which the data or its products are transferred or sold. This asymmetry is secured by design. Power wielders go to great lengths to keep information about their collection, processing, and distributing activities from users by denying them access to the information and in many cases by disguising it.

Similarly, the potential for arbitrary exercise of digital power is very great because the industry has by its nature and design shielded itself from observation by individual users, independent researchers and media, and government regulators. Until recently, there were no public standards governing the collection, retention, use, sale, security of, or access to personal data. Digital platforms asked users to trust them to do the right thing. Without access to relevant information and understanding, individual users lack means of oversight and control. Existing legal frameworks, antitrust and privacy laws for example, were designed for a very different environment utilizing entirely different technologies. Moreover, government regulators typically lack the legal authority and, especially, the technical expertise to exercise any meaningful public oversight over dominant digital platforms.[26]

To recall our earlier image, the loaded weapon is not just sitting on the table waiting to be picked up; it is brandished with nearly unrestrained bravado, and, although it is sometimes used to fend off evils, it can cause many evils on its own. We have explored elsewhere the evils of domination by those who exercise governmental power. We must look more closely at the potential evils of domination by the new Leviathans.

Modes of Digital Domination

The power of digital power wielders lies in their ability to influence the architecture of deliberation and choice of those subject to its power. Of course, the law also seeks to influence the deliberation and choices of its subjects. It does so through addressing norms and reasons to law subjects, engaging their deliberative capacities. In contrast, digital power wielders influence choices and actions by circumventing deliberation and manipulating the resources on which it draws. They can shape the architecture of deliberation and choice itself in several ways: by limiting access to or filtering information that persons might rely on for deliberation, by removing options from their awareness, and by influencing the social environment of discourse and the processes by which they seek to understand, evaluate, and deliberate with information. In addition, digital power wielders can shape the internal technologies of deliberation and choice of people in several ways: for example, by influencing their beliefs and preferences, by altering their emotions or manipulating their vulnerabilities, and by changing the means or modes of communication with others.

Actors in the digital realm also have power over communities. Because digital platforms and social media increasingly function as intermediaries, they are able to facilitate or frustrate, to enable, distort, or distract various forms of interaction—business interactions, political engagement, and mobilization of collective action. They can also affect and direct the flow of information in communities and shape the modes of communication available to its members. They can facilitate or retard the introduction of disinformation and misinformation into deliberation, or flood it with information. They can influence and shape the social environments in which individuals interact, in which they form and reproduce groups and communities. Thus, the potential evils of digital domination are not limited to matters of personal privacy or security; they also include significant public harms, and these two dimensions are interrelated. Two modes of digital domination—surveillance and manipulation—deserve our attention; each of them has a private and a public dimension.

Surveillance
In late January 2020, the *New York Times* Sunday Opinion Section collected several commentaries under the title, "One Nation, Tracked." Stuart A. Thompson

and Charlie Warzel, contributors to this collection, conclude their study of phone tracking this way: "We are living in the world's most advanced surveillance system. . . . The greatest trick technology companies ever played was persuading society to surveil itself."[27] Not just phones track us. The average app has several trackers; and "smart" devices of all kinds listen, watch, and record our every move; they are always on, always tracking and monitoring. Big Tech critic Shoshana Zuboff calls this largely uncontested expression of power "Big Other."[28]

Data retrieved by this pervasive and radically invasive surveillance is merged with mass data from one's surrounding community and the world, and this in turn generates a fearsome power. This surveillance capability in the hands of government is a powerful tool of control. AI technologies significantly enhance, indeed transform, government control capabilities. "Government's most important technique of control is no longer watching or threatening to watch," Jack Balkin warns; "it is analyzing and drawing connections between data."[29] The "social credit" system created by the Chinese government, for example, uses mass personal data to determine the allocation of necessary or desired social and personal benefits.[30] Surveillance is no less worrisome in the hands of nongovernmental entities that are under no constraint to use the extracted information in the public interest or to respect the rights of individuals. Knowledge is power, and, as legal scholar Frank Pasquale reminds us, "to scrutinize others while avoiding scrutiny oneself is one of the most important forms of power."[31]

Surveillance on the massive scale at which digital platforms engage is morally objectionable not just because it can be misused. Such surveillance in itself is harmful to individual human interests. The invasion and the untrammeled taking of information, from the most mundane to the most deeply personal, violates each person's privacy and treats them simply as a means to the ends of others. There is no escape from observation, no sanctuary, no place of one's own. No part of oneself is exclusively one's own, to which others may be admitted only by one's deliberate choice. Another's untrammeled command over one's *labor* is a paradigm of domination; it is no less a form of domination when concentrated digital power puts one's *self* at the disposal of others. This is true, and truly evil and wrong, even when individuals fail to object to or welcome the conditions that enable such power. Indeed, the evil is arguably greater in that case, since the invasion and deprivation is done without the awareness and will of the victims.

Yet the harmful effects of surveillance, profiling, and behavioral targeting extend well beyond privacy concerns. There are also significant *public harms* and loss of valuable public goods.[32] We recognize the security of the nation provided by its military forces as a public good; similarly, the security of our streets and public places, provided by a professionally trained and publicly minded police force is a public good. Such public goods are most notable when they are absent. Security is a key part of the climate or environment of a community, a medium in which social life and interactions flourish. Life in liberal democratic societies, people often say, is characterized by "freedom." This freedom is not merely a matter of what each individual is able to do without interference from others; it is a feature of the social and political environment in which citizens interact and relate to each other. Likewise, markets are "free" not because no rules inhibit behavior, but because social and legal norms create a climate in which parties can interact, trade, and bargain without fear of fraud or duress. Freedom in this dimension, like security, is a public good. Pollution and pervasive fear are public evils, harms suffered by individuals and by the community as a whole. Similarly, pervasive surveillance pollutes the social and political environment; it creates a climate of vulnerability shared by all, not merely experienced by each. They interact, but largely at the good pleasure of others. These systems pose a serious threat to freedom of expression and opinion. It can have a chilling effect on public discourse and the exercise of democratic rights of dissent.[33] It is even worse if we become inured to it, comfortable with it and its impact[34]—when we are not so much chilled as choked.

Nature, of course, can also be hostile and threatening, but we do not regard it as evil. However, the climate created by surveillance is practically, morally, and politically different from nature's threat because it is not impersonal but agential. Resistance and protection must recognize the essentially agential character of its threat. Protection against or effective constraints upon agents exercising digital surveillance is likewise a public good—a good that is nonexclusive (available to all if available to any) and nonrivalrous (enjoyment by some does not preclude enjoyment by other), and it is available to the community through combined efforts of its members or their agents.

Manipulation

Mass surveillance enhances dramatically the ability of digital platforms to manipulate beliefs, emotions, and behavior of individuals and shape the political domain to their liking. The domain of the digital platforms is largely commercial. The digital platforms discovered that they could market the surplus data that they routinely scraped from computers, phones, and the internet to advertisers and merchants who want us to buy their products. Manipulation of this familiar sort lies at the heart of their economic model. The "hidden persuaders" of the twenty-first century can influence buying decisions at a scale unimaginable sixty years ago.[35] Of course, their *modus operandi* is not persuasion, but exploitation of rational biases, emotional vulnerabilities, and social dependencies of many sorts.

As the digital industry has grown, the market for digital manipulation products has expanded beyond the commercial domain. Digital manipulation technologies have great potential value for workplace management and other enterprises. "We are learning how to write the music," a developer of the "internet of things" software said, "and then we let the music make them dance."[36]

Extremely precise, personalized "targetcasting" of messages of all kinds has uses in the private domain and in politics. "Weblining," for example, uses precisely targeted ads and information in the real estate industry.[37] Its use in politics, micro-targeting of information and disinformation for political purposes, has caused the greatest amount of concern.[38] Such targetcasting has the potential, already to some degree realized, to manipulate what we believe and prefer by determining what we see, with whom we see it, and at what emotional temperature. It can channel, concentrate, and amplify our views and our prejudices.

Using advanced analytic technologies and behavioral psychology, wielders of digital power exploit vulnerabilities of people. Old-fashioned advertising operated with a rough idea of widely occurring vulnerabilities; new techniques can precisely personalize their efforts by targeting especially acute emotional vulnerabilities, for example, the recent death of a child or specific health conditions, manic episodes of people with bipolar disorder, or specific mental health issues of elderly persons.[39]

Manipulation is not just a key product of the digital economy; it drives it. Mass data technologies have an unquenchable hunger for data, and the industry has developed highly refined techniques to attract users to their devices and the internet and to keep them there. They begin by creating devices that offer convenience, fun, and connection with others; they keep them connected by making it especially inconvenient and increasingly difficult to leave or to avoid the blandishments offered. These so-called "dark patterns" include making "accept" buttons salient while hiding "decline" buttons, confusing users about their possible choices, and making it difficult for users to identify and express their preferences.[40] Even more troubling are attempts to stimulate a kind of technology "addiction."[41] In 2019, the Stigler Committee on Digital Platforms observed, "[T]here is increasing evidence that many online products are designed to be as addictive as possible, to keep consumers 'hooked' on the platform to increase sales without consideration to well-being."[42] These patterns of manipulation draw on extra-rational features of human psychology and our deep need for social connection. Digital domination has mastered the technique of creating and nurturing dependency and a craving for the domination it offers—in disguise, of course. Users forge their own chains.

Manipulation harms and wrongs individuals in obvious ways. Efforts to influence behavior, not by persuasion, but by manipulation, circumventing our rational and volitional command centers, is an assault on our autonomy and dignity. Through our participation in the digital realm, we are subjected to the arbitrary will of others, a subjection that is shrouded by an algorithmic veil. The effects on individuals of manipulation of their beliefs, attitudes, choices, and behavior are significant and worrisome, but our concerns do not stop there. Our communities can also suffer the evil effects of manipulation; to some degree these effects are already evident. Among the most serious such effects is the deterioration of the public sphere. Two dimensions of public life where such deterioration is possible and evident are worthy of comment.

First, digital platforms present a substantial threat to public deliberative space. In 2017, the US Supreme Court characterized the internet, and especially social media platforms like Facebook, as the "modern public square."[43] This may have been the ambition and fervent hope of the early creators of the World Wide Web, but this hope was dashed with the exponential growth of the digital platforms and their overwhelming economic dominance.[44] This domination threatens to close the virtual Hyde Park and distribute its participants into hermetically sealed windowless monads. (We typically refer to them as "bubbles," but as Adrienne La France suggests, "shrouds" is a better term, since inhabitants of these monads do not know what other people see.[45]) The Stanford Group rightly points out that the effects of the vast economic power of the major digital platforms on the political domain have been devastating.[46] Their control of content dissemination through targetcasting enables the platforms themselves or third parties to deliver specially designed packets of information and disinformation to discrete audiences and to amplify some voices and silence other voices. The potential for undermining our collective ability to think about public matters in a public manner is great. Recent election campaigns in the United States and elsewhere, the vote on Brexit, and other such events demonstrate the extreme difficulty facing publicly minded citizens who seek to engage in conversation across party and ideological lines.

Second, as our social life increasingly migrates to the internet and digital platforms, we risk losing community by losing the public space in which the community is nurtured. As we observed in Chapter 8, public spaces not only enhance our individual lives in manifold ways but they provide an essential public good. In them, people, beyond their intimate relations and regardless of assigned identities, encounter each other and experience together their immediate environment. In this rich soil of public life, more carefully cultivated exchanges of views, arguments, deliberations, and debates can take root, based on a generalized trust, a willingness to engage with people not intimately known to us.

Physical public spaces offer a locus for a kind of human or civic commons, a commons of the *demos*, to which individual strangers contribute, whether intentionally or not, and from which they can draw to establish and replenish a sense of a bond beyond tribe and creed. If interactions among strangers—the mode of interaction in a polity, as opposed to a village—does not take place in this kind of shared public space, the interactions will be alienated. In the absence of interactions in such spaces, lacking the commons they provide, members will not develop the will and skills to meet the demands that the moral ideals of democracy, equality, and mutual respect make on them.

Digital domination (along with other forces) threatens this intangible but utterly vital public. It drives people into virtual ghettos walled off from other ghettos. In the past, political rulers used weakening of public spaces to make it easier for them to control a potentially restive population. Entities of this new form of governing power use it to further their own, largely economic, aims. The fact that individuals willingly if unwittingly participate in such schemes does not diminish the harm of such manipulation, for it is not a matter solely for individual decision. *Communities* victimized by manipulation suffer this harm. Individual members suffer it indirectly. A robust public is a public good. Restoration, protection, and maintenance is a task for the combined efforts of the community. Individuals as members of threatened communities are responsible for participating in these efforts.

Taming the New Leviathan

Digital platforms, large data brokers, and other middle-level digital enterprises wield enormous, largely unconstrained, power over individuals and their communities. They have the resources, opportunities, and motivations to exercise the kind of domination that lies at the center of the rule of law's concern. The *existence* of the power is enough to trigger this concern; we need not demonstrate its extensive *exercise*. Since before Plato, the rule of law sought to tame ruling power of public authorities—the familiar Leviathans. The rise of digital power and the concentration of it in the hands of a small number of nongovernmental enterprises has brought into view a set of new Leviathans that need careful tending and taming as well.

The rule of law uses the law as the instrument for this taming. Some modes of potentially effective intervention may not directly deploy the law—like development of new technologies or platforms that can compete with and thereby constrain the current digital giants—or they may lie beyond the capability of law to deploy. The law's distinctive instrumentalities include setting public standards for the exercise of digital power, devising institutional mechanisms and procedures for public assessment of it, and enabling and mobilizing informal public participation in this accountability-holding. However, efforts to subject digital power to law's rule must keep fully in mind the fact that digital technologies have enormous and not fully charted potential for making our communities more secure, productive, and decent and our lives in them longer, healthier, richer, and more meaningful. Efforts to establish a robustly functioning rule of law in the digital domain must seek to temper, bridle, and properly orient digital power, rather than to disable it.

Accountability

AI technologies utilizing algorithms and machine learning for amassing and analyzing data are the engines of digital power. Any form of governance of digital power must start with what many now call "algorithmic accountability."[47] The rule of law relies heavily on accountability to temper power. The scope of its methods in the digital domain extends beyond algorithmic accountability, but its efforts must begin with this core. Accountability requires *reporting* of (1) the sources and modes of acquiring data inputs, (2) the kinds and sources of data used in training computers to devise their own algorithms and the principles used to guide that training, and (3) the definitions and criteria used for classifying or structuring the data. Accountability also requires that those who are responsible for designing and operating algorithmic processes *explain* and *justify* them. It requires, further, that they *certify* that their predictions are accurate and that they meet internal design and external normative standards. Finally, it requires that mechanisms to mitigate errors and redress harms caused by them are in place and working properly.

It is often said that AI technologies are "black boxes." By nature and design they are complex and impenetrably opaque and, consequently, not amenable to meaningful accountability. However, much about the design, operation, and outputs of algorithmic processes is amenable to inspection and assessment. Human designers determine the inputs, define the targets, goals, and criteria, construct the constraints, and determine the uses of the technologies; further, human beings use the output. Processes, designs, and outputs can be inspected; designers and users can be held to standards.

Transparency is one of the key principles of algorithmic accountability. It is the guiding aim of the reporting task, but it is widely recognized to be insufficient. Access to information about computation processes alone will never be sufficient to making their workings public and assessable, if those who are granted access lack the knowledge and expertise to understand the information and, especially, if the processes are designed in part to enhance its native opacity. Access is not enough; the processes and criteria used must be intelligible ("explainable") to external observers. Of course, most of us lack the background knowledge, training, or time to understand the "explanations." Responsibility for oversight must be given to persons with the expertise needed to exercise governance; and the processes must be explainable to them and to intermediaries who can educate the public and facilitate its role in holding digital power accountable. Also, we can develop technical devices that commit designers of algorithmic systems to certain basic principles and record these commitments. In this way, we can *design* accountability *into* the algorithmic processes.[48] To the extent that these devices are effective and can prevent designers from circumventing or gaming them, they can facilitate accountability without requiring a hard look into the black boxes. Finally, to some degree, the outputs of the algorithmic processes can be tested to determine whether they comply with the standards that are meant to constrain them. For example, if our concern is that algorithms are taught on biased data sets, we can test their results for patterns of systematic bias.

Mechanisms securing access and assessment presuppose the articulation of relevant standards beyond the specific tasks and goals of the technologies to which actors are held accountable by means of these mechanisms. These include standards concerning the fairness or moral-political appropriateness of the processes themselves and the impact of the use of the outputs on the lives of people and their communities. The mechanisms also presuppose clear assignments of responsibility for ensuring proper functioning.

Observers of the current state of play in the digital world report that "accountability mechanisms and legal standards that govern decision processes have not kept pace with technology."[49] Various combinations of standards, standard setters, and authorized accountability holders—I will call them "governance regimes"—have been proposed to tame the new Leviathans. We explore here some of the most salient regimes for their promise to secure people and communities against the arbitrary exercise of digital power.

Governance Regimes

The rule of law seeks to devise legal means effectively and publicly "to challenge automated decision systems," providing time, space, and channels "to test and contest the working of such systems."[50] In some governance regimes, law and legally authorized officials play a significant role; in others, law's role is auxiliary rather than primary. At the limit, the role of law and external regulation is attenuated. We begin our exploration of governance regimes with the lowest level of legal engagement.

Internal Governance

The current mode of governance of wielders of digital power in the United States is internal. Digital platforms exercise control through internal review boards and internally operated mechanisms of algorithmic accountability. They also define the standards by which they judge their performance and, at their discretion, announce these standards, articulated in very broad terms, to the public.

They pursue general approval for their public "commitments," but frequently the commitments hold only until public sentiment shifts or the market calls for a change of strategy. Internal governance works largely on a "trust me" principle: they define the standards by which they wish to be judged; they determine how the standards are to be interpreted; they determine the mechanisms of technical (algorithmic) accountability; and they determine whether they adequately conform to the standards. The law plays very little role in this mode of governance. Indeed, Big Tech platforms have been especially adept in using the law to protect themselves against more searching inspection.

In 2019, Representative Yvette Clarke (in association with Senators Cory Booker and Ron Wyden) introduced an "Algorithmic Accountability Act"[51] into the US House of Representatives. The bill sought to authorize the Federal Trade Commission (FTC) to mandate any corporation that controls personal information of at least one million people or devices and any data broker that buys and sells consumer data to conduct "impact assessments" of any "high risk" automated decision system. The assessment was to evaluate the extent to which the system protects the privacy and security of information, or contributes to inaccurate, unfair, biased, or discriminatory decisions affecting consumers. The impact assessment was to evaluate the system and its training data, the means and duration of storing of the information, and the extent to which the personal information and the output of the system are available to consumers for their inspection and correction.

This bill (which died without a vote) sought to mandate "algorithmic accountability" roughly along the lines described earlier in this chapter. However, it left responsibility for doing the accounting and making any corrections entirely in the hands of the digital corporations. While the bill would authorize the FTC to mandate digital actors to create and operate systems of assessment, it would leave disclosure of the impact assessment to their sole discretion. The entity, presumably, must disclose to the FTC that it has instituted and performs such assessments, but it need not disclose the audit itself. The role of law in this governance regime is vanishingly small, amounting to legally mandated internal review.

Whatever its other merits, this governance regime (had it been legally constituted) fails to meet even minimally core rule-of-law demands. From its inception, the rule of law has never been willing to rely on the goodwill or beneficence of those who wield power. Accountability—the core means by which law rules—necessarily involves giving an account *to another*, to some relevant and appropriate *public*. In the eyes of the rule of law, to be accountable only to self is to be accountable to no one. If H.R. 2231 authorized the FTC to *mandate* public disclosure of the impact assessments by entities subject to the law, it would have brought the governance regime within, if barely, the province of the rule of law.

A robust institution of a free and vigorous press, we learned in Chapter 6, is essential for law's rule of governing power. It is equally critical to law's rule of digital power wielders. It must figure in any governance regime designed to tame the new Leviathans if it is to meet rule-of-law standards.

Of course, as we have seen, disclosure (transparency) is not in itself adequate for effective accountability, even narrowly construed to focus just on auditing the AI technologies used by digital power wielders. At a minimum, explainability to an informed journalist community is essential. Law must also mandate technical certification of the accuracy of the system, and its compliance with critical internal and external standards. Law must play an important role in defining the public norms that govern the operation of the system, including protections of privacy and security of data and promotion of the public goods we mentioned earlier. Moreover, modes of collection and use must also be subjected to scrutiny.

User-Focused Governance

Before we consider governance regimes that rely more heavily on the law, we should consider two proposals of a largely technological kind to curb or counter the power of giant digital platforms. This kind of governance regime combines technological innovations with exploitation of market forces aided by the law. While these proposals depend on innovations in digital technology, they might benefit from some degree of partnership with law. If such a partnership proves feasible and contributes to the effectiveness of control, the rule of law might well smile on it, even if law does not play a principal role in tempering the arbitrary exercise of digital power.

Tim Berners-Lee, mastermind of the World Wide Web in the late 1980s, came to the realization thirty years later that "the web has evolved into an engine of inequity and division; swayed by powerful forces that use it for their own agendas."[52] Too much power and too much personal data, he observed, lie in the hands of giant digital platforms.[53] In the late 2010s, he created an open-source software project he calls Solid and founded a company to spur its adoption. The project aims to empower individuals to create and sustain an equitable, informed, and interconnected society. It seeks to create technology that gives individuals power to control their data and privacy and choose applications and services to meet their needs. Through creation of PODS—personal online data stores—individuals can control their data, the websites they visit, the music they stream, the purchases they make, and the like. Individuals can control access to this data, enabling them to allow companies to use select data for the individuals' purposes. Berners-Lee's aim is to create "Internet 2.0."

His proposal is attractive, but it can hope to curb substantially the power of digital platforms only if it can work its way into the market now utterly dominated by the giants. That can happen only if a sufficiently large number of internet users see for themselves the value in the Solid approach and expect that a sufficiently large number of other users will also see that value and join them. It may be too soon to tell, but success seems unlikely as long as the digital platforms enjoy their monopoly position and continue their highly successful efforts to keep users using. Perhaps, though, with more aggressive antitrust action by government lawyers and regulators, it may have a chance to break into the market.

The second proposal comes from a working group at Stanford University's Program on Democracy and the Internet. Many proposed governance regimes focus on the impact of the activities of digital platforms on individuals; however, the Stanford Group tackles the effects of digital domination in the political domain. "These behemoths . . . pose unique threats to a well-functioning democracy," the Group argues. They "wield so much control over political communication . . . [that they] dominate the dissemination of information and the coordination of political mobilization."[54]

The Group takes aim at the power of digital platforms to curate political content and targetcast it with precision. It seeks to reallocate the rights and powers of editing and curating content through specially designed, individually chosen "middleware," software that mediates between dominant platforms and consumers.[55] Middleware enables users to select providers that offer services catering to the range of user interests that emerge from the market. Consumers can shape their newsfeeds and influence the algorithms that direct content to them. Middleware takes curation out of the hands of digital platforms and puts it in the hands of individuals, thereby catering to their preferences and interests, as they judge them, rather than algorithmic predictions designed ultimately to serve the interests of the digital platforms, advertisers, and purveyors of information and disinformation.

The primary rule-of-law benefit of this regime lies in its promise to dilute the control that digital platforms exercise over the flow of information to individuals and thereby their control over the processes of public deliberation. It also facilitates competition that can spur innovations to enhance communication and political discussion. Clearly, the central player in this proposal is middleware technology. The tempering force on now-dominant digital platforms would come from market competition. The law could play a role as facilitator, requiring platforms to alert users to middleware options and allow them to choose among providers, requiring platforms to use uniform software that allows seamless transfer of content from platform to platform, and holding middleware providers to standards of consistency, transparency, and fairness.[56]

These two innovative proposals are welcome attempts to curb the power of digital platforms. They promise to make inroads into that power; however, their impact is likely to be limited. They both rely entirely on individual end-user decisions and actions. The need for substantial external or public algorithmic accountability is left unaddressed. Moreover, as we have seen, many serious consequences of digital domination by powerful digital actors are public, affecting local and national communities directly and affecting individuals only indirectly. Individuals are not likely to detect these impacts. The Solid project focuses exclusively on user privacy and control of a user's own data. The middleware proposal takes a wider view, targeting the impact of wielders of digital power on the polity, but it is only a partial solution. It leaves too much in the hands of individuals ill-equipped to address public harms. It may even have the unwelcome consequence, as the Stanford Group acknowledges, that middleware enables individuals in a radically polarized polity to cut themselves off even more effectively from the democratic polity.[57]

Wresting a significant degree of control out of the hands of current wielders of digital power requires concerted action of the political community as a whole. Two major obstacles stand in the way of mobilizing our communities for this task: (1) the radical opacity of the technologies and more generally of the activities of digital power giants, and (2) serious collective action problems made worse by political fragmentation. As long as those from whom data is extracted and whose interactions and lives are directed by digital power are fragmented, controllers of the technologies wield all the power. More generally, even if these proposals work effectively according to design, they do not provide rigorous mechanisms for holding digital power accountable to public standards. Thus, there is room for a more active role for law and government in the project of taming digital power.

Law-Enhanced User Control: Property and Contract

One such role is to legally recognize a personal property right in data. A few years ago, John Kennedy, US Senator from Louisiana, introduced a bill he entitled, "Own Your Own Data Act." The proposed bill would establish that "[e]ach individual owns and has an exclusive property right in the data that an individual generates on the internet."[58] Critics of digital power on the right and on the left have argued that, since creation of personal data is a form of labor, the law must treat it as the laborer's property.[59] On this proposal, digital platforms and other users of personal data would be required to negotiate a fair price for the data they propose to extract. When Siri extracts data from listening in on your intimate conversations or Facebook collects information about your favorite leisure activities, the problem, on this view, is not analogous to the government planting a bug on your telephone, but rather to a neighbor's digging up your tulip bulbs and planting them in his garden or selling them at the farmer's market.

The legal framework of contract rather than property provides what might prove to be a more promising approach to regulating digital platforms.[60] Law can recognize actions for breach of contract against platforms that allow app developers and other third parties to use personal data the platforms have promised to protect.[61] The contract frame also brings to bear a range of legal tools to assess the nature of user-given consent and fairness of the agreements between platforms and their users. Courts can analyze contract language to determine whether disclosure of uses of personal information is adequate and terms of the contract are fair and understandable. Especially important, it enables the law to assess the conditions under which users give what passes for consent. Courts can take platform practices of exploitation of user vulnerabilities, especially lack of knowledge and technical expertise, manipulation (nudging), and systematic nontransparency as sufficient grounds for invalidating user consent and the contracts based on them.

The law is more directly involved in these two forms of governance than in the previous governance regimes, because the law's recognition of individual property rights in data and rights to fair treatment in contract relations empowers individuals to control it. It also creates a market to determine the value of personal data and the conditions under which individuals can sell their interest in the data. However, law again puts control exclusively in the hands of individual users. Law underwrites user control. This governance regime does not address the concerns we raised about technology-enabled user control: the demands it places on users to understand digital technologies and the larger processes through which Big Tech and data brokers exercise their power and the obstacles individuals face in mobilizing their opposition to this power. However, the contract frame puts user consent and modes of manipulating, avoiding, or distorting it at the center of regulatory concern.

Nevertheless, these governance regimes are practically infeasible and conceptually confused. The problem is that most data is not personal in a sense that comfortably sits under the concept of property or contractual exchange. We learned earlier that only a very small portion of the data used by digital platforms and data brokers is personal information that is discretely identifiable as such. Much of the data comes from a wide variety of interactions, some intimate, some less so, some while the participants are "at home," some when they are out of doors and using public spaces and infrastructure.[62] It is practically infeasible and maybe conceptually impossible to separate out the individual contributions to the aggregates of information extracted from such interactions and the metadata extracted from it. Indeed, as we have seen, it is not the individual bits of information but their aggregation that yields value for entities that collect it. Thus, the value to any particular individual of some piece of personal information may be vanishingly small, hardly worth the attention of collectors. It is the aggregate mass that's valuable. Consequently, the degree of control that individuals could exert through marketing their information would be extremely limited.

Moreover, if we take the labor theory foundations of the property regime seriously, the digital companies would have a much stronger claim to the vast amount of data they control. This is because the value of this data is due in very large part to the "labor" of aggregating, collating, and analyzing done by their computing devices and processes and the human workers who design and operate them. The data's value is created by aggregation, and the individual and social harms are caused by exploiting this aggregation.[63] But aggregation is the work of the digital actors, not individual users. Neither the property regime nor the contract regime has adequate means to control this potent source of digital power.

Furthermore, the property regime rests on a conceptual mistake: personal data is not plausibly treated as private property. We think of lots of things in our world as "our own," but many of these are not and cannot be "owned." Alicia is "my" daughter, but it is conceptually and morally absurd to think of her as my possession. I take pleasure in hearing a performance of Bach's cello suites and prefer butter pecan to chocolate ice cream, but my pleasure and my preference are not ownable possessions. It is a simple linguistic mistake to move from "my own" to "my owning."

Now think about "my data," that is, some bit of information related to me. A medical condition recently diagnosed is "mine," but it is not something I could plausibly say I own morally or legally. Of course, I might wish that there were limits on the distribution of information about my medical condition that are under my control. I may even have good reason to demand that law protect this control. But I would make this demand by appeal to a prior moral right, say, to privacy, not to my ownership right in it. The same is true of the pleasure I take in hearing Bach and my preference for butter pecan ice cream. From an individual's point of view, a reason to limit others' access to this information may be privacy, but not ownership.

Law-Enhanced User Control: Privacy

Many countries have sought to control access to sensitive information within the frame of a broad right to privacy. In 2019, the American Law Institute (ALI) produced a set of principles for legal governance of digital platforms and data brokers based on a modification of existing privacy law principles.[64] This relatively modest regime is designed to revise but not radically depart from existing US law. In early 2020, California introduced a somewhat more forceful regime, the California Consumer Privacy Act.

The ALI recommendations build on the "notice and consent" strategy of the Fair Information Practice Principles (1973). They require digital actors to respect the confidentiality of user data, to give fair notice to users of operations and use of data, and "heightened" notice for activities that pose significant risk of harm. They permit use of data in the "heightened" category only with explicit opt-in by users. Under these principles, users have a right of access to their data to enable them to correct errors. The principles require digital actors to adopt formats that enable users to move data from one company to another ("data portability"). A "do no harm" principle governs announced primary uses of data, and uses beyond those announced must have a lawful basis. Original collectors of data must exercise due diligence to ensure that other digital actors to which they transfer data also comply with the principles.

The ALI has articulated some important, if relatively modest, standards to protect privacy and data security. The primary burden of implementing them is placed on the shoulders of individual persons from whom data is collected. While the principles bolster the "consent" requirement, they still assume that individuals understand the mechanisms and the consequences of other's use of their data. Moreover, concern about data privacy varies widely across the population,[65] and, of course, individuals are very unlikely to understand or be able to take into account the public harms and consequences for the social and political environment that digital domination can cause. Thus, the problems with nonlegal user-control strategies plague this legal governance regime as well.

Thus, this mode of accountability-holding and tempering of digital power has serious limitations. We need a governance regime that has the resources to address the full nature, size, and scope of the new Leviathans' power over our individual, social, and political lives. Law can and should play a key role in this governance regime. It must set public norms to govern the exercise of digital power and the interface between digital actors and the general public. These norms must allocate responsibility for decision-making under these standards and liability for harmful consequences of exercises of digital power. They must authorize agencies and create processes for robust oversight and accountability. These agencies, if they are adequately funded and employ a staff with high levels of technical and regulatory expertise, can overcome some of the problems of technical understanding, anticipating aggregate consequences, and collective action that severely restrict the effectiveness of user-control governance regimes. These agencies can also encourage, enable, and protect entities and organizations of civil society, like the press, that can assist in oversight and accountability in informal ways. We must complement the privacy-oriented regime by a significant public governance component.

Government Oversight

Several models for digital power governance using law and government oversight have been proposed or are already in place to some degree. One such model calls for enhanced enforcement of antitrust laws by existing government agencies.[66] The general structure of this mode of oversight may be appropriate for governance of digital power, but the remit of such agencies is narrow, since the focus is limited to concern about market fairness. Distortion of markets is just one kind of public consequence of the concentration of power in the hands of digital giants. We have identified additional public concerns.

Recent proposals have envisioned a new specialized governmental agency on the model of the FTC, the Federal Communications Commission, and the Food and Drug Administration in the United States.[67] People with full technical expertise, knowledge of the digital industry, and full legal-regulatory capabilities would staff the agency. It would need full rule-making authority within a statutory frame and comprehensive oversight and accountability authority, shared to some extent with individual users and consumers. The regime must regulate the full range of activities of digital platforms, data brokers, and other major digital actors. The regulated activities include data collection (regarding *what kinds* of data may be collected and *how much* may be collected relative to declared uses), data uses (for example, monitoring and limiting various forms of manipulation), data storage and transfer, and rights of access. We cannot evaluate here the feasibility or other relative merits of such models. However, we can examine from the point of view of central rule-of-law values the differing normative frameworks within which the models work.

In 2018, the European Union implemented its General Data Protection Regulation (GDPR). It is widely regarded as the most comprehensive and ambitious digital governance regime currently in force, combining public governance with protection of individual rights.[68] It has become a model for the rest of the world. It establishes strict rules for collection, processing and transfer of data, and provides special protection for sensitive data. GDPR norms accord data subjects significant rights to be informed about how their data will be used, stored, and transferred to third parties, along with rights of access to their data. US law approaches data privacy as a matter of protecting consumers who are in direct relationships with companies, and so its protections extend only to parties in those relationships. In contrast, the GDPR protects data without regard to whose data it is. Consent is an important ground legitimating use of personal data, but it is not the only such ground. Data must be "processed lawfully"— that is, it may only be used for a specified range of lawful purposes.[69] Moreover, while individual control plays a role in implementing the standards, the regime includes other accountability actors. It recognizes class action rights and in some cases third-party rights of action empowering nongovernmental organizations to sue on behalf of consumers. Importantly, governments also play a large role in enforcing the standards. A core principle of the GDPR is "accountability," according to which a company must demonstrate compliance with the regime. "The GDPR is not just a system of individual rights," write legal scholars Margot E. Kaminski and Meg Leta Jones. "It is, at its core, also a compliance regime, focused on company duties, infrastructure, heuristics, and record-keeping—in short, corporate governance."[70]

This governance regime offers a broad range legal protections and constraints; yet its normative framework remains focused on protection of individual data privacy and security. The responsibility for securing this protection is shared widely, but the grounding value is individual privacy. The potential harm of discrimination to individuals and communities is not addressed; neither is the great potential for manipulation and domination of the public spheres of the communities in which digital actors operate.

Recently, some theorists have suggested that we understand the relation between data subjects and wielders of digital power in *fiduciary* terms. In one version, law would regard Big Tech companies as "information fiduciaries." Because they present themselves as trustworthy, digital actors should be held to fiduciary responsibilities, legal scholar Jack Balkin argues.[71] According to the equitable doctrine of trust, fiduciary duties arise from a dyadic relationship between the parties characterized by dependency and subjection to power,[72] for example, the relationship between attorneys and their clients or between physicians and their patients. Fiduciaries owe duties of care, confidentiality, and loyalty to their principals.

More recently, Brookings scholar Tom Wheeler set his fiduciary notion in the context of law regulating public utilities, rather than the equitable doctrine of trust. His suggestion is that Big Tech companies are providers of goods and services. For many centuries, under common law, the proprietor of a fundamental service, like the ferryman, had a duty to make the service available to all and to take care to identify and mitigate adverse consequences of their activities. Since the late nineteenth century, the doctrine has been extended to providers of electricity, the telegraph, and the telephone. "The ferrymen of the digital era," Wheeler argues, "are platform companies that collect, aggregate, and allocate digital information to create a critical service."[73] On this model, government would hold digital ferrymen to their duties to the service-using consumers, regulating the companies as it does public utilities.

These governance regime proposals provide a broader framework to justify large-scale government regulation. However, they still focus attention on the relationship between digital actors—fiduciaries like doctors and lawyers, or providers of goods and services—and their customers; they still do not include within their purview the full range of activities of digital platforms and other digital actors and the potential for their domination of individuals and communities. All of these proposals, even the two versions of the fiduciary model, assume that the source of digital value and power lies in discrete bits of personal information, contributed willingly or unwillingly by individuals to their digital masters. However, such discrete bits of information are only a small part of the power-generating story. Power lies even more in the aggregation and collation of great masses of such data, produced through digitally monitored interactions of all kinds, and in machine learning operations on this data. Any model that represents the basic normative relationship in digital space exclusively as one between discrete individuals and a digital company—whether that relationship be that of property holder and property appropriator, customer and service provider, or fiduciary and principal—fails to account for the full range of activities and relationships operating in the digital world.

Public Trust Governance

Legal scholar Aziz Huq points out that these proposals fail fully to appreciate the aggregate character of the source of digital power and the potential for large-scale public harm and manipulation that we described earlier in this chapter.[74] Huq defines a normative framework for a more comprehensive governance regime: law should regard mass data as an asset like the air, the sea, and navigable waters. These assets have been recognized since antiquity as common to all people, available for the benefit of all. These common assets are not strictly speaking *owned* by anyone, and the state has strict duties to protect the common heritage as a *public trust*, to be enjoyed by the public at large.[75] The state is charged with managing the trust for the benefit of the public—protecting the interests and rights of individuals affected by the activities of digital actors, seeking to prevent or mitigate public harms that may result, and promoting uses of the asset to provide public benefits. The public trust framework authorizes the agent acting on behalf of the public (namely, the state) to pay special attention to the way control of the common asset can yield great power—power *over* individuals and communities, as well as power *to* achieve large beneficial goals.

Keenly aware of rule-of-law concerns, we may detect a tension in this proposal. Like other similar governance regimes, it calls for robust governmental oversight, depending on state agencies and institutions to have power sufficient to manage nongovernmental digital actors; yet suspicion of concentrated power is baked into the rule of law. The public trust frame is designed to address this tension. It entails two sets of constraints: constraints on private entities who seek to use the asset for commercial gain and constraints on the state to manage uses of it for overall public benefit. The public trust framework at its heart is concerned with the allocation and accountability of the power that stems from the common asset. The state authorizes, enables, and constrains the power that digital actors exercise through exploiting the common asset; and the state is subject to public, democratic oversight, and is oriented to democratic ends, through legislative control *ex ante* and judicial review *ex post*. The public trust, Huq writes, "harnesses 'checks and balances of government' to prevent an asset's misuse, but at the same time reposes no 'blind' trust in the state. It accounts for both market and government failures."[76] The agency must be designed in such a way as to secure its independence from the digital industry. Judicial review of the government agency's management must be engaged to prevent agency capture by entities or interests that might despoil an asset to the public's detriment. Designers of the government agency must also construct a firewall between the national digital governance authority, on the one hand, and political and intelligence agencies, on the other, to prevent abuse by political actors of the power they can wield in the digital domain.

The public trust framework can embrace individual control and individual privacy concerns, while justifying, authorizing, and enabling a government agency to define public norms; and they can step in to protect individuals and communities against digital domination, providing a mechanism of accountability for digital actors that combines formal and informal processes. Thus, the public trust frame enables us to see how the threats of arbitrary exercise of digital power can be met, at least in good part, through recognizable tools of law. The rule of law has an indispensable place in our thought about governance in and of the digital world.

Global Digital Governance

The interference by Russian-government sponsored hackers in the 2016 election awakened the US public to the threat to national security from cyber opportunists. In the last half-decade, many other countries and businesses, private organizations, and municipalities have also suffered greatly from cyberattacks. In a 2020 article in *Foreign Affairs*, Marietje Schaake characterized the global digital domain as a "lawless realm."[77] Schaake argues that large, private digital companies not only operate in the global digital domain nearly free of legal constraint but they also dominate that space. Public authorities around the world, she argues, are at the mercy of private companies. They have even taken on "some key functions of the state, such as the protection of critical infrastructure."[78] She challenges democratic states and international leaders and institutions to wrest control of cybersecurity from private digital companies and to institute norms and regulations at the domestic and international levels to meet current and future threats to cybersecurity around the world. Although the immediate threat comes from state and nonstate opportunists, an even more fundamental threat to security is the widespread practice of states off-loading responsibility for security to digital platforms and major tech companies.

The issue of cybersecurity, of course, is critical because the potential for catastrophic harm is significant. However, Schaake's alarm highlights the more general need for transborder governance of the digital domain. Insofar as digital giants dominate the global digital domain, and they and other state-sponsored and nonstate actors are able to exercise massive power over individuals, communities, commercial and other entities, and even states, rule-of-law principles call for international cooperation to establish effective means of governance in this domain as well.

The global digital domain, we will see in Chapter 15, involves a complex layering of national, regional, and global environments. It is possible for countries to restrict somewhat the movement out of and access to their local internet environments—China and Iran have done so. Some countries have also required that digital companies physically locate their data operations within their borders. However, such activities defy the logic and nature of the internet. The digital domain is only awkwardly limited within national borders. Like the sea in the early modern period, the internet by nature and design—as the "World Wide Web"—has transborder, indeed global, reach. Moreover, digital platform giants operate and exercise their power globally. Indeed, they act like sovereign states, borderless and nonterritorial;[79] or rather, their territory is defined not geographically but by the scope of their command of portions of cyberspace.

The global reach of digital actors and the artificial intelligence technologies they command offer promising resources with which to address some of our most pressing global problems, notably climate change, worldwide pandemics, and poverty. Some of our most fundamental principles of political morality—peace and security, human rights, prevention of discrimination, and protection against domination—have international dimensions and are increasingly interpreted in global terms. Globally and regionally mobilized digital technologies provide indispensable instruments for securing adherence to these principles. At the same time, the enormous concentrated power of digital platforms and other digital actors pose global problems that demand the attention of all international actors. International cooperation is needed to harness the power of the internet and AI technologies and constrain the entities that wield that power.[80]

We will argue in Chapter 15 that rule-of-law principles play a vital role in the global domain. We now see that wielders of digital power are key, perhaps even dominating, actors in this domain. Thus, rule-of-law principles, along with other principles, must guide international cooperative efforts to tame global digital actors. Transnational standards for the exercise of digital power must be defined; regional and global governance institutions, on the model of the World Trade Organization or the International Atomic Energy Agency, must be established, authorized to define and refine international standards, and empowered to mobilize transnational forces to hold digital actors to those standards. We have just begun to think about national governance regimes for digital powers. Efforts to address these global governance issues have not yet reached this level of development. Climate change and global dominance by Big Tech may be the two most pressing issues facing citizens of this planet. It is likely that they are closely linked.

There is, then, a key role for law, and rule-of-law principles, in the endeavor to tame digital Leviathans at the national and global levels. But the exponential growth in the power and reach of artificial intelligence poses a further challenge: AI and machine learning have colonized the law itself. In the next chapter we will assess the prospects of digital domination within the law. Does AI have a useful place within the law, or will AI take the place of law?

14

AI in Law or AI in the Place of Law?

Can you imagine artificial Beethoven? There's no need. You can hear it. At his death in 1827, Beethoven left sketches for a sequel to his magnum opus *9th Symphony*. Recently, musicologists and computer scientists put their heads together and trained a computer to complete his *10th*.[1] A symphony from beyond the grave. *Musica ex machina*. Artificial Bach chorales are also available for your listening pleasure.[2] Music lovers, classical music lovers especially (a rather conservative lot), may find such a thought disconcerting, but the *au courant* say they shouldn't. Apparently, there is no domain of human life where artificial intelligence (AI) fears to tread. Law is no exception.

Artificial Intelligence and Machine Learning in Law

Artificial intelligence and machine learning have been put to a wide variety of uses in the regular operations of law and law-structured governance. Police regularly use algorithms for surveillance purposes, and their commanders use them to determine optimal allocation of personnel across the city. Local and national governments use AI-assisted surveillance to combat the spread of COVID-19. Algorithms come in handy for regulating international travel, granting of visas, and protecting national security at the borders. In the United States, administrative agencies use algorithmic tools to detect fraudulent applications for unemployment or Social Security benefits; the Internal Revenue Service uses them to detect tax fraud and abuse. Environmental protection agencies use them to detect the effects of toxins. AI has made serious inroads into the criminal justice system, aiding bail, sentencing, and parole decisions. It is well known that human decision-making is vulnerable to distortion of heuristics, implicit and explicit bias, and other varieties of cognitive noise. Many believe that properly designed computer programs can assist in securing more reliably impartial and consistent decisions by judges and other governmental officials.

The promise of consistent, fast, cheap, scalable, impartial, and accurate decision-making and more efficient and effective behavioral control has spurred an ever-increasing role for AI in the administration, adjudication, and enforcement of law. We can distinguish between two domains of governance in which

Law's Rule. Gerald J. Postema, Oxford University Press. © Oxford University Press 2022.
DOI: 10.1093/oso/9780190645342.003.0014

the increasing influence of AI is evident: (1) in decision-making of officials involved in civil and criminal adjudicatory processes and the administration of law in government agencies of many kinds, and (2) in government regulation of nongovernmental entities, individual citizens, associations, communities, and business firms.

The ambitions behind this trend toward greater engagement of AI in law vary widely among its advocates. Some see a bright future for pervasive AI influence in these areas and advocate giving "artificial legal intelligence" a wide remit.[3] Others, believing that AI is not suitable for normatively inflected matters, would restrict AI to matters that rely heavily on predictions and have a large empirical element and for which a large base of empirical evidence is available.[4] AI expert Frank Pasquale calls this modest approach a search for legal "intelligence augmentation" (IA rather than AI).[5]

Critics have highlighted reasons why we should hesitate to embrace AI tools even for this modest purpose. Opacity, built-in bias, invasions of privacy, and lack of due process are no less serious on the government side than in the operation of Big Data on the private side. Indeed, the problems are likely to be even more severe, if the vast power that these tools generate cannot be bridled. Authoritarian governments' use of AI for all sorts of surveillance, regulation, and population control is cause for grave worries. It is no less worrisome when liberal and democratic governments deploy the devices. We have reason to ask with urgency whether law can protect against such abuses.

However, the rule-of-law worry that I wish to explore here is different. It concerns proposals for a robust and widely deployed "artificial legal intelligence." Its advocates look to the day, not so very far in the future, they believe, when AI-based computational intelligence and decision-making capabilities exceed the intelligence and capabilities of lawyers, judges, and other legal officials. At that point, it will be possible for artificial legal reasoning to replace legal norms and reasoning in the courts and in the public square, in City Hall and on Main Street.[6] Legal scholar Eugene Volokh invites us to imagine "Chief Justice Robots" and a cadre of artificially intelligent lawyers and bureaucrats. Arguing from the venerable principle that if it looks like a duck, walks and quacks like a duck, then it must be a duck, he writes:

> [I]f an entity performs medical diagnoses reliably enough, it's intelligent enough to be a good diagnostician, whether it is a human being or a computer. . . . Likewise, if an entity writes judicial opinions well enough . . . it's intelligent enough to be a good AI judge . . . If a system reliably yields opinions that we view as sound, we should accept it, without insisting on some predetermined structure for how the opinions are produced.[7]

The future envisioned by these advocates is not one of increased role of AI *in* law but of AI *in the place of* law.

The question for our attention is not how likely this future is, but rather what of value would be lost to us as individuals and to our political community if AI replaces law in a large swath of our political and personal lives. Should we resist changes that would bring about that loss or should we accept it as the price of progress? These questions are important to answer now while the prospect has not yet been realized. We must also ask them if we are to understand the rule of law and its value. The rule of law, recall, is concerned with protection and recourse against the arbitrary exercise of power *through the distinctive instrumentalities of law*. Does Chief Justice Robots offer us merely a model of a more efficient and effective tool for constraining governing power, or does its emergence in our political communities represent a morally disastrous revolution? To answer these questions, we must take a closer look at the *modi operandi* of two forms of intelligence: computational and legal.

Two Forms of Intelligence

Computers are masters of computation. Can they also master legal reasoning? The idea of reasoning as computation is at least as old as Thomas Hobbes's writing in the middle of the seventeenth century. A generation or so later, Gottfried Wilhelm Leibniz turned Hobbes's speculative idea into a research program. He set out to define a mathematically based set of unambiguous atomic symbols and mechanical rules—algorithms, in our idiom—that could serve as a universal language in which topics from metaphysics to morality, from the existence of God to the existence of legal rights and duties, could be discussed and disputes about them settled with finality.[8] The audacity of Leibniz's ambition is astonishing, but the idea that gave birth to it is not all that astonishing. After all, isn't legal reasoning a matter of taking a legal rule that is cast in general terms and applying it to relatively concrete facts to derive a judgment about the rights and duties of specific parties? Isn't this a kind of calculation that once you get the hang of it in one context you can use it pretty much everywhere? Of course, legal rules are often open-ended, so judges must use judgment to fill in the gaps. But if a computer can fill in the very large gaps between the ideas Beethoven sketched for his 10th symphony, why can't it do the same for judging?

The answer—Hobbes, Leibniz, and hosts of other thinkers over the centuries notwithstanding—is that the similarities between computation and legal reasoning are superficial, and they obscure some deeply rooted differences. Upon more careful inspection, AI does not walk or quack like the legal duck. To begin, consider AI's distinctive *modus operandi*, its characteristic mode of reasoning, and its design for social control.

The Intelligence of Artificial Intelligence

Algorithms and the more sophisticated techniques built out of them—the basic currency in the AI economy—are "prediction machines." They take information we have (data) and generate information we don't yet have. Like espionage, this "intelligence" brings us useful information,[9] but it does not engage a capacity for judgment, sagacity, or the disciplined use of reason (capacities Aristotle called *phronēsis*). It produces information that might be critical for decision-making, but it doesn't deliberate; it generates output, but it doesn't make decisions.

The basic structural components of artificial intelligence are algorithms and machine learning. In the early ninth century CE, Persian mathematician, Muhammad ibn Musa al-Khwarizmi (Latinized: Algorithmi), wrote an influential algebra text that devised precise rules for solving algebraic equations.[10] Algorithms, his offspring now ubiquitous in contemporary computing, are "sequences of precise instruction unambiguously specifying how to execute a task or solve a problem,"[11] according to legal and computer scholars Amnon Reichman and Giovanni Sartor. The sequences unequivocally specify a series of operations on data fed to it. Algorithms are deterministic or probabilistic, but always reliably repeatable: once data is provided, they require no fresh cognitive effort by the executor. They are said to yield "predictions," but this is slightly misleading. Their output need not have anything to do with the future. Rather, they uncover correlations, based on statistical analysis of the data fed to them, and on that basis "predict" another correlate. So, for example, algorithms used in many email clients predict the words that we might use to finish a phrase or sentence and produce ads and newsfeeds based on patterns of our internet search behavior.

Computer scientists don't have to write the algorithms themselves anymore. They teach machines how to learn. They have figured out how to train computers to construct and refine their own algorithms. After being fed a set of training data, the computers learn to make correlations, identify patterns through analyzing feedback. The machines generate their own training data through performing repeated trials and analyzing their results. They then develop a model for making further predictions concerning matters not included in the training data set. In 2017, Google created AlphaZero, a chess-playing algorithm. It defeated Stockfish, up to that point the world's most powerful chess engine, after just four hours playing against itself.[12]

Algorithms and machine learning are used in natural language processing. Translation algorithms correlate words in one language with those in another. Sometimes the translations are laughably bad, sometimes astonishingly accurate, but they too simply use statistical correlations. Natural language processing can be used to analyze legal materials and make predictions of how judges will decide cases that come before them. Fed the texts of judicial opinions, they atomize the language into words grouped together in sets of one, two, three, and four "n-grams."[13] If enough data is fed in, a judge's decision can be predicted; the more (and better quality) data, the more accurate the predictions.

However, computers don't "understand" the languages they translate, or even their own mathematical language for that matter. The problem is not that computers lack the mysterious property of consciousness. The problem, rather, is that they don't understand the world. "Understanding language requires understanding the world, and a machine exposed only to language cannot gain such an understanding,"[14] writes computer scholar Melanie Mitchell. And they don't understand or appreciate the propositions, facts, norms, or arguments found in the legal texts fed to them. And, even more, they don't understand the world in which these propositions, facts, and norms are embedded, from which they draw their meanings. Their predictions are not based on reasoning from existing rules and background norms, and their respective roles in the system of norms constituting the legal order. They don't predict in the way Oliver Wendell Holmes, Jr., thought that we, like his notorious "bad man," predict the behavior of the courts. Holmes's mode of "prediction" depended on a keen understanding and appreciation, if not acceptance, of the norms that a lawyer could expect judges to follow.[15] In contrast, algorithms mimic meteorologists predicting the movement of a hurricane. Persuasion, registering the weight of an argument, and assessing reasons for understanding a rule in one way or another play no part in this process. An algorithm works from and analyzes the traces left (exhaust given off) by legal opinions, not from the rules, standards, arguments, and judgments of the opinions themselves. The computing process does not perform legal reasoning tasks more quickly and efficiently than human lawyers and judges; it circumvents them.[16]

The "reasoning" process *simulates* the process of legal reasoning by doing something *altogether different*.[17] This is no *lex ex machina*—computers dropping in at the end of the scene to save rationally challenged human thinkers and decision makers. The judge and the law itself are removed from the scene. Simulation replaces argumentation. AI-driven technologies also promise efficient and effective modes of social ordering. Though, again, they do not just do what law does, but better; they do something altogether different.

Guides, Goads, and Guardrails

We learned in Chapters 3 and 4 that law provides a distinctive mode of social ordering, of structuring and guiding social behavior. When it meets the rule of law's principles, law affirms and nurtures a valued mode of association. Its core technology is *normative guidance*. It addresses rules and norms to agents who must understand and apply them. As we saw in Chapter 2, legal norms mandate certain behavior, but they also structure social interactions by constituting relationships and facilitating efforts of law subjects to order their own lives. Law also, typically, backs up mandating rules with sanctions, but these are not meant to act as goads to behavior but as indicators of the seriousness of the mandates and auxiliary motivations for the reluctant or recalcitrant. AI technologies also enable governments to regulate and order behavior, but the regulatory *modus operandi* of these technologies is very different from those the law deploys. Rather than guide behavior, they channel and goad it.

In his classic analysis, legal scholar Lawrence Lessig distinguished four modes of regulation: law, social norms, market, and architecture.[18] The first two direct behavior by means of formal or informal rules or standards, modeled by, for example, two kinds of road signs. One declares, "Stop" or "Speed Limit 35 mph"; the other reads, "Drive as if your kids live here." The market creates incentives and disincentives to behave in ways desired by a regulating agency. In Lessig's category of "architecture," technology shapes and channels behavior.

A classic example of Lessig-type architecture at work is the speed bump.[19] It slows traffic by making it difficult to sustain any speed faster than is safe for neighborhood streets. Also, in my town, some residential streets are only wide enough for one lane of parked cars and two for traffic moving in opposite directions. City engineers slow traffic on these streets by directing moving traffic in a zigzag pattern every twenty-five yards or so, creating pockets on alternating sides of the street for cars to park. It is surprisingly effective. Another model of architecture is used by various kinds of safety devices. At home, "smart doors" won't close unless users lock them. Computers in "smart cars" detect when the driver is sleepy and, rather than verbally warning the driver, they steer the car to a safe stopping place. They can detect when the driver has had too much to drink and disable the ignition. They don't merely offer directional information to the driver; they make turns, merge onto highways, and take detours, without consulting the driver. This mode of regulation alters the user's deliberative and decision-making frame: it removes options and installs physical or psychological guardrails that channel behavior. The "internet of things" provides regulators with a vast array of technologies for architectural social ordering.

Some commentators on techno-regulation think of these devices, metaphorically of course, as scripts or recipes, but the metaphor is misleading. Scripts and recipes, like social and legal norms, must be grasped, understood, applied, and then followed. They work *within* the deliberative frame of the regulated actors. Architectural regulation works behind the scenes to channel behavior or to reshape the deliberative frame. They work *on* and *alter* the deliberative frame. They construct guardrails, rather than offer guidance; regimentation replaces regulation.

Reasoning Like a Lawyer

Architecture-structured social ordering is a downstream application of AI technologies. It differs in significant ways from law's *modus operandi*. Even more, the core mode of reasoning differs from the law's, from "reasoning like a lawyer," as law-school teachers like to say.

Law is a reasoned thing, we argued in Chapter 2; to bid law to rule is to insist on a central role for law's distinctive mode of practical reasoning in social ordering. Practical reasoning in the mode of law not only produces output that conforms to rules; it also follows the rules in a meaningful, intelligent way. Law's rules function as more than signs of some likely event (like dark clouds heralding rain); they signal things that are to be done. They *prescribe*. Legal rules function as *reasons* to do something. These reasons take their content and force from their place in a constellation of reasons bearing on a range of actions and options. Unlike algorithmic reasoning, applying the law "requires that the decision-maker engages in genuine cognitive effort . . . [involving] interlinked epistemic and practical inquiries,"[20] Reichman and Sartor remind us.

We should notice four key features of law's mode of reasoning. First, it is *practical*. Oriented to action, it uncovers, weighs, assesses reasons for actions and choices among available options for action. In addition, it takes place in and is given shape and content by a disciplined practice of such reasoning, a practice that is public and institutionalized. (We explored this dimension in Chapter 2.)

Second, it essentially involves *judgment* in at least three points in the decision process. (1) Judgment is required to recognize a proposition, utterance, or sign *as a rule*, as something that requires that one follow or comply with it and supplies a reason to do so. (2) Judgment is required to bridge the gap between the rule and its application to concrete circumstances. This is true for all rules and norms, not only for highly general, apparently open-ended standards. To bridge this inevitable gap, we don't merely *pick* an option, or *intuit* the right answer; rather, *reasoning* does the job. The same reasoning enables us to conclude that the object in our path is not a crooked stick, but a sleeping snake; the reasoning at work when, looking at a calendar, we conclude that tomorrow is New Year's Eve, or, looking at a map, determine that we must get off at the next exit. (3) Judgment is required after we determine what concretely the rule requires. For with the rule's application clearly in view, we must still decide *what to do*. We must situate the rule's directive in a larger framework of reasons, assess its weight or authority, and then decide whether to follow it.

Reasoning with and within the law requires that those who deploy it must engage with facts, norms, and values in a variety of ways. Of course, being pretty good at the process, and having settled many of the framing questions in advance, we can often perform these tasks quickly. Sometimes the reasoning takes time and mental energy and the results do not strike us as certain either in advance or after we have done the work.

Third, from what we have said thus far it should come as no surprise that the practical reasoning characteristic of law is fundamentally analogical reasoning.[21] Analogical thinking plays a large part in building the bridge between rules and their concrete applications. It is tempting to think that machine learning might do this job, since it, like analogical thinking, is all about identifying similarities and differences, noticing patterns and correlations. But there is a crucial difference between the two processes. Machine language *counts* to determine relevance of the similarities; analogical reasoning *evaluates*.[22] Relevance is determined not by the number of similarities, but by whether they make practical legal sense. This requires judgment (*phronēsis, prudence*) to situate the target case in a context of comparables, and to identify the pattern or rule that *justifies* treating the target case as relevantly similar to source cases. I have argued elsewhere[23] that to grasp a judicial decision as an example is to locate it in a network of mutually supporting and contrasting judgments. It is no accident that forensic argument typically takes the form of a dialectic of vividly drawing and distinguishing analogies. These judgments, further, are oriented to and constrained by features of the deliberative context that is distinctive of legal practice, most notably its practical, historical, and public dimensions and by a robust sense of justice. Reflective assessment makes room for, indeed greatly depends on, more broadly principled and theoretical concerns, sometimes more sometimes less.

Finally, legal reasoning has an essential moral dimension. I don't mean that it proceeds by appealing at some point to extralegal moral norms or values. I mean, rather, that to exercise judgment entails that reasoning persons are implicated in the practical conclusions they draw. They bear and must take responsibility for them in the sense that they are bound to avow them and are practically liable to other persons assessing their conclusions and the reasoning for them. Rules of mutual accountability apply to the process of legal deliberation and decision-making.

What Is Lost?

Suppose we agree that legal ordering and legal reasoning are different from their AI counterparts. We can still ask why not replace the one with the other, especially if the replacement promises some attractive benefits? What of any value is missing in a world in which Chief Justice Robots has replaced our venerable judges and Justices? Is it really all that comforting to address a human face high on the bench (not to mention wearing a wig)? Aren't human judges and lawyers prone to costly cognitive and moral biases, lapses of attention and judgment? Aren't algorithms consistent, fast, cheap, scalable, and impartial in large part *because* they are impersonal? Isn't the law beyond the grasp of most ordinary people anyway? Don't they have to rely on professionals to make their way in the legal order and doesn't this build in further costs and opportunities for all kinds of human error, not to speak of domination? Similarly, aren't speed bumps more effective than speed limit signs, and a whole lot less costly, since they do the job without police, traffic courts, and fines? What is missing, viewing the matter from the point of view of the rule of law, if we replace our government of laws with a government of machines wherever we can?[24]

To see just what of value is missing, we need to look again at the core concern of the rule of law, which is, of course, power over others that is arbitrarily exercised, and its aim to protect against arbitrary power through the law. Two features of the core aim are critical. We have seen time and again in this study that the aim of the rule of law is (1) to *temper* such power, not to eliminate it, and (2) to temper it *by law*. While the ambition of AI regulation is control, control of circumstances and persons, the aim of the rule of law is ordering and tempering power, giving it meaningful and accountable direction. The choice of law as the means of taming power is not incidental to that purpose. It is not chosen simply because, at the time, it seemed the most effective or efficient or the least costly available means of controlling power. Rather, considerations intrinsic to the rule of law's aim drive the choice of law. The choice of law is a *principled* qualification of that core aim.

The rule of law seeks to *temper power via law* because doing so has its own significance in the moral-political scheme of things. That value—what is lost when it is replaced by AI technology—is, to put it abstractly, *normativity*. Law is important because it is the closest approximation to public deliberative reason that is possible in a large, diverse and divided polity. And it makes possible an especially valued mode of association. As we observed at the outset of this study, rule-of-law advocates recognize that there may be other ways to control power or even provide some sort of recourse when it is abused. The rule of law opts for *law* as its favored means because law promises that those who are ruled and those who rule submit to a regime of public norms, and that people can, through law, constitute themselves as a membership.

We can explore what this means more concretely under two heads: (1) regarding law as a mode of governance, specifically utilizing law's distinctive discipline of practical reasoning, and (2) regarding law as a mode of association reflected in its approach to social ordering. We must keep in mind, however, that we must compare like with like, not AI decision-making at its worst and law at its aspirational finest, or vice versa. No one would argue that we replace law operating at full steam near perfection with a defective digital technology, nor digital technology at its ideal best with law at its saddest and worst.

The Value of Law in Governance

To begin, consider law as a mode of governance, in particular the interface between governing power and ordinary people. What is lost when it is replaced by AI technology? We have seen that governance by algorithm, the intelligence of AI, leaves no room for the mode of practical reasoning that is distinctive of law, and hence no room for judgment, reflection, interpersonal engagement, or personal decision-maker responsibility. Do these intrinsic deficits bring with them disvalued consequences? The answer, I think, is clearly yes, for five reasons.

First, AI has no room for judgment-enhancing human elements like compassion. It cannot understand the meaning of certain acts and their impact on the lives of people; it cannot understand the experience of subordination to others, or limitations on one's freedom imposed by others. These personal and interpersonal elements provide the indispensable context for the proper exercise of judgment. Since AI is "radically solipsistic," as one critic has put it,[25] this context is unavailable to its decision-making. Consequently, its decisions in many cases will lack an essential dimension through which those who are affected by them can understand and appreciate them. Moreover, in some parts of the law, officials lack resources they need to make responsive and responsible decisions; this is especially true where they are expected to exercise mercy or equitable discretion.

Second, AI-dominated adjudication of civil disputes and AI-dominated enforcement of the criminal law provide no opportunity for meaningful participation by immediately affected parties or by the public at large. Determination of governing decisions in these contexts is removed from the relationships among the people affected by them. Decisions are made and imposed, without recognition of the persons they are imposed on. Adjudication of disputed matters among persons is replaced with the administration of things. We might try to capture the value lost thereby in terms of human dignity. That makes sense, I think. Aziz Huq counters that courtrooms and legal processes are hardly paradigms of respect for the dignity of individuals who are subjected to them.[26] However, AI technologies eliminate opportunities for valuable participation by their nature and deep ambitions, whereas the obstacles standing in the way of realizing law's ambition are practical. They are problems of implementation, rather than ambition. We can recognize and value this ambition to accord parties the dignity they are due, measure actual practice against this ambition, and seek to bring practice closer to profession.

Third, replacing law with AI's mode of reasoning would also have an impact on the law itself. For AI-dominated reasoning leaves no room for contesting specific exercises of power; even more importantly, it leaves no room for contesting the alleged warrant for that exercise. Law is not only the *instrument* of governing power; law also affords the resources and forums for *contesting* that power, and *correcting* the law on which governing power relies. Law, as we have seen, is argumentative—it recognizes its own corrigibility, its "resilient fragility."[27] A consequence of this is that law makes its own correction possible. AI-directed decision-making entails the loss of resources for self-correction at the point where its general norms and processes directly engage with the real world of interactions among people, that is, at the point where it is likely to be most effective. Correction or revision of AI-driven regulation is still possible, of course, but this revision takes place at the design level, done by experts who are removed from the lives and interactions of ordinary people.

Fourth, accountability of decision-making is radically changed to the point of being unrecognizable. We observed already the fundamental opacity of the mechanisms deployed by AI systems. This, surely, puts a major obstacle in the way of meaningful accountability of the systems and those who use them for regulatory purposes. But the problem goes deeper. AI technologies replace *accountability* with *accounting*, the process of offering reasons and arguments with counting and calculation. The assurance that proper functioning AI offers is mechanical, shifting attention from performance to design. It is detached from moral as well as legal norms. What passes for "computational accountability" in the AI literature is more accurately described as "explainability."[28] It offers explanations, rather than justifications, assurance of reliability, rather than acceptance and exercise of responsibility. This is fine for thermostats, observes critic Tim Wu,[29] but it is hardly adequate to the task of holding governing power accountable.

The problem is not that such accounting is inefficient or ineffective, but that it is of the wrong kind. It is not the kind that we value when we look to law as the means of protection and recourse against arbitrary power. Reliability does not engage trust; trust is a feature and function of relationships. (See Chapter 10.) The aim of accountability holding is not just ensuring reliability, but maintaining, or where necessary repairing, relationships; thereby sustaining trust. Moreover, by their very nature, AI-technologies deliver accounting entirely into the hands of experts. They cannot function as components in a network of mutual accountability that sweeps up citizens and officials, lay people and legal professionals, and thus it cannot serve the ethos of fidelity that lies at the heart of the rule of law.

Finally, the loss of normativity is evident again when we consider AI as a mode of social ordering. Many render the ambition of the rule of law by the slogan "government of law rather than of human beings." The idea is that to be subject to government by human agents is to be subject to typical human biases and limitations, and inevitably to personal domination. AI technology also transcends the personal and so avoids such domination. However, repeatedly in this book, we have warned against looking to the impersonal as a way of avoiding domination. We must do so here again. AI technologies transcend the personal in problematic ways. In their ambition, they remove regulation from the deliberative domain of those who are regulated, rather than addressing it and engaging it, as law does. Moreover, they remove regulation not only from our participation but also from our awareness. It is not personal or human, but it is no less a form of domination; indeed, it is likely to be an even more insidious domination, by virtue of its being hidden. To the extent that this is true of AI-modeled regulation, we lose something of great value, seen from the perspective of the rule of law.

Law and Membership

In addition to providing guidance for officials and laypersons alike, law provides resources to establish and sustain meaningful forms of social interaction and political recognition that bind the community over time.[30] In contrast, AI's mode of regulation carves up the polity into atomized bits, individual persons, or temporal parts of persons, channeling behavior in ways desired by those who exercise governing power. This kind of regulation may benefit individuals, but it does not help to establish or sustain community among the bits, because it has no transtemporal awareness and provides no resources for constructing personal or communal lives over time. Indeed, its technique of regimentation of behavior is opaque to all but the initiated few, and its vocabulary is radically private and beyond any hope of articulation in or by the public.

Law, in contrast, makes possible a vital and valuable kind of community, one that can aspire to and can approximate the value of membership that we elaborated in Chapter 4. Law affords a vernacular that members can come to understand and use to navigate life in their polity. Law structures potentially meaningful public relationships; it enables members to view themselves as a unity, despite the deep and palpable differences among them, and to regard, respect, and deal with each other as co-members of that unity. Law collects, preserves, and makes available to members the resources they need to address the question of what their common life, its past and its trajectory into the future, commit them to, and to reconcile these commitments with their past, its failures as well as its triumphs.

Moreover, as we saw in Chapter 9, in a community constituted by law and meeting the conditions of the rule of law, members can contest the very terms of association and the shape of its commitments. Law does not presuppose or ensure that all occasions of discord and contention are eliminated, as Hume once argued. On the contrary, it provides a disciplined framework and forums—a public language and public institutions—in which members can address these disputed questions together as members of a political community, and, in so doing, take responsibility for their common life and community over time. Fidelity to the law gives shape to fidelity to the community's existence over time. It is the primary means by which members express fidelity to each other. Law's public, discursive, and time-mindful mode of reasoning, the forums in which it is deployed, and the networks of mutual accountability it institutionalizes all make this mode of association and mode of community-building possible.

All this is lost if AI replaces law as the dominant mode of social ordering. Lost would be a law-constituted public, a vocabulary in which meaningful relationships among members and the shape and character of their shared community can be conceived, articulated, negotiated, and revived. Without such language, individuals and subcommunities are likely to be mutually alienated and thus easily dominated by those who wield power. Deprived of law, members of the community would be deprived of a fundamental means of expressing fidelity to each other. For them, thrown together in thick relations of proximity, the significant value of membership would be beyond reach.

All this, it strikes me, is a very high price to pay for efficient and effective regulation, even if we could be assured that it serves a noble end and its benefits are distributed equitably. Whatever aggregate benefits that AI technologies put in the place of law might bring, high-value public goods, for the community and individual human beings who find themselves in them, would be lost. Thus, there may be a place for AI in the law, but the cost of AI in the place of law is too dear.

15

Rule of Law beyond Borders

The idea of a law of nations or peoples (*ius gentium*) had already taken hold in
Roman Law and was developed further in late medieval Europe in the Natural
Law tradition. It flourished after the Peace of Westphalia (1648), when it took
the distinctive form of law between or among nation-states (*inter gentes*). This
was something of a stretch. Before then it was easy to think of law directing a
sovereign ruler to treat people beyond its jurisdiction in certain ways, but it
was another thing entirely to think that law imposes obligations on sovereign
states governing their interrelations. After all, the transnational domain after
Westphalia was vastly different from familiar domestic polities and the legal orders they established. Indeed, political philosophers in the seventeenth century
were inclined to think of that domain as a state of nature in which law was silent.
Over the next three centuries, further dramatic changes occurred; yet differences
between domestic and transnational domains remain. The differences are so
significant that one might wonder whether the rule-of-law ideal has any credibility in the modern global domain. Perhaps the rule of law is an exclusively
domestic value.

Opinion is divided. On the one hand, it is obvious that opportunities for the
arbitrary exercise of power abound in the global domain. Chapter 2 acquainted
us with, for example, the power of states over states, peoples, and individuals,
the power of international institutions and global governance agencies like the
World Trade Organization (WTO) and International Monetary Fund (IMF),
and the power of global corporations and agents of digital domination. These
power centers can threaten the rights and interests of individuals, groups, peoples, and states. The concerns that motivate us to look to the rule of law in the domestic context do not suddenly vanish when we look beyond national borders.
US President Dwight D. Eisenhower, a decade after the conclusion of World War
II, said, "[T]he world no longer has a choice between force and law. If civilization
is to survive, it must choose the rule of law."[1] Several decades later, Kofi Anan,
then Secretary General of the United Nations, added that the concept of the rule
of law lies "at the very heart of the mission" of the United Nations.[2] Heads of
state from around the world acknowledged "the need for universal adherence to
and implementation of the rule of law at both national and international levels."[3]
In the eyes of UN officials and members, the rule of law is not just a domestic

Law's Rule. Gerald J. Postema, Oxford University Press. © Oxford University Press 2022.
DOI: 10.1093/oso/9780190645342.003.0015

concern but applies to relations among actors in the global domain as well. Since the late twentieth century, the rule of law has become a global ideal and aspiration.[4]

However, the rule-of-law ideal promises protection against arbitrary power *through the instrumentality of law*, and skeptics have argued vigorously that law, as idealized by proponents of the rule of law (that is, law that bridles power and to which all are equally subject), is a myth. In the eyes of the hegemon, they argue, international law is for others, not for itself. International law is either nonexistent or impotent—it's "the law you have if you are not having law."[5]

This challenge is serious, but the present chapter argues to the contrary that the fundamental principles of the rule of law retain their integrity and normative force in the global domain. The core principles and tasks of the rule of law remain, but the global institutions and norms that realize these principles may look rather different. Global law offers resources such for realization; the legal structures enabling mutual accountability needed to constrain the exercise of power can be adapted to relations among global actors. Responsibility for such accountability is distributed across transnational actors. Law, if it is adequately institutionalized, can give shape and content to rule-of-law demands for transparency, deliberative rationality, public review, and broad accountability of those who exercise power in the global domain.

This chapter first explores the distinctive features of law in the global domain. It then addresses and answers the skeptics' challenges. The chapter closes with reflections on the value of the rule of law for denizens of the global community. The thesis of this chapter is that the fundamental question we must address is not whether the rule-of-law ideal can speak credibly and with normative force in this context, but rather whether the global community has created a legal order that approximates the ideal. The critics' challenge properly understood is not a challenge to the intelligibility and force of the ideal in this domain, but to the adequacy of efforts to realize it. The further challenge *for* the rule of law is what can be done to make it more robust. This chapter helps us understand the nature of this challenge; it does not attempt to answer it.

Law in the Global Domain

Does law, and thereby the rule of law, have a valuable role to play in the global domain? To answer this question, we must first explore the nature of this disputed phenomenon—international law and the domain in which it operates. We begin with the conventional understanding—the classical model—of modern international law. It will be immediately apparent that law in the global domain is different in important respects from its domestic counterpart. We will then consider changes—some subtle, some substantial—that have occurred over the past century, expanding the reach of international law, developing its capacities, and (over?) stretching its competence. Finally, this section will survey the resources that contemporary international law provides for constituting and constraining the vast array of power-wielding entities operating in the global domain.

International Law on the Classical Model

On the classical model, public international law governs the domain of nonhierarchical (horizontal) and largely bilateral relations among sovereign nation-states regarded as collectivities aggregating the interests of its citizens and acting as individual agents. Public international law is the law of and for these sovereign entities. The model highlights four related features of law in the global domain.[6]

First, the parties recognized by international law—entities that enjoy "legal personhood"—are states. Other entities or parties—human individuals, cohesive groups, communities, and business firms—are considered by the law only insofar as they are members of and incorporated in nation-states. Their interests and rights, and their agency, have only indirect international legal significance. They have no standing in law in their own right.

Second, states are, on this model, sovereign and equal. Law recognizes them as sovereign; it endows them with a unique bundle of rights and responsibilities, with distinctive standing in law vis-à-vis other states. They are sovereign in the sense that they have exclusive competence to rule within their own territory over their citizens and residents, and they have plenary competence to act in the international domain. No other power has authority over the state's activities within its borders; there it rules supreme, self-governed. It participates as an equal in interactions and relations among other sovereign states. Each state is equal not in power, wealth, or territory, but in the eyes of the law: states enjoy the same rights and privileges and are subject to the same responsibilities and duties under law.

Law constitutes sovereignty; sovereignty is not a property or condition of states that exists apart from the law, merely acknowledged or accepted by it. Sovereignty is a legal status conferred upon entities that participate in relations made possible by law. Thus, as a creature of the law, the state is subject to law, but to no other temporal authority. Yet, as we have learned in this study, to be subject to the law entails liability to be judged by others according to that law—that is, to participate in a network of accountability in which one claims authority to judge others and recognizes the authority of others to judge oneself. William Penn, in the seventeenth century, answered well the objection that by establishing a tribunal to adjudicate disputes states surrender their sovereignty. "If this be called a lessening of their power," he responded, "it must be only because the great fish can no longer eat up the little ones, and each sovereignty is equally defended from injuries and disabled from committing them."[7]

It is a common but mistaken dogma, rooted in this notion of sovereignty, that states are bound only by their own consent. Although states enjoy the power to enter treaties of almost any kind and legally can, on their own motion, derogate from some international obligations, and lift the burden of compliance with some customary laws through their persistent objection, nevertheless, even on the widest understanding of these powers, states are bound by legal norms to which they do not consent. Obviously, a norm binds them to meet their treaty obligations (*pacta sunt servanda*). This is one among a number of norms of customary international law (for example, norms regarding the use of force and norms regarding claims to the continental shelf). Likewise, "general principles of international law" (for example, the "principle of humanity"[8]) are binding on states. Compared with the body of laws binding individuals in domestic legal systems this body is small, but not insubstantial. Sovereignty does not put states above the law or empower them to ignore the responsibilities it imposes on them. Of course, states can, and often do, ignore these responsibilities; they may do so with a degree of impunity, but not with the law's blessing. (Some individuals also manage to get away with violating domestic law, but this does not imply that compliance with laws is voluntary. Rather, we recognize that impunity is due to a failure of domestic enforcement mechanisms.)

This leads us to the third distinctive feature of international law: it lacks centralized enforcement. More generally, the relations among states are nonhierarchical. Although they are not "a-nomic," lacking law, they are "an-archic"—lacking an "archon," a ruler standing above, imposing rules on those subordinate to it and enforcing the rules coercively. Authority relations in the domain of international law are decentralized and distributed. (1) There is no centralized lawmaking body. States make rules largely through bilateral treaties or through their customary practice over time. (2) There is no centralized enforcement agency, no body enjoying a monopoly of force. Rather, states themselves undertake to sanction violators, or to delegate powers of enforcement to a range of other actors. (3) There is no centralized, hierarchically ordered structure of adjudication or tribunals for resolution of disputes. In the twentieth century, various courts of justice were established, but their jurisdiction is not compulsory—parties submit to their procedures and judgments voluntarily—and is limited in scope. States are left largely to their own judgment to determine the nature and scope of their rights and duties under law.

In sum, in the domain governed by international law, we find none of the government institutions familiar to us from our experience of domestic legal systems. This has a further implication. In the domain of international law, the entities subject to the law are at the same time both the sources of that law and the officials who apply and enforce it. Their relationship to law and to other entities that are subject to law differs in a significant way from the relationship individual citizens and private entities bear to the law and to each other. States are *public* entities comparable to officials or agencies of government in domestic polities.[9]

Fourth, on the classical model, the subject matter of international law, the kinds of issues it addresses, is rather limited, at least as compared to the scope of concerns typically found in domestic legal systems. It is restricted to *inter*state matters. International law concerns itself with war and peace, performance of treaties, recognizing and respecting borders, and rights of navigation of common or unclaimed waters, and the like. *Intra*state matters are beyond its remit. Beyond peace and national security there are few universally shared values expressed in international law on the classical model. International law also makes no distinction among kinds of wrongful actions of states; it recognizes no distinction between contractual, tort, and criminal breaches of law.[10]

Recent Developments

The classical model offered a more or less accurate profile of law in the global domain through the first half of the twentieth century. However, after World War II, significant changes have occurred; new rules and arrangements have been created and new institutions and guiding principles have emerged. The changes and developments may not have radically transformed the underlying structure of international law, but they encourage a revision of the classical model in important respects and open new prospects for credible and realistic engagement of the rule-of-law ideal in the global domain. It will be useful for our purposes to sketch developments in three broad areas.

First, contemporary international law addresses a much wider array of parties and entities. States are still the primary subjects of international law, but they are now joined by a range of international organizations created by states, most notably the United Nations and its core agencies. States alone enjoy full legal personhood, but a variety of nonstate entities—international organizations, regional combinations of states (European Union), global governance institutions (WTO, the World Health Organization [WHO], and the like), a variety of nongovernmental organizations, and even at times business firms and corporations—participate in various ways in the formation and application of international law. While corporations are not subject to criminal liability, they are increasingly direct addressees of a wide range of administrative rules and regulations. In addition, individual human beings have become a focus of attention and concern.[11] Under international criminal law individuals bear responsibility for certain offenses (provided they live in states that have agreed to be bound by the International Criminal Court [ICC] statute).

In addition, while international courts do not generally recognize civil claims against individuals, groups and other nonstate actors, a number of states have incorporated international norms into their domestic law and recognize civil claims. In the United States, for example, the Alien Tort Claims Act (codified in 1948, with roots in Judiciary Act of 1789) gives federal courts jurisdiction to hear suits of foreign nationals, "ensuring [them] a remedy for international-law violations in circumstances where the absence of such a remedy might provoke foreign nations to hold the United States accountable."[12] More fundamentally, international humanitarian and human rights law increasingly considers the interests and rights of individuals directly, rather than simply as members of a state. Although only states are autonomous international legal subjects, individuals "are objects [of international law] when it comes to acquiring rights and subjects for the purpose of exercising them."[13]

Accompanying this expansion of the scorecard of players on the field of international law is a richer set of relations among the parties. No longer are relations strictly bilateral, or narrowly multilateral, and horizontal. Layered and overlapping relations bring together entities of various different kinds, some with governmental powers, others coordinating the efforts of states and nonstate actors. Within such communities, relations among the parties are often quasi-hierarchical; some actors make rules for other members of the community and adjudicate behavior of those members governed by those rules. Obligations and commitments are similarly layered and overlapping; some obligations are owed to the world community as a whole (*erga omnes* duties), others are owed to subsets ("publics") defined by common projects of governance.[14]

Second, the scope of international law's subject matter has expanded dramatically. No longer limited to interstate matters, law is now also concerned with intrastate and transnational matters. To its task of reducing or managing interstate conflict and coordination of bilateral interactions, it has added protecting human rights and the environment, realizing projects of international justice, easing poverty, and promoting the development of stable, rule-of-law respecting governing structures within states.

Accompanying this development is the emergence of a set of core common values and principles binding all states qua members of the global community. Not all international obligations claim such universality; some are specific to the particular subcommunities in which states and other entities participate. The binding character of international norms also can vary; some norms are aspirational, urging but not mandating compliance ("soft law"), while some are nearly absolutely binding (for example, so-called *ius cogens* norms which are "non-derogable").

In addition, there is within contemporary international law a strong normative drive toward substantive integration of its norms and regimes under a coherent set of principles. The International Law Commission (ILC) argues that
international law is a system.

> Its rules and principles (i.e. its norms) act in relation to and should be
> interpreted against the background of other rules and principles. As a legal
> system, international law is not a random collection of such norms. There are
> meaningful relationships between them. Norms may thus exist at higher and
> lower hierarchical levels, their formulation may involve greater or lesser gener-
> ality and specificity and their validity may date back to earlier or later moments
> in time.[15]

From an observer's perspective, the norms may appear inconsistent and
fragmented, but this systemic character is not a mere fiction or aspiration; it is,
rather, a normative demand answered through substantive argument, tracing
robust or broken linkages, uncovering principles or themes running through
various parts of the law. Neither observed empirical fact nor pious hope, it is
a regulative idea that calls upon those who bear responsibility for the integrity of the law to resolve deep and fracturing inconsistencies, while also recognizing the value of substantive conflicts to generate movement and progressive
change within the body of law. "We treat the international legal system as an
axiom . . . [while at the same time] we continue to debate the character of the
international system,"[16] writes James Crawford, international law scholar and
judge of the International Court of Justice (ICJ).

In virtue of this systematic character of law, certain typical modes of reasoning
are available in international law as they are in domestic law. International law is
not merely a set of discrete and unrelated rules; it is a system that makes possible,
for example, argument by analogy drawing on resources from various parts of
the system.[17]

Third, following on the above developments and perhaps also driving them
is the remarkable proliferation of global and regional governance institutions—
legislative, adjudicative, and administrative—that are bound together in complex
networks. Some such institutions, like the UN Security Council, have sometimes succeeded in making binding rules of universal application. Similarly, adjudicative institutions have developed. In addition to the ICJ, an assortment of
tribunals have been created with more specific subject-matter jurisdiction. Some
are permanent (for example, the ICC, European Court of Human Rights, and the
International Tribunal for the Law of the Sea); others are occasional and temporary (for example, the International Criminal Tribunal for the former Yugoslavia
and the International Criminal Tribunal for Rwanda).

Perhaps the most remarkable and extensive such development is the emergence of an array of global governance organizations and agencies that combine rule-making and adjudicative functions in a wide variety of regulatory regimes.[18] Already in the nineteenth century, prototypes of such institutions—called "international unions"—were created to deal with transborder matters like postal service and telecommunications. Spurred by increasing global interdependence of states, peoples, firms, and individuals, globally oriented governance and regulatory institutions of many kinds have arisen to address issues of environmental protection, financial regulation, law enforcement, intellectual property, labor standards, food safety, and cross-border migration of people. Sometimes states create these institutions by international treaties; sometimes international organizations or informal intergovernmental networks establish them. Participants in these governance agencies and organizations involve not only transnational nonstate actors but also domestic regulatory officials and agencies, nongovernmental organizations, firms, and sometimes individuals. The main and most familiar such agencies are intergovernmental organizations created by treaty, for example, the WTO, World Bank, WHO, and International Atomic Energy Agency. Also playing important roles in global governance are hybrid public-private agencies like the Internet Corporation for Assigned Names and Numbers (ICANN), which regulates internet address protocols, and the Codex Alimentarius Commission, which adopts international food safety standards. Some private bodies perform similar regulatory functions, for example, the International Standardization Organization (ISO), which adopts standards that harmonize products around the world. Some such agencies seek to direct or influence the conduct of individuals as well as states directly; others focus more sharply on states with the aim of protecting or benefiting individuals or groups.

Challenges of Global Governance

With the growth of global administrative agencies, two challenges to global governance have become salient: accountability of these agencies and fragmentation of the law they create and enforce.

Accountability

The need for effective accountability is one major consequence of the proliferation of administrative tribunals and global governance agencies that has worried observers of contemporary developments in international law. The institutions of global governance make rules, set standards, and enforce them in formal and informal ways, and adjudicate among competing interests. They are, in that respect, law makers and law appliers, and through these activities they exercise a great deal of governing power that must itself be governed.

Thus, in recent decades there has emerged a body of "global administrative law." According to international law scholar Benedict Kingsbury and his associates, global administrative law comprises

> the mechanisms, principles, practices and supporting social understandings that promote or otherwise affect the accountability of global administrative bodies, in particular by ensuring they meet adequate standards of transparency, participation, reasoned decision and legality, and by providing effective review of the rules and decisions they make.[19]

Mechanisms for oversight and accountability are in many cases embryonic, but promising.[20] Domestic institutions, especially domestic courts, often undertake to review and check global administration, providing forums in which rules and decisions of administrative agencies can be formally challenged. In some cases, domestic regulatory officials and parliaments have exercised oversight of a kind by requiring notice and comment opportunities in the standard-setting process or insisting on active participation of their officials in the agency. States influence global institutions by restricting their ability to act, threatening to remove heads of agencies from office, or exerting fiscal pressure on them. Global institutions, responding to public demands, have also adopted a variety of internal mechanisms to ensure transparency, participation, and genuine reason-based decision-making. Occasionally peer organizations and other civil society institutions exert reputational pressure and subject the institutions to public criticism.

It is not surprising, perhaps, that the province of such global governance has grown faster and more sophisticated than mechanisms for their accountability. Critics regularly point out significant accountability deficits, especially with regard to large and powerful organizations like the WTO and the IMF. Political scientists Ruth W. Grant and Robert O. Keohane argue that in fact multilateral institutions are constrained by accountability mechanisms. The problem, as they see it, "is not a lack of accountability as much as the fact that the principal lines of accountability run to powerful states."[21]

Nevertheless, the task of designing an accountability architecture for the constantly changing global domain is daunting. In 1996, the International Law Association, an association of lawyers, jurists, and scholars devoted to the development and understanding of international law, established a Committee on Accountability of International Organizations to assess the current state of accountability in this domain and to consider measures and mechanisms that would secure accountability that is more effective.[22] Mechanisms modeled on hierarchically structured domestic administration may not be the most effective in the pluralistic environment of global governance.[23]

Fragmentation

Another worry is the potential for fragmentation of law in the global domain and the resulting failure of congruence between the law and the behavior of officials, a key rule-of-law demand. This problem has a somewhat different shape, depending on whether we have in view the decisions of tribunals or the activities of transnational governance institutions. Consider the latter first.

Governance institutions often operate in separate domains—for example, environment, financial regulation, internet and big data regulation, cross-border migration of people—and govern more or less discrete "publics." So differences in approach to solving regulatory problems among them may not create serious problems. Even when the principles lying deep beneath the regulatory strategies in one domain are not entirely coherent with those in another, there may be little pressure to force uniformity, since the groups of parties subject to these principles may not greatly overlap. Local coherence may be more desirable and more practically workable than broad universal coherence of principles that may have little more than theoretical elegance going for it.[24] Moreover, sometimes, where the groups of parties subject to inconsistent regimes significantly overlap, the friction created by pluralism of approaches is not always to be regretted. "A law that would fail to articulate the experienced differences between fact-situations or between the interests or values that appear relevant in particular problem-areas would seem altogether unacceptable."[25] The friction, in fact, may generate positive and progressive change over time in one or more regime. To require a single right legal answer may yield results inimical to especially vulnerable constituencies of international law, for example, WTO's principled solutions to problems of free trade might weaken protections of human rights.[26]

However, the proliferation of tribunals and courts in the global domain presents a different profile of problems because their decisions are often not limited to subject-matter niches. Concerns about doctrinal fragmentation and incoherence have been raised as different adjudicative institutions issue conflicting equally authoritative pronouncements on matters of law. Such conflicting judgments are common in domestic legal systems, but they are usually resolved by a higher court settling the matter. There is no such hierarchy among international tribunals and courts.

Yet we must not exaggerate this contrast. Even in hierarchical legal systems like that in the United States, the Supreme Court does not eliminate the possibility of conflicting rulings; courts tend to work out their differences over time, as judges explore the divergent arguments and the way they play out in practice. Something like this common-law-like process occurs also in the global domain.[27]

In a nonhierarchical structure, there is greater room and need for cooperation and dialogue among adjudicative institutions. The ILC's Fragmentation Group observed that "although fragmentation may create problems, they are neither altogether new nor of such nature that they could not be dealt with through techniques international lawyers have used to deal with the normative conflicts that may have arisen in the past." Through disciplined use of "the wealth of techniques in the traditional law for dealing with tensions or conflicts between legal rules and principles," many, perhaps most, conflicts are resolved converging toward a coherent solution.[28]

If courts are guided by a principle of comity that counsels tribunals to weigh their own jurisdiction against the interests of parties and the jurisdiction of other courts, they can work to maintain a reasonably coherent, but also flexible and nimble, body of law that approximates systemic coherence.[29]

The International Law's Toolbox

Although law in the global domain differs in important respects from domestic law, it also shares salient features that enable the rule of law to make good on its promise to provide significant protection and recourse against the arbitrary exercise of power. However, due to its decentralized form, we cannot look exclusively to explicit law-making and law-applying institutions to define and validate international legal norms. Rather, many of these norms emerge from the practice of states and other international actors.

This practice is essentially interactive; it involves actions oriented toward other international actors. "In international relations, where authoritative determinations . . . are the exception, the parties themselves must constantly interpret each other's moves and renegotiate the reality in which they operate."[30] This interaction "is discursive: an interlocutory process of exhortation, expiation, explanation, and exposition."[31] It is a matter of "claim and counter claim, assertion and reaction,"[32] carried on in an articulated discursive mode, through offering interpretations, reasons, and arguments drawing on the resources of past practice and common understandings of it. "A discursive process of explanation, justification, and persuasion is a central attribute of international affairs," write legal scholars Abram and Antonia Chayes.[33]

As a matter of practical necessity (caused by deep and broad interdependence and the strong need for an effective international system), global actors are forced to give reasons for their past or proposed actions, to characterize their deeds, and to explain and justify them to the relevant transnational publics. In turn, other parties review, evaluate, reinterpret, accept, or challenge these proffered interpretations and justifications. These activities invite further argumentative response from the original actors and others.[34] From this process of claim and counterclaim, explanation and argument, rules emerge and are modified, strengthened, or weakened.[35]

Like domestic law, international law guides conduct through providing a disciplined practice of public practical reasoning.[36] Law in this domain has a discursive structure broadly similar to domestic law. However, the global context of discourse is more diffuse and decentralized, the global parties play a much larger role in making and interpreting the norms, and the authority or validity of norms and standards depends less on formal criteria and institutional affirmation and more on the strength of argument.[37]

Law in the global domain provides a "mode of contestation."[38] The primary resource provided to actors in the global domain is not fixed and determinate rules, but rather a grammar and forums for disputing and determining the content of its norms and orienting and coordinating efforts to hold wielders of power in the global domain accountable.

Skeptical Challenges

To the main question of this chapter—Can the rule-of-law ideal speak with credibility in the global domain?—the answer from many observers of international relations is simple: it cannot. Seeking to establish global rule of law is a fool's errand. Most critics find ground for skepticism primarily in two manifest features of what goes by the name of international law. First, it lacks all the necessary features of law as we know it: strictly speaking, international *law* does not exist. Second, what passes for law in the global domain *can't rule*: it is *impotent*, so it cannot do the work that the rule-of-law ideal requires of it. Other critics, impressed with the power of international law, argue in the alternative that law rules, but it enhances rather than constrains that power. It serves rather than curbs domination.

Whether chimera, weakling, or ideological mask, law cannot serve the ends of the rule of law beyond domestic borders, critics charge. The rule of law is an ideal for domestic consumption only. Like other challenges we have considered in this book, we can meet this challenge. We begin by bringing global law out of the shadow of domestic law.

The Dark Shadow of Domestic Law

"There is no law there," skeptics boldly charge. Can't we just as boldly respond, with Prosper Weil, "*Le droit international existe: je l'ai recontré*" ("Of course there is, we've met it!")?[39] However, critics, not easily silenced, reply, "The 'it' you met isn't *law*; what you met is something interested parties (primarily powerful states, when they wish to legitimate their domination, or weak states when they wish to mobilize support for resistance against such domination) like to call 'law.'" "But, surely," we might counter, "interested parties treating something as law is often thought to be a strong marker of something *as law*. What more do we need?" To this, critics again have a ready reply: "For it to be law it must have a certain institutional structure; in short, it must look like familiar domestic law."

What *passes* for law in the global domain, critics argue, is law without government.[40] It has none of the key institutional features of proper government, namely, centralized ruling power, articulated in legally authorized law-making bodies, a centralized and hierarchically structured court system, and mechanisms for effectively enforcing the norms made and applied. In contrast, international "law" consists of norms made without enactors or promulgators, applied and adjudicated without unified courts with compulsory jurisdiction, and only weakly enforced by those who are also supposed to be subject to them. Relations among rulers and ruled are radically decentralized. Norms and rules are diffuse, lacking sharp lines; they are constantly contested, shifting with the winds of custom and honored largely in the breach. When some matters are more or less settled, this is not due to authoritative public determination by courts empowered to make such determinations, but due to a fragile, temporary convergence of the behavior and views of parties subject to them. What passes for law is largely self-imposed and self-enforced. No sovereign power makes, imposes, or enforces its norms. The contrast between this phenomenon and law properly so called, they insist, cannot be sharper.

Although this description of contemporary international law is exaggerated, it has a ring of truth. Law in the global domain, even as it has changed in recent decades, is manifestly different from domestic law. However, the critics' argument fails, not (only) because it exaggerates these differences but because it assumes that law can only exist in the form developed in and for the modern nation-state. Law in the global domain falls in the dark shadow of the domestic paradigm. Removed from that shadow, as we attempted to do earlier in this chapter, international law emerges as a transnational normative structure in its own right, one that, despite disanalogies, also bears striking analogies with familiar law.

Over the last two centuries, the law of the modern nation-state has mesmerized legal philosophers in the business of policing the conceptual boundaries of the province of jurisprudence. The spell is beginning to lift in part due to a growing willingness of legal thinkers to cast their gaze to earlier periods and different social and political arrangements in which something like law has played a crucial ordering role. This reflection has uncovered illuminating similarities between modern domestic law and normative structures in political communities of more widely dispersed power and varying degrees of cohesion. For example, in the Middle Ages, an effective body of norms and practices emerged (*lex mercatoria*) governing commercial transactions among traders moving throughout Europe.

Moreover, domestic legal systems themselves vary in the degree to which they fit the model. For example, domestic constitutional law—which is of special interest to the rule of law—does not fit neatly into the orthodox paradigm of formal rules of fixed and determinate meaning, that are made, identified, applied, and enforced by institutions and officials that stand apart from those subject to them. International law scholar Ian Brownlie writes:

> The addressees of the rules [of international law] are normally and primarily the Governments themselves. . . . This feature is shared by public law in States. Like the law of the constitution, international law addresses the very agents who should apply the rules: the rules are essentially principles of self-limitation and, for Governments, they are immanent and not external.[41]

Constitutional law is made, applied, and enforced by a government that at the same time is bound by it. Moreover, its norms often are in many ways indeterminate and regularly and hotly contested.[42] Nevertheless, we have traced in earlier chapters the lineaments of this law and its important role in realizing the rule of law. If there is no point seeking to realize the rule of law in the global domain, our efforts on the most important plane of domestic rule are equally pointless.

Further, critics who rely on the domestic paradigm overlook features of law in the global domain that are similar in important respects to features of domestic law. We observed in earlier chapters that the law on which the rule of law relies consists of more than fixed, determinate, and formally validated rules. Crucial to law's rule is its disciplined practice of practical reasoning. Interactions among those who exercise power, and interactions between them and parties subject to their rule, are shaped and directed by practical reasoning disciplined in this way. Law in the global domain, as we have seen, deploys this same modality. In both domestic and global domains, law does not displace disagreement onto the articulated will of some entity set beyond all disagreement, but rather disciplines it and gives opportunity, focus, forums, and resources for deliberatively oriented accountability of those who exercise ruling power.

Thus, the skeptics' initial challenge, denying that international law exists, is not serious. Our basic concern is whether seeking to realize the fundamental aims of a global rule of law makes sense, whether there are available resources fit for this task. The question is not whether international law looks like domestic law, but whether it can function in ways appropriate to this purpose. It is at this point that critics drive home their second challenge. Call it "law" if you like, they argue, but it cannot do crucial rule-of-law work because it is fundamentally impotent.

Varieties of Realism

In 1951, Hans Morgenthau, dean of the Realist school of international relations, formulated his "iron law of international politics," according to which "legal obligations must yield to national interest."[43] Morgenthau's Realism lies behind the skeptics' charge that law in the global domain is impotent, but his iron law can be read in three different ways, depending on how we understand "must" in his formulation. It could refer to a psychological "must," a practical reasoning "must," or a moral "must." To these correspond three forms of the skeptics' impotence challenge: Power Realism, Practical Reason Realism, and Fiduciary Realism. Let us consider these each in turn.

Power Realism
Power Realism argues that international law cannot effectively constrain the power of states. Domestic law is effective precisely because and just when it wields coercive power against all parties subject to it. International law lacks any credible mechanism to coerce states to comply. So, for all realistic and practical purposes, this international law is law manqué. This challenge combines two skeptical claims: international law is institutionally deficient, lacking necessary coercive enforcement institutions, and it is, in any case, utterly ineffective, states can exercise their power with impunity, international law notwithstanding.

The first claim, of course, merely lets the domestic paradigm blind us to the resources of international law and the weaknesses of domestic law. Skeptics focus on the resources of domestic law to motivate compliance by private wielders of power—for example, individual citizens, business firms, and associations—by wielding greater power. However, this view ignores the critical problem at the core of the rule-of-law idea: how to guard the guardians. That is, the lack of a centralized coercive mechanism with which to motivate compliance is a fundamental feature of law *within* the state regarding the exercise of ruling power.[44] This is a challenge for the rule of law, of course, but a familiar one. In previous chapters, we have explored a variety of mechanisms that hold those who wield ruling power to the law that constitutes and constrains them. These mechanisms tend to operate not only on the "vertical" level but also on a "horizontal" level, employing different parts of the ruling structure to check the power of other parts—institutionalizing a network of mutual accountability. Relatively rarely do these mechanisms deploy explicitly coercive measures and even more rarely are they to any significant degree centralized. We constantly face questions of the efficacy of the mechanisms of mutual accountability favored by the rule of law; and we acknowledge that they are fragile. Nevertheless, they are recognizable mechanisms that the rule of law deploys for its purpose of bridling the exercise of power within the state.

Recent scholars have pointed out features of international law typically overlooked by Realist critics. These devices tend to be nonhierarchical, but promise a substantial degree of efficacy in motivating compliance. Legal scholars Oona Hathaway and Scott Shapiro have described the dominant form of law enforcement in the global domain as "outcasting."[45] Without denying that sometimes states use brute force, they argue that the more common mechanism of enforcement involves denial of the benefits of cooperation or ultimately membership to noncompliant actors. While it is, in a sense, coercive, it is nonviolent; and it is decidedly decentralized, not depending on police forces or hierarchical bureaucratic institutions. States sanction other states or other global actors. In addition, as we have seen earlier in this chapter, international law has developed a variety of accountability mechanisms that also, while not deploying physical force, utilize the power of public criticism, challenges to legitimacy or right, and similar devices. These devices may not resemble the police forces that carry out verdicts of formal courts familiar in domestic legal systems, but they do bear a closer resemblance to the constitutional devices deployed to hold ruling power in check.

However, this response does not impress Power Realists. The power of states in the global domain is of an entirely different magnitude than those that domestic legal systems deal with, they argue. The power of some states is vast and the distribution of power is vastly unequal. To powerful states, deference to law is a strategy of the weak.[46] It may prove useful to powerful states to appear to comply, but only when convenient. Unlike the weak, who praise virtues of cooperation, negotiation, and recognition of common obligations, the powerful always have the capacity and will to act with impunity. Philosopher Susan Neiman captured the spirit of this view as follows.

> What's real is (military and economic) power. Those who have it can afford to be honest about what drives them; those who lack it resort to a series of ruses designed to cripple their stronger neighbors just as surely as the Lilliputians tied Gulliver's hands. If you can win wars, you will consider war a viable part of international relations. If you cannot, you will praise the virtues of negotiation.[47]

The problem of controlling power in the global domain, on this view, is far more acute than in the domestic domain. Law is no match for this power.

Even a casual observer of international relations will recognize that there are limits to the effectiveness of law to constrain behavior of states, especially powerful ones. But that highlights a task for international law, the task of seeking ways to enhance law's effectiveness, not its irrelevance. Moreover, in many contexts, states comply with law, even when it does not seem convenient for them. Nearly fifty years ago, legal scholar Louis Henkin made the subsequently oft-quoted observation: "Almost all nations observe almost all principles of international law and almost all of their obligations almost all of the time."[48] Even Morgenthau conceded that "to deny that international law exists at all as a system of binding legal rules flies in the face of all evidence." In many areas, matters are "routinely determined by reference to international law."[49]

But critics are not impressed because they believe compliant behavior does not demonstrate law's efficacy. This response stems from a subtler form of Realist skepticism: Practical Reason Realism.

Practical Reason Realism

These Realists argue that international law is epiphenomenal; it doesn't count when it counts. What passes for law in the global domain does not count *in the way* that law counts. This form of Realism does not rely on superficial observation of the existence and operation of formal institutions. It relies on the deeper thesis that law functions properly *as law*, in the distinctive manner of law, just when it plays a key role in the practical reasoning of international actors. Practical Reason Realists deny that international law does or can operate in this way. Law does not operate as guiding and binding norms. It does not and cannot do so because international actors, especially states, act only from their understanding of their national self-interest. As Jack Goldsmith and Eric Posner, major advocates of this form of Realism, put it: "States do not act in accordance with a rule that they feel obliged to follow; they act because it is in their interests to do so."[50] Posner adds, "Because states have no intrinsic desire to comply with international law, all international law is limited by the rational choice of self-interested actors. . . . States cannot bootstrap cooperation by creating rules and calling them 'law.' "[51]

On this view, states are exclusively self-interest maximizing rational actors. Rational national officials, of course, carefully weigh the costs and benefits (to national self-interest) of cooperation, reciprocity, and reputation, and seek to avoid costly sanctions. Indeed, they may make a big deal of their compliance with the law when it is widely visible and likely to induce other states to comply. Still, it is not law that counts, but only their assessments of the nation's interest in visibly complying. When compliance is inconvenient, and they can get away with it, they will follow the lead that their interest provides, feeling no need for apology or excuse. When it counts—that is, when complying with law is inconvenient—law doesn't count. This explains, perhaps more deeply than Power Realists can, why the more powerful a state is the less likely it is to act as if law is a serious constraint.

Despite its popularity among international relations and international law scholars, and its attractive conceptual simplicity, Practical Reason Realism does not succeed in showing that there is no role for the rule of law in the global domain. It has a very narrow and implausible understanding of how law *could* and *does* count for purposes of realizing and implementing the rule of law. Practical considerations count *in the way law counts*, on the Realist view, only if agents *obey* its rules *for the sake of the rules alone*; they can function to constrain behavior of these agents in the way law does only if *those rules alone* determine conclusively the choices and actions of the agents. However, we do not ask of domestic officials this kind of practical single-mindedness; we don't need to ask it of international actors either. Rather, we ask, at minimum, that international actors take law to play the role of a *policy* or *plan* in their practical reasoning. Plans are a kind of practical resolution that parties stick to when they are caught in nets of high stakes interaction where long-range commitments are needed to prevent the interaction collapsing into self-defeating and destructive struggle.[52] Such plans are "sticky" and require actors to look beyond immediate gains or losses to the longer-term benefits of cooperation. *Rational* actors do not focus only on case-by-case assessments of advantage, but engage such plans and resources in their practical environment for building and sustaining such plans; they feel "bound" by them. Law provides just such resources. Their commitment to the law-shaped plans may rest ultimately on considerations of self-interest, but it may also converge with consideration of the good of a wider community and the shared benefits of mutual commitments over time.

The Practical Reason Realist reduces a potentially rich practical landscape to monochrome shades of self-interest. To say, "It's just self-interest at work," is like saying that Bach's *Cello Suite #5* is just a lot of notes played in succession. Social cooperation, reciprocity, reputation, and retaliation, at the international level, no less than the interpersonal level, have richly normative dimensions. The global actors do not just predict behavior of other actors; contrary behavior may not be a surprise, but is seen as a violation. That is, norms shape the interactions, giving meaning to expectations and playing a meaningful role in the deliberative economy of interacting agents.

Norms and standards of law play this role in the deliberative economy of law subjects. Laws define the horizons of their deliberation, constitute and highlight options, and give meaningful shape and salience to a range of potentially competing reasons and exclude others from consideration. The domain of actions and reactions is in certain ways expanded and in other ways narrowed by the law; it helps to give publicly recognizable shape to individual and collective aims. It provides grounds for claims and demands that each can make on the actions of others, resources for vindicating one's actions in the eyes of other agents, and challenging those of others. On this basis, reciprocity is sustained among agents caught in nets of interaction, and retaliation is understood, affirmed, resisted, and protested. Reciprocity requires not only that we look around to see whether other implicated parties are complying or likely to comply but also that we do what we can (relative to costs of doing so, of course) to encourage compliance of other, responding to their behavior in regime-appropriate ways, calling out deviations. Thus, the external and internal dimensions are tightly woven together. For this, law is indispensable.

We ask our domestic officials to give this role to law in their practical reasoning. In the name of law's rule, we require it of them. We also ask that they take responsibility for active participation in available networks of accountability as an expression of their fidelity to law. This, however, does not exclude, but often heavily depends on, consideration of the behavioral and discursive responses of others, the likelihood and meaningful shape of their reciprocity, and its promise for future interaction and cooperation. For law to count as law, and for law to rule, compliance need not be motivated solely by a single-minded and abstract sense of duty; it is enough that law plays the role in the deliberative economy of law-subjects described in the previous paragraph. This applies not only to law in the domestic domain but also to interactions among global actors.

International law provides "not merely the vocabulary of inter-state relations, but its underlying grammar."[53] International disputes and conflicts are rarely limited to legal matters; nevertheless, conflict is carried on at least in part in the vocabulary of international law, through the process of claim and counterclaim we described earlier in this chapter. Law provides a common if disputed frame of reference that enables quarreling states to understand and anticipate the moves of their opponents and often through that disputing find solutions.[54] Respect for the law itself may not be the principal motive for acts of state conformity, but law shapes the actions of international actors, their defenses of their actions, and the responses of other international actors. The behavior of states and other international actors has its meaning in good part from the context of rules and norms of international law. The appropriate characterization of a deed in this domain is not determined by the intentions of international actors, but by its uptake in the transnational community. We have good reason to conclude, then, that law in the global domain is not inert, merely an epiphenomenon of the reality of struggles of nations for domination and survival.

Fiduciary Realism

A rather different form of Realism, and consequent skepticism regarding the rule of law, remains. Unlike the previous forms, Fiduciary Realism takes a decidedly moral stance. Critics argue that states act only through the actions of state officials who are charged with acting in the name of and for the interests of the state and nation as a whole. Officials are morally bound to do so, because they are agents of the state and must act only in the interest of their principal. This fiduciary duty is the bedrock principle of their offices. State interests can depart from the interests of the individual officials, of course. In that case, officials are duty-bound to do that which best promotes state interests, notwithstanding their own. Moreover, when international law calls for actions not strictly in line with state interests, officials are bound by their fiduciary duty to serve state interests even against the demands of law. Thus, morality itself, not sheer power, nor rational (state) self-interest, drives officials to pay no more than lip service to international law.

This argument draws on our ordinary understanding of interpersonal fiduciary relationships. However, that understanding does not support the narrow conception of state officials' fiduciary obligations assumed by Fiduciary Realism. In ordinary fiduciary relationships, the interests of the fiduciary are secondary to those of the principal, but the fiduciary is not entitled to promote the interests of the principal without regard to the consequences for third parties. This is so for two reasons. First, as we noted in Chapter 10, the trust relationship is morally inflected. One can honor the trust placed in one while failing to act as the trustor expects—one may not betray that trust—when doing what is expected of the trustee does a greater wrong to another person, or requires the trustee to shoulder costs greater than the trustor can reasonably ask the trustee to bear.

Second, the principal, presumably, is subject to moral and legal constraints, to duties and responsibilities. The principal's interests must find their proper place among those duties and responsibilities, and those interests may be defeated by overriding duties in some cases. The fiduciary may not attend only to the principal's interests narrowly construed, but must pursue those interests as cabined by the principal's moral and legal responsibilities. This makes sense, of course, because otherwise one could escape any onerous moral or legal duty simply by engaging a fiduciary to do one's dirty work.

The same must be true for officials acting as agents of a state. That state is subject to moral and especially legal duties and responsibilities, as outlined by international law. Faithful pursuit of the state's interest by its officials must be constrained by the moral and legal limits of the principal. The state does not get to offload its legal responsibilities by binding an agent to duties to serve its interests alone. There is no credible basis for state officials only taking seriously the demands and responsibilities of international law when it is convenient from the point of view of the state's interests. Fiduciary Realism fails as a basis for skepticism about law's role and law's rule in the global domain.

Mask or Project?

From a rather different quarter, critics argue that law's rule in the global domain must be resisted rather than welcomed because global "rule of law serves the strong and those who have made the law."[55] International law doesn't constrain dominance, they argue, but rather hands hegemonic states effective tools to dominate weak states and global actors.[56] Law masks power rather than bridling it.[57]

Law fails; we know that. But failure of law's rule does not entail the poverty of the ideal. The rule of law requires good faith participation of actors in the global domain in networks of mutual accountability; that is, it requires not only that hegemonic powers hold weaker states accountable to legal norms but also that they acknowledge the standing of other international actors to hold them accountable to those same norms. Hegemonic exceptionalism—holding other actors to account while refusing to be judged by them, evident, for example, in the stance of the United States toward the ICC[58]—is a blatant violation of a fundamental tenet of the rule of law. The reflexivity and fidelity principles clearly condemn it. However, to acknowledge this violation is not to concede that the rule-of-law ideal has no place in the global domain. On the contrary, it presupposes the relevance, and recognizes the force, of that demand.

Moreover, global law provides invaluable resources of protection and recourse against hegemonic power. For one thing, while states can use international law as a tool of domination, it also affords weaker states resources to resist domination.[59] In addition, like domestic law, international law that meets demands of the rule of law provides the infrastructure needed for protection of human rights, national security, popular self-determination, and domestic and global democratic values.

Surely, states can turn international law from a plowshare for peace, security, and protection of human rights into a sword of hegemonic domination, but this would be an abuse of law, condemned by the rule of law. Frank recognition of defects of current international law highlights the need for more effective ways to realize the rule of law and enable its beneficiaries to enjoy its blessings. Thus, the pressing question for us is, what values can we hope to serve by realizing global rule of law? Why undertake this project?

Moral Foundations of Global Rule of Law

It is not obvious what sort of values lie at the foundations of the global rule of law. To begin, we must recognize that, for the most part, the primary direct beneficiaries of robust rule of law in the global domain are states and large transnational entities, while individual human beings or groups benefit only indirectly.

Thus, we might look to broad state-regarding values of peace and security, effective coordination of global international actors, or promotion of economic prosperity to ground the rule of law. However, these seem to be welcome collateral benefits of established rule-of-law regime rather than components of its deep moral foundation. Alternatively, we might argue, following legal philosopher Jeremy Waldron, that we do not find the ground of the rule of law in respect for the freedom or dignity of states, but rather in concern to promote the freedom and dignity, and more generally the well-being, of individual human beings.[60] States are trustees of such well-being and promoting the good of states is morally justified to the extent that states are well fitted to serve this trustee role. The measure of the value of the rule of law must be, then, its promised service to the well-being, freedom, and dignity of individuals.

Waldron's approach is correct in one respect and in need of correction in another. It correctly regards the moral value of benefiting states and other international institutions as largely contingent on their being fit to serve or respect the good of individuals. It correctly treats the interests and well-being of individual human persons as moral bedrock. It needs correction because it fails to acknowledge the value of a variety of human associations and attachments that are important constituents of individuals' good and their role in grounding the global rule of law. In Chapter 4, we learned how freedom, dignity, and equality are bound up with a commitment to community in the composite value of *membership*. Building on the argument of Chapter 4 and the discussion of the relationship between human rights and the rule of law in Chapter 5, I propose the following understanding of the complex moral foundation of global rule of law.

When global rule of law is established, the freedom, dignity, and fundamental well-being of individual human beings is served in several ways. (1) It promotes and enhances the capacity of integral political communities (primarily, states) to respect and protect the good of membership for their members. (2) It protects the security of these political communities and promotes peace and cooperation among them. (3) It provides institutional resources with which to articulate and defend fundamental human rights on a global scale. Finally, (4) it tempers the power of nonstate transnational actors in order to promote one or more of these interrelated ends. This proposal builds on the account developed and defended in Chapter 4. Let us look at the key elements of this proposal.

To begin, consider element (1). The security and integrity of certain forms of human association are more than instrumental to the good of their individual members. Such communities are often objects of valued attachment for their members; they are constituent elements of the good of such persons—components of their well-being. Communities that foster and sustain the value of membership are valued in this way.

Communities in which freedom, dignity, and equality can flourish have a complex kind of intrinsic value we called membership. Each member occupies a valued place in the community (dignity) and stands in the eyes of others as a peer (equality), not subject to the arbitrary wills of others (freedom). This standing is articulated in a set of reciprocal rights and responsibilities and is recognized in the attitudes and actions of members who not only care for and about other members but also about their relationship and about other members' care for the relationship. The dignity and equality of each is woven into the value expressed in the mutual responsibilities that define the relationship and the benefits that members enjoy in it.

Political communities are among the possible sites of the value of membership, and the rule of law, when it is realized in a national political community, underwrites its citizens' enjoyment of this value. Members of a community protected by the rule of law are accorded the dignity and equality appropriate to incumbents in a membership relationship. As *subjects of* a common body of laws, rather than being *subject to* the power or authority of others,[61] their status as peers is recognized and protected; mutuality is given structure and direction in their common responsibilities of accountability-holding.

In the modern world, states are the sites of more or less integrated political communities, and well-ordered political communities realize to varying extents the value of membership. States are not only trustees of the well-being of its citizens but also guardians and promoters of the value of membership for them. Governing power in the global domain constituted and constrained by international law enhances the capacities of national and transnational communities to foster and secure the good of membership for their members.

Regarding elements (2) and (4): transnational peace and security and international cooperation among states, while valuable in their own right, are important for rule of law purposes because they also underwrite and secure the efforts of political communities to provide the good of membership. Similarly, efforts to temper power of nonstate actors in the global domain serves individual dignity and equality, especially as woven into the fabric of membership in their political communities.

Finally, regarding (3): legal norms and institutions provide the international community resources to protect against a wide variety of modes of domination proscribed by widely recognized principles of human rights. The rule of law does not itself entail these principles, but its principles safeguard the integrity of norms and processes by which the rights are protected and recourse against violation of them is secured (see Chapter 5).

The Idea of a Global Community

These blessings are likely to be enjoyed only if a robust rule of law obtains in the global community, the community that it fosters is not irremediably unjust,[62] and the law provides at least minimal protection for certain fundamental human rights. The rule of law and these complementary values demand the allegiance of the global community as a whole. But this assumes that a coherent global community exists.

Key doctrines of international law do so as well. Since the middle of the twentieth century, and increasingly in recent decades, international law has sought to identify and articulate universal norms that bind all members of the global community regardless of their consent. They are thought to impose obligations *owed to* the community as a whole, obligations to which that whole community has a stake in compliance (obligations *erga omnes*); moreover, these obligations claim overriding legal force (*jus cogens*).

However, a clear-eyed observer of the global domain may see no global community but only a motley aggregate of state, substate, and suprastate entities. A clear precondition of law's rule appears to be absent from the global domain. Even Lon Fuller, the rule of law's most ardent advocate, seemed to counsel despair. We cannot build community on law, he seemed to argue.[63]

Yet we must not despair too quickly. Community is a matter of degree. It depends on some amount of shared understanding and, importantly, a significant degree of proximity (density of interactions, frequency of dealing, and entanglements of disputes). But, in our era of globalization, proximity no longer depends on physical contiguity, and shared understanding does not require uniformity of culture or commitments. Moreover, law does not depend one-sidedly on preexisting community. Law and global community are interdependent. Fuller's counsel, if we listen carefully, was moderate rather than despairing. We cannot build global community with law *alone*, he argued; rather, "law and community of purpose must develop together."[64] Law and community depend on each other for development and movement toward greater maturity.

A political community is an association constituted by a common framework of norms that define rights and responsibilities. This framework is not necessarily robust or detailed, and certainly not uncontested nor simply mirror an already existing body of shared values. Community is neither a precondition of functional law, nor simply a product of its ruling. Rather, law provides a nascent community with resources to build and sustain itself.[65] The need for common values or articulated norms emerges from the proximity of international actors and their appreciation of the need for cooperation that it creates. Law provides forums and a common vocabulary for articulating these values and reshaping the community's commitment to them. In law's forums, members can deploy this vocabulary to articulate and manage disputes that threaten to divide the nascent community. Through this process we can explore and assess the nature, scope, and depth of the community bond. These are not matters for empirical discovery but for discursive, deliberative determination; and dissonance sounding in these forums may signal strength rather than disintegration.

Law, then, presupposes community—in the domestic and the global domain—but only in the thin sense that potential members, existing in conditions of proximity that generate the need and motivation for some degree of union, are committed to making use of the deliberative resources of law rather than sheer power to articulate, manage, or resolve their disputes. In a global domain with this profile, law has a vocation. At the same time, the *rule of law* is necessary, because power does not vanish from this scene. Indeed, power may have to be more effectively organized, enabled, and constrained by law. The commitment to resort to law rather than brute force is fragile. A global community ordered by transnational law is neither a rock-hard reality, nor a pious wish. It is an ongoing project. Effective realization of the rule of law is a key contributor to the stability of order in such a global community.

Epilogue

When I began work on the topic of this book nearly a decade ago, I became aware of much controversy and confusion, and even skepticism, about the rule of law; however, they were largely limited to scholars. People outside academia, if they were aware of the notion, embraced it, sensed its political value, celebrated its successes, and in some circles sought to promote it around the world. Over the intervening years, threats and challenges to the rule of law have become more intense, widespread, and publicly visible. Once-secure fortresses of the rule of law have begun to decay and rot, once-strong convictions have weakened with complacency, proud beacons have grown dim from exposed hypocrisy. Watching other nations struggle to turn back assaults on their core rule-of-law institutions, people have begun to ask each other, "Can it happen here?" Journalists, pundits, political leaders, and people on the street regularly utter and debate questions about the intelligibility, moral force, and viability of the rule of law.

Even as I write these concluding words, news of a blatant challenge to the rule of law—not to speak of human rights and human decency—dominates the media, as Russia seeks to crush Ukraine's attempt to embrace democracy and the rule of law. Russia's President Vladimir Putin, as historian Timothy Snyder compellingly relates, has explicitly and publicly championed *proizvol*—arbitrariness, lawlessness—and *bespredel*—absence of limits on the ability of the leader to do anything—portraying the rule of law as a dangerous alien fiction destructive of true civilization.[1] Putin has used this rhetoric to excuse his contempt for and defiance of international legal norms.

It is time to bring our reflections to a close; but, aware of these historical developments, we cannot bring them to an end. Classical composers sometimes write "attacca" over the last few bars of a symphony movement. The word signals that players must not pause, but must proceed immediately to the opening bars of the next movement. We are at an attacca point in our thinking about the rule of law; the cadence of this work yields no sustained caesura, but rather launches us into the next movement. The work has brought us not to an ending but to an *understanding*, to a *conviction*, a *commitment*, and a *project*; not to a conclusion, but a *charge*.

The aim of this work has been to reclaim, articulate, and ground a fundamental ideal of political morality and foundation of constitutional democracies. It was motivated by the thought that, even in times of crisis like ours, we do well not to rush to concoct policies or programs to remedy our perceived dangers, but rather to "oust the intense and familiar imagination of disaster,"[2] by lingering for a while with the ideal, feeling its weight, sounding its depth, listening to its call. We have learned that the rule of law is not merely a (contested) vision or pleasing aspiration, but an ideal of normative force powerful enough to command our allegiance, deep enough to anchor our convictions and inspire our commitment to its service, and rich enough to guide efforts toward its realization.

Understanding. At its core, the rule of law promises protection and recourse against the arbitrary exercise of power using the distinctive tools of the law. The organizing aim is to temper the exercise of power to avoid its arbitrary exercise, and law is the chosen means of serving this aim. Law, on this understanding, provides a bulwark of protection, a bridle on the powerful, and a bond constituting and holding together the political community and giving expression to an ideal of association that we called "membership." It models a mode of governance and a mode of association.

Three principles follow immediately from this core idea: sovereignty of law, equality in the eyes of the law, and fidelity. Sovereignty demands that those who exercise ruling power *govern with* law (legality), that law *governs them* (reflexivity), and only acts that are ordained by law are legitimate (exclusivity). Equality requires that law's protection and recourse be made available on an equal basis for all who are also bound by it. Fidelity requires that all of the members of the political community, and not merely the legal or ruling elite, take responsibility for holding each other, and especially law's officials, accountable under the law.

The rule of law is an institutionally realized ideal, existing only insofar as institutions, norms, and practices give concrete expression to its principles in historical political communities. As one value or principle of political morality, the rule of law exists alongside, complements, and sometimes conflicts with other fundamental principles. Hence, the rule of law faces limits in the material and cultural circumstances of particular communities in which it seeks to take hold, and in occasional competition with other principles of political morality. Never fully realized and never enjoying a guaranteed future, the rule of law is vulnerable to a variety of threats, including sabotage of its sustaining institutions and norms, and corruption and coarsening of the moral culture needed to sustain it. The rule of law so understood faces a number of serious challenges, but they have proved to be challenges *for* the rule of law resolutely to address and seek to answer, not ultimate challenges *to* its intelligibility, normative force, or feasibility.

Conviction and commitment. Our convictions regarding the rule of law are anchored not in worship of Law, or belief in its magical power, but in a realistic recognition that law is an indispensable means by which the dignity, equality, and common membership of each person in their community is acknowledged and served. Every member of the community owes the duty of fidelity not to the law or to government, but to each other; keeping faith with the law is a primary means of keeping faith with each other. Commitment to respecting and serving the rule of law springs from a commitment to work in concert to resist arbitrary rule and domination and to create conditions in which the community can unite to seek justice. In this effort, the rule of law marches arm in arm with democracy and key fundamental human rights.

Project. This understanding and the commitment it inspires a charge to accept the responsibility to realize the rule of law in our political communities. The rule of law is a bold and demanding ideal, a dare. Often we think of the rule of law in terms of rules, procedures, formalities, and institutions; however, the most fundamental thesis of this book urges us to look beyond them to the animating spirit of the rule of law: the ethos of the people who seek the rule of law for their community. Law rules in a political community only when there is in that community a deeply rooted ethos of fidelity. Fidelity is practiced when all members of the community, official and nonofficial alike, take responsibility for holding each other to account under the law. We must recognize that the rule of law cannot protect itself. Neither courts nor Congress can save it without the committed and mobilized engagement of the people. As Justice Brandeis wrote, "[T]he greatest menace to freedom [sc. rule of law] is an inert people."[3]

"The people" refers, of course, to individual citizens. For they—we—individually must recognize, appreciate, and internalize value of the rule of law and its principles, and respect the norms that have evolved in their particular polity to serve those principles. The rule of law demands of us personal integrity; we must refuse to sacrifice rule-of-law principles (and with them cognate principles of democracy and human rights) for personal or partisan gain. It also demands that we resist efforts of allies as well as opponents to sabotage these principles, norms, and practices, while also joining common efforts to revise and reform them. This is a large task, a heavy burden. Nevertheless, each citizen, especially those who hold public office, bears this responsibility.

This is a task to be undertaken collectively. Heraclitus challenged his fellow Ephesians to fight for their law as they would fight for the walls of their city. Like city walls, the rule of law is a communal good; its protection is a common task. The protests in Kyiv's Maidan Nezalezhnosti (Independence Square) illustrate the power of concerted, coordinated, and committed action, as they offer sobering a lesson.[4] In the early months of 2014, committed Ukrainians gathered to demonstrate in defense of the rule of law, urging an end to corruption and closer association with the European Union. Ukrainians created informal horizontal associations and forced significant political changes, restoring the 2004 constitution, limiting the powers of the presidency, and forcing impeachment of Russia-leaning President Viktor Yanukovych.

However, popular efforts like these to uphold the rule of law and hold ruling power accountable can be sustained only when rooted in strong, resilient institutions of civil society. What we need, Jonathan Rauch reminds us, is institutional, as well as intestinal, fortitude.[5] From our study, two critical resources stand out. First, the people need public spaces in which they can randomly interact, exchange greetings, and acknowledge each other and the world around them. Doing so, they learn to engage each other; they learn of the good will and solidarity of others. In the assurance of this good will, they are emboldened to participate in cooperative efforts, trusting the like participation of others. Second, success of their common efforts depends on networks of associations, organizations, and institutions that transform individual energy into disciplined and effective collective effort over time. These formal and informal structures enliven, enable, enlarge, encourage, and educate individual and collective efforts. They lead, support, and heal. They build capacity, bridges, hope, and resilience.

What, then, is to be done? How do we, who have achieved this understanding of the rule of law and are inspired to respect and promote it, respond to this charge? This book offers no blueprint, but only the observation that we can only discern the answers to this question as we learn to speak the vernacular of the rule of law in the political communities in which we find ourselves. We learn this vernacular when we take to the streets, engage in "corporeal politics";[6] when we join efforts to build, fund, and sustain public spaces; when we resist the urge to isolate ourselves and resist political and media forces that channel us into filter bubbles. We learn it when we participate in efforts to build the will and skills to work together across religious, racial, cultural, and political divides.[7] We practice our vernacular skills when we sustain essential norms of decency, fairness, and respect, norms that give concrete content to our rule-of-law convictions and when we call out violators and hearken to calls for their reform.

The work is hard and likely to be costly. Resignation and despair may be hard to resist. It may be easier to join enclaves, protecting ourselves and letting the rest of the world fight or suffer. However, if we do not resist the pathologies of the rule of law when we see them, we will soon lose our ability to see them clearly; we will contribute to defining the deviancy and pathology down,[8] regarding as normal, if regrettable, what was once appalling. Still, our efforts are likely to be partial or modest. Nothing is inevitable—neither success nor failure. History is not at an end, neither is the hope of progress; but history is in our hands, and therein lies our hope. When our efforts fail, we must, as Beckett admonished, "Try again. Fail again. Fail better."[9] Attacca.

Acknowledgments

Work on this project spans a decade. My thoughts on the topic made their first public appearance in my Boutwood Lecture, during my tenure as Arthur L. Goodhart Visiting Professor of Legal Science, Cambridge University. I have since presented various portions of the argument of the chapters in this book to universities and conferences in Melbourne, Australia; Toronto, Canada; Zhengzhou and Beijing, China; Athens and Rethymnon, Greece; Catanzaro, Italy; Kyoto, Japan; Oslo, Norway; Krakow, Poland; Istanbul, Turkey; Auckland, New Zealand; Cambridge, Oxford, London, United Kingdom; and Boston, Durham, Greensboro, Iowa City, and New Orleans, United States. I am grateful for comments and challenges from participants at and after these events, especially Matthew Adler, Trevor Allan, Lisa Austin, Steven Burton, Thomas Bustamante, Peter Cane, James Crawford, Thiago Decat, Timothy Endicott, Evan Fox-Decent, Paul Gowder, Matthew Harding, Michihiro Kaino, Matthew Kramer, Massimo La Torre, George Letsas, David Lyons, Marcin Matczak, Paul B. Miller, Robert T. Miller, Konstantinos Papageorgiou, Nicole Roughan, Kristen Rundle, Wojciech Sadurski, Kim Lane Scheppele, Julian Sempill, Michael Sevel, Nigel Simmonds, Tomasz Stawecki, Tomasz Gizbert-Studnicki, John Tasioulas, Isabel Trujillo, Catherine Valcke, Xiaobo Zhai, and Benjamin Zipursky.

Martin Krygier's extraordinary work on the rule of law was a constant inspiration for me, as was the work of Jeremy Waldron and David Dyzenhaus. I acknowledge with gratitude their insights, arguments, and challenges.

I am grateful for the careful attention and wise counsel of colleagues who read and critically advised on substantial portions of the text, especially Alexander Campbell, Edward Fiske, Matthew Harding, Larry May, Barak Richman, Giovanni Sartor, and Leslie Winner. I owe an immense debt of gratitude to Leslie, who has encouraged me in this project from its inception and read with her sympathetic critical eye much of the text. Without her, this text would not have been.

At various points, I have drawn on small portions of previously published work, especially the following.

"Law's Rule: Reflexivity, Mutual Accountability, and the Rule of Law," in *Bentham's Theory of Law and Public Opinion*, Xiaobo Zhai and Michael Quinn, eds., Cambridge University Press, 2014, 7–39.

"Fidelity in Law's Commonwealth," in *Private Law and the Rule of Law*, Lisa M. Austin and Dennis Klimchuk, eds., Oxford University Press, 2014, 17–40.

"Trust, Distrust, and the Rule of Law," in *Fiduciaries and Trust: Ethics, Politics, Economics and Law*, Paul B. Miller and Matthew Harding, eds., Cambridge: Cambridge University Press, 2019, 242–272.

"Fidelity, Accountability and Trust: Tensions at the Heart of the Rule of Law," in *Philosophy of Law as an Integral Part of Philosophy: Essays on Jurisprudence of Gerald J. Postema*, Thomas Bustamante and Thiago Decat, eds., Oxford: Hart Publishing Co., 2020, 33–60.

"From Law's Existence to Law's Rule: Reflections on Kramer's Understanding of the Rule of Law," in *Without Trimmings: The Legal, Moral, and Political Philosophy of Matthew Kramer*, Mark McBride and Visa A.J. Kurki, eds., Oxford, University Press, 2022, 167–88.

"Constitutional Norms—Erosion, Sabotage and Response," *Ratio Juris* 35 (2022), 99–122.

Notes

Prologue

1. "The Rule of Law at the National and International Levels," United Nations General Assembly, 67th Session, A/67/PV.3 (September 24, 2012), 2.
2. International Bar Association, Rule of Law Resolution, Prague (September 29, 2005).
3. 2021 Rule of Law Report: The Rule of Law Situation in the European Union, Brussels (July 7, 2021), 1, https://eur-lex.europa.eu/legal-content/EN/TXT/?qid=1634551652 872&uri=CELEX%3A52021DC0700.
4. World Justice Project, "European Union's Top Court Rules Against Hungary and Poland in Rule of Law Showdown" (February 16, 2022), https://worldjusticeproject. org/news/european-union%E2%80%99s-top-court-rules-against-hungary-and-pol and-rule-law-showdown; Wojciech Sadurski, *Poland's Constitutional Breakdown* (Oxford: Oxford University Press, 2019), v.
5. International Institute for Democracy and Electoral Assistance, "The Global State of Democracy 2021: Building Resilience in a Pandemic Era" (Stockholm, 2021).
6. Alan Feuer, Maggie Haberman, Michael S. Schmidt, and Luke Broadwater, "Trump Had a Role in Seizing Voting Machines," *New York Times*, January 31, 2022.
7. "Face the Nation," *CBS News*, January 2, 2022.
8. András Sajó, *Ruling by Cheating* (Cambridge: Cambridge University Press, 2021).
9. Judith N. Shklar, "Political Theory and the Rule of Law," in A.C. Hutchinson and P. Menahan, eds., *The Rule of Law: Ideal or Ideology?* (Toronto: Carswell, 1987), 1; Martin Loughlin, *Foundations of Public Law* (Oxford: Oxford University Press, 2010), 313.
10. George Fletcher, *Basic Concepts of Legal Thought* (New York: Oxford University Press, 1996), 11.

Chapter 1

1. F.D. Miller, Jr., "The Rule of Law in Ancient Greek Thought," in M. Sellers and T. Tomaszewski, eds., *The Rule of Law in Comparative Perspective* (Dordrecht: Springer, 2010), 11–12.
2. Sollom Emlyn relates this story in his preface to Matthew Hale, *History of the Pleas of the Crown* (London, 1736), vi.

3. Gerald J. Postema, ed., *Matthew Hale on the Law of Nature, Reason, and Common Law: Selected Jurisprudential Writings* (Oxford: Oxford University Press, 2017), xv–xix.

4. Sir Edward Coke, 4 *Institutes* 41, Steve Sheppard, ed., *The Selected Writings of Sir Edward Coke* (Indianapolis: Liberty Fund, 2003), 1143.

5. Henri de Bracton, *On the Laws and Customs of England*, Samuel E. Thorne, tr. (Cambridge, MA: Belknap Press, 1968), II, 305.

6. W. Ecenbarger, *Kids for Cash* (New York: The New Press, 2012).

7. Ian Urbina, "Despite Red Flags About Judges, a Kickback Scheme Flourished," *New York Times*, March 27, 2009.

8. Ecenbarger, *Kids for Cash*, 232.

9. Albert Venn Dicey, *Introduction to the Study of Law of the Constitution*, 8th edition, 1915 (Indianapolis: Liberty Classics, 1982). *The Oxford English Dictionary* mentions the first use of "rule of law" in a translation of Aristotle's *nomon archein* (law-rule).

10. Jens Meierhenrich, "*Rechtsstaat* versus the Rule of Law," in Jens Meierhenrich and Martin Loughlin, eds., *The Cambridge Companion to the Rule of Law* (Cambridge: Cambridge University Press, 2021), 39–67.

11. Johannes Althusius, *Politica* X.4, Frederick S. Carney, ed. and tr. (Indianapolis: Liberty Fund, 1964), 80.

12. M. Gagarin and P. Woodruff, eds., *Early Greek Political Thought from Homer to the Sophists* (Cambridge: Cambridge University Press, 1995), 293, 294 (Iamblichus), 153 (Heraclitus), 108 (Thucydides). The latter two wrote in the fifth century BCE.

13. Quoted in M. Canevaro, "The Rule of Law as the Measure of Political Legitimacy in the Greek City States," *Hague Journal of the Rule of Law* 9 (2017), 213.

14. Euripides, *Suppliant Maidens*, ll. 433–7, in Gagarin and Woodruff, *Early Greek Political Thought*, 65.

15. Quoted in John Phillip Reid, *Rule of Law: The Jurisprudence of Liberty in the Seventeenth and Eighteenth Centuries* (DeKalb: Northern Illinois University Press, 2004), 51.

16. Thomas Hobbes, *Leviathan*, ch. XXX, para. 21, translation of the Latin edition, Edwin Curley, ed. (Indianapolis: Hackett, 1994), 229.

17. W. Bradley Wendel, *Lawyers and Fidelity to Law* (Princeton: Princeton University Press, 2010), 60.

18. Marbury v. Madison, 5 U.S. (1 Cranch) (1803), 163. I am indebted to John Goldberg and Benjamin Zipursky for this reference. See John Goldberg and Benjamin Zipursky, *Recognizing Wrongs* (Cambridge, MA: Belknap, 2020), 36.

19. Coke, 2 *Institutes* 55–56; Sheppard, *Selected Writings of Coke*, 870.

20. Plato, *The Laws*, 715d, Malcolm Schofield, ed., Tom Griffith, tr. (Cambridge: Cambridge University Press, 2016), 156.

21. Aristotle, *Politics* IV. 4, 1292a34; C.D.C. Reeve, tr. (Indianapolis: Hackett, 2017), 90.

22. Aristotle, *Politics* III.16, 1287a29–30; Reeve, 79.

23. Whitney v. California, 274 U.S. 357, at 375 (Brandeis concurring).

24. Plato, *The Statesman*, Julia Annas, ed., Robin Waterfield, tr. (Cambridge: Cambridge University Press, 1995), 59–70.

25. Aeschylus, "Prometheus Bound" ll. 323–324, David Grene, tr., in *Aeschylus I*, David Grene and Richmond Lattimore, eds. (Chicago: University of Chicago Press, 2013), 187.

26. Herodotus, *The Histories of Herodotus*, Harry Carter, tr. (New York: Heritage Press, 1958), III, 80.

27. C.L. Kingsford, ed., *Song of Lewes* (Oxford: Clarendon Press, 1963), xxviii.

28. Bracton, *On the Laws and Customs of England*, II, 306.

29. See B. Tierney, "'The Prince Is Not Bound by the Laws': Accursius and the Origins of the Modern State," *Comparative Studies in Society and History* 5 (1963), 391.

30. Bracton, *On the Laws and Customs of England*, II, 306.

31. Richard Hooker, *Of the Laws of Ecclesiastical Polity* (published 1648), Arthur Stephen McGrade, ed. (Cambridge: Cambridge University Press, 1989), 147, 217.

32. Bracton, *On the Laws and Customs of England*, II, 110.

33. Translation of the 1297 version in Anthony Arlidge and Igor Judge, eds., *Magna Carta Uncovered* (Oxford: Hart, 2014), 189.

34. R.C. van Caenegem, "Galbert of Bruges on Serfdom, Prosecution of Crime, and Constitutionalism (1127–1128)," in B.S. Bachrach and D. Nicholas, eds., *Law, Custom, and the Social Fabric in Medieval Europe* (Kalamazoo: Medieval Institute Publications, 1990), 89–112.

35. George Garnett, ed. and tr., *Vindiciae, contra Tyrannos* (Cambridge: Cambridge University Press, 1994).

36. Althusius, *Politica* X.8, at 82; XVIII.95, at 111.

37. *Politica*, XVIII.48, 63–66, at 99, 103–104.

38. *Politica*, XX.19–20, at 134.

39. *Politica*, XVIII.98, at 112.

40. James Harrington, *The Commonwealth of Oceana and A System of Politics*, J.G.A. Pocock, ed. (Cambridge: Cambridge University Press, 1992), 25.

41. Gagarin and Woodruff, *Early Greek Political Thought*, 294.

42. M.I. Finley, *The Ancient Greeks* (New York: The Viking Press, 1963), 42.

43. Cicero, *De Re Publica*, I. 32 (49), Clinton Walker Keyes, tr., Loeb Classical Library (Cambridge, MA: Harvard University Press, 1928), 75–77.

44. James Morice in lectures on the royal prerogative at the Middle Temple in 1579, BL Additional MS 36,081 fol. 231, quoted by Christopher W. Brooks in "The Ancient Constitution in Sixteenth Century Legal Thought," in Ellis Sandoz, ed., *The Roots of Liberty* (Columbia: University of Missouri, 1993), 71.

45. Harrington, *Commonwealth of Oceana*, 8.

46. Althusius, *Politica*, I.1–2, at 17.

47. Romans 12.5; Ephesians 4.25.

48. *Politica*, I.7–10, at 19.

49. Annabel S. Brett, *Changes of State: Nature and the Limits of the City in Early Modern Natural Law* (Princeton: Princeton University Press, 2011), 91.

50. *Politica*, XVIII.73, at 105–106. Brian Tierney, *Religion and the Growth of Constitutional Thought 1150–1650* (Cambridge: Cambridge University Press, 1982), 56–60. Tierney traces the principle to Azo of Bologna in the early thirteenth century.

51. *Politica*, XVIII.15, at 94–95.
52. *Politica*, XVIII.106, at 115; see IX.21, at 71 and XIX.7–8, at 121.
53. Geoffrey de Q. Walker, *The Rule of Law* (Melbourne: Melbourne University Press, 1988), 3.
54. Martin Krygier, "Rule of Law (and *Rechtsstaat*)," in Neil J. Smelser and Paul B. Baltes, eds., *International Encyclopedia of the Social & Behavioral Sciences*, 2nd edition (Amsterdam: Elsevier, 2015), vol. 20, at 785.
55. Lon L. Fuller, *The Morality of Law*, 2nd edition (New Haven: Yale University Press, 1969).
56. Joseph Raz, "The Rule of Law and Its Virtue," in Joseph Raz, *The Authority of Law* (Oxford: Oxford University Press, 1979); Jeremy Waldron, "The Rule of Law and the Importance of Procedure," in James E. Fleming, ed., *NOMOS 50: Getting to the Rule of Law* (2011), 3–31.
57. United Nations Security Council, "The Rule of Law and Transitional Justice in Conflict and Post-Conflict Societies," Report of the Secretary-General, UN/S/2004/616, August 23, 2004.
58. For discussion of various competing conceptions of the rule of law in contemporary China, see R. Peerenboom, *China's Long March toward Rule of Law* (Cambridge: Cambridge University Press, 2002), ch. 3.
59. Ivor Jennings, *The Law and the Constitution*, 5th edition (London: University of London Press, 1959), 60.
60. Jeremy Waldron, "The Rule of Law as an Essentially Contested Concept," in Meierhenrich and Loughlin, eds., *The Cambridge Companion to the Rule of Law*, 121–136.
61. Martin Krygier, "Rule of Law (and *Rechtsstaat*)," 784.
62. Martin Krygier, "Inside the Rule of Law," *Rivista di Filosofia del Diritto* 3 (2014), 89.
63. Quoted in Walker, *The Rule of Law*, 2.
64. David Kennedy, "Speaking Law to Power: International Law and Foreign Power," *Wisconsin International Law Journal* 23 (2005), 173–182.
65. *Political Education* (1582), quoted in David P. Henreckson, *The Immortal Commonwealth: Covenant, Community, and Political Resistance in Early Reformed Thought* (Cambridge: Cambridge University Press, 2019), 91.
66. Martin Krygier, "What's the Point of the Rule of Law?" *Buffalo Law Review* 67 (2019), 743–791; "The Rule of Law: Legality, Teleology, Sociology," in Gianluigi Palombella and Neil Walker, eds., *Relocating the Rule of Law* (Oxford: Hart, 2008), 45–69.
67. By "normative force," I mean that the rule of law ideal is not merely an attractive goal, good to consider and perhaps hope for; rather, it imposes strong demands on our institutions and practices, demands that are backed by compelling reasons and that do not permit being set aside when some other attractive goal occurs to us. The "force" is the force of reasons to act; it is normative in the sense that its demands are categorical or at least not subject to easy trade-offs.

Chapter 2

1. Quoted in H.L.A. Hart, *Essays on Bentham* (Oxford: Oxford University Press, 1982), 25.

2. Note: the term "agents" refers to persons who act on their own behalf, not those who act for a principal, as in the legal usage of the term.

3. Xenophon, *Memorabilia*, bk. I, ch. 2, para. 44, in *Xenophon: Apology and Memorabilia I*, M.D. MacLeod, tr. (Oxford: Oxbow Books, 2008), 89.

4. Quoted in Gilbert Osofsky, ed. *Puttin' on Ole Massa: The Slave Narratives of Henry Bibb, William Wells, and Solomon Northrup* (New York: Harper & Row, 1969), 9.

5. Frederick Douglass, *My Bondage and My Freedom* (1855) (New York: Dover Publications, 1969), 161, quoted in Frank Lovett, *A General Theory of Domination and Justice* (Oxford: Oxford University Press, 2010), 45–46.

6. Steven Lukes, *Power: A Radical View* (Houndmills: MacMillan Education, 1975), 24.

7. Lovett, *General Theory of Domination*, 52–53.

8. Mark Haugaard and Philip Pettit, "A Conversation on Power and Republicanism," *Journal of Political Power* 10 (2017), 26–27.

9. Philip Pettit, *On the People's Terms* (Cambridge: Cambridge University Press, 2012), 63.

10. I am grateful to Leslie Winner for encouraging me to think about such examples and the power of position more generally.

11. Edmund Burke, *The Writings and Speeches of Edmund Burke*, vol. VI, *India: The Launching of the Hastings Impeachment 1786–1788*, P.J. Marshall, ed. (Oxford: Clarendon Press, 1991), 351.

12. Robert Kirsch, Unclassified Attorney Notes Regarding Hadj Boudella, in "Report on Torture and Cruel, Inhuman, and Degrading Treatment of Prisoners at Guantanamo Bay, Cuba," Center for Constitutional Rights, 2006.

13. William Shakespeare, *King Lear*, VI. I.

14. William Shakespeare, *Macbeth*, V. I.

15. Aeschylus, "Prometheus Bound" ll. 323–324, in Grene and Lattimore, eds., *Aeschylus I*, 187.

16. Frederick Hayek, *The Constitution of Liberty* (Chicago: University of Chicago Press, 1960).

17. John Steinbeck, *The Grapes of Wrath*, Chapter 5. In Chapter 9 of *The Trial*, Franz Kafka unnervingly depicts the arbitrariness of impersonal power.

18. Martin Krygier, "Tempering Power," in Maurice Adams, Anne Meuwese, and Ernest Hirsch Ballin, eds., *Constitutionalism and the Rule of Law: Bridging Idealism and Realism* (Cambridge: Cambridge University Press, 2016), 36.

19. Juvenal, *Satires* VI, ll, 347–348.

20. Julian A. Sempill, "The Lions and the Greatest Part: The Rule of Law and the Constitution of Employer Power," *Hague Journal of the Rule of Law* 9 (2017), 312.

21. Robin West, "The Limits of Process," in James E. Fleming, ed., *NOMOS 50: Getting to the Rule of Law* (New York University Press, 2011), 45, 47.

22. U.S. v. Columbia Steel Co., 334 U.S. 495, 536 (1946).

23. Elizabeth Anderson, *Private Government: How Employers Rule Our Lives (and Why We Don't Talk about It)* (Princeton: Princeton University Press, 2017), xi, 44–45.

24. Marsh v. Alabama, 326 U.S. 501, 506, and 508–510 (1946).

25. Margaret J. Radin, "Boilerplate and Democratic Degradation: Taking the Rule of Law Private," in Lisa M. Austin and Dennis Klimchuk, *Private Law and the Rule of Law* (Oxford: Oxford University Press, 2014), 288–305.

26. Lisa Austin, "The Power of the Rule of Law," in Lisa M. Austin and Dennis Klimchuk, *Private Law and the Rule of Law* (Oxford: Oxford University Press, 2014), 269–287.

27. 675 F.2d 1342 (1982).

28. As Leslie Winner, attorney of record for the plaintiffs in this case, reminded me.

29. 463 F.2d 853 (D.C. Cir. 1972), at 871; discussed in Margaret J. Radin, "Reconsidering the Rule of Law," *Boston University Law Review* 69 (1989), 781, 782, 817–819.

30. Benedict Kingsbury, "The Concept of 'Law' in Global Administrative Law," *European Journal of International Law* 20 (2009), 25. See also Richard Stewart, "The Global Regulatory Challenge to U.S. Administrative Law," *New York University Journal of International Law & Policy* 37 (2005), 695.

31. Ruth W. Grant and Robert O. Keohane, "Accountability and Abuses of Power in World Politics," *American Political Science Review* 99 (2005), 29–43.

32. Norwegian Consumer Council, "Out of Control: How Consumers Are Exploited by the Online Advertising Industry," January 14, 2020, at 12, https://fil.forbrukerradet.no/wp-content/uploads/2020/01/2020-01-14-out-of-control-final-version.pdf.

33. Francis Fukuyama, Barak Richman, Ashish Goel, Roberta R. Katz, Douglas Melamed, and Marietje Schaake, "Report of the Working Group on Platform Scale," 11; available at https://cyber.fsi.stanford.edu/publication/report-working-group-platform-scale.

34. Jeremy Waldron, "The Concept and Rule of Law," *Georgia Law Review* 43 (2008), 20.

35. Lon L. Fuller, *The Anatomy of the Law* (New York: Praeger, 1968), 5.

36. Lon L. Fuller, "Forms and Limits of Adjudication," in Lon L. Fuller, *The Principles of Social Order: Selected Essays of Lon L. Fuller*, revised edition, Kenneth I. Winston, ed. (Oxford: Hart, 2001).

37. Neil MacCormick, "Rhetoric and the Rule of Law," in David Dyzenhaus, ed., *Recrafting the Rule of Law* (Oxford: Hart Publishing, 1999), 172–173.

38. Aristotle, *Politics*, III. 16. 1287a29.

39. Whitney v. California, 274 U.S. 357, at 375 (Brandeis concurring).

40. MacCormick, "Rhetoric and the Rule of Law," 174.

41. Waldron, "The Concept and the Rule of Law," 56.

42. Gerald J. Postema, "Law's System: The Necessity of System in Common Law," *New Zealand Law Review* (2014), 69–105.

43. John Stuart Mill, *Utilitarianism* (Indianapolis: Hackett, 2002), ch. 4.

44. Joel Feinberg, "The Nature and Value of Rights," *Journal of Value Inquiry* 4 (1970), 243–257.

45. My reflections and terminology in this section are much influenced by Martin Krygier's essay, "Tempering Power," 34–59.

46. Jeremy Waldron, "Constitutionalism—A Skeptical View," in Tom Christiano and John Christman, eds., *Contemporary Debates in Political Philosophy* (Malden, MA: Wiley-Blackwell, 2009), 273.

47. Stephen Holmes, "Constitution and Constitutionalism," in Michel Rosenfeld and András Sajó, eds., *Oxford Handbook of Comparative Constitutional Law* (Oxford: Oxford University Press, 2012), 202.

48. Jeremy Waldron, "The Rule of Law as a Theater of Debate," in Justine Burley, ed., *Dworkin and His Critics* (Oxford: Blackwell, 2004), 319–336.

Chapter 3

1. Bryan Stevenson tells this story in Bryan Stevenson, *Just Mercy* (New York: Spiegel and Grau, 2014), 105–114.

2. Isabel Wilkerson, *The Warmth of Other Suns* (New York: Vintage Books, 2010), 17–179.

3. See Isabel Wilkerson, *Caste: The Origins of Our Discontents* (New York: Random House, 2020).

4. Martin Krygier and Whit Mason, "Violence, Development and the Rule of Law," in G. Mavrotas, ed., *Security and Development* (Cheltenham: Edward Elgar, 2011), 137–138.

5. United Nations Security Council, "The Rule of Law and Transitional Justice in Conflict and Post-Conflict Societies"—Report of the Secretary-General, UN/S/2004/616, August 23, 2004.

6. Geoffrey de Q. Walker, *The Rule of Law: Foundation of Constitutional Democracy* (Melbourne: University of Melbourne Press, 1988), 5.

7. He Weifang, *In the Name of Justice* (Washington, D.C.: Brookings Institution Press, 2012), xxxvii.

8. Lon L. Fuller, *The Morality of Law*, 2nd edition (New Haven: Yale University Press, 1969), 204–208.

9. Stephen Holmes, "Lineages of the Rule of Law," in José María Maravall and Adam Przeworski, eds., *Democracy and the Rule of Law* (Cambridge: Cambridge University Press, 2003), 21.

10. He Weifang, *In the Name of Justice*, xxxvii.

11. https://teachingamericanhistory.org/document/transcript-of-david-frosts-interview-with-richard-nixon/.

12. Fuller, *The Morality of Law*.

13. Kim Lane Scheppele, "The 2000 Election and the Rule of Law," *University of Pennsylvania Law Review* 149 (2001), 1375.

14. Wojciech Sadurski, *Poland's Constitutional Breakdown* (Oxford: Oxford University Press, 2019).

15. David Hume, *The History of England* (Indianapolis: Liberty Classics, 1983), vol. 2, at 143.

16. Jothie Rajah, *Authoritarian Rule of Law: Legislation, Discourse and Legitimacy in Singapore* (Cambridge: Cambridge University Press, 2012).

17. U.S. v. Lee, 106 U.S. 196, 220 (1882).

18. Norman Marsh, International Commission of Jurists, *The Rule of Law in a Free Society* (1959), 196.

19. Jeremy Waldron, *Torture, Terror, and Trade-Offs* (Oxford: Oxford University Press, 2010), 250.

20. Andre Marmor, "The Rule of Law and Its Limits," *Law and Philosophy* 23 (2004), 3–4.

21. Ernst Fraenkel, *The Dual State: A Contribution to the Theory of Dictatorship* (1981), E.A. Shils, tr. (Oxford: Oxford University Press, 2017).

22. Fraenkel, *The Dual State*, 4.

23. Fraenkel, *The Dual State*, 57.

24. Matthew Hale, "Reflections on Mr. Hobbes His Dialogue of the Law," in Gerald J. Postema, *Matthew Hale: On the Law of Nature, Reason, & Common Law* (Oxford: Oxford University Press, 2017), 197.

25. John Locke, *Second Treatise of Government*, C.B. Macpherson, ed. (Indianapolis: Hackett, 1980), sec. 160.

26. A.V. Dicey, *The Law of the Constitution*, 8th edition (1915) (Indianapolis: Liberty Fund, 1982), 282.

27. David Dyzenhaus, *The Constitution of Law: Legality in the Time of Emergency* (Cambridge: Cambridge University Press, 2006), 1–3, 196–204.

28. Dyzenhaus, *The Constitution of Law*, 196.

29. U.S. v. Lee, 106 U.S. 196, 220 (1882).

30. Jeremy Waldron, "Are Sovereigns Entitled to the Benefit of the International Rule of Law?" *The European Journal of International Law* 22 (2011), 337–342; John Gardner, "The Twilight of Legality," *Australasian Journal of Legal Philosophy* 43 (2018), 7.

31. Translation in Anthony Arlidge and Igor Judge, eds., *Magna Carta Uncovered* (Oxford: Hart, 2014), 189.

32. 28 Edward III, cap. 3; *Statutes of the Realm* I, 345. Discussed in Paul Gowder, *The Rule of Law in the Real World* (Cambridge: Cambridge University Press, 2016), 131–132.

33. U.S. v. Lee, 106 U.S. 196, 208–209 (1882).

34. Euripides, *Suppliant Maidens*, ll. 429–436, in M. Gagarin and P. Woodruff, eds., *Early Greek Political Thought from Homer to the Sophists* (Cambridge: Cambridge University Press, 1995), 65.

35. Quoted in Gowder, *The Rule of Law in the Real World*, 235.

36. Philip Pettit, *Just Freedom* (New York: Norton, 2104), xxvi, 98–100.

37. Edward Coke 2 *Institutes* 55–56; Steve Sheppard, ed., *The Selected Writings of Sir Edward Coke* (Indianapolis: Liberty Fund, 2003), 870.

38. John C.P. Goldberg and Benjamin C. Zipursky, *Recognizing Wrongs* (Cambridge, MA: Belknap, 2020), 3, 31, 112. The authors limit their discussion to private wrongs of tort law. I have taken the liberty to enlarge the scope of the recourse idea.

39. Michael Oakeshott, "The Rule of Law," in *On History and Other Essays* (Indianapolis: Liberty Fund, 1999).

40. Quoted in James Miller, *Rousseau: Dreamer of Democracy* (New Haven: Yale University Press, 1984), 250.

41. Immanuel Kant, "On the Common Saying: That may be correct in theory, but it is of no use in practice," in Immanuel Kant, *Practical Philosophy*, Mary J. Gregor, ed. and tr. (Cambridge: Cambridge University Press, 1996), 292–293.

42. James Harrington, *The Commonwealth of Oceana* (1676), J.A.G. Pocock, ed. (Cambridge: Cambridge University Press, 1992), 8.

43. Philip Selznick, "Legal Cultures and the Rule of Law," in M. Krygier and A. Czarnota, eds., *The Rule of Law after Communism* (Aldershot: Ashgate, 1999), 37.

44. Brian Tamanaha, "The History and Elements of the Rule of Law," *Singapore Journal of Legal Studies* 2012 (2012), 246.

45. Howard Ball, *Justice in Mississippi: The Murder Trial of Edgar Ray Killen* (Lawrence: University of Kansas Press, 2006), 10.

46. Adam Ferguson, *An Essay on the History of Civil Society* (1767), Fania Oz-Salzberger, ed. (Cambridge: Cambridge University Press, 1995), 249.

47. Thomas Hobbes, *Leviathan*, R. Tuck, ed. (Cambridge: Cambridge University Press, 1996), 504.

48. Nicolò Machiavelli, "Belfagor Arcidiavolo," quoted in Inez Kotterman-van de Vosse, "Hayek on the Rule of Law," in Jack Birner and Rudy van Zijp, eds., *Hayek, Coordination, and Evolution* (London: Routledge, 1994), 255.

49. Mark Tushnet, "Authoritarian Constitutionalism," *Cornell Law Review* 100 (2015), 391–461; Stephen Holmes, "Lineages of the Rule of Law," in José María Maravall and Adam Prezworski, eds., *Democracy and the Rule of Law* (Cambridge: Cambridge University Press, 2003), 20–21.

50. Philip Hunton, *A Treatise of Monarchy* and *A Vindication of the Said Treatise* (London: E. Smith, 1689), 14.

51. Immanuel Kant, "Perpetual Peace," in Immanuel Kant, *Practical Philosophy*, M.J. Gregor, ed. and tr., 323.

52. Hobbes, *Leviathan*, ch. 29, para. 9.

53. Hunton, *Treatise*, 15.

54. Craig T. Borowiak, *Accountability and Democracy: Promises and Pitfalls* (New York: Oxford University Press, 2011), 88.

55. See D.K. Androff, Jr., "Can Civil Society Reclaim Truth? Results from a Community-Based Truth and Reconciliation Commission," *The International Journal of Transitional Justice* 6 (2012), 296–317.

56. The Commission's Executive Summary is available at http://www.greensborotrc.org/exec_summary.pdf.

57. Sarina Tavernise, "Citizens, Not the State, Will Enforce New Abortion Law in Texas," *New York Times*, July 9, 2021.

58. The US Supreme Court's decision (Dobbs v. Jackson Women's Health Organization, 597 U.S. ____ 2022) removed the constitutional prohibition on legal limitations of abortions in the United States, but it did not address the Texas law's mode of enforcement of its abortion ban.

59. *Vindiciae Contra Tyrannos*, first published 1579, George Garnett ed. and tr. (Cambridge: Cambridge University Press, 1994), 38. First published in Latin and French. A facsimile edition of the English translation of 1689 by William Walker is available at http://archive.org/details/vindiciaecontrat00lang.

60. *Vindiciae Contra Tyrannos* (Walker translation), 27.

61. Babylonian Talmud, Sotah 37 a–b, quoted in Michael Walzer, Menachem Lorberbaum, and Noam J. Zohar, eds., *Jewish Political Tradition* (New Haven: Yale University Press, 2000), vol. 1, at 35.

62. United Nations Security Council, "The Rule of Law and Transitional Justice in Conflict and Post-Conflict Societies"—Report of the Secretary-General, UN/S/2004/616, August 23, 2004.

Chapter 4

1. E.P. Thompson, *Whigs and Hunters: The Origin of the Black Act* (Harmondsworth: Penguin Books, 1976), 267.

2. Michael Ignatieff, *Blood and Belonging* (New York: Farrar, Straus and Giroux, 1995), 189.

3. UN Commission on Legal Empowerment of the Poor, *Making the Law Work for Everyone*, Final Report (New York, 2008), vol. 1, at 3, https://www.un.org/ruleoflaw/files/Making_the_Law_Work_for_Everyone.pdf.

4. UN General Assembly, Sixty-seventh Session, *Declaration of the High-level Meeting of the General Assembly on the Rule of Law at the National and International Levels* (September 19, 2012), 2, https://www.un.org/ruleoflaw/files/A-RES-67-1.pdf.

5. Martin Loughlin, "The Apotheosis of the Rule of Law," *The Political Quarterly* 89 (2018), 664.

6. World Bank, *Governance and Law: World Development Report 2017* (Washington, D.C.: World Bank, 2017), 95.

7. See, for example, Stephen Haggard and Lydia Tiede, "The Rule of Law and Economic Growth: Where Are We?" *World Development* 39 (2010), 673–685.

8. Philip Pettit, *Just Freedom* (New York: Norton, 2014); Philip Pettit, *A Theory of Freedom* (Oxford: Polity, 2001).

9. Cicero, "Pro Cluentio," para. 146 in Cicero, *Orations*, C.D. Yonge, and B.A. London, trs. (London, 1856).

10. Frederick Hayek, *The Constitution of Liberty* (Chicago: Henry Regnery, 1960), 142.

11. 505 U.S. 833 (1992), 833.

12. Timothy A.O. Endicott, "The Impossibility of the Rule of Law," in Timothy A.O. Endicott, *Vagueness in Law* (Oxford: Oxford University Press, 2000), 185–203.

13. Michel de Montaigne, "Of Experience," in *Michel de Montaigne: The Complete Essays*, M.A. Screech, tr. (London: Penguin Books, 2003), 1208.

14. Endicott, "The Impossibility of the Rule of Law," 203.

15. David Luban, "Misplaced Fidelity," *Texas Law Review* 90 (2012), 688.

16. Jeremy Waldron, "Torture and the Rule of Law," in Jeremy Waldron, *Torture, Terror, and Trade-offs* (Oxford: Oxford University Press, 2010), 202.

17. Gerald J. Postema, *Bentham and the Common Law Tradition*, 2nd edition (Oxford: Clarendon Law Series, 2019), 273–279.

18. Frances Bacon, "Examples of a Treatise on Universal Justice," in *De Augmentis Scientiarum* (facsimile edition) (New York: Garland, 1978), bk. 8, aphorism 85.

19. Frederick Hayek, *Law, Legislation and Liberty—Volume 1: Rules and Order* (Chicago: University of Chicago Press, 1973), 118.

20. Antonin Scalia, "The Rule of Law as the Rule of Rules," *University of Chicago Law Review* 56 (1989), 1175–1188.

21. Cicero, *De Re Publica* I.32 (49); Immanuel Kant, "On the Common Saying: That may be correct in theory, but it is of no use in practice," in Immanuel Kant, *Practical Philosophy*, Mary J. Gregor, ed. and tr. (Cambridge: Cambridge University Press, 1996), 292–293.

22. Edmund Burke, "Speech on the Conciliation with the Colonies," in Francis Canavan, ed., *Selected Works* (Indianapolis: Liberty Fund, 1999), vol. 1, at 240.

23. Jedediah Purdy, *A Tolerable Anarchy: Rebels, Reactionaries, and the Making of American Freedom* (New York: Knopf, 2009), 31.

24. See, for example, Wendell Berry, *The Wild Birds* (San Francisco: North Point Press, 1986).

25. https://www.un.org/en/about-us/universal-declaration-of-human-rights.

26. International Commission of Jurists, *The Rule of Law in a Free Society* (1959), 197.

27. Steven Pinker, "The Stupidity of Dignity," *The New Republic*, May 28, 2008, 28–31.

28. Scholars give this quote a date in August 1858, but they are unsure where he may have said these words.

29. Gregory Vlastos, "Justice and Equality," in Jeremy Waldron, ed., *Theories of Rights* (Oxford: Oxford University Press, 1984), 55.

30. Danielle Allen, "Invisible Citizens: Political Exclusion and Domination in Arendt and Ellison," in Melissa A. Williams and Stephen Macedo, eds., *NOMOS 46: Political Exclusion and Domination* (New York: New York University Press, 2005), 48–61.

31. Nico Kolodny, "Rule Over None II: Social Equality and Justification and Democracy," *Philosophy and Public Affairs* 42 (2014), 306.

32. Philip Pettit, *Just Freedom*, xxvi, 98–100.

33. Aristotle, *Nicomachean Ethics*, Terence Irwin, tr. (Indianapolis: Hackett, 1985), bk. viii; Paul W. Ludwig, *Rediscovering Political Friendship: Aristotle's Theory and Modern Identity, Community, and Equality* (Cambridge: Cambridge University Press, 2020).

34. Ephesians 4.25 and 5.21; see also Romans 12.5.

35. Micheal O'Siadhail, "*Après Vous, Monsieur!*" in Micheal O'Siadhail, *Collected Poems* (Tarset, Northumberland: Bloodaxe Books, 2013), 573.

36. Bernard Williams, "The Idea of Equality," in Bernard Williams, *Problems of the Self* (Cambridge: Cambridge University Press, 1973), 236.

37. Danielle Allen, "Invisible Citizens," 63.

38. R. Jay Wallace, *The View from Here* (Oxford: Oxford University Press, 2013), 25–29.

39. I have defended this claim in Gerald J. Postema, "Time in Law's Domain," *Ratio Juris* 31 (2018), 160–182.
40. Bernard Williams, *Moral Luck* (Cambridge: Cambridge University Press, 1981), 29.
41. Ronald Dworkin, *Law's Empire* (Cambridge, MA: Belknap Press, 1986), chs. 6–7; see Gerald J. Postema, "Time in Law's Domain," and Gerald J. Postema, "Integrity: Justice in Workclothes," *Iowa Law Review* 82, (1997), 821–855.
42. Kristen Rundle, *Forms Liberate: Reclaiming the Jurisprudence of Lon L Fuller* (Oxford: Hart, 2014), 134, 139.

Chapter 5

1. Alexander B. Grosart, ed., *Works in Verse and Prose Verse and Prose Complete of the Honourable Fulke Greville* (New York: AMS Press, 1966), vol. 1, at 94–95.
2. For the text of the law, see http://www.compromise-of-1850.org/fugitive-slave-act-of-1850/.
3. David Lyons, *The Moral Aspects of Legal Theory* (Cambridge: Cambridge University Press, 1993), ix.
4. Joseph Raz, "The Rule of Law and Its Virtue," in Joseph Raz, *The Authority of Law* (Oxford: Oxford University Press, 1979), 214–218.
5. Raz, "The Rule of Law and Its Virtue," 221.
6. Tom Bingham, *The Rule of Law* (London: Penguin Books, 2010), 67.
7. World Justice Program, *WJP Rule of Law Index: 2021*, at 13, https://worldjusticeproj ect.org/sites/default/files/documents/WJP-INDEX-21.pdf.
8. Martin Krygier, "Rule of Law: An Abuser's Guide," in A. Sajó, ed., *Abuse: The Dark Side of Fundamental Rights* (The Hague: Eleven International Publishing, 2006), 141.
9. Jeremy Waldron, "The Rule of Law as an Essentially Contested Concept," in Jens Meierhenrich and Martin Loughlin, eds., *The Cambridge Companion to the Rule of Law* (Cambridge: Cambridge University Press, 2021).
10. John Tasioulas, "The Rule of Law," in John Tasioulas, ed., *The Cambridge Companion to the Philosophy of Law* (Cambridge: Cambridge University Press, 2019), 128.
11. John Finnis, *Natural Law and Natural Rights* (Oxford: Clarendon Press, 1980), 273.
12. Stephen Holmes, "Lineages of the Rule of Law," in José María Maravall and Adam Przeworski, eds., *Democracy and the Rule of Law* (Cambridge: Cambridge University Press, 2003), 21.
13. Holmes, "Lineages," 20.
14. See Gerald J. Postema, *Legal Philosophy in the Twentieth Century: The Common Law World* (Dordrecht: Springer, 2011), 161–162.
15. Martin Krygier, "The Hart-Fuller Debate, Transitional Societies, and the Rule of Law," in Peter Cane, ed., *The Hart-Fuller Debate in the Twenty-First Century* (Oxford: Hart Publishing, 2010), 118.
16. Paul Gowder, *The Rule of Law in the Real World* (Cambridge: Cambridge University Press, 2016), 45.

17. Gowder, *The Rule of Law in the Real World*, 145–147.

18. Venice Commission (European Commission for Democracy through the Rule of Law), *Rule of Law Checklist*, 2016, https://www.venice.coe.int.

19. For a very useful strategy for defending human rights claims, see James W. Nickel's classic, *Making Sense of Human Rights*, 2nd edition (Malden, MA: Blackwell Publishing, 2007), chs. 4–5.

20. Tasioulas, "The Rule of Law," 127.

21. Julian A. Sempill, "Law, Dignity and the Elusive Promise of a Third Way," *Oxford Journal of Legal Studies* 38 (2018), 223.

22. Jeremy Waldron, "The Rule of Law," *Stanford Encyclopedia of Philosophy*, https://plato.stanford.edu/entries/rule-of-law/; Jeremy Waldron, "The Rule of Law and the Importance of Procedure," in James Fleming, ed., *NOMOS 50: Getting to the Rule of Law* (New York: New York University Press, 2011), 3–31.

23. Martin Krygier, "Democracy and the Rule of Law," in Meierhenrich and Loughlin, eds., *Cambridge Companion to the Rule of Law*, 407.

24. John Locke, *Second Treatise of Government*, C.B. Macpherson, ed. (Indianapolis: Hackett, 1980), chs. VIII–X.

25. Tamas Gyorfi, *Against the New Constitutionalism* (Northampton, MA: Elgar, 2016), 62–63.

26. Larry Diamond and Leonardo Morlino, eds., *Assessing the Quality of Democracy* (Baltimore: Johns Hopkins University Press, 2005), xv.

Chapter 6

1. Martin Krygier and Whit Mason, "Violence, Development and the Rule of Law," in George Mavrotas, ed., *Security and Development* (Cheltenham: Edgar Elgar, 2011), 131.

2. The classic discussion can be found in Lon L. Fuller, *The Morality of Law*, 2nd edition (New Haven: Yale University Press, 1969); see Matthew Kramer, *Objectivity and the Rule of Law* (Cambridge: Cambridge University Press, 2007), 101–186.

3. The distinction between "formal" and "substantive" is fraught. See John Gardner, "The Supposed Formality of the Rule of Law," in John Gardner, *Law as a Leap of Faith* (Oxford: Oxford University Press, 2012); Jeremy Waldron, "The Rule of Law and the Importance of Procedure," in James E. Fleming, ed., *NOMOS 50: Getting to the Rule of Law* (New York: New York University Press, 2011).

4. Neal Kumar Katyal, "Internal Separation of Powers: Checking Today's Most Dangerous Branch from Within," *Yale Law Journal* 115 (2006), 2314–2349.

5. Eric Posner and Adrian Vermeule, *The Executive Unbound* (Oxford: Oxford University Press, 2010).

6. Posner and Vermeule, *The Executive Unbound*, 10, 89–90.

7. Akil Reed Amar, *America's Unwritten Constitution* (New York: Basic Books, 2012); Keith E. Whittington, "The Status of Unwritten Constitutional Conventions in the

United States," *University of Illinois Law Review* 2013 (2013), 1847–1870; Lawrence H. Tribe, *The Invisible Constitution* (Oxford: Oxford University Press, 2008).

8. Adrian Vermeule, "Conventions of Agency Independence," *Columbia Law Review* 113 (2013), 1163–1238.

9. Daphna Renan, "Presidential Norms and Article II," *Harvard Law Review* 131 (2018), 2187–2282; Neil S. Siegel, "Political Norms, Constitutional Conventions, and President Donald Trump," *Indiana Law Journal* 93 (2017), 177–205.

10. Steven Levitsky and Daniel Ziblatt, *How Democracies Die* (New York: Crown, 2018), 102–112.

11. Neil Siegel, "Law Is Not Enough," *Ohio Northern University Law Review* 45 (2019), 197–232.

12. Julia R. Azari and Jennifer K. Smith, "Unwritten Rules: Informal Institutions in Established Democracies," *Perspectives on Politics* 10 (2012), 41–42.

13. Samuel Issacharoff and Trevor Morrison, "Constitution by Convention," *California Law Review* 108 (2020), 1913–1954.

14. Tribe, *Invisible Constitution*, 38, 149–151.

15. Kim Lane Scheppele, "Autocratic Legalism," *University of Chicago Law Review* 85 (2018), 566.

16. Kim Lane Scheppele, "The Rule of Law and the Frankenstate: Why Governance Checklists Do Not Work," *Governance: An International Journal of Policy, Administration, and Institutions* 26 (2013), 559–562.

17. Katyal, "Internal Separation of Powers"; John Braithwaite, "Tempered Power, Variegated Capitalism, Law and Society," *Buffalo Law Review* 67 (2019), 527–594; John Braithwaite, "On Speaking Softly and Carrying Big Sticks: Neglected Dimensions of a Republican Separation of Powers," *University of Toronto Law Journal* 47 (1997), 305–361; Gillian E. Metzger, "The Interdependent Relationship between Internal and External Separation of Powers," *Emory Law Journal* 59 (2009), 423–458.

18. Shirin Sinnar, "Protecting Rights from Within? Inspectors General and National Security Oversight," *Stanford Law Review* 65 (2013), 1027–1086.

19. Mark Moore, Jr., and Margaret Jane Gates, *Inspectors General: Junkyard Dogs or Man's Best Friend* (New York: Russell Sage Foundation, 1986).

20. Margo Schlanger, "Offices of Goodness: Influence without Authority in Federal Agencies," *Cardozo Law Review* 36 (2014), 53–117.

21. 6 U.S.C. para. 345(a)(4) (2012).

22. Jeremy Bentham, *Works*, John Bowring, ed. (Edinburgh: William Tait, 1838–1843), vol. iv, at 316.

23. Jeremy Bentham, *Political Tactics* (1791, 1816), M. James, C. Blamires, and C. Pease-Watkin, eds. (Oxford: Clarendon Press, 1999), 37.

24. Martin Krygier, "Virtuous Circles: Antipodean Reflections on Power, Institutions, and Civil Society," *East European Politics and Societies* 11 (1997), 62. The title of this subsection comes from page 46 of Krygier's essay.

25. For a study of the wide range of such organizations deployed in countries around the world, see Taeku Lee and Sina Odugbemi, eds., *Accountability Through Public Opinion* (Washington, D.C.: World Bank, 2011), especially Harry Blair, "Gaining

State Support for Social Accountability," 37–52, from which some of the examples mentioned here are taken.

26. See D.K. Androff, Jr., "Can Civil Society Reclaim Truth? Results from a Community-Based Truth and Reconciliation Commission," *The International Journal of Transitional Justice* 6 (2012), 296–317.

27. Project Democracy, *Towards Non-Recurrence: Accountability: Options for Trump-Era Transgressions*, https://protectdemocracy.org/project/towards-non-recurrence-acc ountability/.

28. C. Smulovitz and E. Peruzzotti, "Societal and Horizontal Controls: Two Cases of a Fruitful Relationship," in S. Mainwaring and C. Welna, eds., *Democratic Accountability in Latin America* (Oxford: Oxford University Press, 2003), 317–323.

29. 2021 World Justice Challenge Winners, https://worldjusticeproject.org/world-just ice-challenge-2022/word-justice-challenge-2021.

30. Brian Tamanaha, "The History and Elements of the Rule of Law," *Singapore Journal of Legal Studies* 2012 (2012), 244.

31. David Luban, *Legal Ethics and Human Dignity* (Cambridge: Cambridge University Press, 2007), 143.

32. Lon L. Fuller, "The Lawyer as an Architect of Social Structure," in Lon L. Fuller, *The Principles of Social Order: Selected Essays of Lon L. Fuller*, revised edition, Kenneth I. Winston, ed. (Oxford: Hart, 2001).

33. David Luban, "The Rule of Law and Human Dignity: Re-examining Fuller's Canons," *Hague Journal on the Rule of Law* 2 (2010), 45.

34. William Shakespeare, *Henry VI*, Part 2, Act 4.

35. Ambrose Bierce, *The Devil's Dictionary*, https://www.gutenberg.org/ebooks/972.

36. Aziz Z. Huq, "Legal or Political Checks on Apex Criminality: An Essay on Constitutional Design," *UCLA Law Review* 65 (2018), 1530.

37. Wojciech Sadurski, "On the Relative Irrelevance of Constitutional Design: Lessons from Poland," Sydney Law School Research Paper No. #19/34 (June 13, 2019), https://ssrn.com/abstract=3403327.

38. Adam Ferguson, *An Essay on the History of Civil Society* (1767), Fania Oz-Salzberger, ed. (Cambridge: Cambridge University Press, 1995), 249.

Chapter 7

1. Andrea Mazzurco and Brent K. Jesiak, "Learning from Failure: Developing a Typology to Enhance Global Service-Learning Engineering Projects," *American Society of Engineering Education* (2014), http://www.asee.org/public/conferences/32/papers/10075/view.

2. David Marshall, Introduction to *The International Rule of Law Movement: A Crisis of Legitimacy and the Way Forward*, David Marshall, ed. (Cambridge, MA: Harvard University Press, 2014), xiv. See also Thomas Carothers, "The Problem of Knowledge," in Thomas Carothers, ed., *Promoting the Rule of Law Abroad: In Search of Knowledge* (Washington, D.C.: Brookings Institution Press, 2006).

3. Martin Krygier, "Rule of Law (and *Rechtsstaat,*)" in James D. Wright, ed., *International Encyclopedia of the Social & Behavior Sciences,* 2nd edition (Oxford: Elsevier, 2015), 784.

4. Brian Z. Tamanaha, "The Rule of Law and Legal Pluralism in Development," *The Hague Journal on the Rule of Law* 3 (2011), 15.

5. Raoul Wallenberg Institute, *Rule of Law: A Guide for Politicians* (2012), 22, https://rwi.lu.se/publications/rule-law-guide-politicians/.

6. See Katherina Pistor, "The Standardization of Law and Its Effect on Developing Economies," *American Journal of Comparative Law* 50 (2002), 101–107; and generally Kevin E. Davis and Michael J. Trebilcock, "The Relationship Between Law and Development: Optimists vs Skeptics," *American Journal of Comparative Law* 56 (2008), 895, 904–905.

7. Kim Lane Scheppele, "The Rule of Law and the Frankenstate: Why Government Checklists Do Not Work," *Governance: An International Journal of Policy, Administration, and Institutions* 26 (2013), 559–562. See also Barbara Brabowska-Moroz, "Understanding the Best Practices in the Area of the Rule of Law," *Reconnect,* April 30, 2020, https://papers.ssrn.com/sol3/papers.cfm?abstract_id=3600029.

8. David Hume, *Enquiry Concerning the Principles of Morals* (1751), Tom L. Beauchamp, ed. (Oxford: Oxford University Press, 1998), sec. 3, pt. 1; John Rawls called these "the circumstances of justice." John Rawls, *A Theory of Justice,* revised edition (Cambridge, MA: Belknap Press, 1991), 109–122.

9. Martin Krygier and Whit Mason, "Violence, Development and the Rule of Law," in G. Mavrotas, *Security and Development* (Cheltenham: Edward Elgar, 2011), 137–138.

10. Guillermo O'Donnell puts these words in the mouth of a shady Argentinian executive, who also said, "to be powerful is to have [legal] immunity." In Guillermo O'Donnell, "Why the Rule of Law Matters," *Journal of Democracy* 15 (2004), 40.

11. Thomas Reid, "Essays on the Active Powers of the Mind," in Thomas Reid, *Philosophical Works,* Sir William Hamilton, ed., 8th edition (Edinburgh, 1895, Hildesheim, 1967), vol. II, at 660.

12. Stephen Holmes, "Lineages of the Rule of Law," in José Maria Maravall and Adam Przeworski, eds., *Democracy and the Rule of Law* (Cambridge: Cambridge University Press, 2003), 59

13. Cass Sunstein, *Why Societies Need Dissent* (Cambridge, MA: Harvard University Press, 2003), 159.

14. Paul Gowder argues for a similar conclusion from rather different premises in *The Rule of Law in the Real World,* chs. 1–4.

15. The phrase, common in American constitutional discourse, is usually traced to Justice Robert Jackson's dissent in *Terminiello v. Chicago,* 337 U.S. 1, 36 (1949).

16. Robert Jackson's Opening Statement before the International Military Tribunal (Nuremberg, November 21, 1945) can be found at https://www.roberthjackson.org/speech-and-writing/opening-statement-before-the-international-military-tribunal/.

17. Robert H. Jackson, "Address at the University of Buffalo Centennial Convocation, October 4, 1946," *Buffalo Law Review* 60 (2012), 287.

18. Martin Krygier, "The Rule of Law: Abuser's Guide," in András Sajó, ed., *Abuse: The Dark Side of Fundamental Rights* (The Hague: Eleven International Publishing, 2006), 145.

19. See David Dyzenhaus's discussion of the case of Bram Fischer in his essay, David Dyzenhaus, "'With Benefit of Hindsight': Dilemmas of Legality," in Emilios Christodoulidis and Scott Veitch, eds., *Lethe's Law: Justice, Law and Ethics in Reconciliation* (Oxford: Hart Publishing, 2001), 65–89.

20. Noah Feldman, "This Is the Story of How Lincoln Broke Our Constitution," *New York Times*, November 2, 2021, https://www.nytimes.com/2021/11/02/opinion/constitut ion-slavery-lincoln.html. Noah Feldman, *The Broken Constitution: Lincoln, Slavery, and the Refounding of America* (New York: Farrar, Straus and Giroux, 2021).

21. Simone Weil, "The Needs of the Soul," in Siân Miles, ed., *Simone Weil: An Anthology* (London: Penguin, 2005), 107.

22. See Gerald J. Postema, "Self-Image, Integrity, and Professional Responsibility," in David Luban, ed., *The Good Lawyer* (Totowa, NJ: Rowman and Allenheld, 1983), 286–314.

23. George Bundy Smith and Thomas J. Hall, "Limits on the Exercise of 'Sole and Absolute' Discretion," *New York Law Journal*, December 16, 2011.

24. Carl Schmitt, *Political Theology: Four Chapters on the Concept of Sovereignty*, George Schwab, tr. (Chicago: University of Chicago Press, 2005), 13.

25. John Gardner, "The Twilight of Legality," *Australasian Journal of Legal Philosophy* 43 (2019), 4–5.

26. Ian Shapiro, "On Non-Domination," *University of Toronto Law Journal* 62 (2012), 334.

27. See H.L.A. Hart, "Positivism and the Separation of Law and Morals," *Harvard Law Review* 71 (1958), 618–621; Lon Fuller, "Positivism and Fidelity to Law: A Reply to Professor Hart," *Harvard Law Review* 71 (1958), 652–657.

28. Barak Richman, *Stateless Commerce: The Diamond Network and the Persistence of Relational Exchange* (Cambridge, MA: Harvard University Press, 2017), ch. 2.

29. Richman, *Stateless Commerce*, 52.

Chapter 8

1. Larry Diamond, "January 6 and the Paradoxes of America's Democracy Agenda," *Foreign Affairs*, January 6, 2022, https://www.foreignaffairs.com/articles/united-sta tes/2022-01-06/january-6-and-paradoxes-americas-democracy-agenda.

2. H.R. Khanna, "Rule of Law" (1977) 4 SCC (Jour) 7.

3. Sanford Levinson quotes John P. Roche, "The Iron Cage of Veneration," *Verfassungsblog*, December 27, 2021; available at https://verfassungsblog.de/the-iron-cage-of-veneration/.

4. Laurent Pech and Kim Lane Scheppele, "Illiberalism Within: Rule of Law Backsliding in the European Union," *Cambridge Yearbook of European Legal Studies* 19 (2017).

5. I follow Tom Daly's terminology in Tom Daly "Democratic Decay: Conceptualising an Emerging Research Field," *Hague Journal on the Rule of Law* 11 (2019), 17.

6. Montesquieu, *Considerations on the Causes of the Greatness of the Romans and Their Decline*, David Lowenthal, ed. (London: Hackett, 1999), 129, quoted by Gábor Attila Tóth, "Constitutional Markers of Authoritarianism," *Hague Journal on the Rule of Law* 11 (2019), 37.

7. Ozan O. Varol, "Stealth Authoritarianism," *Iowa Law Review* 100 (2015), 1673–1742; Adam Przeworski, "Subversion by Stealth," http://conciliumcivitas.pl/subversion-by-stealth/.

8. Kim Lane Scheppele, "On Being the Subject of the Rule of Law," *Hague Journal on the Rule of Law* 11 (2019), 467.

9. See, for example, *2021 Rule of Law Report*, 2–4. On "black holes," see David Dyzenhaus, *The Constitution of Law* (Cambridge: Cambridge University Press, 2006), 42, 196–220.

10. Scheppele, "On Being the Subject of the Rule of Law," 467.

11. For a detailed account, see Wojciech Sadurski, *Poland's Constitutional Breakdown* (Oxford: Oxford University Press, 2019); and Marcin Matczak, "Poland's Constitutional Crisis: Facts and Interpretations," https://www.fljs.org/polands-con stitutional-crisis-facts-and-interpretations.

12. Wojciech Sadurski, "Constitutional Design: Lessons from Poland's Democratic Backsliding," *Constitutional Studies* 6 (2020), 60; Laurent Pech, "Protecting Polish Judges from Political Control," *Verfassungsblog*, July 20, 2021, https://verfassungsb log.de/protecting-polish-judges-from-political-control/.

13. https://pace.coe.int/en/news/7766.

14. Sadurski, *Poland's Constitutional Breakdown*, 255.

15. Center for Ethics and the Rule of Law, *Report on the Department of Justice and the Rule of Law*, October 12, 2020, https://www.penncerl.org/files/report-on-the-doj-and-the-rule-of-law/. DOJ Alumni Statement on the Events Surrounding the Sentencing of Roger Stone, https://medium.com/@dojalumni/doj-alumni-statement-on-the-events-surrounding-the-sentencing-of-roger-stone-c2cb75ae4937. "Mr. Trump's War on Accountability," *New York Times*, Editorial, May 6, 2020, https://www.nyti mes.com/2020/05/04/opinion/inspector-general-trump-coronavirus.html. Doha Modani, "Trump Pardons Roger Stone, Paul Manafort, Charles Kushner and Others," *NBC News*, December 23, 2020, https://www.nbcnews.com/politics/politics-news/trump-pardons-roger-stone-paul-manafort-charles-kushner-others-n1252307.

16. For a more detailed discussion, see Gerald J. Postema, "Constitutional Norms—Erosion, Sabotage and Response," *Ratio Juris* 35 (2022), 99–122.

17. Timothy Snyder uses these terms in Timothy Snyder, "The American Abyss," *New York Times Magazine*, January 9, 2021, https://www.nytimes.com/2021/01/09/magazine/trump-coup.html?referringSource=articleShare.

18. Sherman L. Cohn, "*Ex Injuria Non Jus Oritur*: A Principle Misapplied," *Santa Clara Lawyer* 3 (1962), 23–42.

19. Gerald Gaus, *The Tyranny of the Ideal* (Princeton: Princeton University Press, 2016), 61–74.

20. Mark Tushnet, "Constitutional Hardball," *John Marshall Law Review* 37 (2004), 523–553.
21. David Hume, *A Treatise of Human Nature*, David Fate Norton and Mary J. Norton, eds. (Oxford: Oxford University Press, 2000), 343.
22. Khanna, "Rule of Law," 7.
23. Cass R. Sunstein, "What Is Normal," Harvard Public Law Working Paper No. 21–24, June 12, 2021; available at http://dx.doi.org/10.2139/ssrn.3865681.
24. Daniel Patrick Moynihan, "Defining Deviancy Down," *The American Scholar* 62 (1993), 17–30.
25. Grant Tudor and Justin Florence, "Taking Stock: Accountability for January 6th and the Risks of Recurrence," Preface to *Project Democracy: Towards Non-Recurrence*, December, 2020, https://protectdemocracy.org/project/towards-non-recurrence-acc ountability/.
26. Quoted in David Frum, *Trumpocalypse: Restoring American Democracy* (New York: Harper, 2020), 190.
27. Plato, *Republic*, 414b–415d, G.M.A. Grube, tr. (revised C.D.C Reeve) (Indianapolis: Hackett, 1992), 91–92.
28. Masha Gessen, *Surviving Autocracy* (New York: Riverhead Books, 2020), 107.
29. Simone Weil, "Draft for a Statement of Human Obligations," in Siân Miles, ed., *Simone Weil: An Anthology* (London: Penguin Books, 1986), 228.
30. Tom Ginsburg and Aziz Z. Huq, *How to Save a Constitutional Democracy* (Chicago: University of Chicago Press, 2018), 231.
31. 2021 *Rule of Law Report*, 20.
32. Yehudi Amichai, "The Place Where We Are Right" (Stephen Mitchell, tr.), in Robert Alter, ed., *The Poetry of Yehuda Amichai* (New York: Farrar, Straus and Giroux, 2015), 66.
33. John Stuart Mill, *On Liberty* (Indianapolis: Hackett, 1978), ch. 2.
34. Adam Ferguson, *An Essay on the History of Civil Society* (1767), Fania Oz-Salzberger, ed. (Cambridge: Cambridge University Press, 1995), 249.

Chapter 9

1. Graves v. New York ex rel. O'Keefe (Frankfurter, J. concurring), 306 U.S. 446 (1939).
2. Henry M. Hart, Jr. and Albert M. Sacks, *The Legal Process: Basic Problems in the Making and Application of Law*, William N. Eskridge, Jr. and Philip P. Frickey, eds. (Westbury, NY: Foundation Press, 1995), 4.
3. Larry D. Kramer, *The People Themselves: Popular Constitutionalism and Judicial Review* (Oxford: Oxford University Press, 2004), 105–110, 135–136; Michael Stokes Paulsen, "The Most Dangerous Branch: Executive Power to Say What the Law Is," *Georgetown Law Journal* 83 (1994), 217–346. See Richard H. Fallon, Jr., "Judicial Supremacy, Departmentalism, and the Rule of Law in a Populist Age," *Texas Law Review* 96 (2018), 487–551.

4. Peter W. Hogg and Allison A. Bushell, "The Charter Dialogue between Courts and Legislatures," *Osgood Hall Law Journal* 35 (1997), 75–105.

5. Luc B. Tremblay, "The Legitimacy of Judicial Review: The Limits of Dialogue between Courts and Legislatures," *International Journal of Constitutional Law* 3 (2005), 617–648.

6. Maartje de Visser, *Constitutional Review in Europe: A Comparative Analysis* (Oxford: Hart, 2015), ch. 1.

7. de Visser, *Constitutional Review in Europe*, 16–18.

8. de Visser, *Constitutional Review in Europe*, 7, 20–22.

9. Stephen Gardbaum, *The New Commonwealth Model of Constitutionalism: Theory and Practice* (Cambridge: Cambridge University Press, 2013); Stephen Gardbaum, "Decoupling Judicial Review from Judicial Supremacy," in Thomas Bustamante and Bernardo Gonçalves Fernandes, eds., *Democratizing Constitutional Law: Perspectives on Legal Theory and the Legitimacy of Constitutionalism* (Springer International Publishers, 2016).

10. For example, Canadian legislatures may directly override the judicial decision nullifying their law in accordance with Section 33 of Canada's Charter of Rights and Freedoms. See Kent Roach, "Constitutional and Common Law Dialogues between the Supreme Court and Canadian Legislatures," *Canadian Bar Review* 80 (2001), 481–533.

11. Daniel Epps and Ganesh Sitaraman, "How to Save the Court," *Yale Law Journal* 129 (2019), 181–185.

12. See John G. Grove's assessment of the merits of this proposal in "Reforming the Court," *National Affairs* (Winter 2020), https://www.nationalaffairs.com/publications/detail/reforming-the-court.

13. Marsh v. Alabama, 326 U.S. 501, 506, and 508–510 (1946).

14. Shuttlesworth v. City of Birmingham, 394 U.S. 147, 151 (1969).

15. In a decision three years earlier that is not easy to reconcile with *Shuttlesworth*, the Court sustained convictions of other participants in the same march for contempt of an eleventh hour, ex parte order enjoining the march. The Court argued in Walker v. Birmingham, 338 U.S. 307 (1966), that the marchers could not challenge the constitutionality of the ordinance in its defense, despite the fact that it was unconstitutional, because they had not sought to challenge the injunction before marching.

16. As reported by Bart Gellman, "January 6 was Practice," *The Atlantic*, January/February 2022, at 32.

17. See, for example, A. Shinar, "Dissenting from Within: Why and How Public Officials Resist the Law," *Florida State University Law Review* 40 (2013), 634–636.

18. Mario Lopez v. Heckler, 725 F. 2d 1489, 1483–1484 (9th Cir. 1984).

19. U.S. v. Lee, 106 U.S. 196, 220 (1882).

20. The letter is available at https://assets.documentcloud.org/documents/3438879/Letter-From-Sally-Yates.pdf.

Chapter 10

1. Anonymous Iamblichi, in Michael Gagarin and Paul Woodruff, eds., *Early Greek Political Thought from Homer to the Sophists* (Cambridge: Cambridge University Press, 1995), 293, 294.

2. David Hume, "Of the Independency of Parliament," in David Hume, *Essays Moral, Political and Literary*, Eugene F. Miller, ed. (Indianapolis: Liberty Classics, 1985), 42–43.

3. Thomas Jefferson, "Resolutions Relative to the Alien and Sedition Acts," in Philip Kurland and Ralph Lerner, eds., *The Founders' Constitution* (Chicago: University of Chicago Press, 1987), vol. 1, at 292–293.

4. Jeremy Bentham, *The Works of Jeremy Bentham*, John Bowring, ed. (Edinburgh: William Tait, 1838–1843), vol. ix, at 6.

5. Bentham, Works, vol. iv, at 316–317.

6. Jeremy Bentham, *Securities Against Misrule and Other Constitutional Writings for Tripoli and Greece*, Philip Schofield, ed. (Oxford: Clarendon Press, 1990), 139.

7. Jeremy Bentham, *Political Tactics*, Michael James, Cyprian Blamires, and Catherine Pease-Watkin, eds. (Oxford: Clarendon Press, 1999), 37.

8. Russell Hardin, "Liberal Distrust," *European Review* 10 (2002), 73–89; Margaret Levi, "A State of Trust," in Valerie Braithwaite and Margaret Levi, eds., *Trust and Governance* (New York: Russell Sage Foundation, 1998), 81.

9. Philip Pettit, "Republican Theory and Political Trust," Braithwaite and Levi, *Trust and Governance*, 309.

10. Jonathan Wolff, "Fairness, Respect and the Egalitarian Ethos," *Philosophy and Public Affairs* 27 (1998), 108.

11. This section draws on a large contemporary philosophical literature on trust. For references, see Gerald J. Postema, "Trust, Distrust, and the Rule of Law," in Paul B. Miller and Matthew Harding, eds., *Fiduciaries and Trust: Ethics, Politics, Economics and Law* (Cambridge: Cambridge University Press, 2019).

12. Philip Pettit, "The Cunning of Trust," *Philosophy and Public Affairs* 24 (1995), 208.

13. Daniel Weinstock, "Building Trust in Divided Societies," *The Journal of Political Philosophy* 7 (1999), 293.

14. Annette Baier, "What Is Trust?" in David Archard et al., eds., *Reading Onora O'Neill* (New York: Routledge, 2013), 178.

15. Victoria McGeer, "Trust, Hope and Empowerment," *Australasian Journal of Philosophy* 86 (2008), 247.

16. Philip Pettit, "The Cunning of Trust," *Philosophy and Public Affairs* 24 (1995), 205–207; and Victoria McGeer and Philip Pettit, "The Empowering Theory of Trust," in Paul Faulkner and Thomas Simpson, eds., *The Philosophy of Trust* (Oxford: Oxford University Press, 2016), 14–34.

17. McGeer, "Trust, Hope and Empowerment," 240; Patti Tamara Lenard, *Trust, Democracy and Multicultural Challenges* (Philadelphia: University of Pennsylvania Press, 2012), 31.

18. Karen Jones, "Trusting Interpretations," in Pekka Mäkelä and Cynthia Townley, eds., *Trust: Analytic and Applied Perspectives* (Amsterdam: Brill, 2013), 15.

19. Bernd Lahno, "Institutional Trust: A Less Demanding Form of Trust?" *Revista Latinoamericana de Estudios Avanzados* 15 (2001), 31.

20. Jones, "Trusting Interpretations," 20–21.

21. McGeer, "Trust, Hope and Empowerment," 242, 247–248; Pettit, "Cunning of Trust," 212–217.

22. Edna Ullmann-Margalit, "Trust, Distrust, and In Between," in Russell Hardin, ed., *Distrust* (New York: Russell Sage Foundation, 2004), 60–82.

23. Lenard, *Trust, Democracy and Multicultural Challenges*, 59.

24. Ullmann-Margalit, "Trust, Distrust, and In Between," 72.

25. David Hume, *A Treatise of Human Nature*, David Fate Norton and Mary J. Norton, eds. (Oxford: Oxford University Press, 2000), 206.

26. Kenneth Newton, Dietlind Stolle, and Sonja Zmerli, "Social and Political Trust," in Eric M. Uslaner, ed., *The Oxford Handbook of Social and Political Trust* (Oxford: Oxford University Press, 2018), 49.

27. Annette Baier, *The Commons of the Mind* (Chicago: Open Court, 1997).

28. Robert Putnam, *Bowling Alone: The Collapse and Revival of American Community* (New York: Simon & Schuster, 2000).

29. Martin Krygier, "Virtuous Circles: Antipodean Reflections on Power, Institutions, and Civil Society," *East European Politics and Societies* 11 (1997), 71.

30. Ullmann-Margalit, "Trust, Distrust and In Between," 77.

31. Adam Smith, *A Theory of Moral Sentiments*, D.D. Raphael and A.L. MacFie, eds. (Indianapolis: Liberty Fund, 1982), 111.

32. Stephen Darwall and Brandan Dill, "Moral Psychology as Accountability," in Justin D'Arms and Daniel Jacobson, eds., *Moral Psychology and Human Agency: Philosophical Essays on the Science of Ethics* (Oxford: Oxford University Press, 2014), 43, 44.

33. Stephen Darwall, *The Second-Person Standpoint* (Cambridge, MA: Harvard University Press, 2006), 100–104.

34. Stephen Darwall, "Respect and Honor as Accountability," in Stephen Darwall, *Honor, History, and Relationship: Essays in Second-Personal Ethics II* (Oxford: Oxford University Press, 2013), 12–13.

35. John Braithwaite, "Institutionalizing Distrust: Enculturating Trust," in Braithwaite and Levi, *Trust and Governance*, 343–375.

36. Roderick M. Kramer, "Trust and Distrust in Organizations: Emerging Perspectives, Enduring Questions," *Annual Review of Psychology* 50 (1999) 591–592; Lahno, "Institutional Trust," 47.

37. Bruno S. Frey, "A Constitution for Knaves Crowds Out Civic Virtue," *The Economic Journal* 107 (1997) 1043–1053; Geoffrey Brennan and Philip Pettit, *The Economy of Esteem* (Oxford: Oxford University Press, 2004), 260–263.

38. Piotr Sztompka, *Trust: A Sociological Theory* (Cambridge: Cambridge University Press, 2000), 146.

39. Brennan and Pettit, *The Economy of Esteem*, 260–263.

40. Abraham Lincoln, "Communication to the People of Sangamon County (March 9, 1832)," in Abraham Lincoln, *Collected Works*, Ray P. Basler, ed. (New Brunswick: Rutgers University Press, 1953), vol. 1, at 8.

41. David Hume, "Of the Dignity or Meanness of Human Nature," in Hume, *Essays Moral, Political and Literary*, 86.

42. James Madison, "Federalist No. 55 (1788)," in Ian Shapiro, ed., *The Federalist Papers* (New Haven: Yale University Press, 2009), 285.

Chapter 11

1. Sir Edward Coke, 4 *Institutes* 41, Steve Sheppard, ed., *The Selected Writings of Sir Edward Coke* (Indianapolis: Liberty Fund, 2003), 1143.

2. Xenophon, *Cyropaedia*, Henry Graham Dakyns, tr., Project Gutenberg E-text, https://www.gutenberg.org/files/2085/2085-h/2085-h.htm#2H_4_0011, bk. 8, ch. 1, secs. 7–8, 22.

3. Plato, *The Statesman*, Julia Annas, ed., Robin Waterfield, tr. (Cambridge: Cambridge University Press, 1995), 59–70.

4. Aristotle, *Politics* III. 15–16.

5. Edward Coke, *Rooke's Case*, 5 *Reports* 99b, Sheppard, *Selected Writings of Sir Edward Coke*, 143.

6. Coke, 4 *Institutes* 41 ["*discretio est discernere per legem quid sit justum*,"] Shepherd, *Selected Writings of Sir Edward Coke*, 1144.

7. Aristotle, *Nicomachean Ethics*, bk. 5, ch. 10. Dennis Klimchuk, "Aristotle at the Foundations of the Law of Equity," in Dennis Klimchuk, Irit Samet, and Henry E. Smith eds., *Philosophical Foundations of the Law of Equity* (Oxford: Oxford University Press, 2020), 32–51. Early on, the official view in English law was that Equity operated as a correction of Common Law; however, over time, and especially after passage of the Judicature Act in the 1870s, jurisdictional equity developed its own general doctrines and strict and formal rules.

8. "The equitable man is . . . no stickler for justice in a bad sense but tends to take less than his share though he has the law on his side." Aristotle, *Nicomachean Ethics*, bk. 5, ch. 10, 1137b28–1138a1.

9. Panco v. Rogers, 87 A.2d 770, 773 (N.J. Ch. Div. 1952). Emily Sherwin, "Equitable Correction of Law," in Dennis Klimchuk et al., eds., *Philosophical Foundations of the Law of Equity*, 258.

10. Patel v. Ali [1984] 48 P & CR 118; Sherwin, "Equitable Correction," 259.

11. Hollywood Silver Fox Farm v. Emmett [1936] 2 KB 468. I follow the description of this case by Dennis Klimchuk, "Equity and the Rule of Law," in Lisa M. Austin and Dennis Klimchuk, eds., *Private Law and the Rule of Law* (Oxford: Oxford University Press, 2014), 257.

12. Riggs v. Palmer, 115 N.Y. 506 (1889).

13. Frederick Pollock, ed., *Table Talk of John Selden* (London: Quaritch, 1927), 43 (*Table Talk* was compiled from Selden's private conversations and first published posthumously in 1689).

14. William Camden, *Discourse Concerning the Prerogative of the Crown* (1615), published in Frank Smith Fussne, "William Camden's 'Discourse Concerning the Prerogative of the Crown,'" *Proceedings of the American Philosophical Society* 101 (1957), 205.

15. Robert Chambers, *A Course of Lectures on the English Law* (1767–1773), Thomas M. Curley, ed. (Madison: University of Wisconsin Press 1986), vol. 2, at 231.

16. Christopher St. German, "What Is Equytie," ch. 16, quoted in Zofia Rueger, "Gerson's Concept of Equity and Christopher St. German," *History of Political Thought* 3 (1982), 17. Gerson, the canonist, whom St German followed, wrote *summa ius summa est iniustia*; Rueger, 11.

17. Martha Nussbaum, "Equity and Mercy," *Philosophy and Public Affairs* 22 (1993), 83–125.

18. Lauren Winner introduced me to this useful notion. She called it "characteristic damage." See Lauren F. Winner, *The Dangers of Christian Practice: On Wayward Gifts, Characteristic Damage, and Sin* (New Haven: Yale University Press, 2018).

19. F.W. Maitland, *Equity: A Course of Lectures* (1936), A.H. Chaytor and W.J. Whittaker, eds. (Cambridge: Cambridge University Press, 2011), 19.

20. Henry E. Smith, "Equity as Meta-Law," *Yale Law Journal* 130 (2020), 1050–1144.

21. Smith, "Equity as Meta-Law," 1056, 1071–1081.

22. Smith, "Equity as Meta-Law," 1084–1089.

23. Smith, "Equity as Meta-Law," 1113–1129.

24. Matthew Harding, "Equity and the Rule of Law," *Law Quarterly Review* 132 (2016), 278–302; Matthew Harding, "Equity and the Value of Certainty in Commercial Life," in Peter Devonshire and Rohan Havelock, eds., *The Impact of Equity and Restitution in Commerce* (Oxford: Hart, 2019), 147–164.

25. Wojciech Sadurski, *Poland's Constitutional Breakdown* (Oxford: Oxford University Press, 2019), 249.

26. Aziz Huq introduced this useful phrase in Aziz Z. Huq, "The Difficulties of Democratic Mercy," *California Law Review* 103 (2015), 1684.

27. Seneca, *On Mercy*, bk. I, esp. I.11.4, in Seneca, *Moral and Political Essays*, John Cooper and J.F. Procopé, eds. and trs. (Cambridge: Cambridge University Press, 1995), 131–157, esp. 143.

28. Talmud, *Vayikra Rabbah*, 29.4; *Lev. R.*, Emor, xxix, 3.

29. Midrash, *Bereishit Rabbah*, 12.15.

30. Martha Nussbaum, *Upheavals of Thought* (Cambridge: Cambridge University Press, 2001), 366.

31. Seneca, *De Clementia* II.7 (fragment), quoted in Nussbaum, "Equity and Mercy," 102.

32. William Shakespeare, *The Merchant of Venice*, IV. i. 193–198.

33. William Shakespeare, *Measure for Measure*, II. 2, ll. 166–168.

34. Selections from Matthew Hale's diary of autumn, 1668, are reproduced in Maija Jansson, "Matthew Hale on Judges and Judging," *Journal of Legal History* 9 (1988),

209, 210. See also Susan A. Bandes, "Compassion and the Rule of Law," *International Journal of Law in Context* 13 (2017), 184–196.

35. Nussbaum, *Upheavals of Thought*, 446.

36. Henry Fielding, *The History of Tom Jones, A Foundling* (Harmondsworth: Penguin, 1985), bk. III, ch. 10.

37. Ross Harrison, "The Equality of Mercy," in Hyman Gross and Ross Harrison, eds., *Jurisprudence: Cambridge Essays* (Oxford: Clarendon Press, 1992), 107–125.

38. Carla Johnson "Seasoning Justice," *Ethics* 99 (1989), 556–558; Michael Davis, "Sentencing: Must Justice Be Even-Handed?" *Law & Philosophy* 1 (1982), 111–112.

39. Martha Nussbaum, *Upheavals of Thought*, 19–33, 301–327. See also Maksymilian Del Mar, "Imagining by Feeling: A Case for Compassion in Legal Reasoning," *International Journal of Law in Context* 13 (2017), 144–147.

40. Nussbaum, *Upheavals of Thought*, 316; Del Mar, "Imagining by Feeling," 148–152.

41. Del Mar, "Imagining by Feeling," 153, n.16.

42. Nussbaum, *Upheavals of Thought*, 386.

43. Nussbaum, *Upheavals of Thought*, 368–385.

44. Nietzsche, *The Gay Science*, Bernard Williams, ed., Josefine Nauckhoff, tr. (Cambridge: Cambridge University Press, 2001), 191.

45. Immanuel Kant, "Doctrine of Virtue," in Immanuel Kant, *Ethical Philosophy*, James W. Ellington, tr. (Indianapolis: Hackett, 1983), 122.

46. Nussbaum, *Upheavals of Thought*, 370–371.

47. R. Antony Duff, "Mercy," in John Deigh and David Dolinko, eds., *The Oxford Handbook of the Philosophy of Criminal Law* (Oxford: Oxford University Press, 2011), 467–492; R. Antony Duff, "The Intrusion of Mercy," *Ohio State Journal of Criminal Law* 4 (2007), 361–389.

48. John Tasioulas, "Mercy," *Proceedings of the Aristotelian Society* 103 (2003), 101–132; John Tasioulas, "Punishment and Repentance," *Philosophy* 81 (2006), 279–322; John Tasioulas, "Where Is the Love?" in Rowan Cruft, Matthew Kramer, and Mark Reiff, eds., *Crime, Punishment, and Responsibility* (Oxford: Oxford University Press, 2011), 37–53.

49. Tasioulas, "Where Is the Love," 44; Tasioulas, "Punishment and Repentance," 283.

50. Tasioulas, "Punishment and Repentance," 205; Andrew Brien, "Mercy in Legal Justice," *Social Theory and Practice* 24 (1998), 102.

51. Tasioulas, "Mercy," 115.

52. Shakespeare, *Measure for Measure*, I.3, ll. 28, 30.

53. Nussbaum, *Upheavals of Thought*, 396.

54. G.K. Chesterton, "Twelve Men," in G.K. Chesterton, *Tremendous Trifles* (New York: Sheed and Ward, 1955), 57–58.

55. Jean Hampton, "The Retributive Idea," in Jeffrie Murphy and Jean Hampton, *Forgiveness and Mercy* (Cambridge: Cambridge University Press, 1988), 124–138.

56. Dante Alighieri, *Inferno*, Robert Hollander and Jean Hollander, trs. (New York: Anchor Books, 2000), Canto V, lines 73–142.

57. Dante Alighieri, *Purgatorio*, D.M. Black, tr. (New York: New York Review Books, 2021), Canto II, line 75.

58. Alex Kozinski, "Teetering on the High Wire," *University of Colorado Law Review* 68 (1997), 1219, quoted in Susan A. Bandes's account of this story in "Compassion and the Rule of Law," 193–194.

59. For a discussion, see Gerald J. Postema, "Cemented with Diseased Qualities," *Hume Studies* 31 (2006), 359–408.

60. O. Henry, "Law and Order," in O. Henry, *100 Selected Stories* (Hertfordshire: Wordsworth Classics, 1995), 487–498. Carol Steiker brought O. Henry's story to my attention. Carol Steiker, "Tempering or Tampering? Mercy and the Administration of Criminal Justice," in Austin Sarat and Nasser Hussain, eds., *Forgiveness, Mercy and Clemency* (Stanford: Stanford University Press, 2007), 17–18.

61. Tasioulas, "Mercy," 121.

62. Tasioulas, "Mercy," 131.

63. Midrash, *Bereishit Rabbah*, 12.15.

64. Seneca, *On Mercy*, 1.6.1, in Seneca, *Moral and Political Essays*, 135.

65. *Leges Henrici Primi* [Laws of Henry the First], L.J. Downer, ed. and tr. (Oxford: Clarendon Press, 1972), 88, 6a–b.

66. Barak Richman, *Stateless Commerce: The Diamond Network and the Persistence of Relational Exchange* (Cambridge, MA: Harvard University Press, 2017), 52–60, esp. 52, 59.

Chapter 12

1. Austin Sarat and Nasser Hussain, "On Lawful Lawlessness: George Ryan, Executive Clemency, and the Rhetoric of Sparing Life," *Stanford Law Review* 56 (2004), 1307, 1329.

2. In re Sapp, 118 F.3d 460, 465 (6th Cir. 1997).

3. Quoted in Bob Bauer and Jack Goldsmith, "How to Reform the Pardon Power," *Lawfare*, February 26, 2020, https://www.lawfareblog.com/how-reform-pardon-power.

4. Cesare Beccaria, *On Crimes and Punishments*, Aaron Thomas, ed. (Toronto: University of Toronto Press, 2008), 84; Immanuel Kant, *The Metaphysics of Morals: Doctrine of Right*, Mary Gregor, tr. (Cambridge: Cambridge University Press, 1991), 145; Montesquieu, *The Spirit of the Laws*, Anne M. Cohler, Basia C. Miller, and Harold S. Stone, eds. (Cambridge: Cambridge University Press, 1989), pt. I, bk. 6, ch. 21.

5. Matthew Hale, Lincoln's Inn Hargrave MS9, ch. 12, at 95.

6. U.S. Constitution, art. II, § 2, cl. 1.

7. Sullivan v. Askew, 348 So. 2d, 312, 315 (Fla. 1977).

8. Sarat and Hussain, "Lawful Lawlessness," 1329.

9. Linda Ross Meyer, "The Merciful State," in Austin Sarat and Nasser Hussain, eds., *Forgiveness, Mercy, and Clemency* (Palo Alto: Stanford University Press, 2007), 65.

10. Quoted in Bauer and Goldsmith in "How to Reform the Pardon Power."

11. Rachel E. Barkow and Mark Osler, "We Know How to Fix the Clemency Process. So Why Don't We?" *New York Times*, July 13, 2021.

12. Home Building & Loan Association v. Blaisdell (Judge George Sutherland, dissenting), 298 U.S. 398 (1934), 483.

13. Kim Lane Scheppele, "Law in a Time of Emergency: States of Exception and the Temptations of 9/11," *University of Pennsylvania Journal of Constitutional Law* 6 (2004), 1004.

14. 10 Coke Rep. 139a (1609).

15. François Tanguay-Renaud, "Basic Challenges for Governance in Emergencies," in A. MacLachlan and A. Speight, eds., *Justice, Responsibility and Reconciliation in the Wake of Conflict* (Dordrecht: Springer, 2013), 65, 68.

16. See Tom Ginsburg and Mila Versteeg, "The Bound Executive: Emergency Powers During the Pandemic," *International Journal of Constitutional Law* 19 (2021), 13.

17. Alexander Hamilton, "Federalist, No. 23," in George W. Carey and James McClellan, eds., *The Federalist* (Indianapolis: Liberty Fund, 2001), 113.

18. Carl Schmitt, *Political Theology: Four Chapters on the Concept of Sovereignty*, George Schwab, tr. (Chicago: University of Chicago Press, 2005), 13.

19. Eric A. Posner and Adrian Vermeule, *The Executive Unbound* (New York: Oxford University Press, 2010), 4, 33.

20. Posner and Vermeule, *Executive Unbound*, 9.

21. Quoted in James Taranto, "A Strong Executive," *Wall Street Journal*, January 28–29, 2006, A8.

22. Schmitt, *Political Theology*, 13.

23. Michael Walzer, *Just and Unjust Wars* (New York: Basic Books, 1977), 251.

24. Hamilton, "Federalist No. 41," *The Federalist*, 209.

25. Eric A. Posner and Adrian Vermeule, "Crisis Governance in the Administrative State," *University of Chicago Law Review* 76 (2009), 1614.

26. Posner and Vermeule, *Executive Unbound*, 9.

27. Saikrishna B. Prakash and Michael D. Ramsey, "Goldilocks Executive," *Texas Law Review* 90 (2012), 985–992.

28. Ginsburg and Versteeg, "The Bound Executive," 18–30.

29. Posner and Vermeule, *Executive Unbound*, 33.

30. Hamilton, "Federalist No. 70," *The Federalist*, 363.

31. Scheppele, "Law in a Time of Emergency," 3.

32. Youngstown Sheet & Tube Co. v. Sawyer, 343 U.S. 579, 650 (1952) (Jackson, J. concurring).

33. Stephen Holmes, *The Matador's Cape* (Cambridge: Cambridge University Press, 2007), 233.

34. Stephen Holmes, "In Case of Emergency: Misunderstanding Tradeoff in the War on Terror," *California Law Review* 97 (2009), 345.

35. Holmes, "In Case of Emergency," 311–355.

36. Holmes, "In Case of Emergency," 301–302, 310.

37. Holmes, "In Case of Emergency," 305.

38. Holmes, *Matador's Cape*, 6.

39. Home Building & Loan Association v. Blaisdell, 290 U.S. 398, 426 (1934) (Charles Evans Hughes, CJ, majority opinion).

40. Ryan Alford, *Permanent State of Emergency* (Montreal: McGill-Queen's University Press, 2017), 26, summarizing the Report of the Rio Congress of the International Commission of Jurists, 1962.

41. Ginsburg and Versteeg, "The Bound Executive," 14; Christian Bjørnskov and Stefan Voigt, "The Architecture of Emergency Constitutions," *International Journal of Constitutional Law* 16 (2108), 101.

42. Scheppele, "Law in Time of Emergency," 74.

43. See Scheppele, "Law in a Time of Emergency," 64–66, 72–73.

44. See, for example, *Convention on Civil and Political Rights, General Comment No. 29: Article 4: Derogations during a State of Emergency*, August 31, 2001, CCPR/C/21/Rev.1/Add.11, available at https://www.refworld.org/docid/453883fd1f.html.

45. *European Commission for Democracy Through Law (Venice Commission) Compilation of Venice Commission Opinions and Reports on States of Emergency* (2020), https://rm.coe.int/09000016809e38a6.

46. Andrew Ladley, "New Zealand and COVID-19: Parliamentary Accountability in Time of Emergencies," April 7, 2020, http://constitutionnet.org/news/new-zealand-and-covid-19-parliamentary-accountability-time-emergencies.

47. David Dyzenhaus suggested this image.

48. David Cole, "The Priority of Morality," *Yale Law Journal* 113 (2004), 1762.

49. Aziz Z. Huq, "Binding the Executive (by Law or by Politics)," *University of Chicago Law Review* 79 (2012), 826.

Chapter 13

1. David Reinsel, John Gantz, and John Ryding, "The Digitization of the World from Edge to Core," IDC White Paper, November 2018, 2, https://www.seagate.com/files/www-content/our-story/trends/files/idc-seagate-dataage-whitepaper.pdf.

2. Giles Harvey, "The Age of Ishiguro," *New York Times Magazine*, February 28, 2021, reviewing Kazuo Ishiguro, *Klara and the Sun* (New York: Knopf, 2021).

3. Norwegian Consumer Counsel, "Out of Control: How Consumers Are Exploited by the Online Advertising Industry," January 14, 2020, https://fil.forbrukerradet.no/wp-content/uploads/2020/01/2020-01-14-out-of-control-final-version.pdf.

4. Stigler Committee on Digital Platforms (Stigler Committee), Final Report, September 2019, at 14; available at https://research.chicagobooth.edu/stigler/media/news/committee-on-digital-platforms-final-report.

5. Ronald J. Deibert, "Three Painful Truths about Social Media," *Journal of Democracy* 30 (2019), 28–31.

6. Francis Fukuyama, Barak Richman, Ashish Goel, Roberta R. Katz, Douglas Melamed, and Marietje Schaake, "Report of the Working Group on Platform Scale," (Stanford Group), 8; available at https://cyber.fsi.stanford.edu/publication/report-working-group-platform-scale.

7. Alex Engler, "The Devil Is in the Data," *Lawfare*, October 9, 2020. https://www.lawf areblog.com/devil-data.

8. Tom Wheeler, "A Federal Agency Is Necessary to Oversee Big Tech," *Brookings Blueprints for American Renewal & Prosperity*, https://www.brookings.edu/research/a-focused-federal-agency-is-necessary-to-oversee-big-tech/.

9. Shira Ovide, "Big Tech Has Outgrown This Planet," *New York Times*, July 29, 2021.

10. Bruce Schneier, *We Have Root* (Indianapolis: Wiley, 2019), 54.

11. Siva Vaidhyanathan, *Antisocial Media* (Oxford: Oxford University Press, 2018), 99.

12. Norwegian Consumer Counsel, "Out of Control," 12.

13. Stanford Group, 8.

14. Norwegian Consumer Counsel, "Out of Control," 12, 25–28.

15. See several articles in "One Nation, Tracked," *New York Times: Opinion Section*, January 26, 2020.

16. Stanford Group, 11.

17. 47 U.S. Code, sec. 230. See Stewart Baker, "What Should We Do About Section 230?" *Lawfare*, February 19, 2020, https://www.lawfareblog.com/what-should-we-do-about-section-230.

18. Stigler Committee, 3–4.

19. Jane R. Bambauer, Saura Masconale, and Simone M. Sepe, "Cheap Friendship," *University of California, Davis, Law Review* 54 (2021), 2341–2352.

20. Shoshana Zuboff, *The Age of Surveillance Capitalism* (New York: Public Affairs, 2019), 180, quoting Eric Schmidt and Jared Cohen, *The New Digital Age: Transforming Nations, Businesses, and Our Lives* (New York: Vintage, 2014), 9–10.

21. Bruce Schneier, *Data and Goliath* (New York: Norton, 2015), 27.

22. See the Stigler Committee and Stanford Group reports.

23. See Norwegian Consumer Counsel, "Out of Control," 14–15, 17–25.

24. Aziz Z. Huq, "The Public Trust in Data," *Georgetown Law Journal* 110 (2021), 343.

25. For a grasp of the range of such evils, see Stanford Group; Stigler Committee; Norwegian Consumer Counsel, "Out of Control"; Zuboff, *Surveillance Capitalism*; and Schneier, *Data and Goliath*.

26. Todd Feathers, "Why It's So Hard to Regulate Algorithms," *The Markup*, January 4, 2022, https://themarkup.org/news/2022/01/04/why-its-so-hard-to-regulate-algorithms.

27. Stuart A. Thompson and Charlie Warzel, "12 Million Phones, One Dataset, Zero Privacy," *New York Times Opinion*, January 26, 2020, 3.

28. Shoshana Zuboff, "Big Other: Surveillance Capitalism and the Prospects of an Information Civilization," *Journal of Information Technology* 30 (2015), 75–89.

29. Jack M. Balkin, "The Constitution in the National Surveillance State," *Minnesota Law Review* 93 (2008), 12.

30. Nicole Kobie, "The Complicated Truth About China's Social Credit System," *Wired*, June 7, 2019, https://www.wired.co.uk/article/china-social-credit-system-explained; Rogier Creemers, "China's Social Credit System: An Evolving Practice of Control" (May 9, 2018); available at SSRN: https://ssrn.com/abstract=3175792 or http://dx.doi.org/10.2139/ssrn.3175792.

31. Frank Pasquale, *The Black Box Society* (Cambridge, MA: Harvard University Press, 2015), 3.

32. Norwegian Consumer Counsel, "Out of Control," 43. The Stanford Group is a rare and welcome study of the public effects of digital domination. See also Lisa M. Austin and David Lie, "Safe Sharing Sites," *New York University Law Review* 94 (2019), 581–623; and Stigler Committee, 271–327.

33. Amnesty International, "Surveillance Giants: How the Business Model of Google and Facebook Threatens Human Rights," https://www.amnesty.org/download/Docume nts/POL3014042019ENGLISH.PDF.

34. Vaidhyanathan, *Antisocial Media*, 68.

35. See Tim Wu, *The Attention Merchants: The Epic Scramble to Get Inside Our Heads* (New York: Knopf, 2016). Vance Packard's *Hidden Persuaders* was published in 1957.

36. Zuboff, *Surveillance Capitalism*, 295, see 294–297.

37. Schneier, *Data and Goliath*, 128–129.

38. Tom Wheeler, "Can Social Media Targetcasting and Democracy Co-exist?" *Brookings*, November 13, 2019, https://www.brookings.edu/blog/techtank/2019/11/13/can-social-media-targetcasting-and-democracy-coexist/;Francis Fukuyama, Barak Richman, and Ashish Goel, "How to Save Democracy from Technology," *Foreign Affairs* 100 (2021), 98–103.

39. Stigler Committee, 240–241.

40. Stigler Committee, 238–239.

41. Deibert, "Three Painful Truths," 29.

42. Stigler Committee, 8–9. The Committee cites Adam Alter, *Irresistible: The Rise of Addictive Technology and the Business of Keeping Us Hooked* (New York: Penguin, 2017).

43. Packingham v. North Carolina, 137 S. Ct. 1730 (2017), cited in Stanford Group, 5.

44. Tim Berners-Lee, "One Small Step for the Web," October 22, 2018, https://inrupt. com/one-small-step-for-the-web. Steve Lohr, "He Created the Web. Now He's Out to Remake the Digital World, *New York Times*, January 10, 2021, https://www.nytimes. com/2021/01/10/technology/tim-berners-lee-privacy-internet.html.

45. Adrienne La France, "Facebook Is a Doomsday Machine," *The Atlantic*, December 15, 2020, https://www.theatlantic.com/technology/archive/2020/12/facebook-dooms day-machine/617384/. In the eighteenth-century philosophy of Gottfried Wilhelm Leibniz, windowless monads are isolated, atomic entities unable to perceive or interact with any other such entity.

46. Stanford Group, 17–18; Fukuyama et al., "How to Save Democracy," 102. See also Stigler Committee, 271, 277, 281.

47. Robyn Caplan, Joan Donovan, Lauren Hanson, and Jeanna Matthews, "Algorithmic Accountability: A Primer," April 18, 2018; available at https://datasociety.net/libr ary/algorithmic-accountability-a-primer/; Joshua A. Kroll, Joanna Huey, Solon Barocas, Edward W. Felton, Joel R. Reidenberg, David G. Robinson, and Harlan Yu, "Accountably Algorithms," *University of Pennsylvania Law Review* 165 (2017), 633–705.

48. Kroll et al., "Accountable Algorithms," 637, 640.

49. Kroll et al., "Accountable Algorithms," 636.
50. Mireille Hildebrandt, "Law as Computation in an Era of Artificial Legal Intelligence," *University of Toronto Law Journal* (Supplement 1), 68 (2018), 34.
51. H.R. 2231, https://www.congress.gov/bill/116th-congress/house-bill/2231/text.
52. Tim Berners-Lee, "One Small Step for the Web," https://inrupt.com/one-small-step-for-the-web.
53. Steve Lohr, "He Created the Web."
54. Francis Fukuyama et al., "How to Save Democracy from Technology," 98; see also Stigler Committee, 293–305.
55. Stanford Group, 31–34.
56. Stanford Group, 36–37.
57. Stanford Group, 35.
58. S. 806, Own Your Own Data Act of 2019 (March 14, 2019), https://www.congress.gov/bill/116th-congress/senate-bill/806.
59. Eric A. Posner and E. Glen Weyl, *Radical Markets: Uprooting Capitalism and Democracy for a Just Society* (Princeton: Princeton University Press, 2018), 243–249; and Zuboff, *Surveillance Capitalism*, 19.
60. Giovanni Sartor, Francesca Lagioia, and Federico Galli, *Regulating Targeted and Behavioural Advertising in Digital Services: How to Ensure Users' Informed Consent*, July 2021, at 92–106, https://www.dropbox.com/s/tf7iw8sqyewy67l/SartorLagioi aGalli2021Study%20Regulating%20targeted%20and%20behavioural%20advertis ing.pdf?dl=0.
61. See, for example, In Re: Facebook, Inc., Pretrial Order #20 (N.D. Ca. 2019).
62. Austin and Lee, "Safe Sharing Sites," 581–585.
63. Huq, "The Public Trust in Data," 46.
64. Daniel J. Solove and Paul M. Schwartz, "ALI Data Privacy: Overview and Black Letter Text," *UCLA Law Review* 68 (2022), 1252–1300.
65. Stigler Committee, 214.
66. Stigler Committee, 27–121; Stanford Group, 23–25 and references given there.
67. Stigler Committee, 13, 309–311.
68. Margot E. Kaminski and Meg Leta Jones, "An American's Guide to the GDPR," *Denver Law Review* 98 (2020), 93, 107; Margot E. Kaminski, "Binary Governance: Lessons from the GDPR's Approach to Algorithmic Accountability," *Southern California Law Review* 92 (2019), 1582–1611.
69. Kaminski and Jones, "An American's Guide," 108.
70. Kaminski and Jones, "An American's Guide," 110; see Kaminski, "Binary Governance," 1560, 1602, 1611.
71. Jack Balkin and Jonathan Zittrain "A Grand Bargain to Make Tech Companies Trustworthy," *The Atlantic*, October 3, 2016; available at https://www.theatlantic.com/technology/archive/2016/10/information-fiduciary/502346/. Jack Balkin "The Fiduciary Model of Privacy," *Harvard Law Review* 132 (2020), 11, 13–16; see also Lina M. Khan and David E. Pozen, "A Skeptical View of Information Fiduciaries," *Harvard Law Review* 133 (2019), 497–541.

72. Gerald J. Postema, "Trust, Distrust and the Rule of Law," in Paul B. Miller and Matthew Harding, *Fiduciaries and Trust: Ethics, Politics, Economics and Law* (Cambridge: Cambridge University Press, 2020), 263.

73. Tom Wheeler, "A Focused Federal Agency Is Necessary to Oversee Big Tech."

74. Huq, "The Public Trust in Data," 40, 45–46.

75. Huq, "The Public Trust in Data," 40–53.

76. Huq, "The Public Trust in Data," 49.

77. Marietje Schaake, "The Lawless Realm: Countering the Real Cyberthreat," *Foreign Affairs* 99 (November/December 2020), 27–33.

78. Schaake, "The Lawless Realm," 28.

79. Darrell M. West and John R. Allen, *Turning Point: Policymaking in the Era of Artificial Intelligence* (Washington, D.C.: Brookings Institution Press, 2020), 13; Adrienne La France, "Facebook Is a Doomsday Machine," *The Atlantic*, December 15, 2020, https://www.theatlantic.com/technology/archive/2020/12/facebook-doomsday-machine/617384/.

80. Joshua P. Melzer and Cameron F. Kerry, "Strengthening International Cooperation on Artificial Intelligence," *Brookings Blueprints for American Renewal and Prosperity*, February 17, 2021, https://www.brookings.edu/research/strengthening-international-cooperation-on-artificial-intelligence/; Kate Jones and Emily Taylor, "The U.S. and Europe Can't Each Go It Alone Against Big Tech," *World Politics Review*, February 22, 2021, https://www.worldpoliticsreview.com/articles/29437/the-u-s-and-europe-can-t-each-go-it-alone-regulating-big-tech; World Health Organization, "COVID-19 Shows Why United Action Is Needed for More Robust International Health Architecture," March 30, 2021, https://www.who.int/news-room/commentaries/detail/op-ed—-covid-19-shows-why-united-action-is-needed-for-more-robust-international-health-architecture; Amnesty International, "Surveillance Giants: How the Business Model of Google and Facebook Threatens Human Rights," https://www.amnesty.org/download/Documents/POL301404 2019ENGLISH.PDF.

Chapter 14

1. Ahmed Elgammal, "How a Team of Musicologists and Computer Scientists Completed Beethoven's Unfinished 10th Symphony," https://theconversation.com/how-a-team-of-musicologists-and-computer-scientists-completed-beethovens-unfinished-10th-symphony-168160. The article includes a short clip from a performance of the piece.

2. At https://arxiv.org/abs/1612.01010.

3. Benjamin Alarie, "The Path of Law: Towards Legal Singularity," *University of Toronto Law Journal* 66 (2016), 443–455; Eugene Volokh, "Chief Justice Robots," *Duke Law Journal* 68 (2019), 1135–1192; Lawrence B. Solum, "Artificially Intelligent Law," *BioLaw Journal* 1 (2019), 53–62; for a critique, see Mireille Hildebrandt, "Law as

Computation in the Era of Artificial Legal Intelligence: Speaking Law to the Power of Statistics," *University of Toronto Law Journal* 68 (2018), 12–35.

4. Aziz Z. Huq, "A Right to a Human Decision," *Virginia Law Review* 106 (2020), 634.

5. Frank Pasquale, *New Laws of Robotics: Defending Human Expertise in the Age of AI* (Cambridge, MA: Belknap Press, 2020), 199. See also Solum, "Artificially Intelligent Law."

6. Benjamin Alarie, "The Path of Law: Toward Legal Singularity," *University of Toronto Law Journal* 66 (2016), 443–455. For discussions of such proposals, see Richard M. Re and Alicia Solo-Niederman, "Developing Artificially Intelligent Justice," *Stanford Technology Law Review* (2019), 242–289; and Simon Deakin and Christopher Markou, eds., *Is Law Computable* (Oxford: Hart Publishing, 2020), especially Deakin and Markou's essay, "From Rule of Law to Legal Singularity," and "*Ex Machina Lex*: Exploring the Limits of Legal Computability."

7. Volokh, "Chief Justice Robots," 1138.

8. Deakin and Markou, "From Rule of Law to Legal Singularity," 9–12.

9. Ajay Agrawal, Joshua Gans, and Avi Goldfarb, *Prediction Machines: The Economics of Artificial Intelligence* (Boston: Harvard Business Review Press, 2018), 24, 29.

10. Amnon Reichman and Giovanni Sartor, "Algorithms and Regulation," in Giovanni De Gregorio, Hans Micklitz, Oreste Pollicino, Amnon Reichman, Andrea Simoncini, and Giovanni Sartor, eds., *Constitutional Challenges in the Algorithmic Society* (Cambridge: Cambridge University Press, 2021), 132.

11. Reichman and Sartor, "Algorithms and Regulation," 131.

12. https://www.chess.com/terms/alphazero-chess-engine.

13. Frank Pasquale and Glyn Cashwell, "Prediction, Persuasion, and the Jurisprudence of Behaviorism," *University of Toronto Law Journal* 68 (2018), 64–73.

14. Melanie Mitchell, "What Does it Mean for AI to Understand," *Quanta Magazine*, December 16, 2021, https://www.quantamagazine.org/what-does-it-mean-for-ai-to-understand-20211216/#.

15. Oliver Wendell Holmes, Jr., "The Path of Law," *Harvard Law Review* 10 (1897), 457. I defend this reading of Holmes in Gerald J. Postema, *Legal Philosophy in the Twentieth Century: The Common Law World* (Dordrecht: Springer, 2011), ch. 2.

16. Reichman and Sartor, "Algorithms and Regulation," 152.

17. Mireille Hildebrandt, "Law as Computation in the Era of Artificial Intelligence," *University of Toronto Law Journal* 68 Supplement 1 (2018), 23, 29–30.

18. Lawrence Lessig, *Code 2.0* (New York: Basic Books, 2006).

19. Mireille Hildebrandt, "Technology and the End of Law," in Eric Claes, Wouter Devroe, and Bert Keirsbilck, eds., *Facing the Limits of Law* (Berlin: Springer Verlag, 2009), 453.

20. Reichman and Sartor, "Algorithms and Regulation," 136.

21. Gerald J. Postema, "*A Similibus ad Similia*: Analogical Thinking in Law," in Douglas E. Edlin, ed., *Common Law Theory* (Cambridge: Cambridge University Press, 2007), 102–133.

22. Cass R. Sunstein, "Of Artificial Intelligence and Legal Reasoning," *University of Chicago Law School Roundtable* 8 (2001), 32.

23. Postema, "*A Similibus ad Similia.*"
24. Emily Berman, "A Government of Laws and Not of Machines," *Boston University Law Review* 98 (2018), 1277–1356.
25. Frank Pasquale, "The Resilient Fragility of Law," in Simon Deakin and Christopher Markou, eds., *Is Law Computable* (Oxford: Hart Publishing, 2020), viii.
26. Aziz Z. Huq, "A Right to a Human Decision," *Virginia Law Review* 106 (2020), 611–688.
27. Frank Pasquale, "The Resilient Fragility of Law."
28. Maranke Wieringa, "What to Account for When Accounting for Algorithms," *Conference on Fairness, Accountability, and Transparency*, January 2020, Barcelona, https://doi.org/10.1145/3351095.3372833. See Chapter 13.
29. Tim Wu, "Will Artificial Intelligence Eat the Law? The Rise of Hybrid Social-Ordering Systems," *Columbia Law Review* 119 (2019), 2021.
30. In this paragraph and the next, I follow Gerald J. Postema, "Law in Time's Domain," *Ratio Juris* 31 (2018), 176–180. See Chapter 4.

Chapter 15

1. Arthur Larson, *Eisenhower: The President Nobody Knew* (London: Frewin, 1969), 119.
2. Report of the Security Council on the Rule of Law and Transitional Justice in Conflict and Post Conflict Societies (2004), UN Doc. S/2004/616, para. 6.
3. UN General Assembly, 2005 World Summit Outcome, UN Doc. A/Res/60/1 (2005), para. 134.
4. *The Rule of Law: A Guide for Politicians* (Lund: Raoul Wallenberg Institute, 2012), 6.
5. James Crawford, *Chance, Order, Change: The Course of International Law* (The Hague: Hague Academy of International Law, 2014), 31. Crawford's book is an extended answer to this skepticism.
6. The following profile is drawn from *inter alia*, James Crawford, *State Responsibility: The General Part* (Cambridge: Cambridge University Press, 2013); James Crawford, *Chance, Order, Change*; Gleider Hernández, *International Law* (Oxford: Oxford University Press, 2019); Antonio Cassese, *International Law* (Oxford: Oxford University Press, 2005); Malcolm Shaw, *International Law* (Cambridge: Cambridge University Press, 2021); John Tasioulas and Samantha Besson, eds., *The Philosophy of International Law* (Oxford: Oxford University Press, 2010).
7. William Penn, *Essay towards the Present and Future Peace in Europe* (1623), quoted in Deutsch, *International Rule of Law*, xxv.
8. Elena Carpanelli, "General Principles of International Law: Struggling with a Slippery Concept," https://lawexplores.com/principles-of-international-law-struggling-with-a-slippery-concept/.
9. Jeremy Waldron, "Are Sovereigns Entitled to Benefit of International Law?" *The European Journal of International Law* 22 (2011), 327–342.
10. Crawford, *State Responsibility*, 51–53.

11. Crawford, *State Responsibility*, 79–80.

12. Jesner v. Arab Bank, 138 S. Ct. 1386, 1406 (2018).

13. Anne Peters, *Beyond Human Rights* (Cambridge: Cambridge University Press, 2016).

14. Benedict Kingsbury, "International Law as Inter-Public Law," in Henry Richardson and Melissa Williams, eds., *NOMOS 49: Moral Universalism and Pluralism* (New York: York University Press, 2008), 167–204. Some international law scholars contest this notion.

15. International Law Commission, Report of the Study Group on Fragmentation of International Law, UN Doc. A/CN.4/L.682 (2006), 177, para. 251.

16. Crawford, *Chance, Order, Change*, 22.

17. Gerald J. Postema, "Law's System: The Necessity of System in Law," *New Zealand Law Review* (2014), 69–105.

18. Benedict Kingsbury, Nico Krisch, and Richard B. Stewart, "The Emergence of Global Administrative Law," *Law and Contemporary Problems* 68 (2005),15–61; Nico Krisch and Benedict Kingsbury, "Global Governance and Global Administrative Law in the International Legal Order," *European Journal of International Law* 17 (2006), 1–13; Benedict Kingsbury, "Frontiers of Global Administrative Law in the 2020s," IILJ Working Paper 2020/2; available at https://www.iilj.org/publications/frontiers-of-glo bal-administrative-law-in-the-2020s/; Eyal Benvinisti, *Law of Global Governance*, Hague Academy of International Law (Leiden: EJ Brill, 2014).

19. Kingsbury, Krisch, and Stewart, "The Emergence of Global Administrative Law," 17, 28.

20. Kingsbury, Krisch, and Stewart, "The Emergence of Global Administrative Law," 31–37; Ruth W. Grant and Robert O. Keohane, "Accountability and Abuses of Power in World Politics," *American Political Science Review* 99 (2005), 29–43.

21. Grant and Keohane, "Accountability and Abuses of Power in World Politics," 37. See also Eisuke Suzuki and Suresh Nanwani, "Responsibility of International Organizations: The Accountability Mechanisms of Multilateral Development Banks," *Michigan Journal of International Law* 27 (2005), 177.

22. See ILA Committee on Accountability of International Organizations, Final Report, *Berlin Conference* (2004).

23. Krisch and Kingsbury, "Global Governance and Global Administrative Law," 10.

24. Postema, "Law's System," 23–24.

25. International Law Commission Report of the Study Group on Fragmentation of International Law, "Fragmentation of International Law: Difficulties Arising from the Diversification and Expansion of International Law," UN Doc. A/CN.4/L.682 (2006), para. 16.

26. Liam Murphy, "Law Beyond the State," *European Journal of International Law* 28 (2017), 215.

27. See Crawford, *Chance, Order, Change*, 282–297.

28. ILC Report of the Study Group on Fragmentation, paras. 14, 18. See also Murphy, "Law Beyond the State," 216. The ILC report details a wide variety of techniques and principles.

29. Crawford, *Chance, Order, Change*, 298–303.

30. Frederich Krachtowil, *Rules, Norms, and Decisions* (Cambridge: Cambridge University Press, 1989), 102.
31. Thomas Franck, *Fairness in International Law and Institutions* (Oxford: Clarendon Press, 1995), 477.
32. M.H. Mendelson, *The Formation of Customary International Law, Recueil des cours*, Académie de droit international, vol. 272 (The Hague: Martinus Nijhoff, 1999), 189–191.
33. Abram Chayes and Antonia H. Chayes, *The New. Sovereignty* (Cambridge, MA: Harvard University Press, 1995), 127.
34. Chayes and Chayes, *The New Sovereignty*, 25–6, 28, 118–123.
35. Mendelson, *Formation of Customary International Law*, 190.
36. Franck, *Fairness in International Law and Institutions*, 14.
37. Wojciech Sadurski, "Conceptions of Public Reason in Supranational Sphere and Legitimacy Beyond Borders," in Wojciech Sadurski, Michael Sevel, and Kevin Walton, eds., *Legitimacy: The State and Beyond* (Oxford: Oxford University Press, 2019), 175.
38. World Bank, *Governance and Law* (Washington, D.C., 2017), 83, 91.
39. Quoted by H. Thirlway, "Concepts, Principles, Rules and Analogies: International and Municipal Legal Reasoning," in *Collected Courses of The Hague Academy of International Law* (Leiden: EJ Brill, 2003), vol. 294, at 302.
40. Eric Posner, *Perils of Global Legalism* (Chicago: University of Chicago Press, 2009), xiii, 16.
41. Ian Brownlie, *The Rule of Law in International Affairs* (The Hague: Martinus Nijhoff, 1998), 14.
42. Jack Goldsmith and Daryl Levinson, "Law for States: International Law, Constitutional Law, Public Law," *Harvard Law Review* 122 (2009), 1794 and passim.
43. Hans J. Morgenthau, *In Defense of National Interest: A Critical Study of American Foreign Policy* (New York: Knopf, 1951), 144.
44. Goldsmith and Levinson, "Law for States," 1842.
45. Oona Hathaway and Scott Shapiro, "Outcasting: Enforcement in Domestic and International Law," *Yale Law Journal* 121 (2011), 252–349.
46. Department of Defense, *National Defense Strategy of the United States of America* (March 2005), 5.
47. Susan Neiman, *Moral Clarity: A Guide for Grow-Up Idealists* (Princeton: Princeton University Press, 2009), 37. Neiman challenges this view.
48. Louis Henkin, *How Nations Behave*, 2nd edition (New York: Columbia University Press, 1979), 47.
49. Hans Morgenthau, *Politics among Nations: The Struggle for Power and Peace*, 2nd edition (New York: Knopf, 1954), 251.
50. Jack L. Goldsmith and Eric A. Posner, *The Limits of International Law* (Oxford: Oxford University Press, 2005), 39.
51. Eric A. Posner, "Do States Have a Moral Obligation to Obey International Law?" *Stanford Law Review* 55 (2003), 1919.

52. Jens David Ohlin directs this classic Humean argument against the Practical Reason Realists in Jens David Ohlin, *The Assault on International Law* (Oxford: Oxford University Press, 2015).

53. James Crawford, ed., *Brownlie's Principles of International Law*, 8th edition (Oxford: Oxford University Press, 2012), 15.

54. Malcolm Shaw, *International Law* (Cambridge: Cambridge University Press, 2021), 5.

55. Charles Sampford, "Reconceiving the Rule of Law in Globalizing World," in Spencer Zifcak, ed., *Globalisation and the Rule of Law* (New York: Routledge 2004), 22.

56. B.S. Chimni, "Legitimating the International Rule of Law," in James Crawford and Martti Koskenniemi, eds., *Cambridge Companion to International Law* (Cambridge: Cambridge University Press, 2012), 299–302.

57. See Michael Byers and George Nolte, eds., *United States Hegemony and the Foundations of International Law* (Cambridge: Cambridge University Press, 2003).

58. As legal scholar, Evan Fox-Decent, wrote, "It is perhaps not surprising that the United States of America has withdrawn its ratification of the International Criminal Court. Imperial power does not permit itself to be judged and sentenced." Evan Fox-Decent, "Is the Rule of Law Really Indifferent to Human Rights?" *Law and Philosophy* 27 (2008), 27.

59. Nico Krisch, "International Law in Times of Hegemony: Unequal Power and the Shaping of the International Legal Order," *The European Journal of International Law* 16 (2005), 372, 408.

60. Jeremy Waldron "Are Sovereigns Entitled to the Benefit of the International Rule of Law?" *The European Journal of International Law* 22 (2011), 315–343; Jeremy Waldron, "The Rule of International Law," *Harvard Journal of Law & Public Policy* 30 (2006), 15–30.

61. Kristen Rundle, *Forms Liberate: Reclaiming the Jurisprudence of Lon L Fuller* (Oxford: Hart, 2012), 134, 139.

62. Crawford, *Choice, Order, Change*, 343, 468–507.

63. Lon L. Fuller, "Forms and Limits of Adjudication," *Harvard Law Review* 92 (1978), 378.

64. Fuller, "Forms and Limits of Adjudication," 378–379.

65. See Monica Hakimi, "Constructing an International Community," *American Journal of International Law* 111 (2017), 317–356.

Epilogue

1. Timothy Snyder, *The Road to Unfreedom* (New York: Tim Duggan Books, 2018), 81–82.

2. Denise Levertov, "Making Peace," in *Breathing the Water* (New York: New Directions, 1987).

3. Whitney v. California, 274 U.S. 357, 372 (Brandeis, J. concurring).

4. Snyder, *Road to Unfreedom*, 128–131.

5. Jonathan Rauch, *The Constitution of Knowledge* (Washington, D.C.: Brookings, 2021), 234.

6. Snyder, *Road to Unfreedom*, 130.

7. One impressive effort along these lines is the North Carolina Leadership Forum; see https://sites.duke.edu/nclf/.

8. Daniel Patrick Moynihan, "Defining Deviancy Down," *The American Scholar* 62 (1993), 17–30.

9. Samuel Beckett, *Worstward Ho* (New York: Grove Press, 1983).

Index

For the benefit of digital users, indexed terms that span two pages (e.g., 52–53) may, on occasion, appear on only one of those pages.